Shojo Beat

ORESAMA TEACHER

Vol. 4

Story & Art by
Izumi Tsubaki

Chapter 18

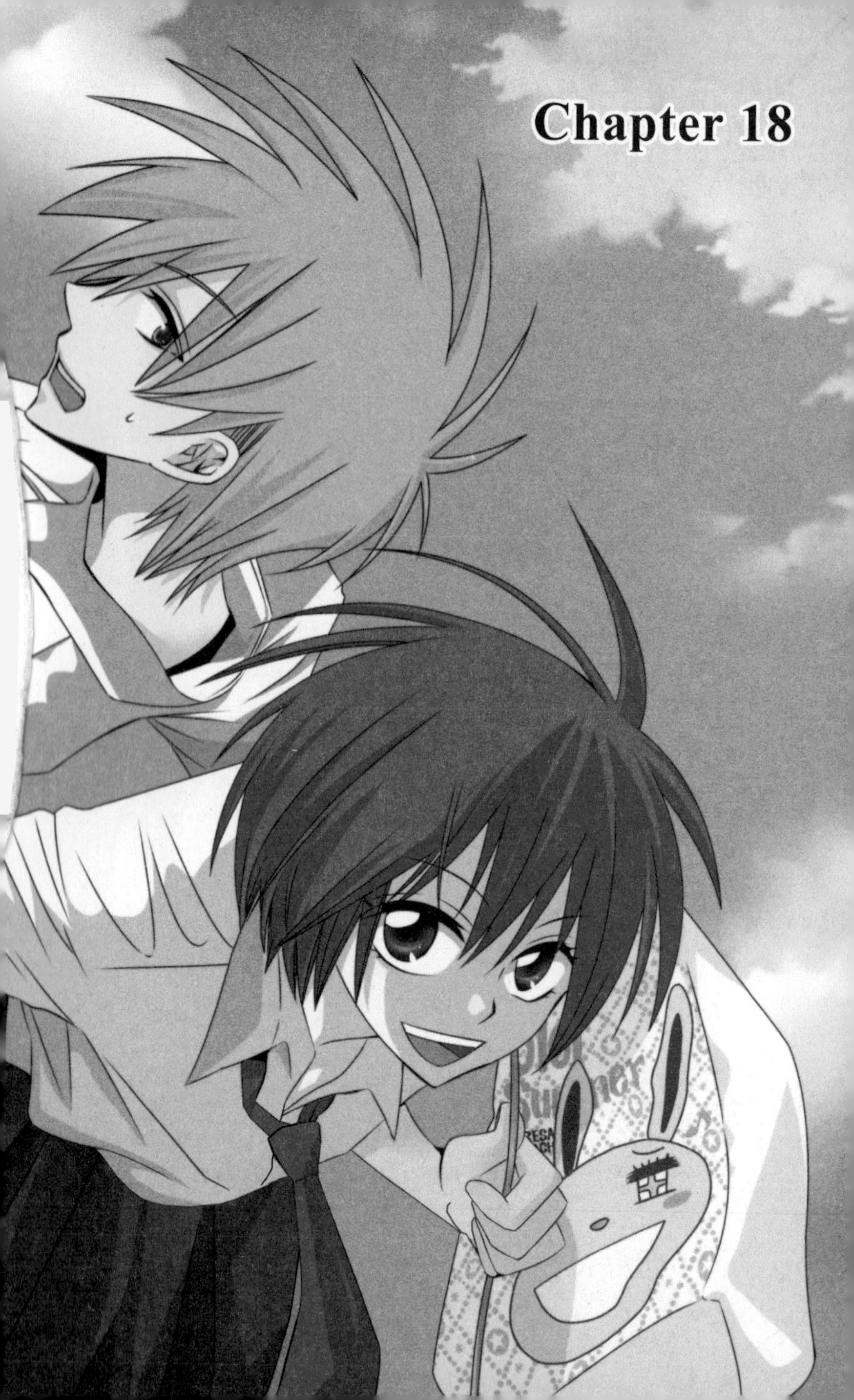

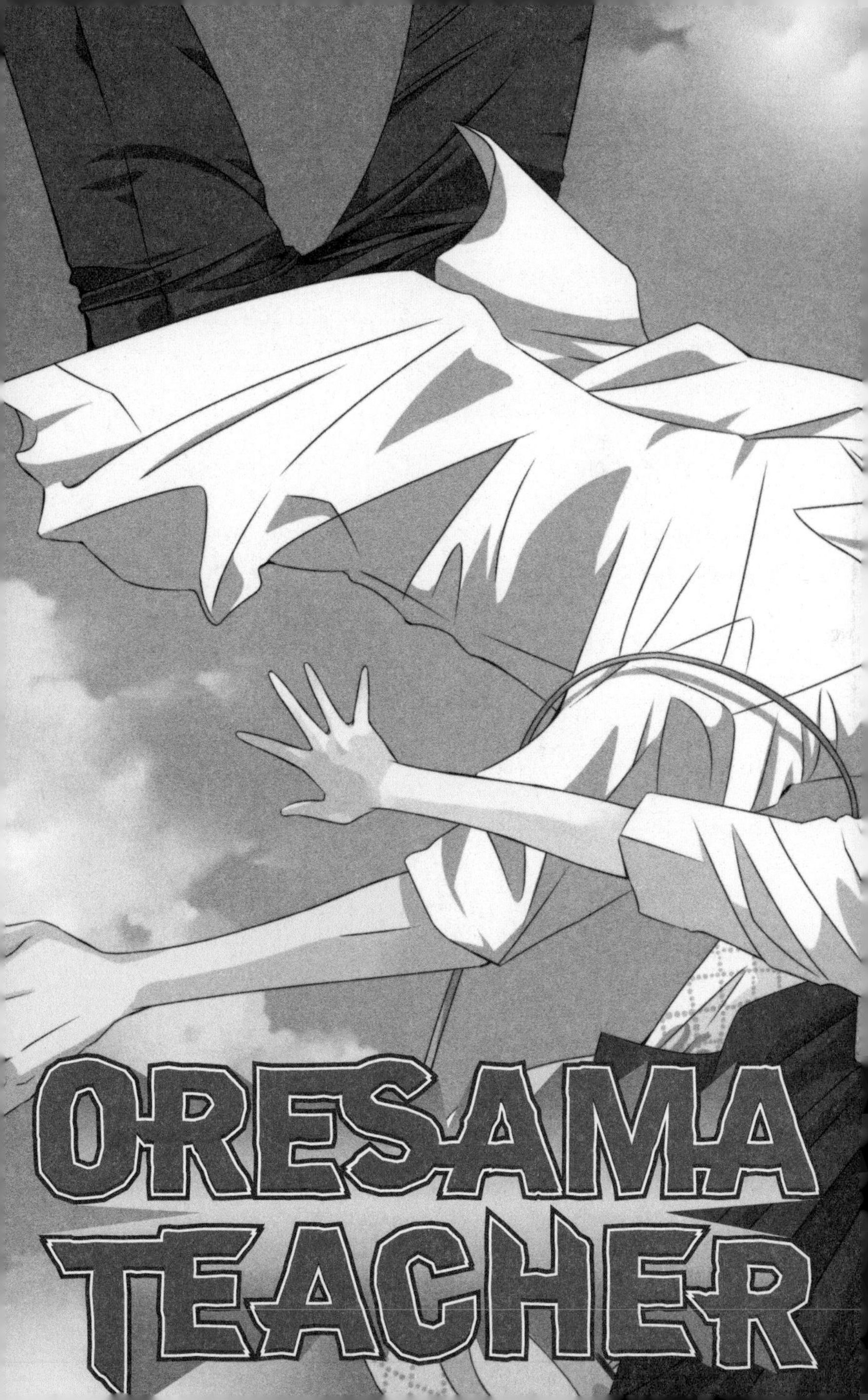
ORESAMA
TEACHER

ORESAMA TEACHER

Volume 4
CONTENTS

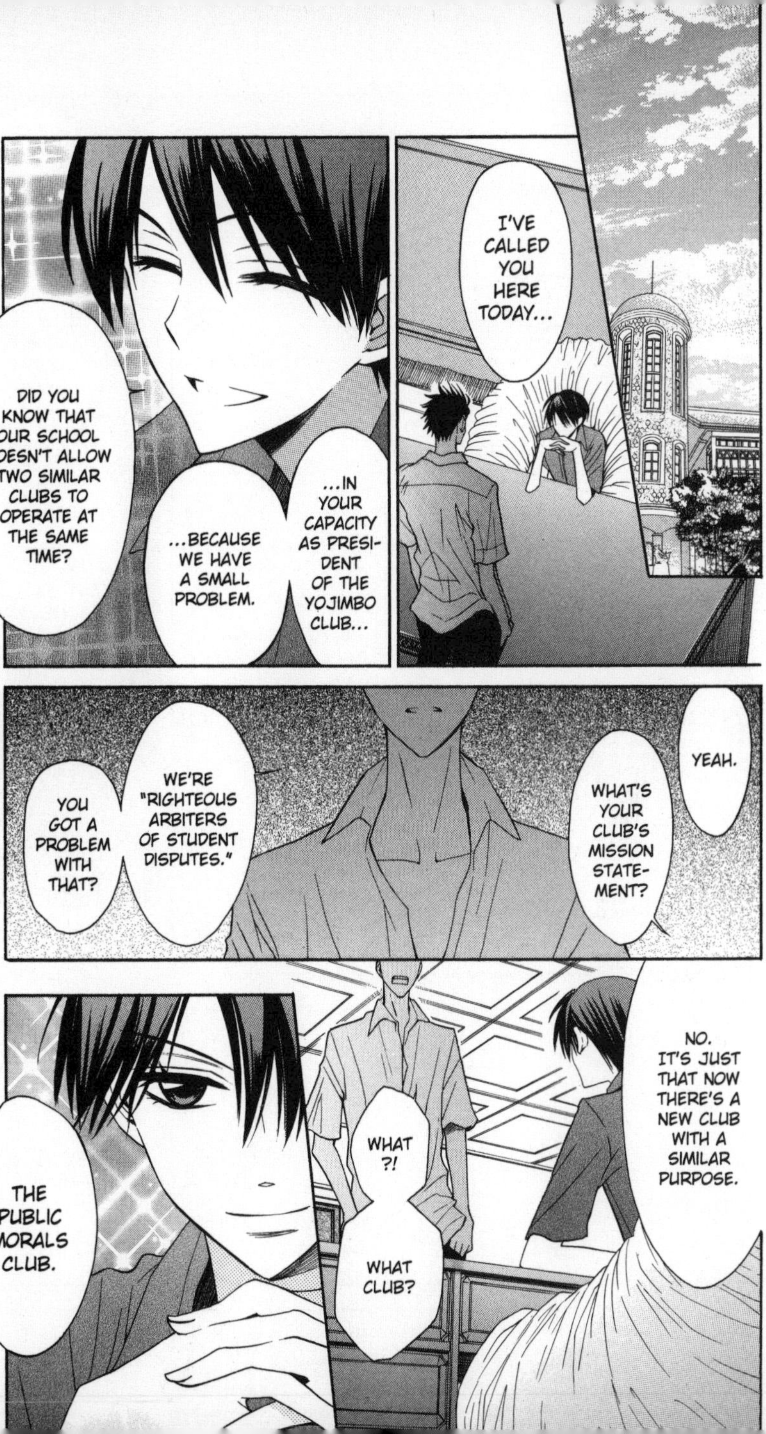
I'VE CALLED YOU HERE TODAY...
...IN YOUR CAPACITY AS PRESIDENT OF THE YOJIMBO CLUB...
...BECAUSE WE HAVE A SMALL PROBLEM.
DID YOU KNOW THAT OUR SCHOOL DOESN'T ALLOW TWO SIMILAR CLUBS TO OPERATE AT THE SAME TIME?
YEAH.
WHAT'S YOUR CLUB'S MISSION STATEMENT?
WE'RE "RIGHTEOUS ARBITERS OF STUDENT DISPUTES."
YOU GOT A PROBLEM WITH THAT?
NO. IT'S JUST THAT NOW THERE'S A NEW CLUB WITH A SIMILAR PURPOSE.
WHAT?!
WHAT CLUB?
THE PUBLIC MORALS CLUB.

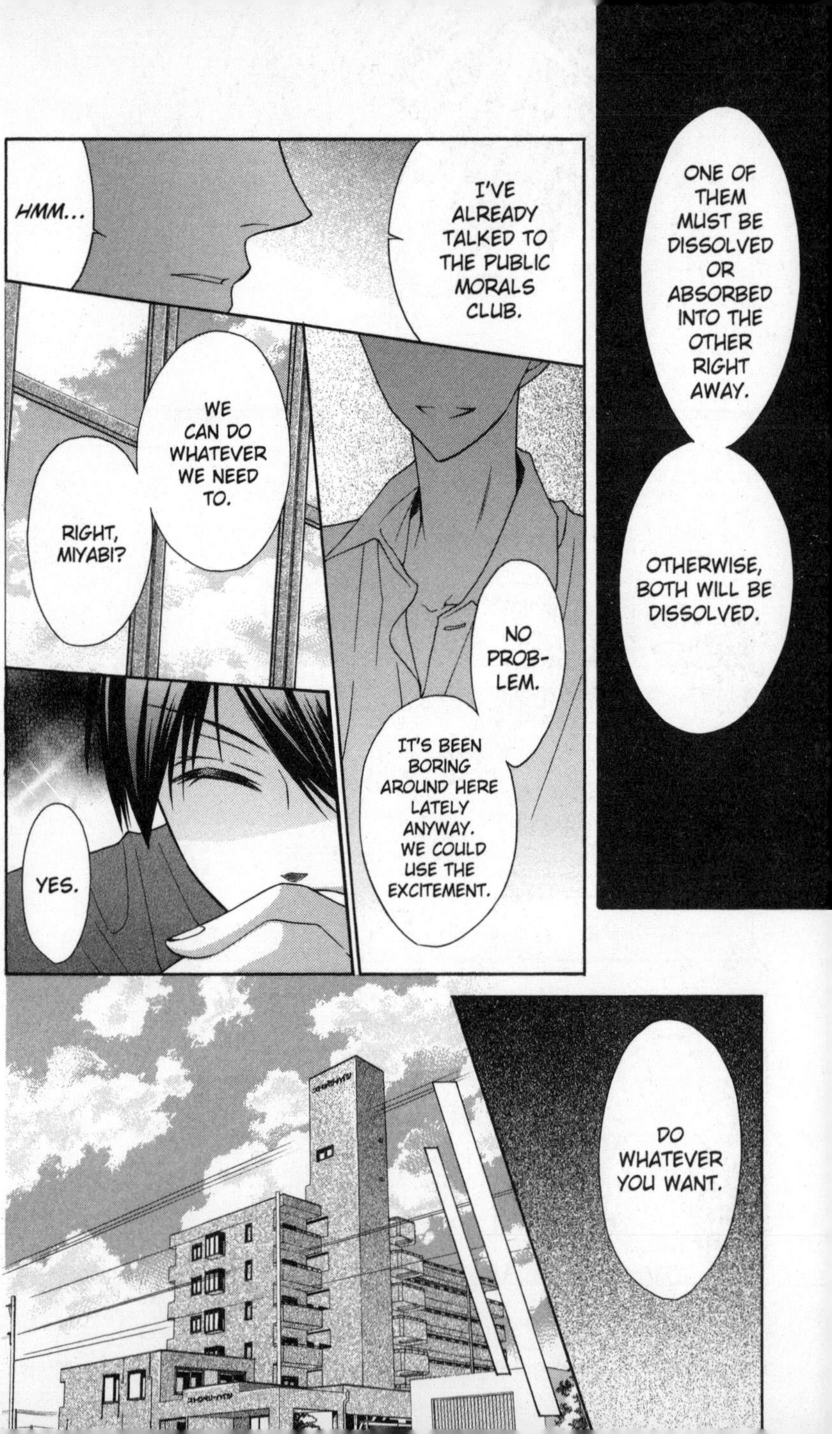
ONE OF THEM MUST BE DISSOLVED OR ABSORBED INTO THE OTHER RIGHT AWAY.
OTHERWISE, BOTH WILL BE DISSOLVED.
I'VE ALREADY TALKED TO THE PUBLIC MORALS CLUB.
HMM...
WE CAN DO WHATEVER WE NEED TO.
RIGHT, MIYABI?
NO PROB-LEM.
IT'S BEEN BORING AROUND HERE LATELY ANYWAY. WE COULD USE THE EXCITEMENT.
YES.
DO WHATEVER YOU WANT.

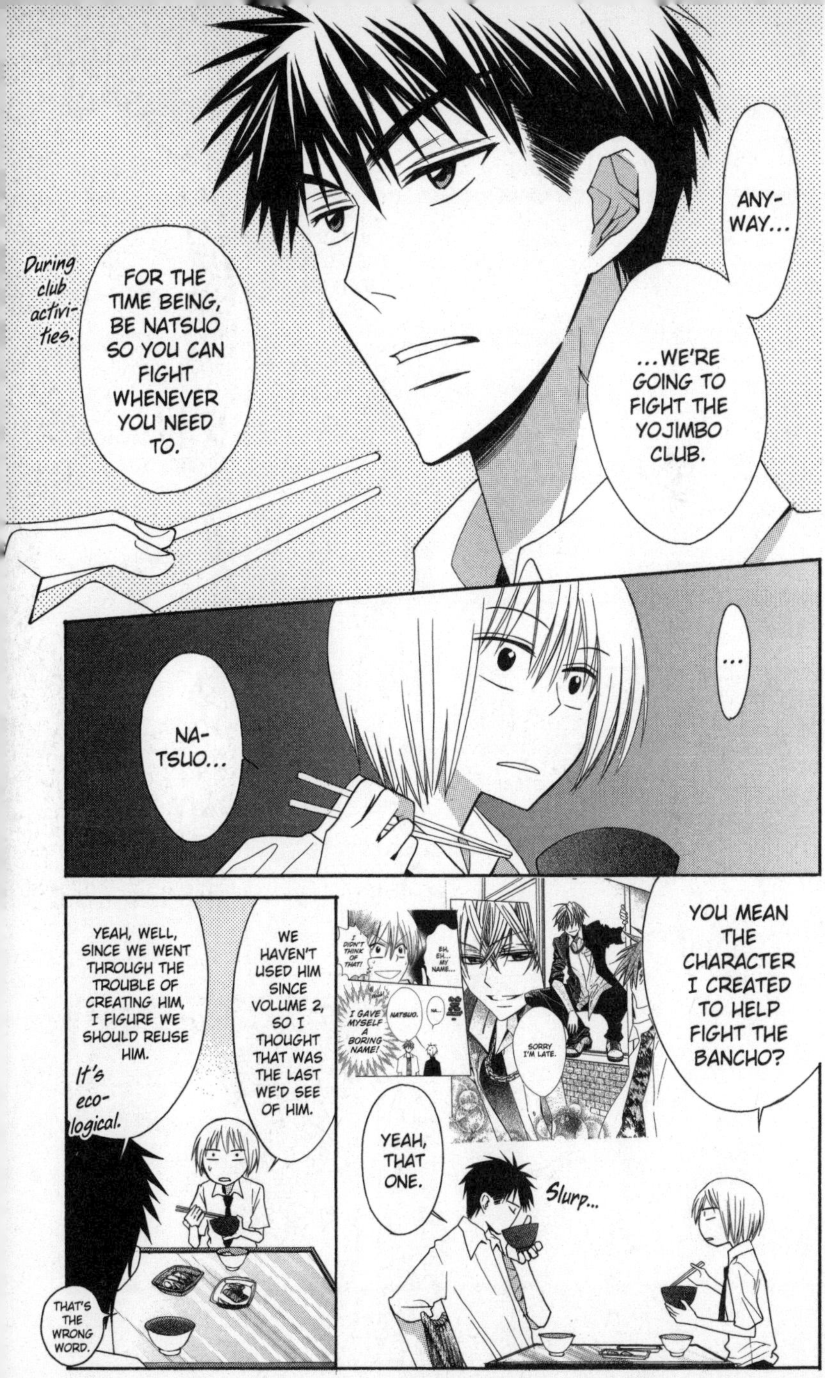
ANY-WAY...
...WE'RE GOING TO FIGHT THE YOJIMBO CLUB.
FOR THE TIME BEING, BE NATSUO SO YOU CAN FIGHT WHENEVER YOU NEED TO.
During club activi-ties.
...
NA-TSUO...
YOU MEAN THE CHARACTER I CREATED TO HELP FIGHT THE BANCHO?
SORRY I'M LATE.
EH, EH... MY NAME...
NA...
NATSUO.
I DIDN'T THINK OF THAT!
I GAVE MYSELF A BORING NAME!
YEAH, THAT ONE.
Slurp...
WE HAVEN'T USED HIM SINCE VOLUME 2, SO I THOUGHT THAT WAS THE LAST WE'D SEE OF HIM.
YEAH, WELL, SINCE WE WENT THROUGH THE TROUBLE OF CREATING HIM, I FIGURE WE SHOULD REUSE HIM.
It's eco-logical.
THAT'S THE WRONG WORD.

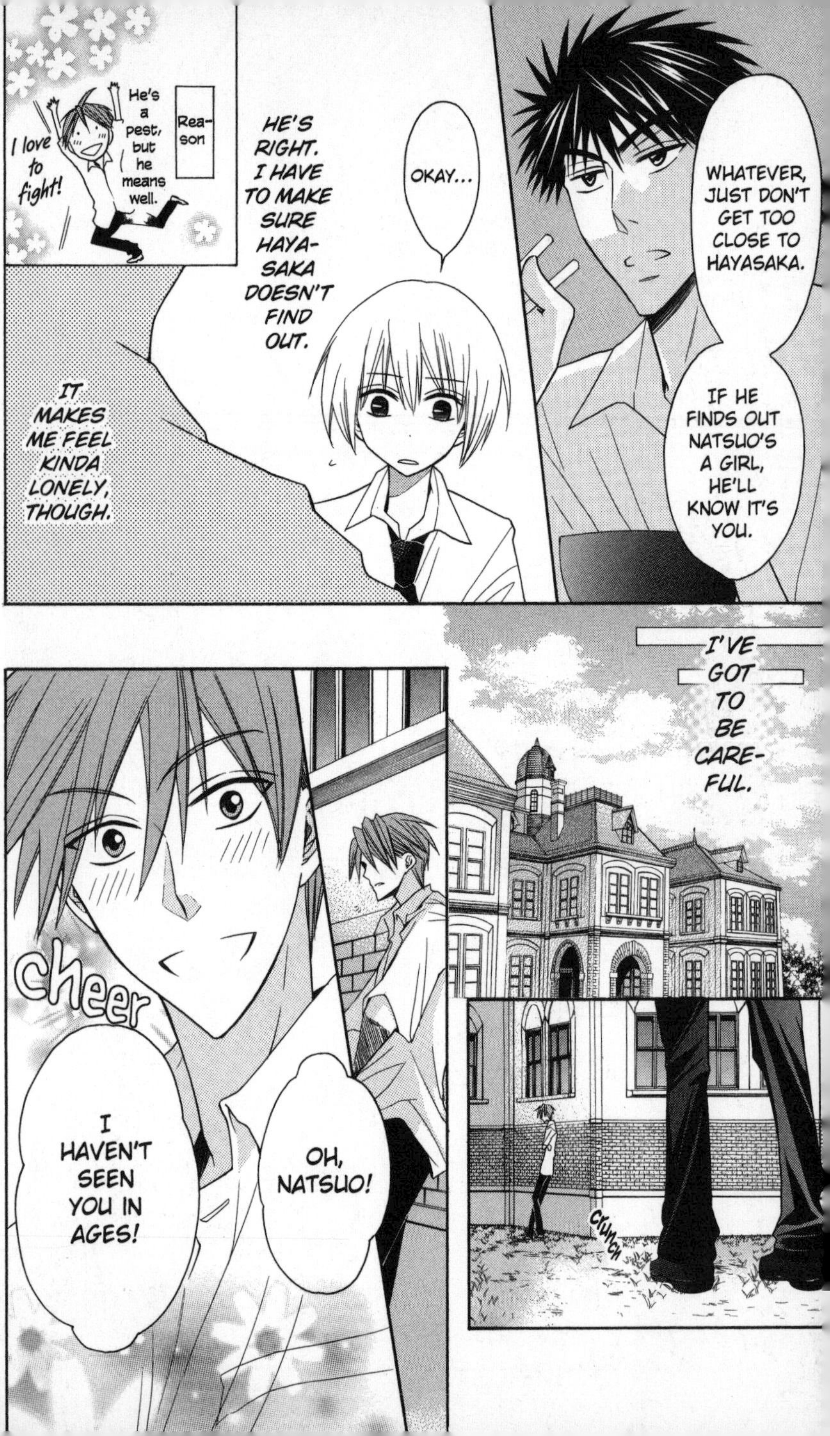
WHATEVER, JUST DON'T GET TOO CLOSE TO HAYASAKA.
IF HE FINDS OUT NATSUO'S A GIRL, HE'LL KNOW IT'S YOU.
OKAY...
HE'S RIGHT. I HAVE TO MAKE SURE HAYA-SAKA DOESN'T FIND OUT.
IT MAKES ME FEEL KINDA LONELY, THOUGH.
Rea-son
He's a pest, but he means well.
I love to fight!
I'VE GOT TO BE CARE-FUL.
crunch
cheer
OH, NATSUO!
I HAVEN'T SEEN YOU IN AGES!

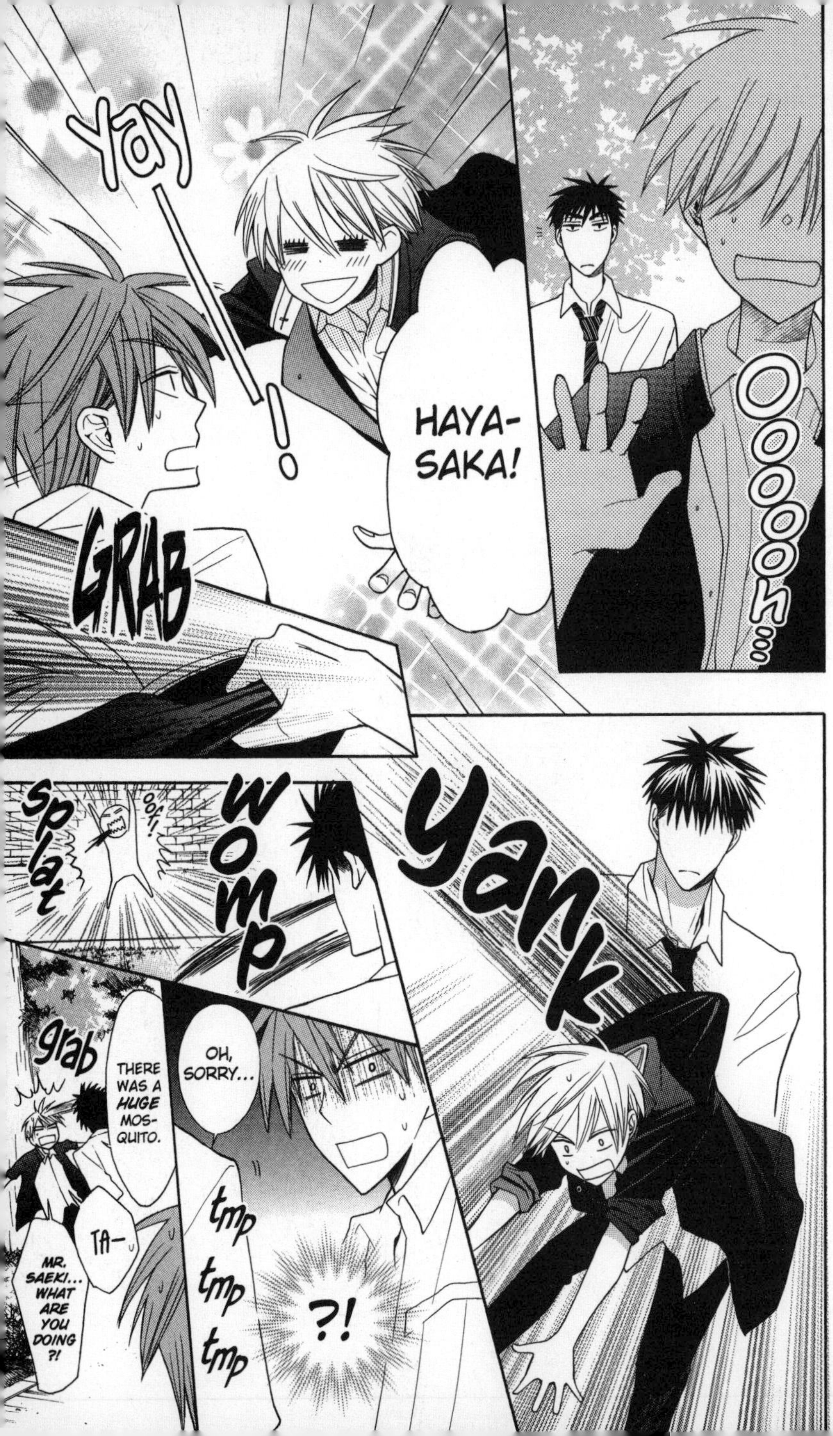
Oooooh...
Yay!
HAYA-SAKA!
GRAB
yank
womp
oof!
splat
OH, SORRY...
THERE WAS A HUGE MOSQUITO.
grab
tmp tmp tmp
?!
TA-
MR. SAEKI... WHAT ARE YOU DOING?!

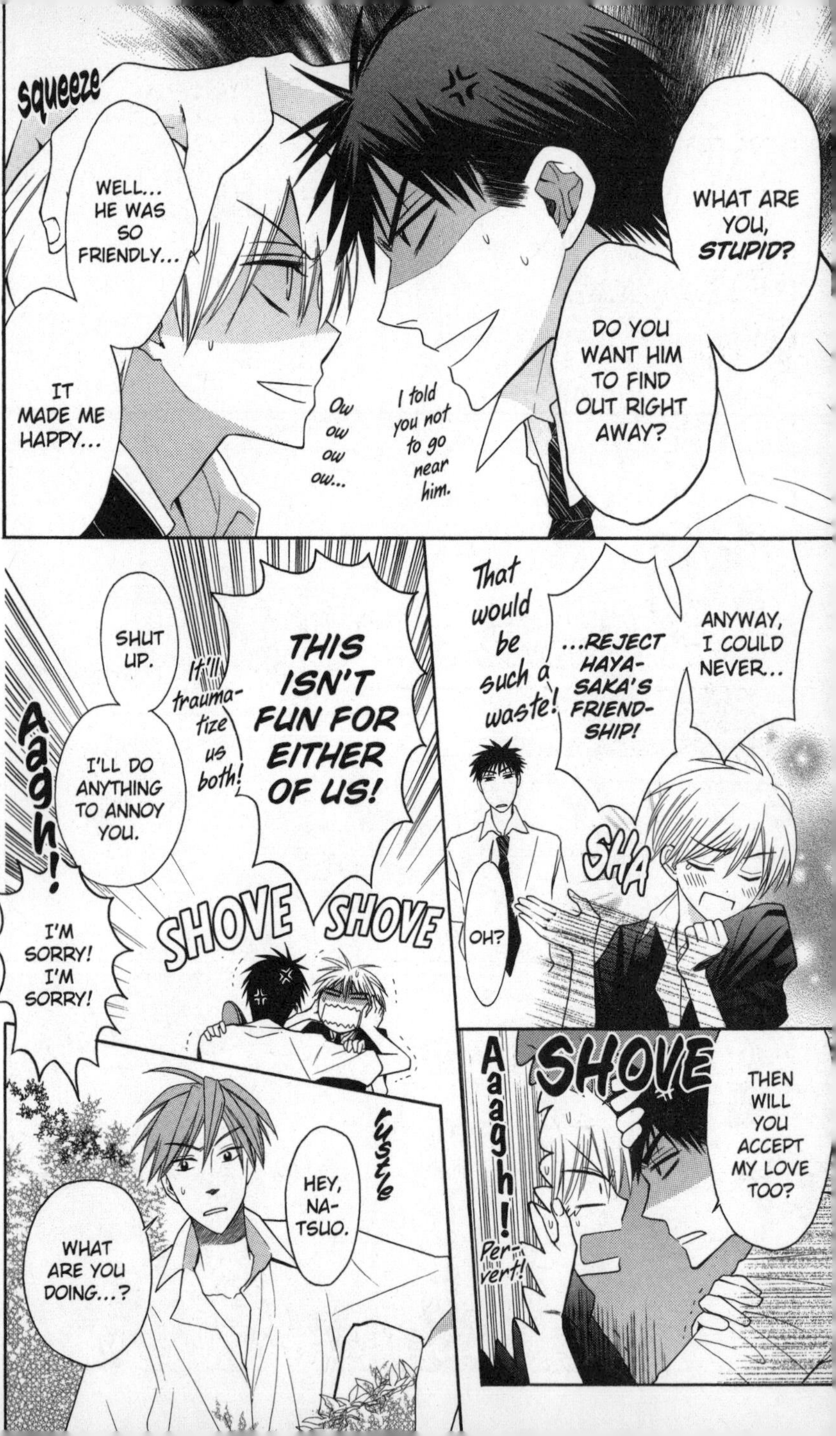
WHAT ARE YOU, STUPID?
DO YOU WANT HIM TO FIND OUT RIGHT AWAY?
I told you not to go near him.
Ow ow ow ow...
squeeze
WELL... HE WAS SO FRIENDLY...
IT MADE ME HAPPY...
ANYWAY, I COULD NEVER...
...REJECT HAYA-SAKA'S FRIEND-SHIP!
That would be such a waste!
SHA
OH?
SHOVE
THEN WILL YOU ACCEPT MY LOVE TOO?
Aaagh!
Per-vert!
THIS ISN'T FUN FOR EITHER OF US!
It'll trauma-tize us both!
SHUT UP.
I'LL DO ANYTHING TO ANNOY YOU.
Aagh!
SHOVE SHOVE
I'M SORRY! I'M SORRY!
rustle
HEY, NA-TSUO.
WHAT ARE YOU DOING...?

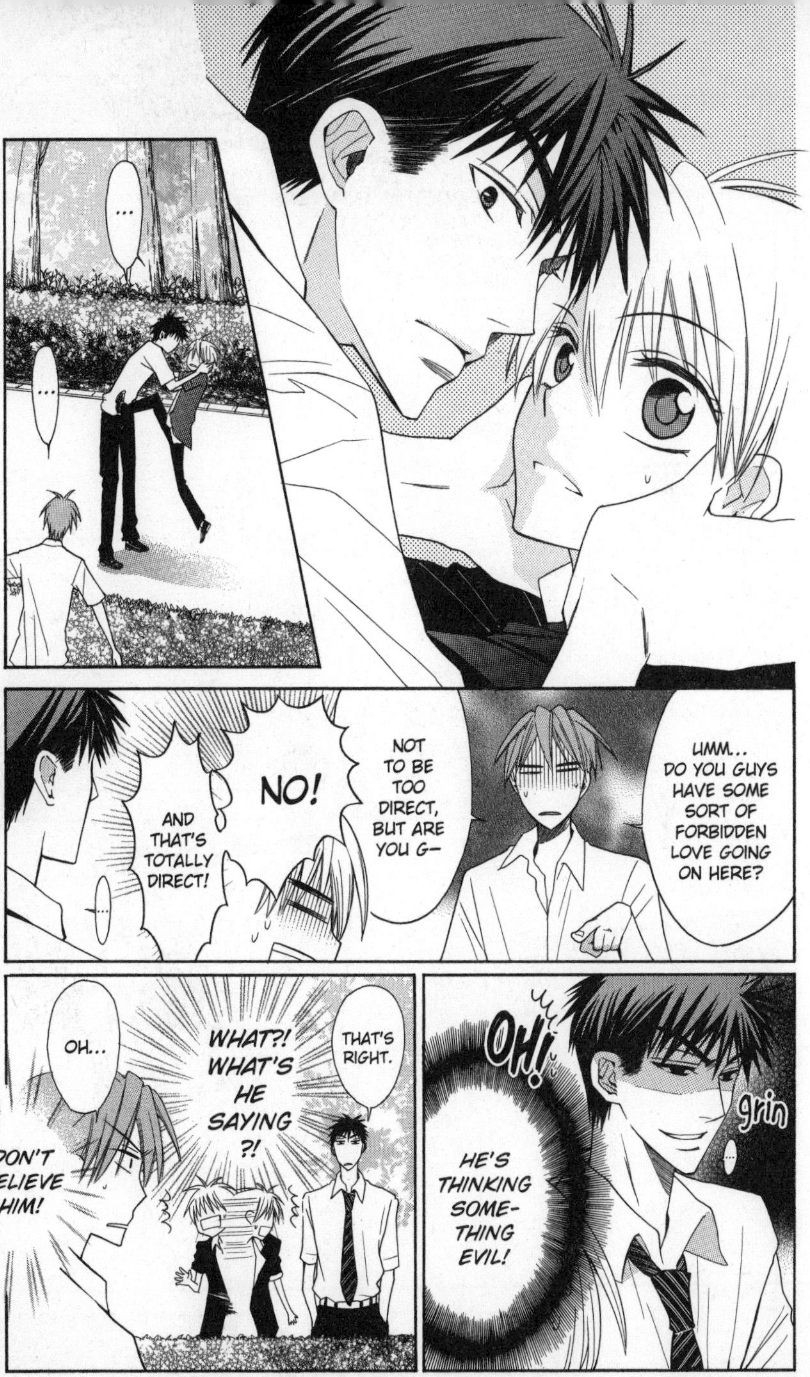
...
...
UMM... DO YOU GUYS HAVE SOME SORT OF FORBIDDEN LOVE GOING ON HERE?
NOT TO BE TOO DIRECT, BUT ARE YOU G—
NO!
AND THAT'S TOTALLY DIRECT!
...
OH!
grin
...
HE'S THINKING SOME-THING EVIL!
THAT'S RIGHT.
WHAT?! WHAT'S HE SAYING?!
OH...
DON'T BELIEVE HIM!

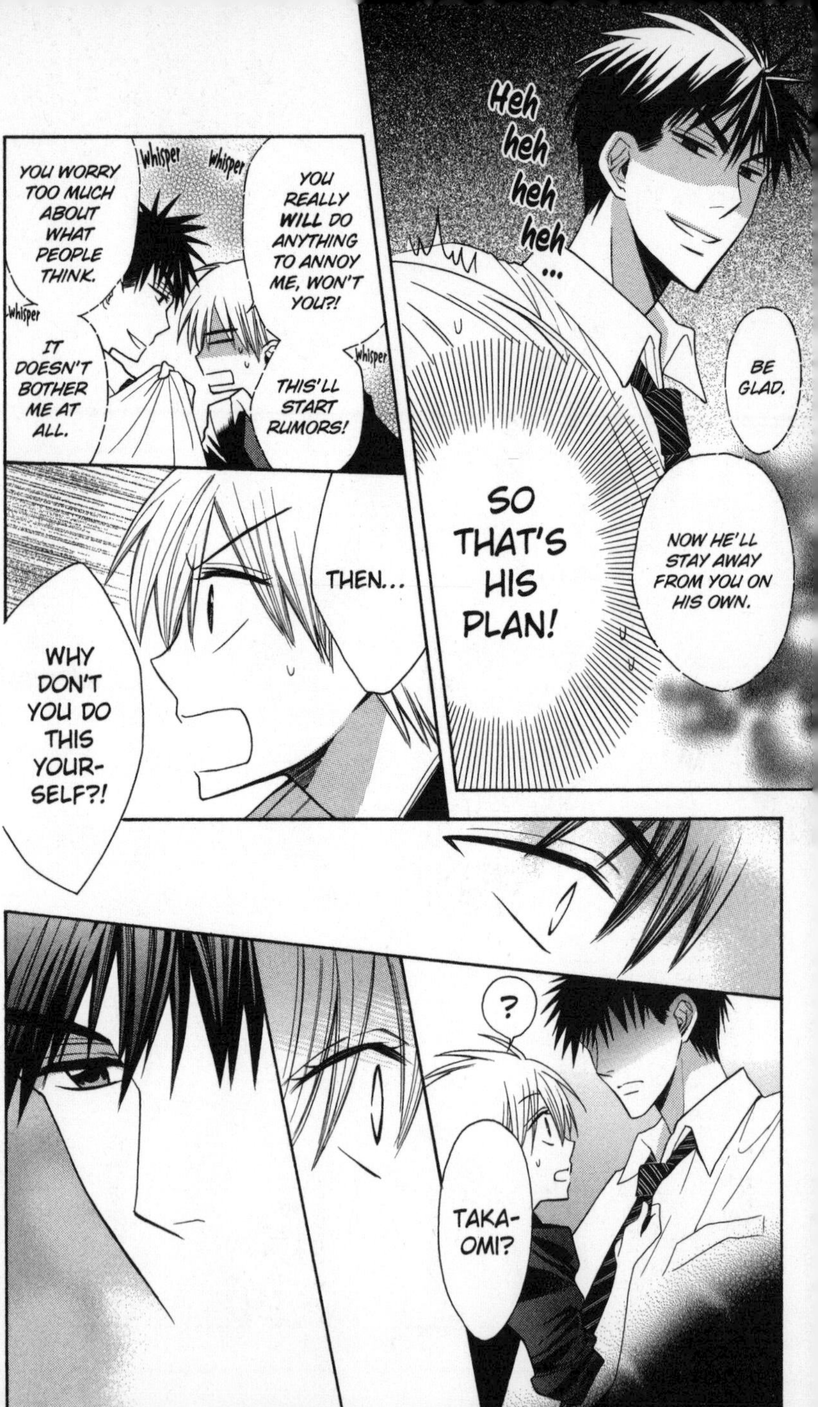
Heh heh heh heh...
BE GLAD.
NOW HE'LL STAY AWAY FROM YOU ON HIS OWN.
SO THAT'S HIS PLAN!
whisper
whisper
YOU REALLY WILL DO ANYTHING TO ANNOY ME, WON'T YOU?!
whisper
THIS'LL START RUMORS!
YOU WORRY TOO MUCH ABOUT WHAT PEOPLE THINK.
whisper
IT DOESN'T BOTHER ME AT ALL.
THEN...
WHY DON'T YOU DO THIS YOUR-SELF?!
?
TAKA-OMI?

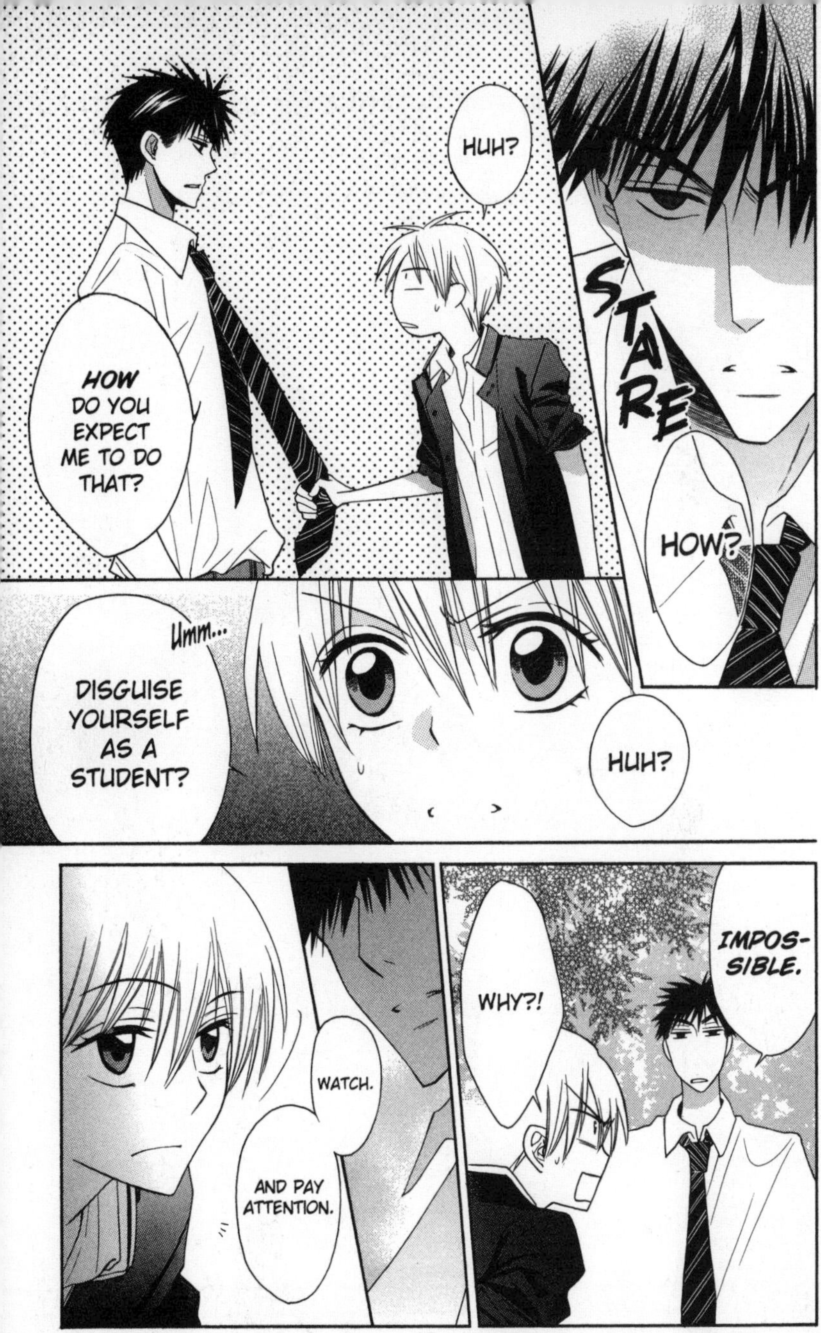
STARE
HOW?
HUH?
HOW DO YOU EXPECT ME TO DO THAT?
Umm...
DISGUISE YOURSELF AS A STUDENT?
HUH?
IMPOSSIBLE.
WHY?!
WATCH.
AND PAY ATTENTION.

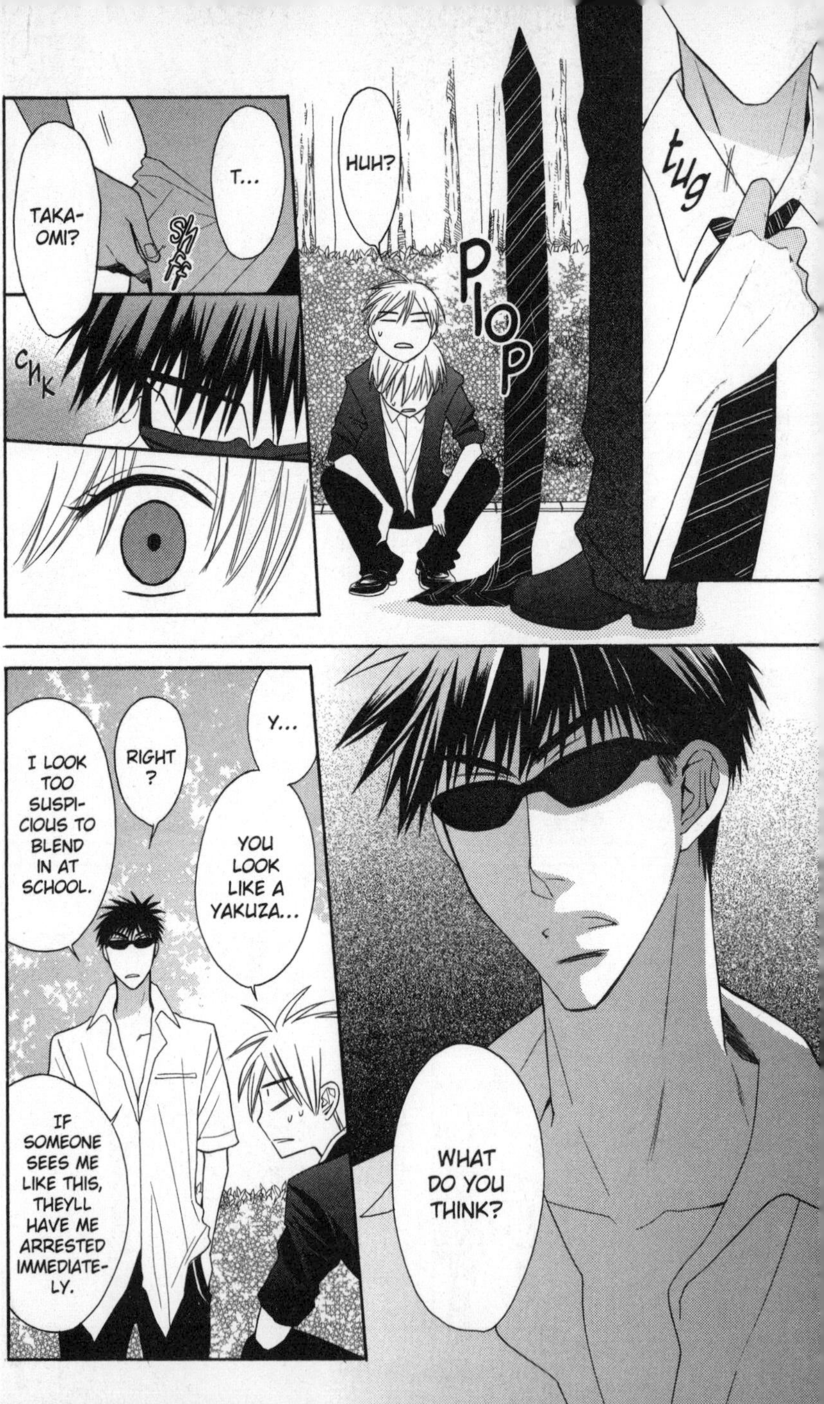
tug
HUH?
PLOP
T...
TAKA-OMI?
shff
CNK
WHAT DO YOU THINK?
Y...
YOU LOOK LIKE A YAKUZA...
RIGHT?
I LOOK TOO SUSPICIOUS TO BLEND IN AT SCHOOL.
IF SOMEONE SEES ME LIKE THIS, THEYLL HAVE ME ARRESTED IMMEDIATE-LY.

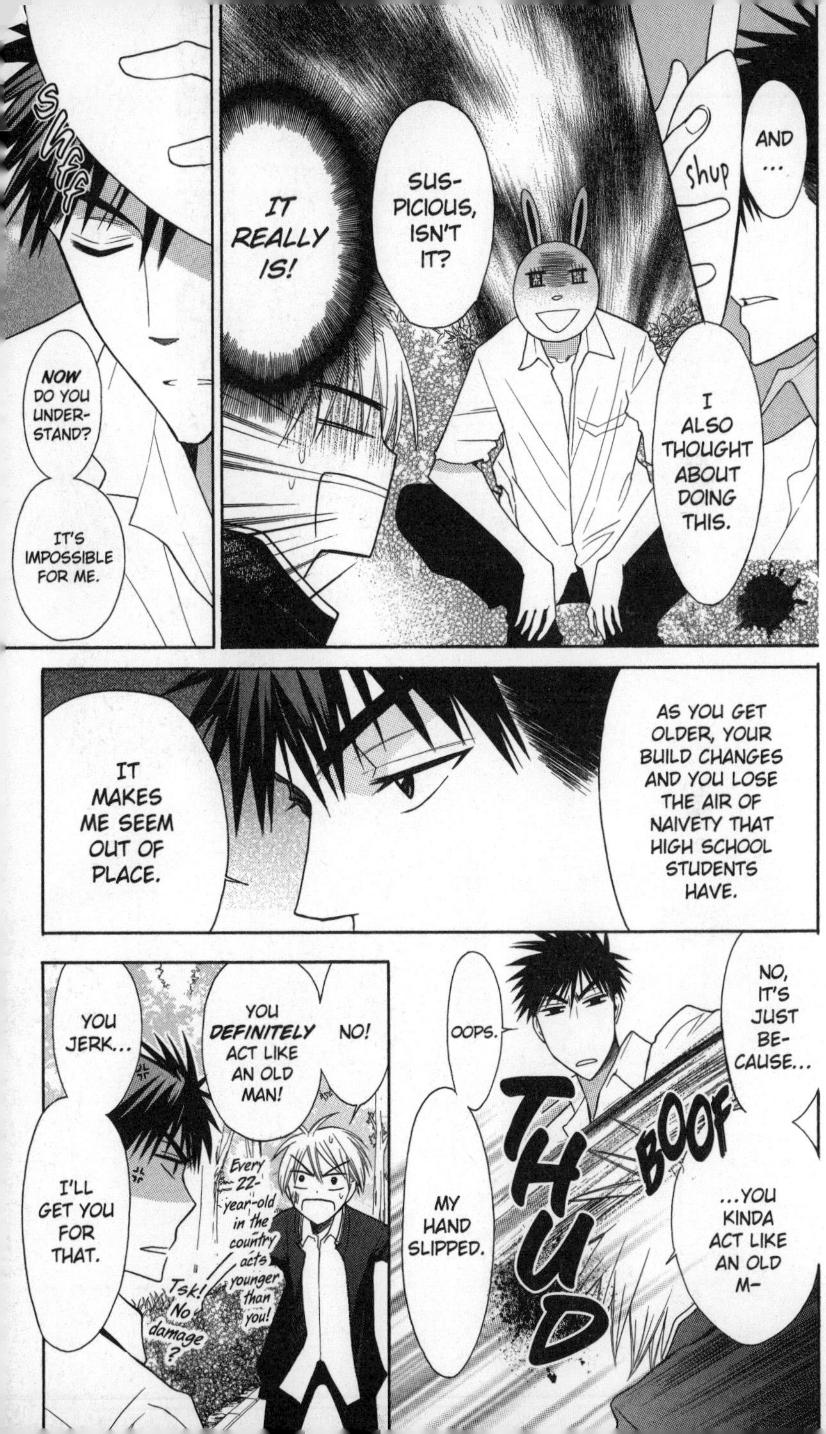
AND...
shup
I ALSO THOUGHT ABOUT DOING THIS.
SUS-PICIOUS, ISN'T IT?
IT REALLY IS!
SHFF
NOW DO YOU UNDER-STAND?
IT'S IMPOSSIBLE FOR ME.
AS YOU GET OLDER, YOUR BUILD CHANGES AND YOU LOSE THE AIR OF NAIVETY THAT HIGH SCHOOL STUDENTS HAVE.
IT MAKES ME SEEM OUT OF PLACE.
NO, IT'S JUST BE-CAUSE...
OOPS.
...YOU KINDA ACT LIKE AN OLD M-
BOOF
THUD
MY HAND SLIPPED.
NO!
YOU DEFINITELY ACT LIKE AN OLD MAN!
YOU JERK...
Every 22-year-old in the country acts younger than you!
I'LL GET YOU FOR THAT.
Tsk! No damage?

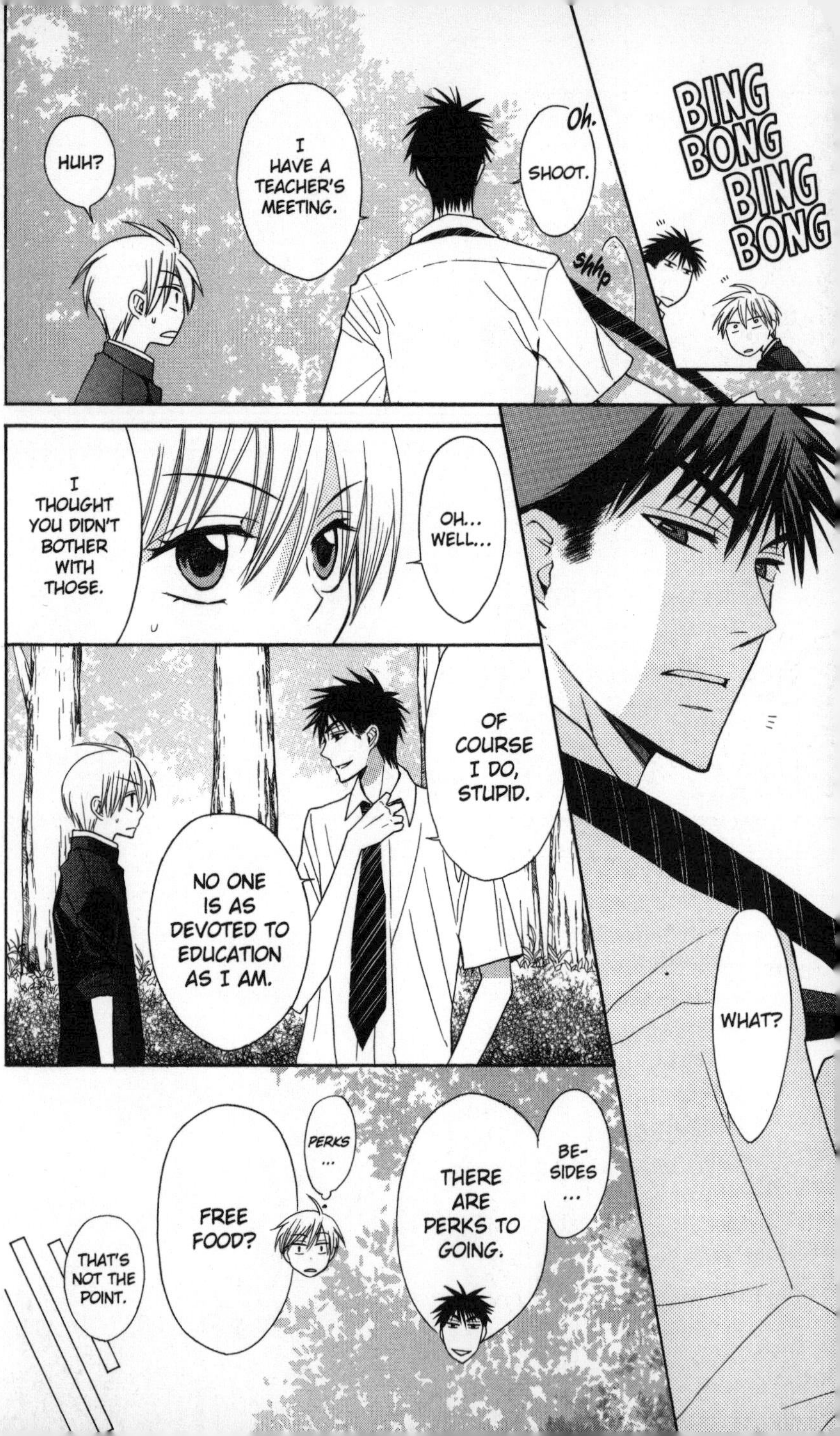
BING BONG BING BONG
shhp
Oh.
SHOOT.
I HAVE A TEACHER'S MEETING.
HUH?
WHAT?
OH... WELL...
I THOUGHT YOU DIDN'T BOTHER WITH THOSE.
OF COURSE I DO, STUPID.
NO ONE IS AS DEVOTED TO EDUCATION AS I AM.
BE-SIDES...
THERE ARE PERKS TO GOING.
PERKS...
FREE FOOD?
THAT'S NOT THE POINT.

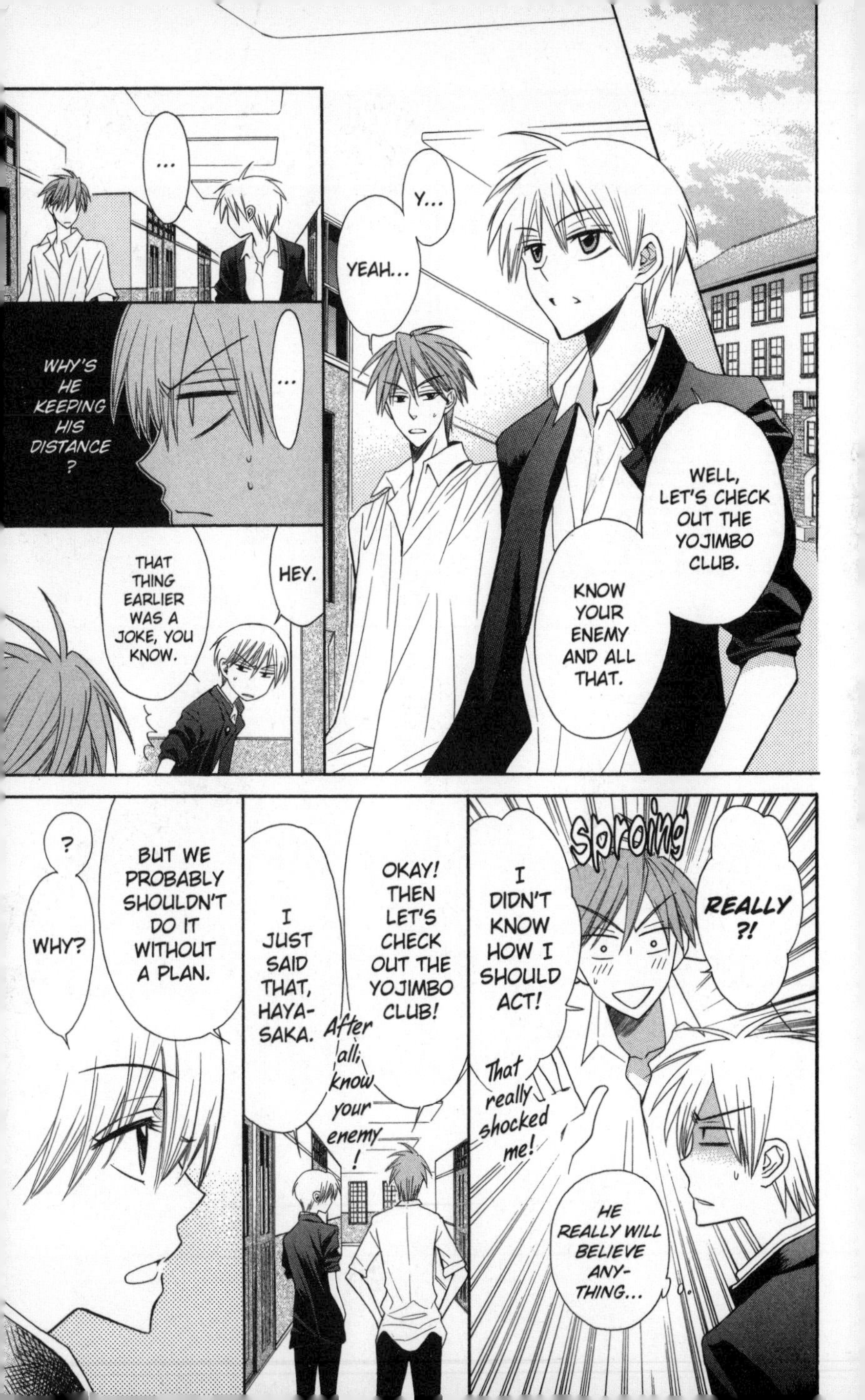
WELL, LET'S CHECK OUT THE YOJIMBO CLUB.
KNOW YOUR ENEMY AND ALL THAT.
Y... YEAH...
...
WHY'S HE KEEPING HIS DISTANCE?
...
HEY.
THAT THING EARLIER WAS A JOKE, YOU KNOW.
REALLY?!
sproing
I DIDN'T KNOW HOW I SHOULD ACT!
That really shocked me!
HE REALLY WILL BELIEVE ANYTHING...
OKAY! THEN LET'S CHECK OUT THE YOJIMBO CLUB!
I JUST SAID THAT, HAYA-SAKA.
After all, know your enemy!
BUT WE PROBABLY SHOULDN'T DO IT WITHOUT A PLAN.
?
WHY?

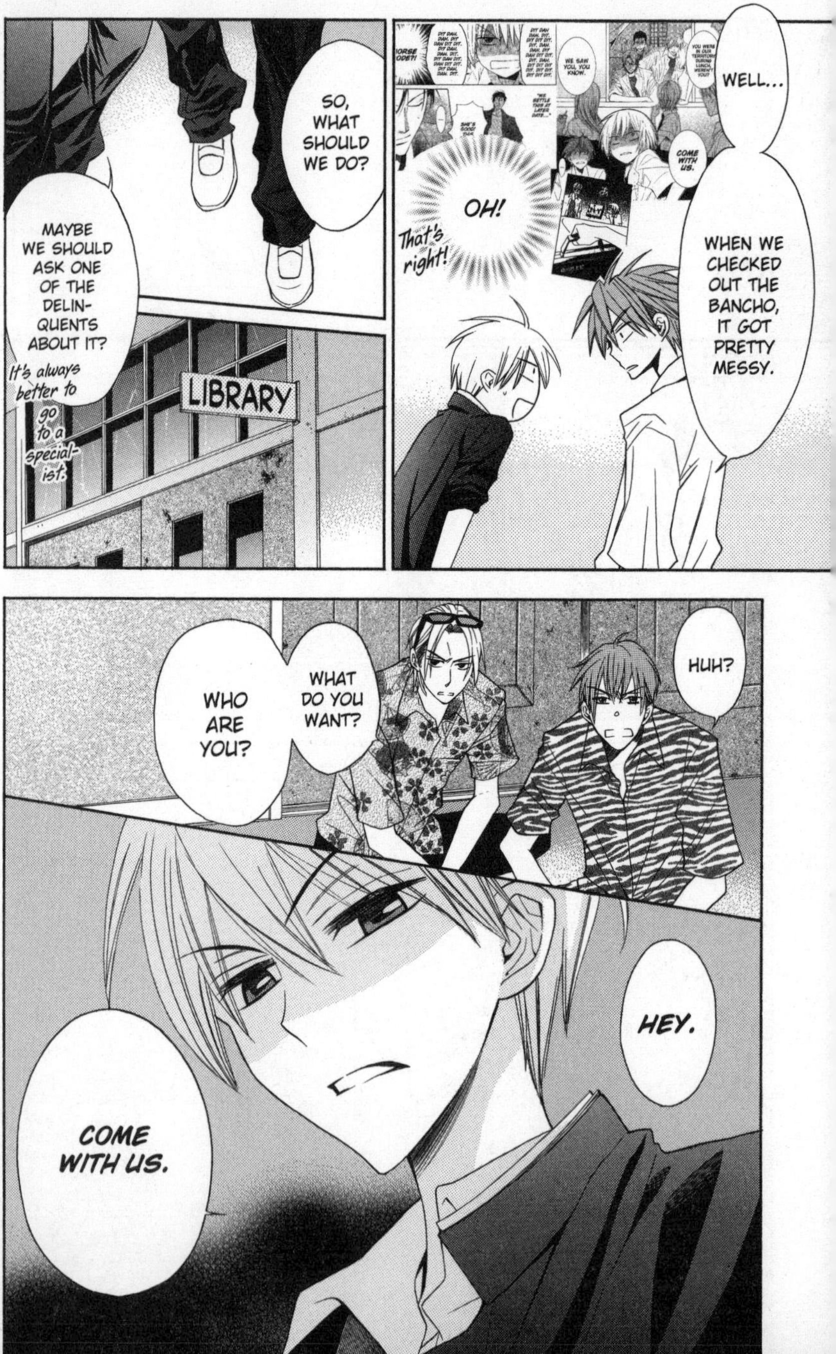
WELL...
YOU WERE IN OUR TERRITORY DURING LUNCH, WEREN'T YOU?
WE SAW YOU, YOU KNOW.
COME WITH US.
WHEN WE CHECKED OUT THE BANCHO, IT GOT PRETTY MESSY.
OH!
That's right!
SO, WHAT SHOULD WE DO?
MAYBE WE SHOULD ASK ONE OF THE DELINQUENTS ABOUT IT?
It's always better to go to a specialist.
LIBRARY
HUH?
WHAT DO YOU WANT?
WHO ARE YOU?
HEY.
COME WITH US.

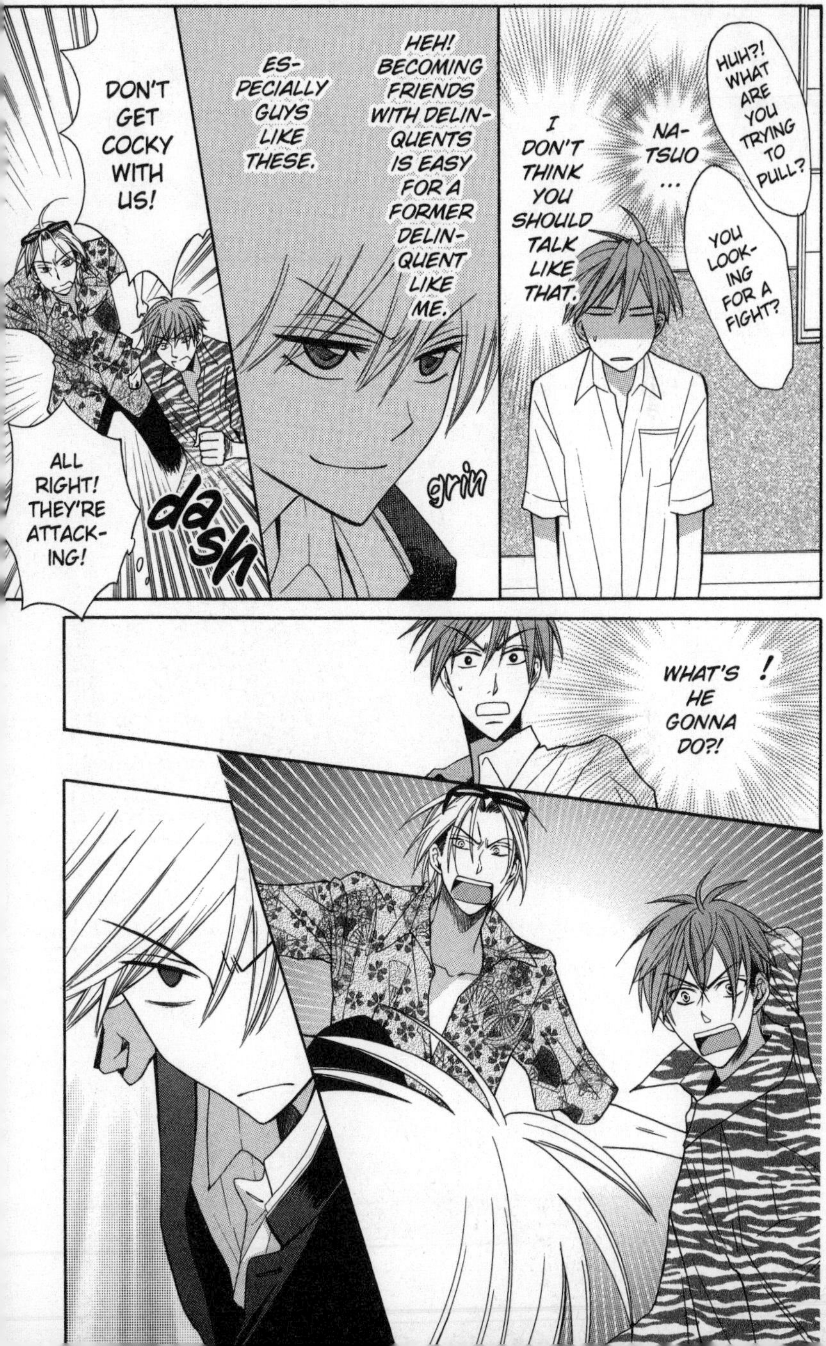
HUH?! WHAT ARE YOU TRYING TO PULL?
YOU LOOKING FOR A FIGHT?
NA-TSUO...
I DON'T THINK YOU SHOULD TALK LIKE THAT.
HEH! BECOMING FRIENDS WITH DELIN-QUENTS IS EASY FOR A FORMER DELIN-QUENT LIKE ME.
ES-PECIALLY GUYS LIKE THESE.
grin
DON'T GET COCKY WITH US!
dash
ALL RIGHT! THEY'RE ATTACK-ING!
!
WHAT'S HE GONNA DO?!

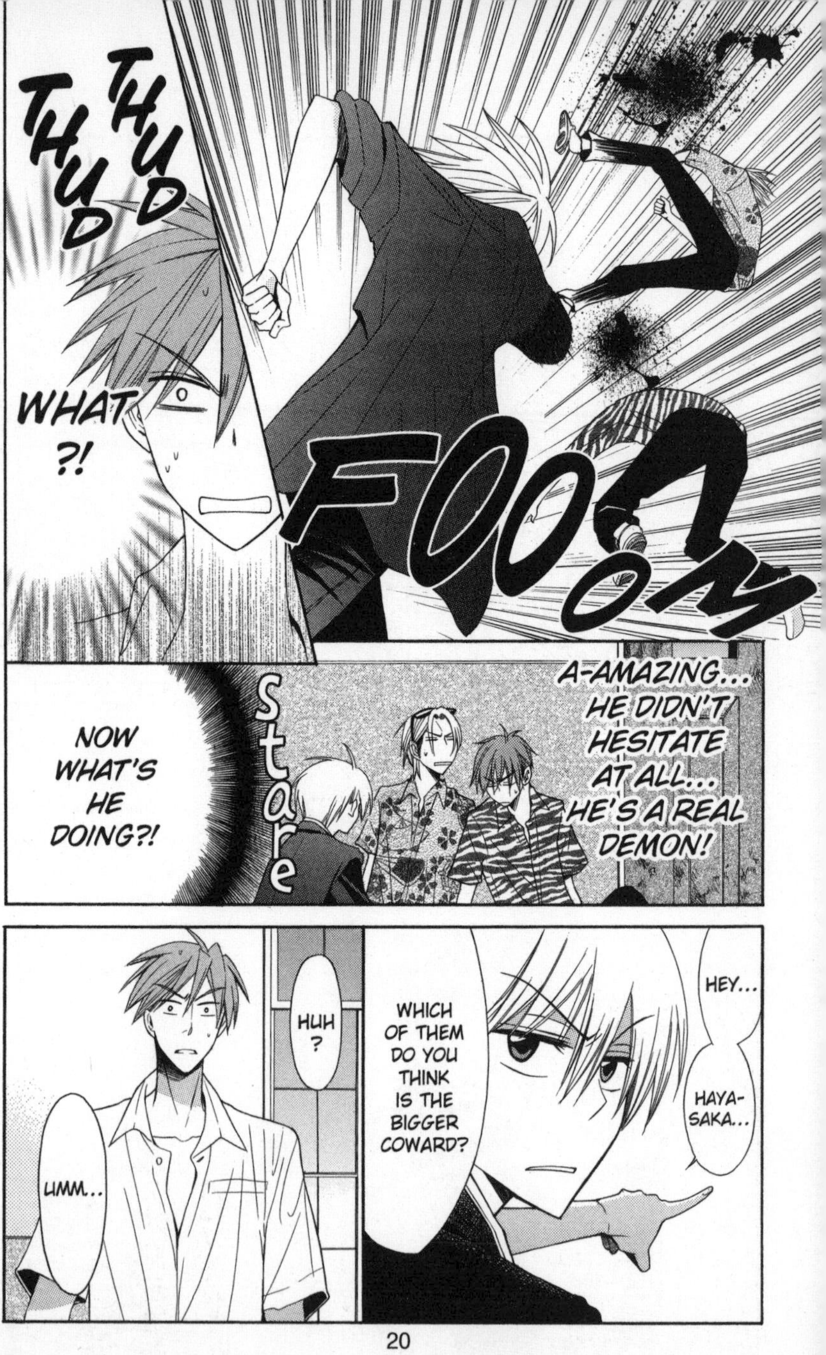
THUD THUD
FOOOOM
WHAT?!
A-AMAZING... HE DIDN'T HESITATE AT ALL... HE'S A REAL DEMON!
stare
NOW WHAT'S HE DOING?!
HEY... HAYA-SAKA...
WHICH OF THEM DO YOU THINK IS THE BIGGER COWARD?
HUH?
UMM...

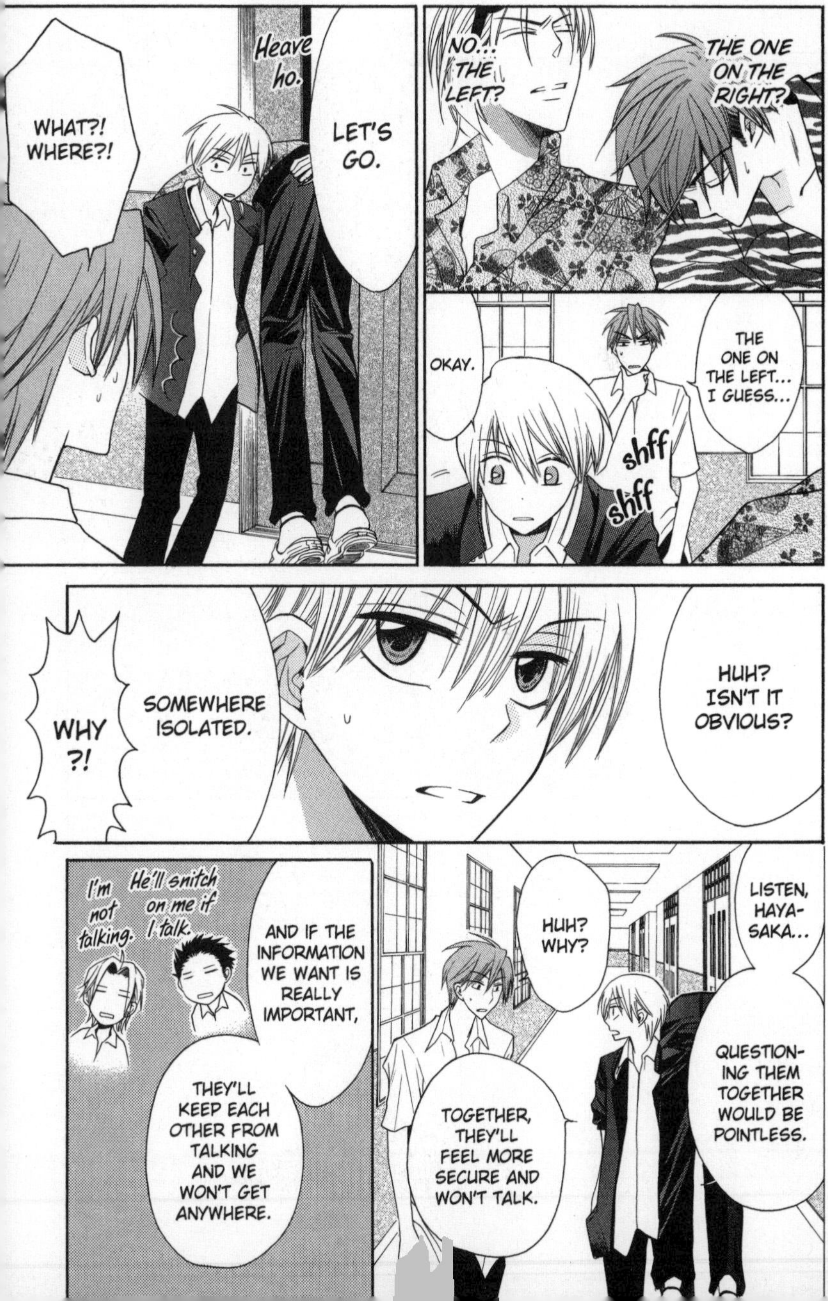
THE ONE ON THE RIGHT?
NO... THE LEFT?
THE ONE ON THE LEFT... I GUESS...
shff
shff
OKAY.
LET'S GO.
Heave ho.
WHAT?! WHERE?!
HUH? ISN'T IT OBVIOUS?
SOMEWHERE ISOLATED.
WHY ?!
LISTEN, HAYA-SAKA...
HUH? WHY?
QUESTION-ING THEM TOGETHER WOULD BE POINTLESS.
TOGETHER, THEY'LL FEEL MORE SECURE AND WON'T TALK.
AND IF THE INFORMATION WE WANT IS REALLY IMPORTANT,
He'll snitch on me if I talk.
I'm not talking.
THEY'LL KEEP EACH OTHER FROM TALKING AND WE WON'T GET ANYWHERE.

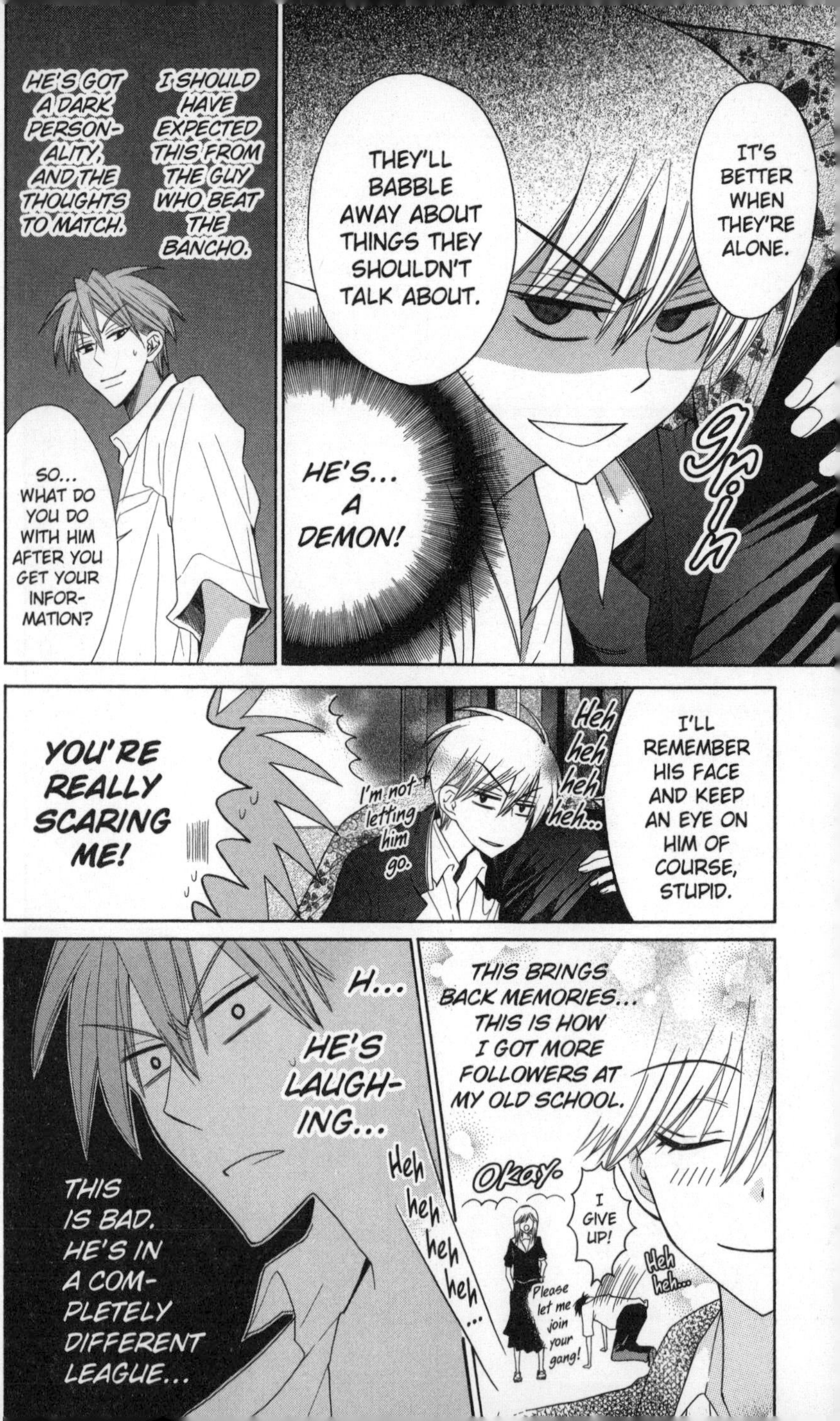
IT'S BETTER WHEN THEY'RE ALONE.
THEY'LL BABBLE AWAY ABOUT THINGS THEY SHOULDN'T TALK ABOUT.
grin
HE'S... A DEMON!
I SHOULD HAVE EXPECTED THIS FROM THE GUY WHO BEAT THE BANCHO.
HE'S GOT A DARK PERSON-ALITY, AND THE THOUGHTS TO MATCH.
SO... WHAT DO YOU DO WITH HIM AFTER YOU GET YOUR INFOR-MATION?
I'LL REMEMBER HIS FACE AND KEEP AN EYE ON HIM OF COURSE, STUPID.
Heh heh heh heh...
I'm not letting him go.
YOU'RE REALLY SCARING ME!
THIS BRINGS BACK MEMORIES... THIS IS HOW I GOT MORE FOLLOWERS AT MY OLD SCHOOL.
Okay.
I GIVE UP!
Please let me join your gang!
Heh heh...
H...
HE'S LAUGH-ING...
Heh heh heh heh...
THIS IS BAD. HE'S IN A COM-PLETELY DIFFERENT LEAGUE...

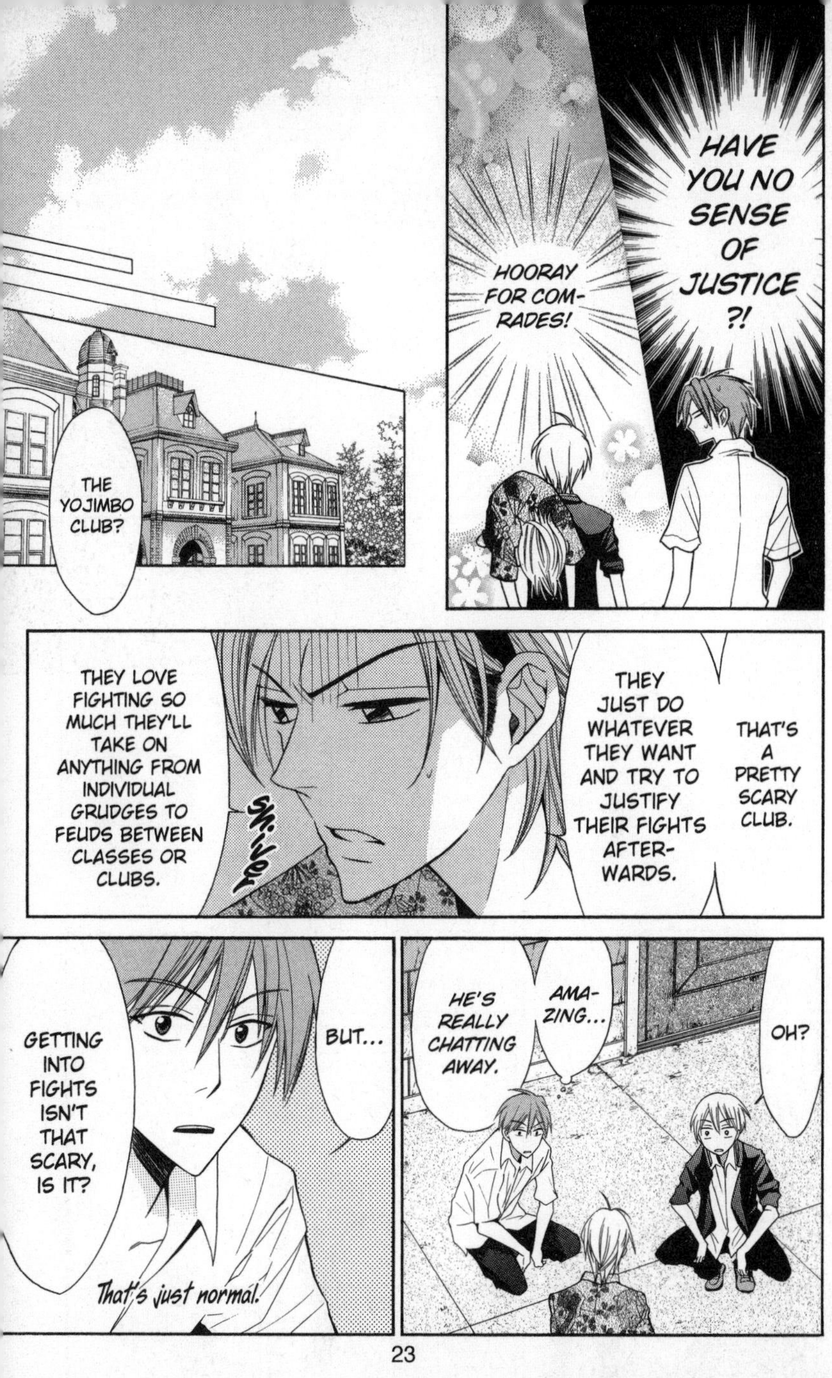
HAVE YOU NO SENSE OF JUSTICE?!
HOORAY FOR COM-RADES!
THE YOJIMBO CLUB?
THAT'S A PRETTY SCARY CLUB.
THEY JUST DO WHATEVER THEY WANT AND TRY TO JUSTIFY THEIR FIGHTS AFTER-WARDS.
shiver
THEY LOVE FIGHTING SO MUCH THEY'LL TAKE ON ANYTHING FROM INDIVIDUAL GRUDGES TO FEUDS BETWEEN CLASSES OR CLUBS.
OH?
AMA-ZING...
HE'S REALLY CHATTING AWAY.
BUT...
GETTING INTO FIGHTS ISN'T THAT SCARY, IS IT?
That's just normal.

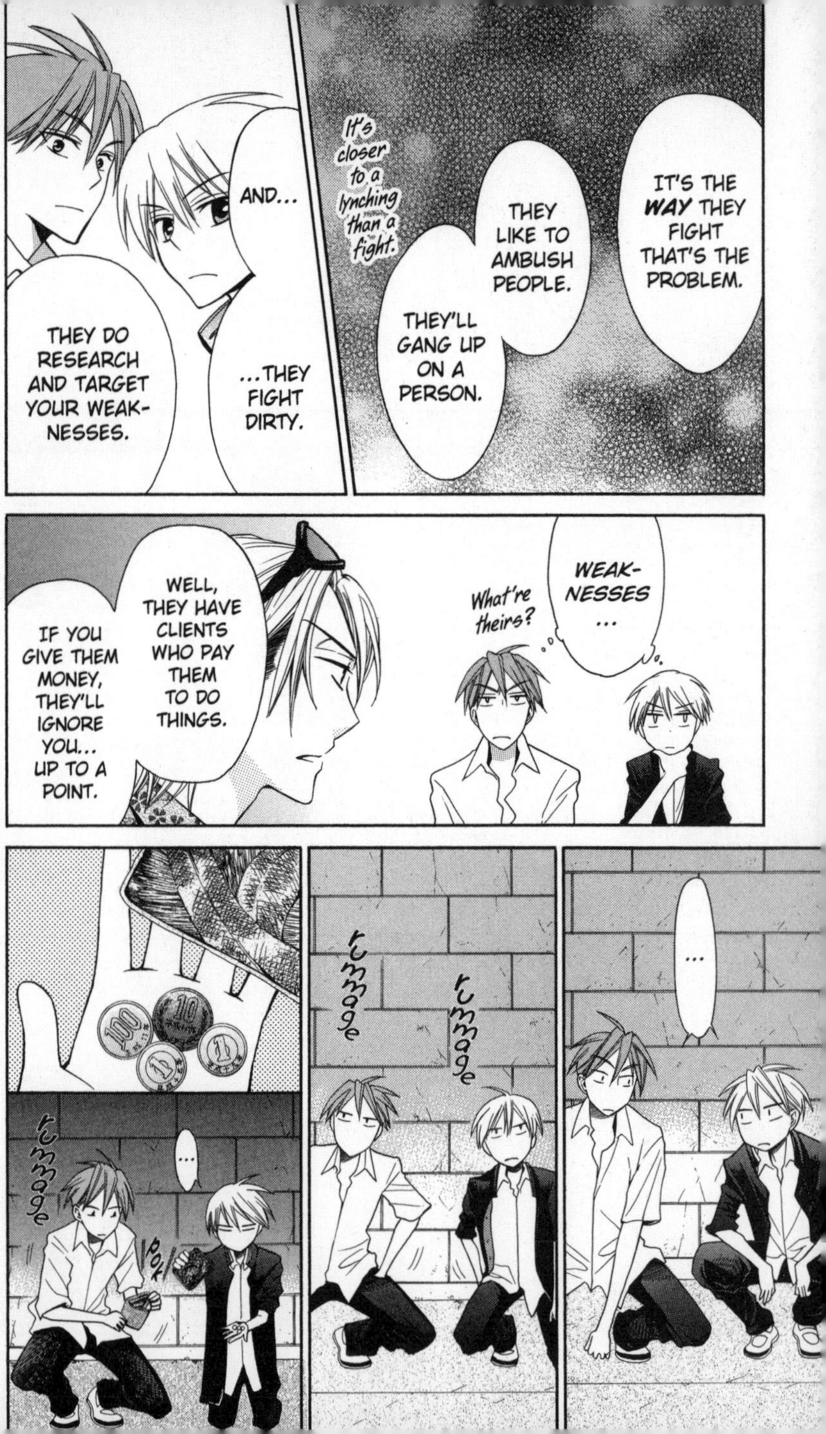
IT'S THE WAY THEY FIGHT THAT'S THE PROBLEM.
THEY LIKE TO AMBUSH PEOPLE.
THEY'LL GANG UP ON A PERSON.
It's closer to a lynching than a fight.
AND...
...THEY FIGHT DIRTY.
THEY DO RESEARCH AND TARGET YOUR WEAK-NESSES.
WEAK-NESSES ...
What're theirs?
WELL, THEY HAVE CLIENTS WHO PAY THEM TO DO THINGS.
IF YOU GIVE THEM MONEY, THEY'LL IGNORE YOU... UP TO A POINT.
...
rummage
rummage
10
100
1
1
rummage
...
pok

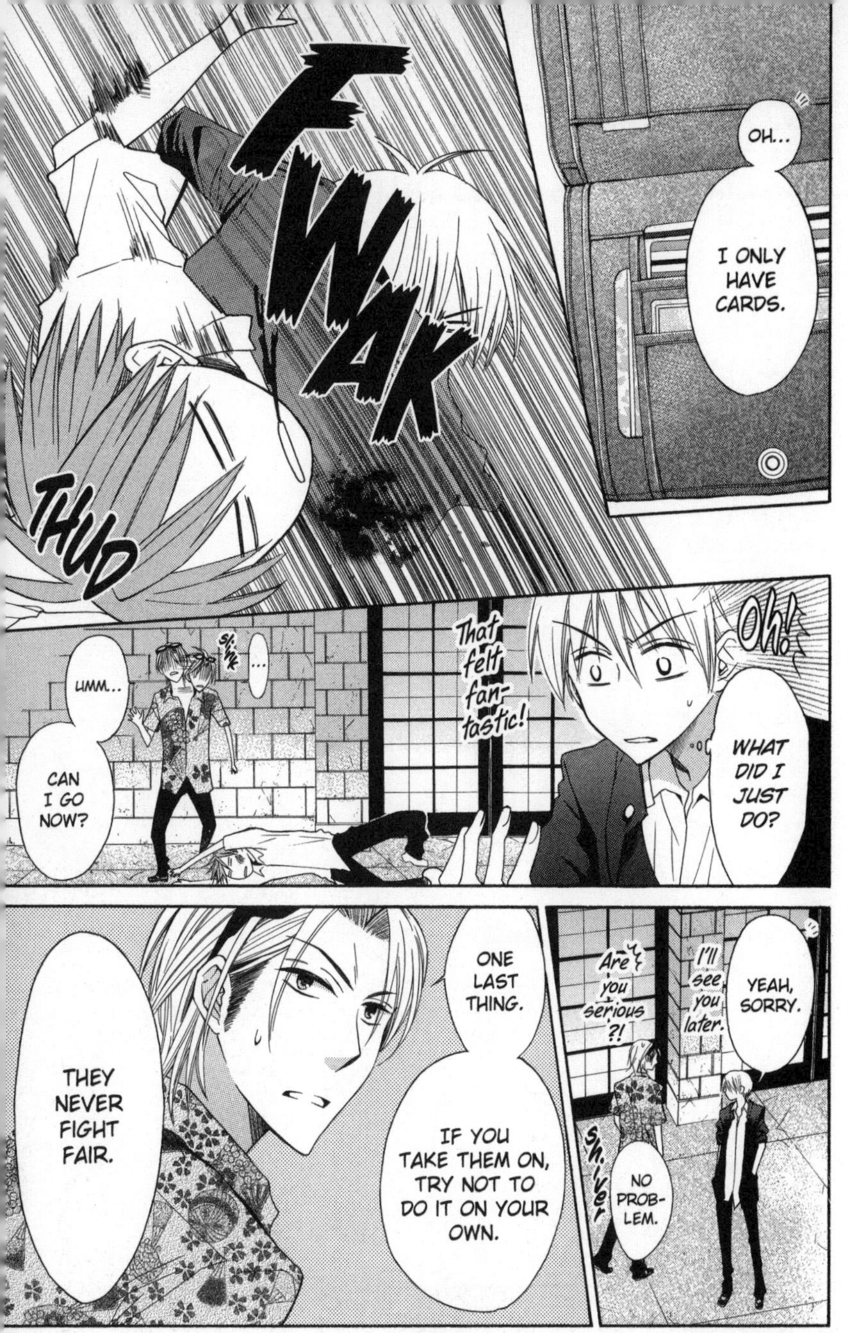
OH...
I ONLY HAVE CARDS.
WHAK
THUD
Oh!
WHAT DID I JUST DO?
That felt fan-tastic!
...
slink
UMM...
CAN I GO NOW?
YEAH, SORRY.
I'll see you later.
Are you serious?!
shiver
NO PROB-LEM.
ONE LAST THING.
IF YOU TAKE THEM ON, TRY NOT TO DO IT ON YOUR OWN.
THEY NEVER FIGHT FAIR.

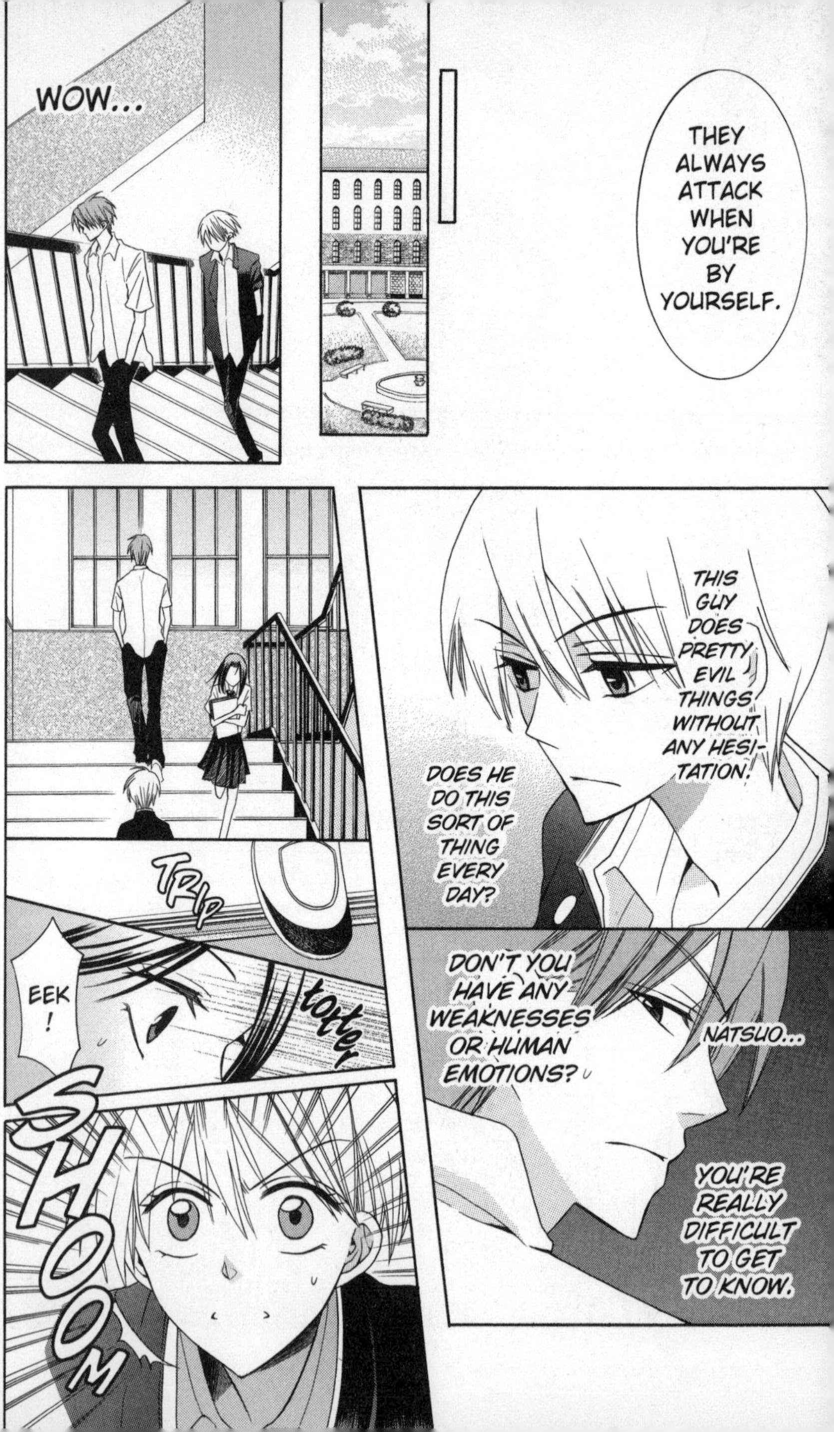

THEY ALWAYS ATTACK WHEN YOU'RE BY YOURSELF.
WOW...
THIS GUY DOES PRETTY EVIL THINGS WITHOUT ANY HESI-TATION.
DOES HE DO THIS SORT OF THING EVERY DAY?
DON'T YOU HAVE ANY WEAKNESSES OR HUMAN EMOTIONS?
NATSUO...
YOU'RE REALLY DIFFICULT TO GET TO KNOW.
TRIP
EEK!
totter
SHOOM

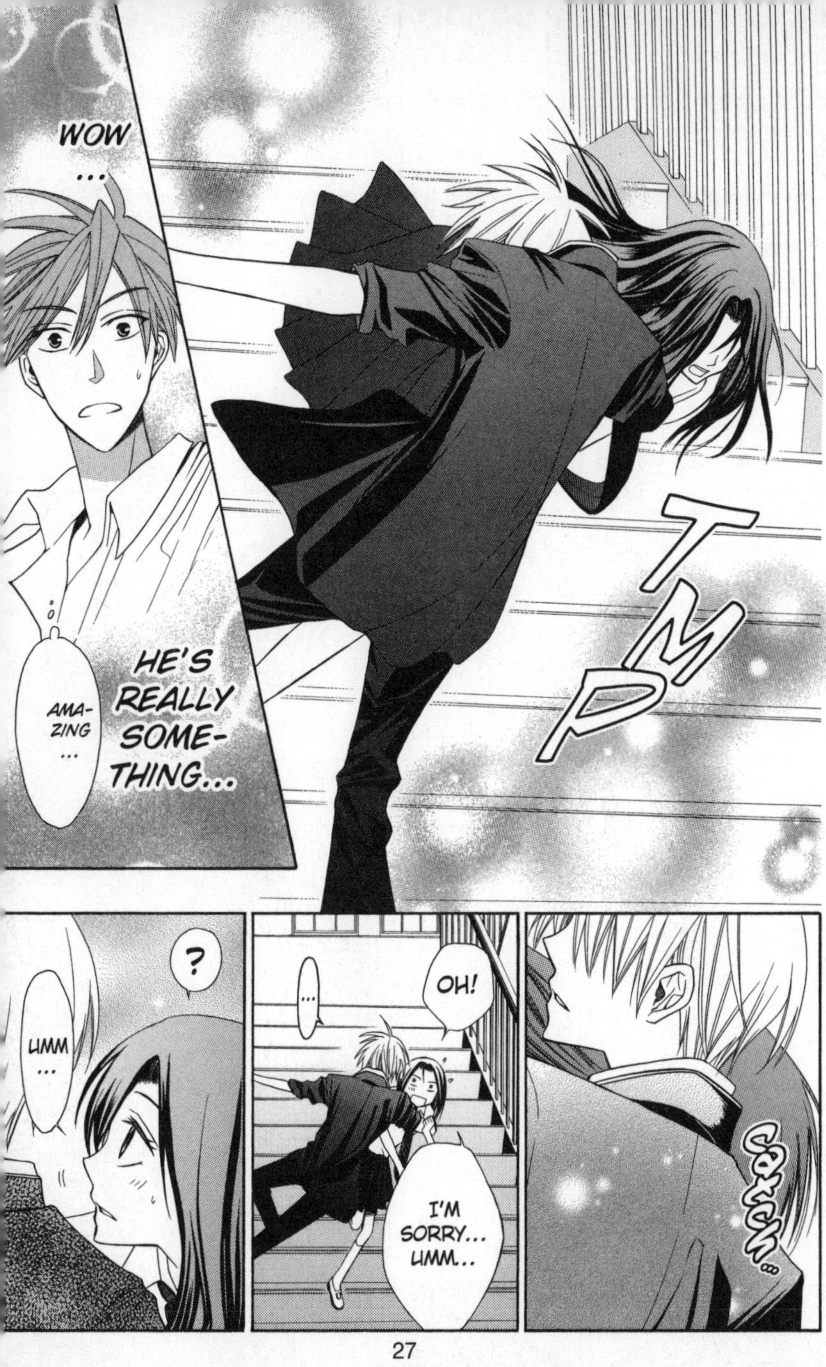
TMP
WOW ...
HE'S REALLY SOMETHING...
AMA-ZING ...
catch..
OH!
...
I'M SORRY... UMM...
?
UMM ...

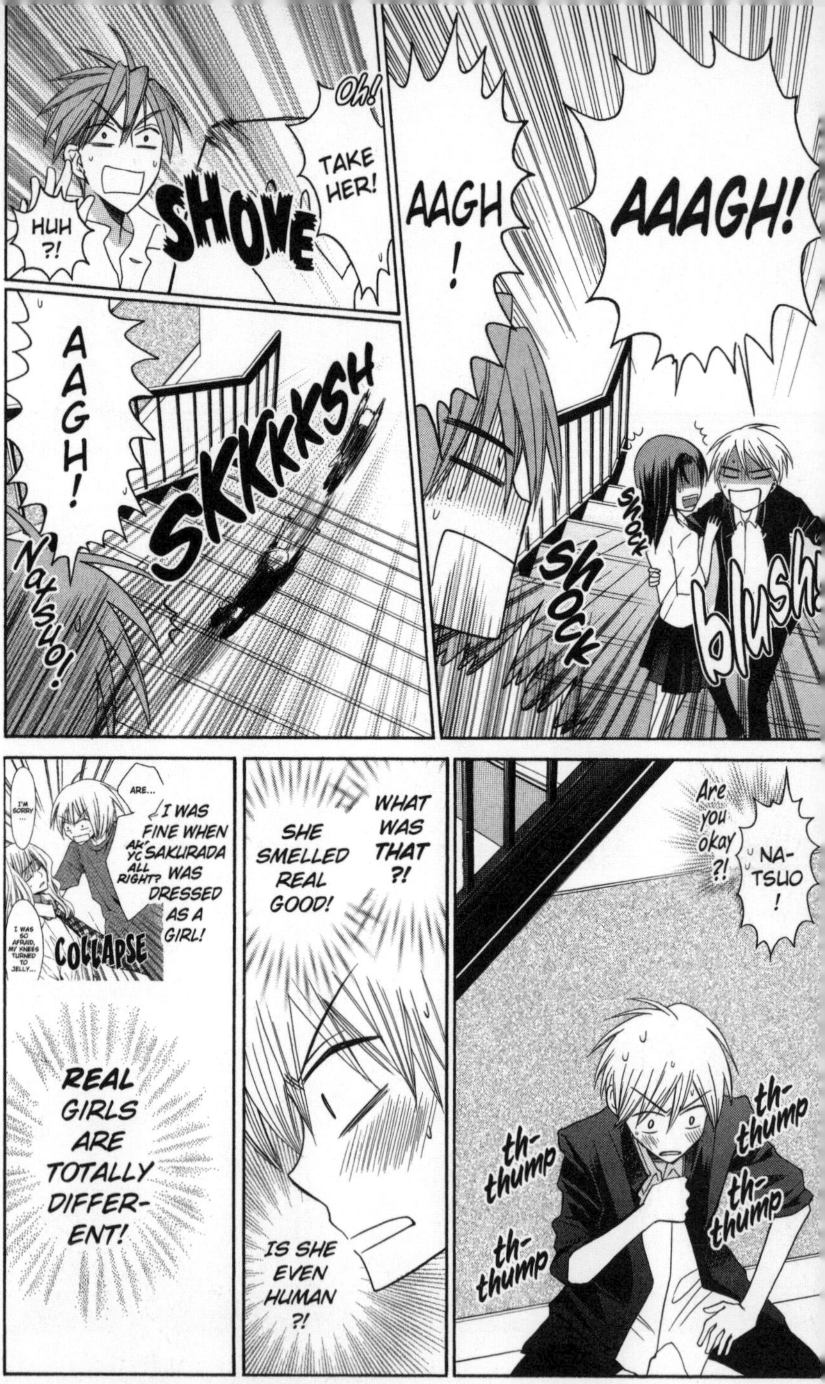
AAAGH!
AAGH!
SHOCK
SHOCK
blush
Oh!
TAKE HER!
SHOVE
HUH?!
AAGH!
SKKKKSH
Natsuo!
Are you okay?!
NA-TSUO!
th-thump
th-thump
th-thump
th-thump
WHAT WAS THAT?!
SHE SMELLED REAL GOOD!
IS SHE EVEN HUMAN?!
ARE...
I WAS FINE WHEN SAKURADA WAS DRESSED AS A GIRL!
I'M SORRY...
ALL RIGHT?
I WAS SO AFRAID, MY KNEES TURNED TO JELLY...
COLLAPSE
REAL GIRLS ARE TOTALLY DIFFER-ENT!

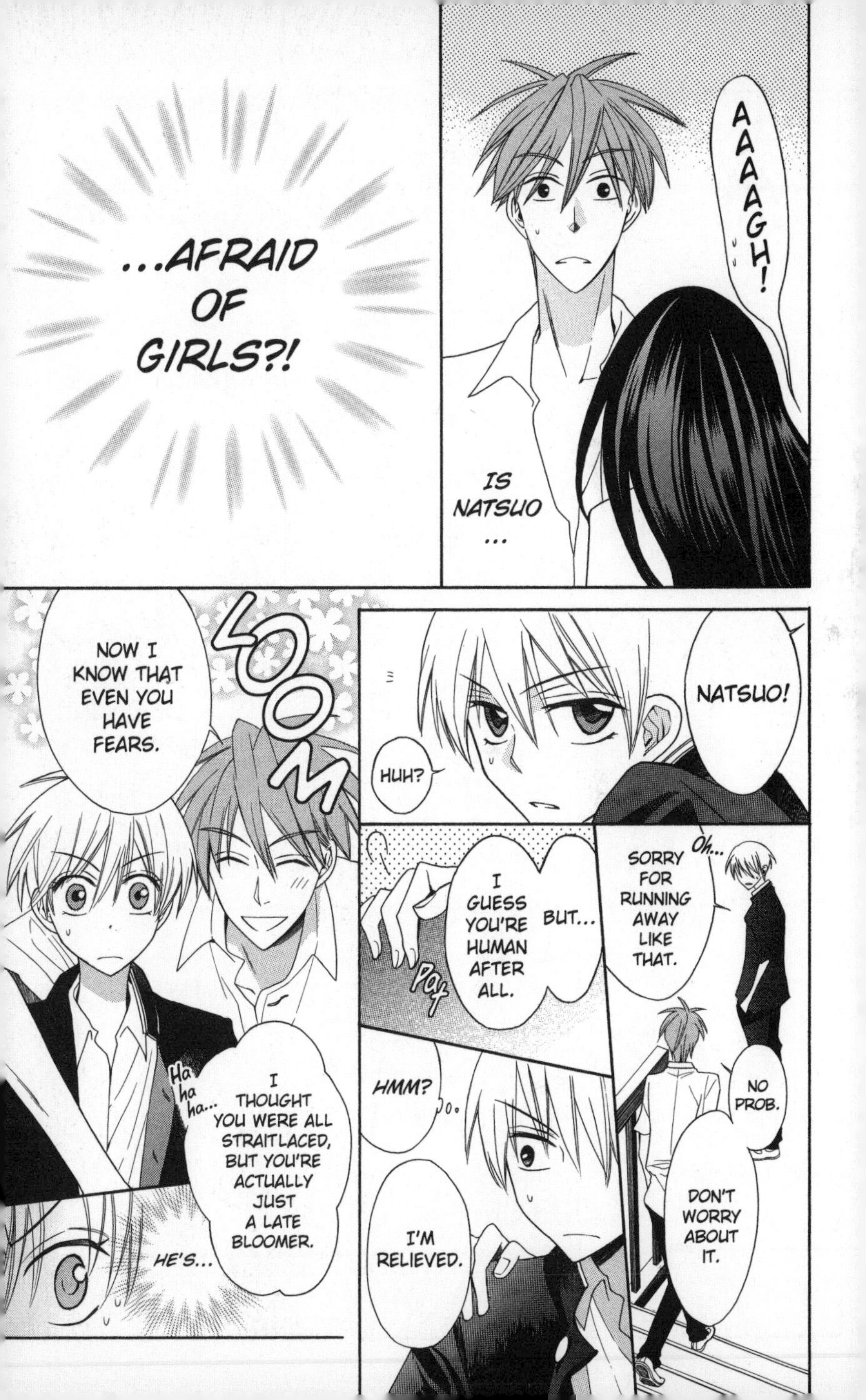
AAAAGH!
IS NATSUO...
...AFRAID OF GIRLS?!
NATSUO!
HUH?
Oh...
SORRY FOR RUNNING AWAY LIKE THAT.
NO PROB.
DON'T WORRY ABOUT IT.
Pat
I GUESS YOU'RE HUMAN AFTER ALL.
BUT...
HMM?
I'M RELIEVED.
NOW I KNOW THAT EVEN YOU HAVE FEARS.
LOOM
Ha ha ha...
I THOUGHT YOU WERE ALL STRAITLACED, BUT YOU'RE ACTUALLY JUST A LATE BLOOMER.
HE'S...

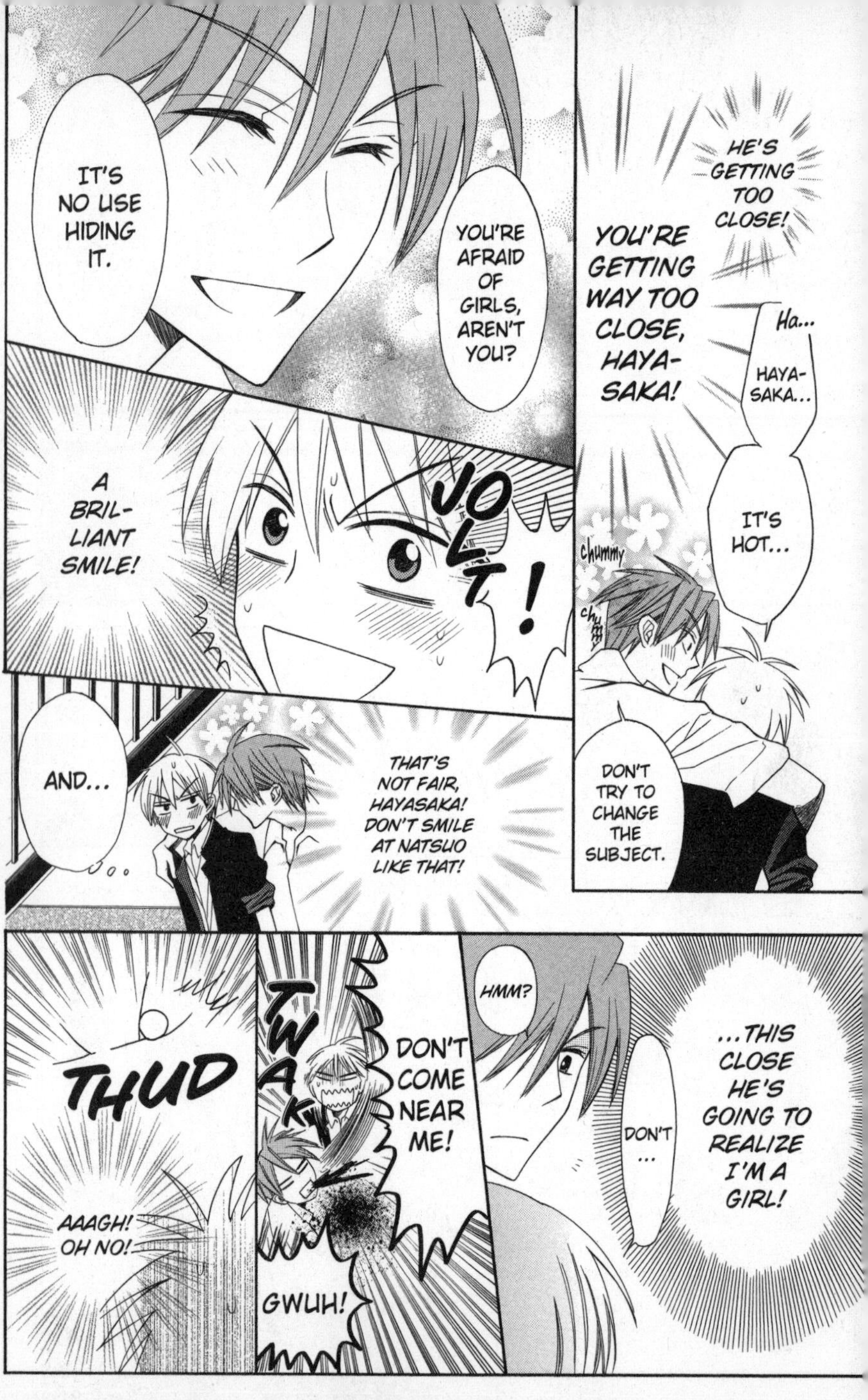
HE'S GETTING TOO CLOSE!
YOU'RE GETTING WAY TOO CLOSE, HAYA-SAKA!
Ha...
HAYA-SAKA...
IT'S HOT...
chummy
chu
DON'T TRY TO CHANGE THE SUBJECT.
YOU'RE AFRAID OF GIRLS, AREN'T YOU?
IT'S NO USE HIDING IT.
JOLT!
A BRIL-LIANT SMILE!
THAT'S NOT FAIR, HAYASAKA! DON'T SMILE AT NATSUO LIKE THAT!
AND...
HMM?
...THIS CLOSE HE'S GOING TO REALIZE I'M A GIRL!
DON'T ...
DON'T COME NEAR ME!
TWAK
GWUH!
THUD
AAAGH! OH NO!

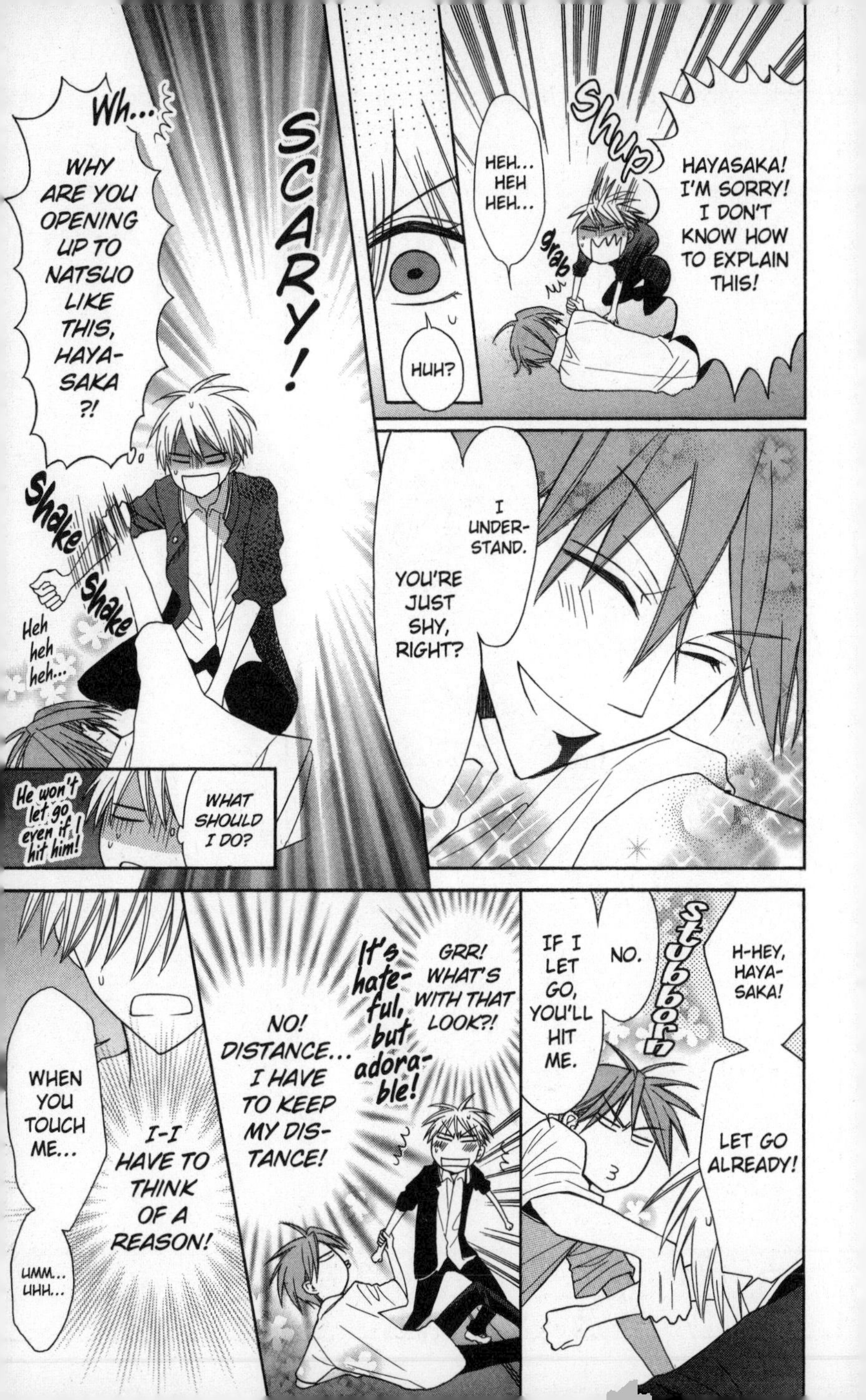
Shup
HAYASAKA! I'M SORRY! I DON'T KNOW HOW TO EXPLAIN THIS!
grab
HEH... HEH HEH...
HUH?
I UNDERSTAND.
YOU'RE JUST SHY, RIGHT?
Wh...
WHY ARE YOU OPENING UP TO NATSUO LIKE THIS, HAYA-SAKA ?!
SCARY!
Shake shake
Heh heh heh...
WHAT SHOULD I DO?
He won't let go even if I hit him!
H-HEY, HAYA-SAKA!
LET GO ALREADY!
stubborn
NO.
IF I LET GO, YOU'LL HIT ME.
GRR! WHAT'S WITH THAT LOOK?!
It's hate-ful, but adora-ble!
NO! DISTANCE... I HAVE TO KEEP MY DIS-TANCE!
I-I HAVE TO THINK OF A REASON!
WHEN YOU TOUCH ME...
UMM... UHH...

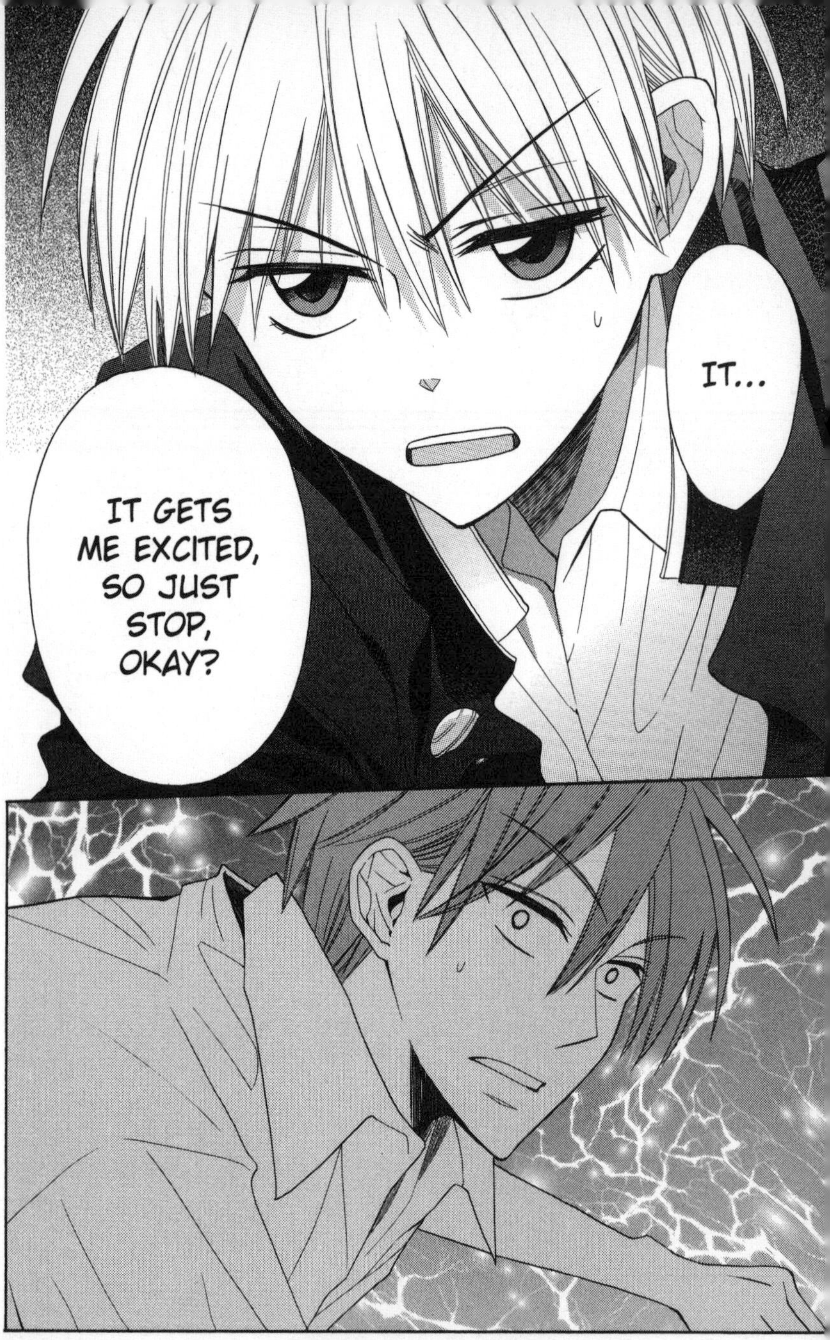
IT...
IT GETS ME EXCITED, SO JUST STOP, OKAY?

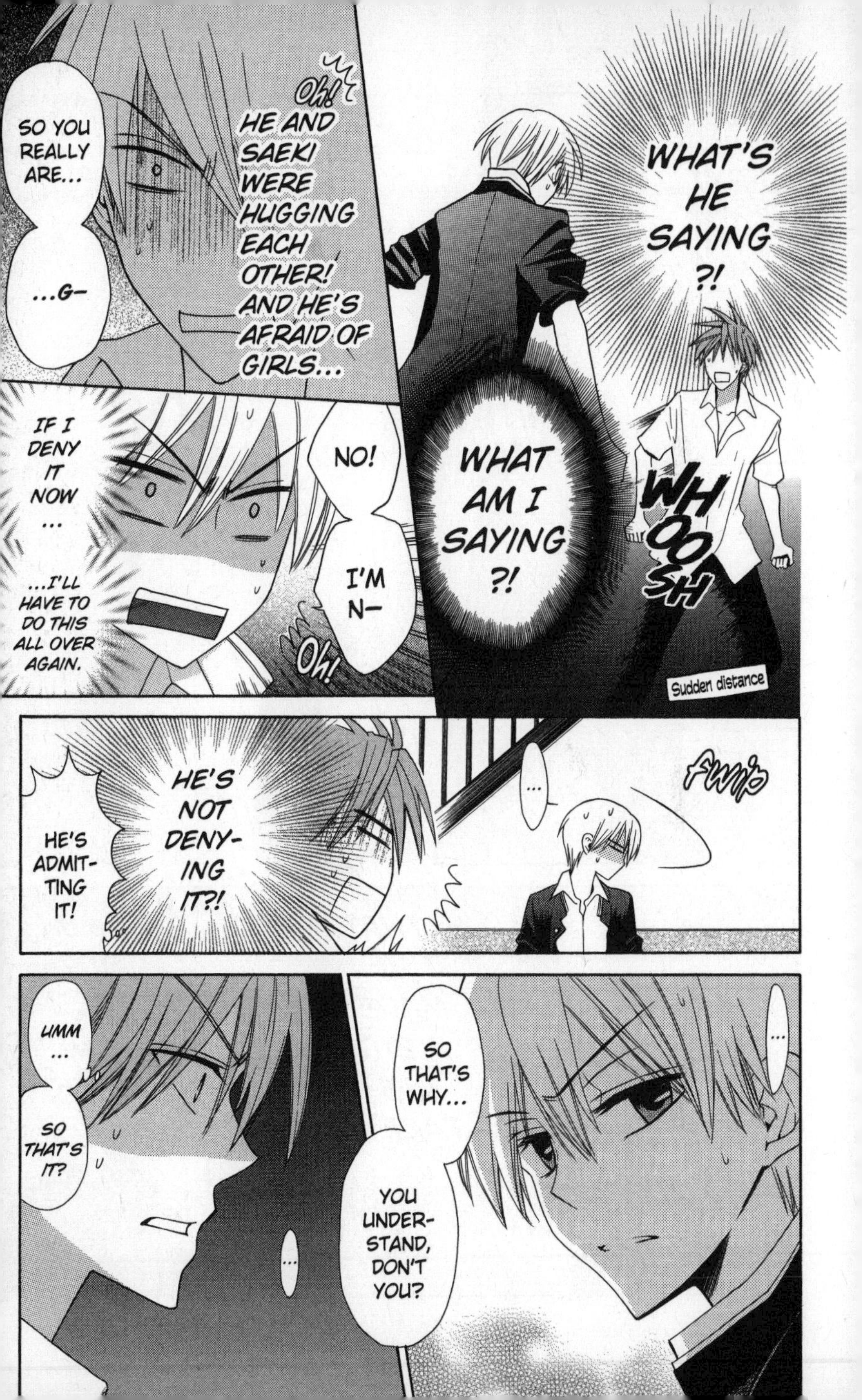
WHAT'S HE SAYING?!
WHAT AM I SAYING?!
WHOOSH
Sudden distance
Oh!
HE AND SAEKI WERE HUGGING EACH OTHER! AND HE'S AFRAID OF GIRLS...
SO YOU REALLY ARE...
...G-
NO!
I'M N-
Oh!
IF I DENY IT NOW...
...I'LL HAVE TO DO THIS ALL OVER AGAIN.
fwip
...
HE'S NOT DENYING IT?!
HE'S ADMITTING IT!
...
SO THAT'S WHY...
YOU UNDERSTAND, DON'T YOU?
...
UMM...
SO THAT'S IT?

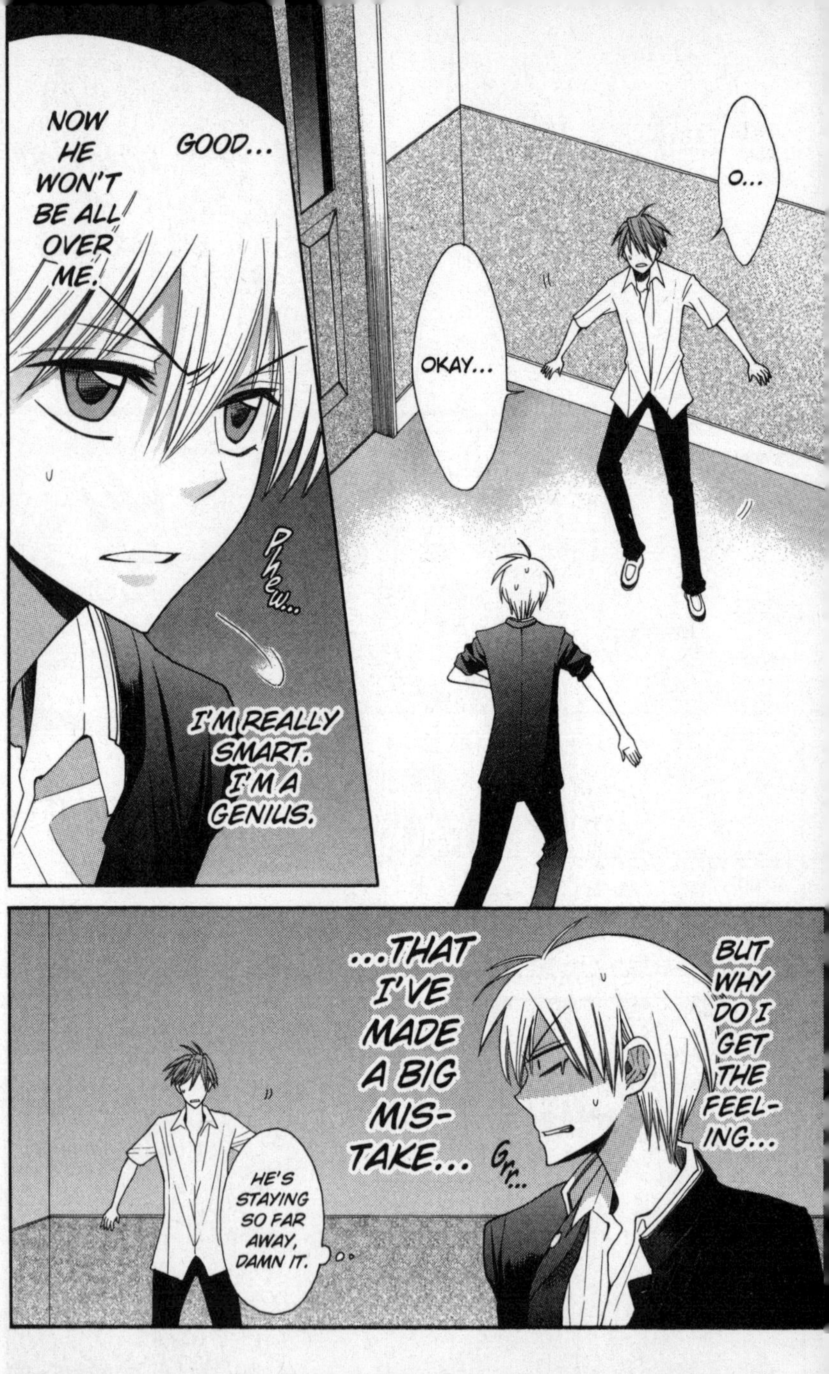
O...
OKAY...
GOOD...
NOW HE WON'T BE ALL OVER ME.
Phew...
I'M REALLY SMART. I'M A GENIUS.
BUT WHY DO I GET THE FEEL-ING...
...THAT I'VE MADE A BIG MIS-TAKE...
Grr...
HE'S STAYING SO FAR AWAY, DAMN IT.

Chapter 19

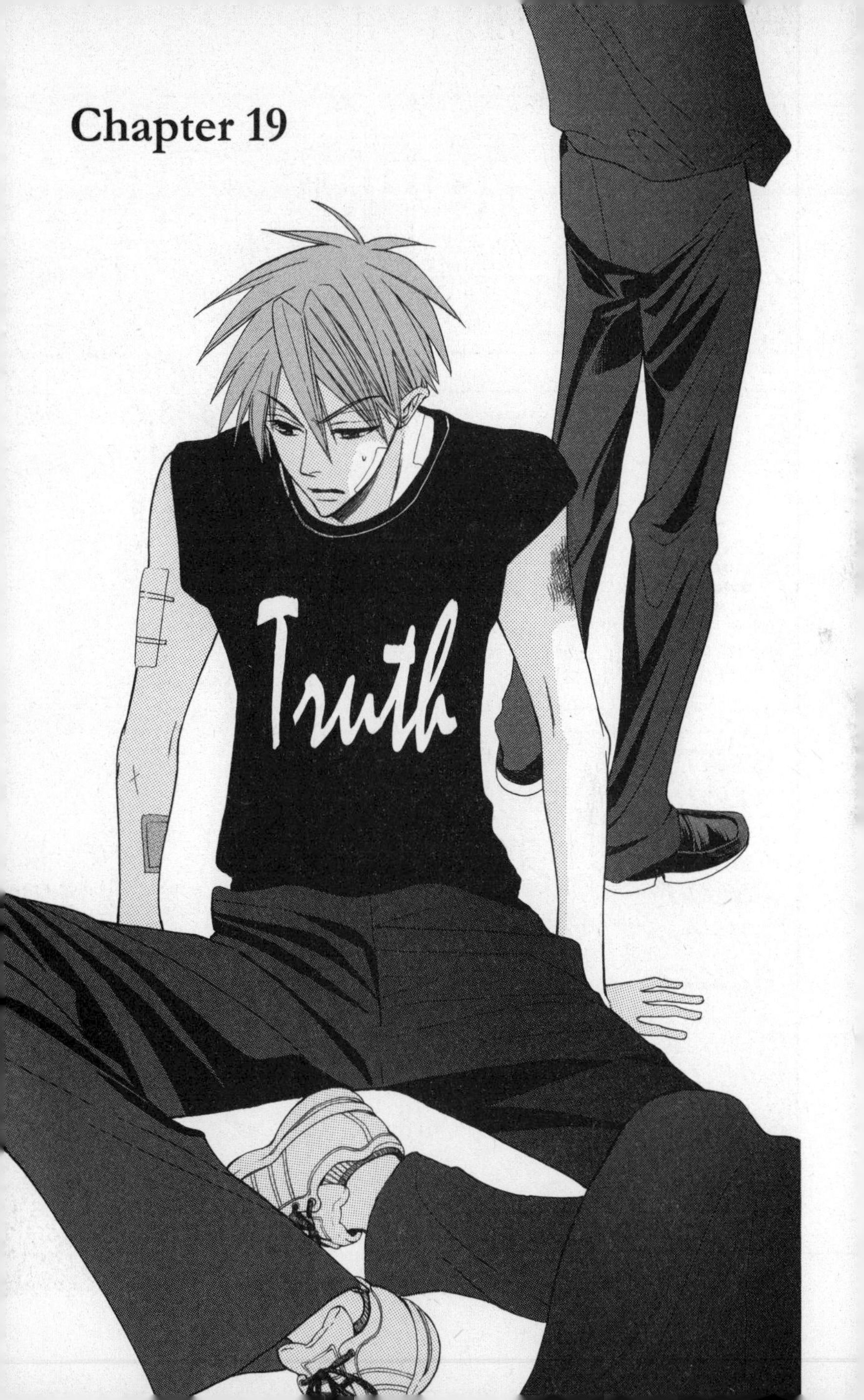
Truth

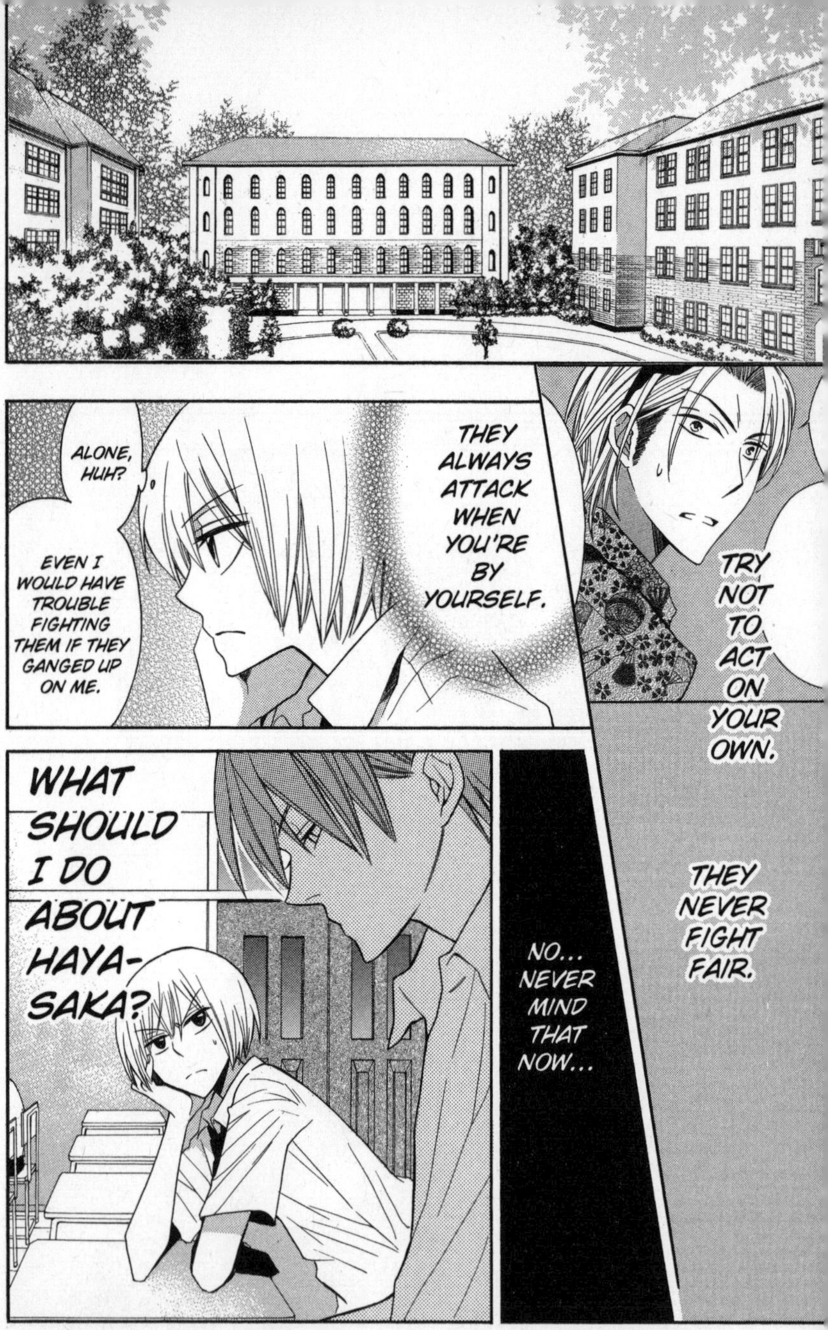
TRY NOT TO ACT ON YOUR OWN.
THEY NEVER FIGHT FAIR.
THEY ALWAYS ATTACK WHEN YOU'RE BY YOURSELF.
ALONE, HUH?
EVEN I WOULD HAVE TROUBLE FIGHTING THEM IF THEY GANGED UP ON ME.
NO... NEVER MIND THAT NOW...
WHAT SHOULD I DO ABOUT HAYA-SAKA?

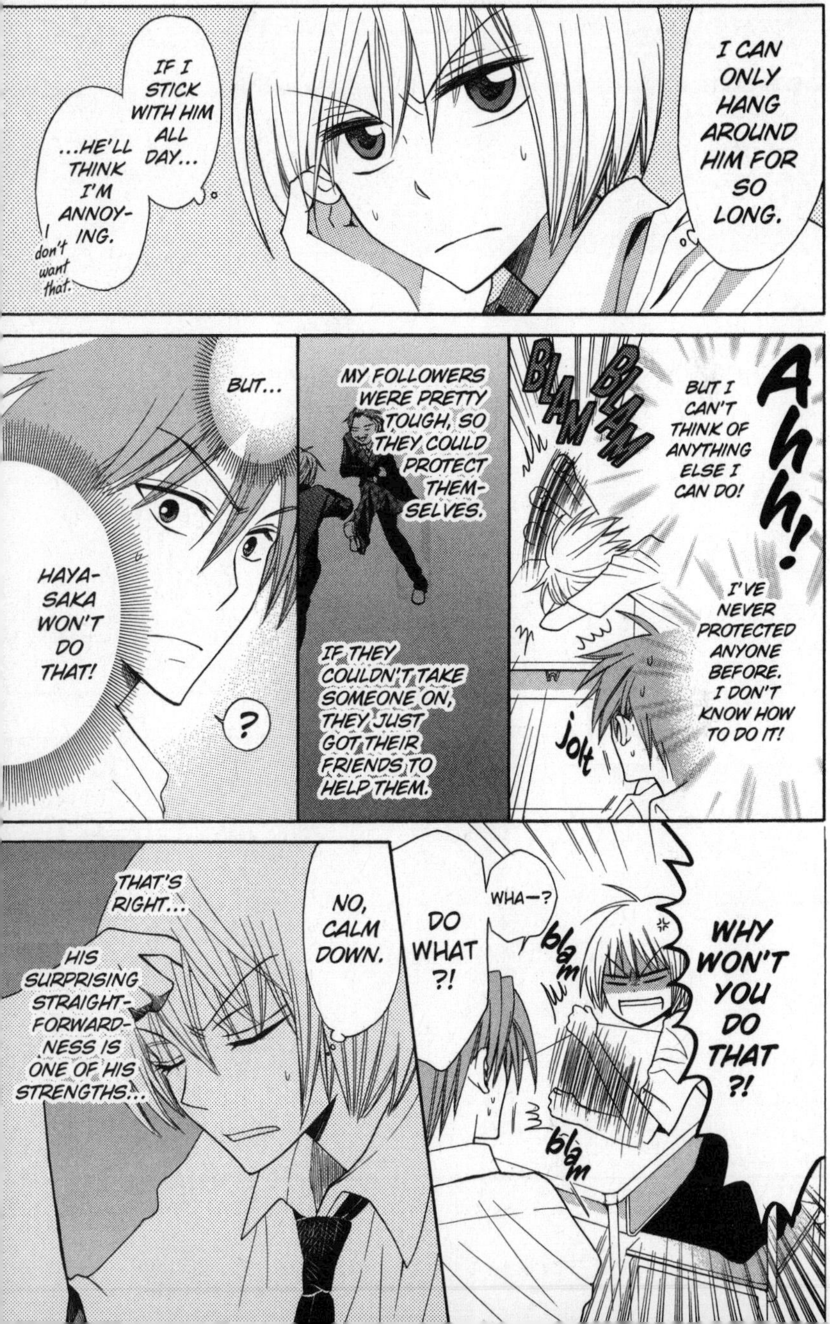
I CAN ONLY HANG AROUND HIM FOR SO LONG.
IF I STICK WITH HIM ALL DAY...
...HE'LL THINK I'M ANNOYING.
I don't want that.
BLAM BLAM
Ahh!
BUT I CAN'T THINK OF ANYTHING ELSE I CAN DO!
I'VE NEVER PROTECTED ANYONE BEFORE. I DON'T KNOW HOW TO DO IT!
jolt
MY FOLLOWERS WERE PRETTY TOUGH, SO THEY COULD PROTECT THEMSELVES.
IF THEY COULDN'T TAKE SOMEONE ON, THEY JUST GOT THEIR FRIENDS TO HELP THEM.
BUT...
HAYASAKA WON'T DO THAT!
?
WHY WON'T YOU DO THAT?!
blam
blam
WHA—?
DO WHAT?!
NO, CALM DOWN.
THAT'S RIGHT...
HIS SURPRISING STRAIGHTFORWARDNESS IS ONE OF HIS STRENGTHS...

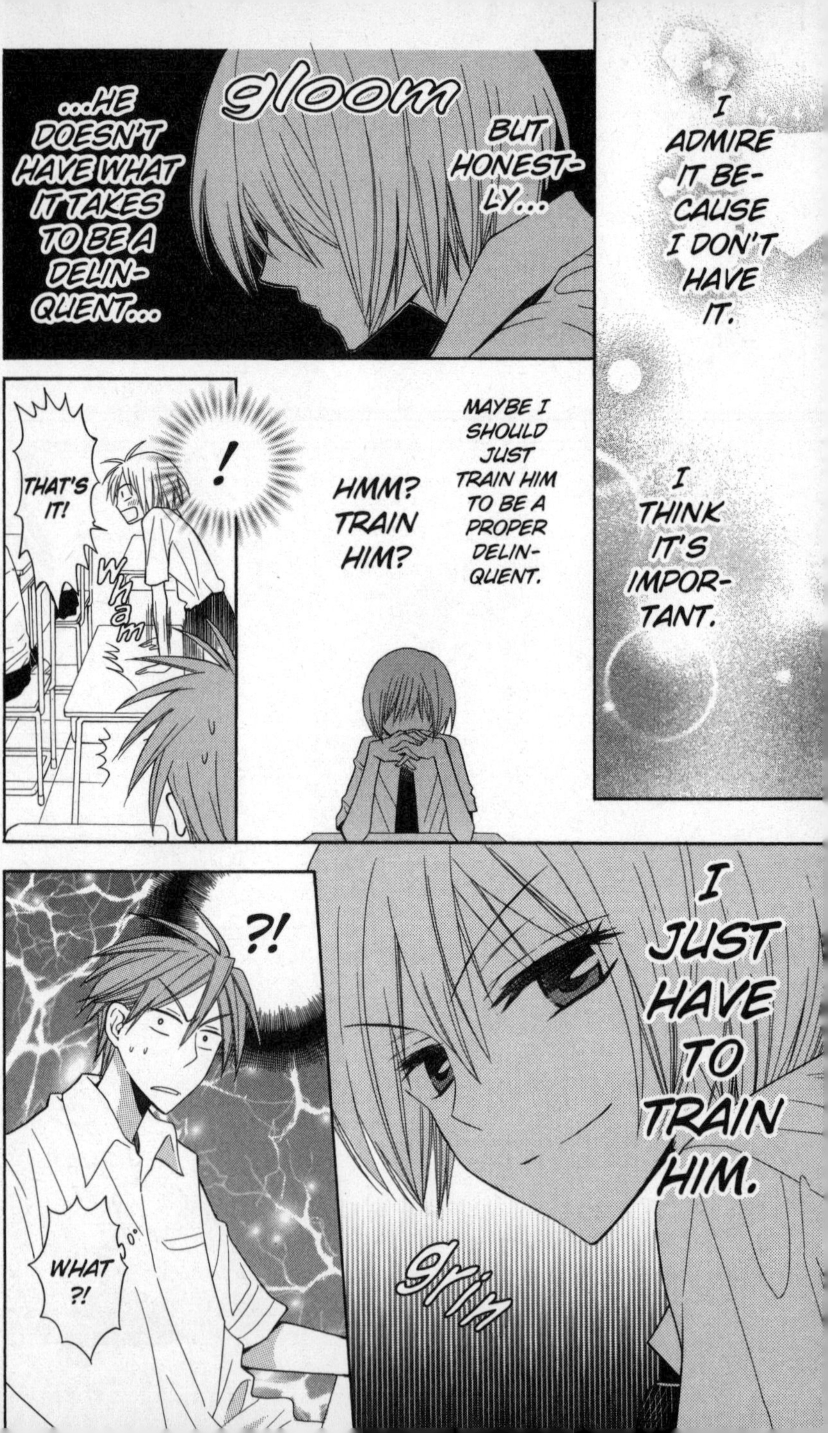
I ADMIRE IT BE-CAUSE I DON'T HAVE IT.
I THINK IT'S IMPOR-TANT.
gloom
BUT HONEST-LY...
...HE DOESN'T HAVE WHAT IT TAKES TO BE A DELIN-QUENT...
MAYBE I SHOULD JUST TRAIN HIM TO BE A PROPER DELIN-QUENT.
HMM? TRAIN HIM?
!
THAT'S IT!
Wham
I JUST HAVE TO TRAIN HIM.
grin
?!
WHAT ?!

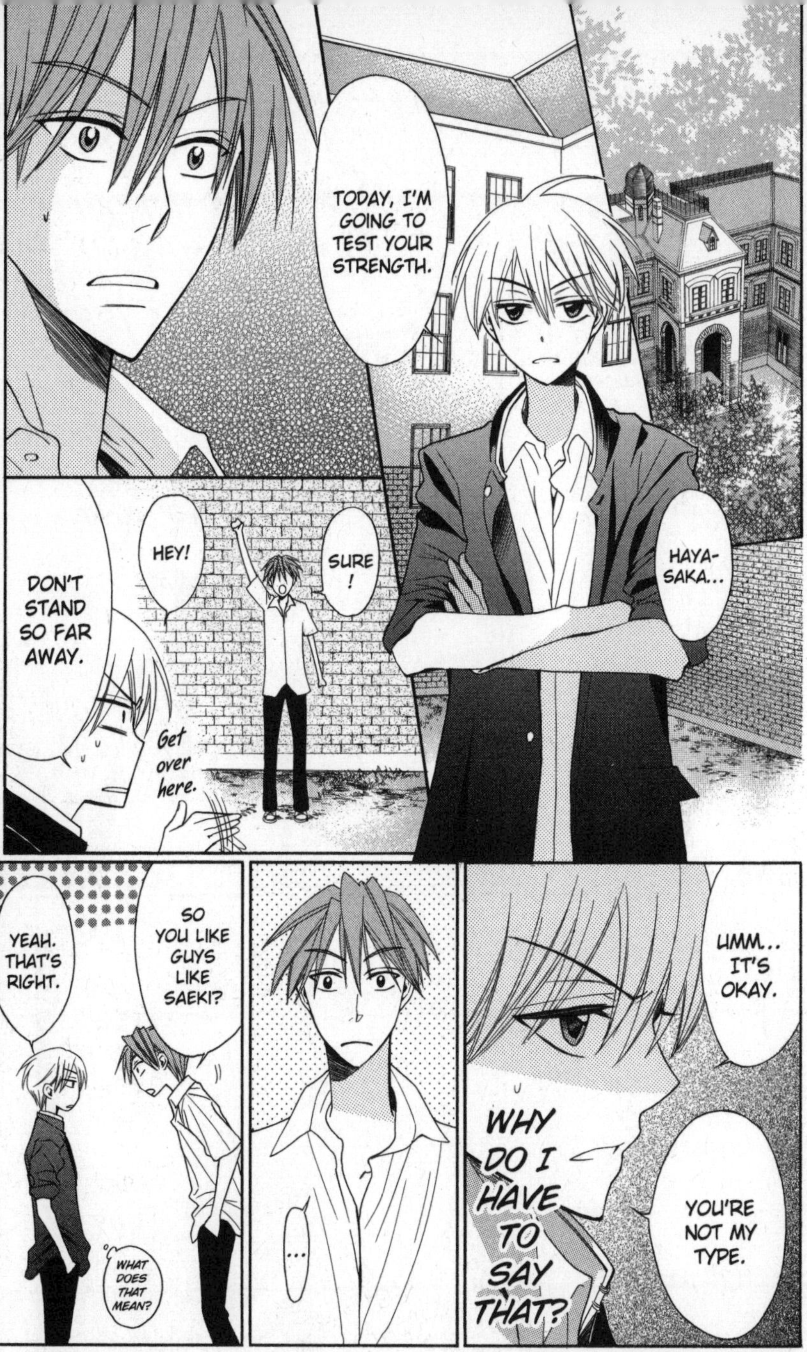
TODAY, I'M GOING TO TEST YOUR STRENGTH.
HAYA-SAKA...
HEY!
SURE!
DON'T STAND SO FAR AWAY.
Get over here.
UMM.. IT'S OKAY.
YOU'RE NOT MY TYPE.
WHY DO I HAVE TO SAY THAT?
...
SO YOU LIKE GUYS LIKE SAEKI?
YEAH. THAT'S RIGHT.
WHAT DOES THAT MEAN?

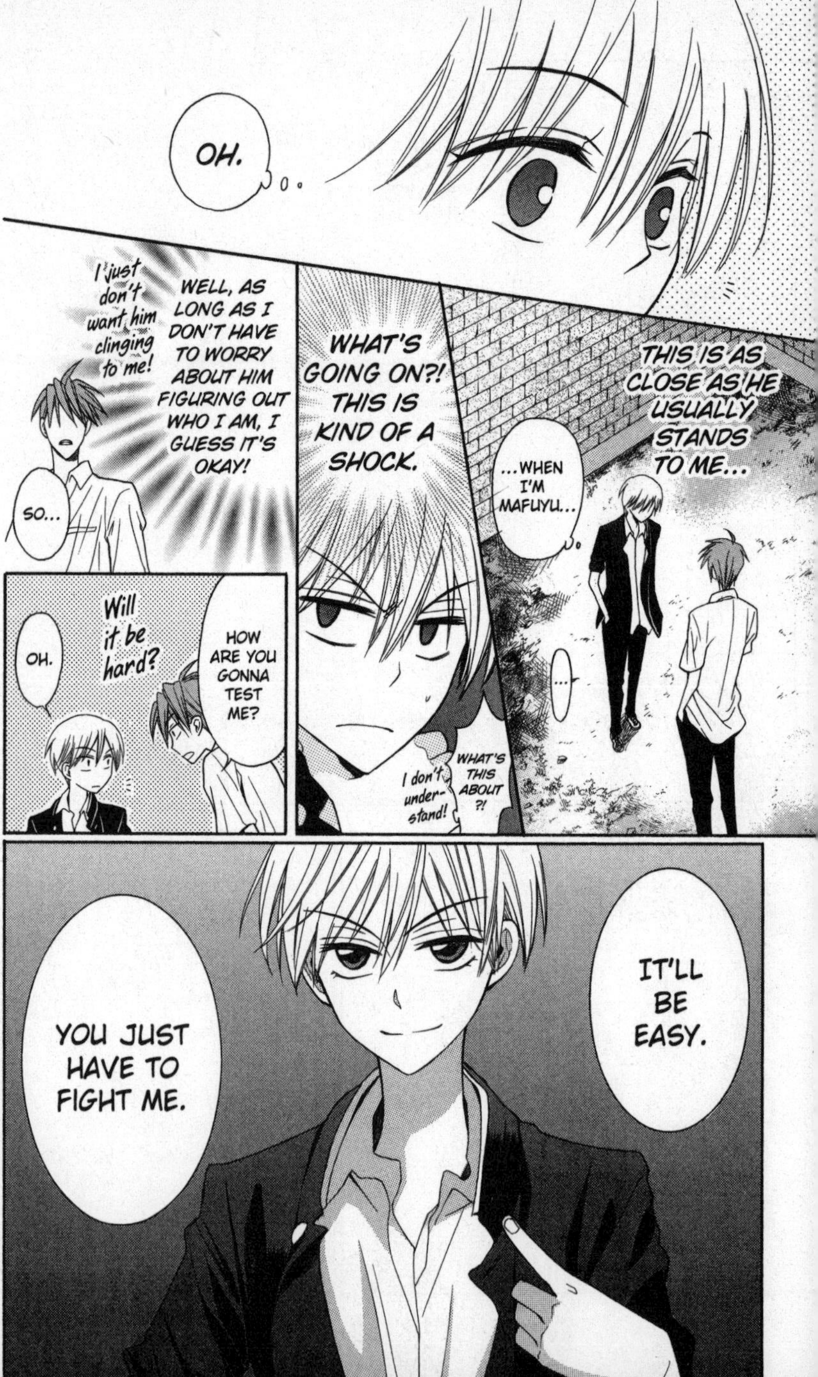
OH.
THIS IS AS CLOSE AS HE USUALLY STANDS TO ME...
...WHEN I'M MAFUYU...
...
WHAT'S GOING ON?! THIS IS KIND OF A SHOCK.
WHAT'S THIS ABOUT?!
I don't under-stand!
WELL, AS LONG AS I DON'T HAVE TO WORRY ABOUT HIM FIGURING OUT WHO I AM, I GUESS IT'S OKAY!
I just don't want him clinging to me!
SO...
HOW ARE YOU GONNA TEST ME?
Will it be hard?
OH.
IT'LL BE EASY.
YOU JUST HAVE TO FIGHT ME.

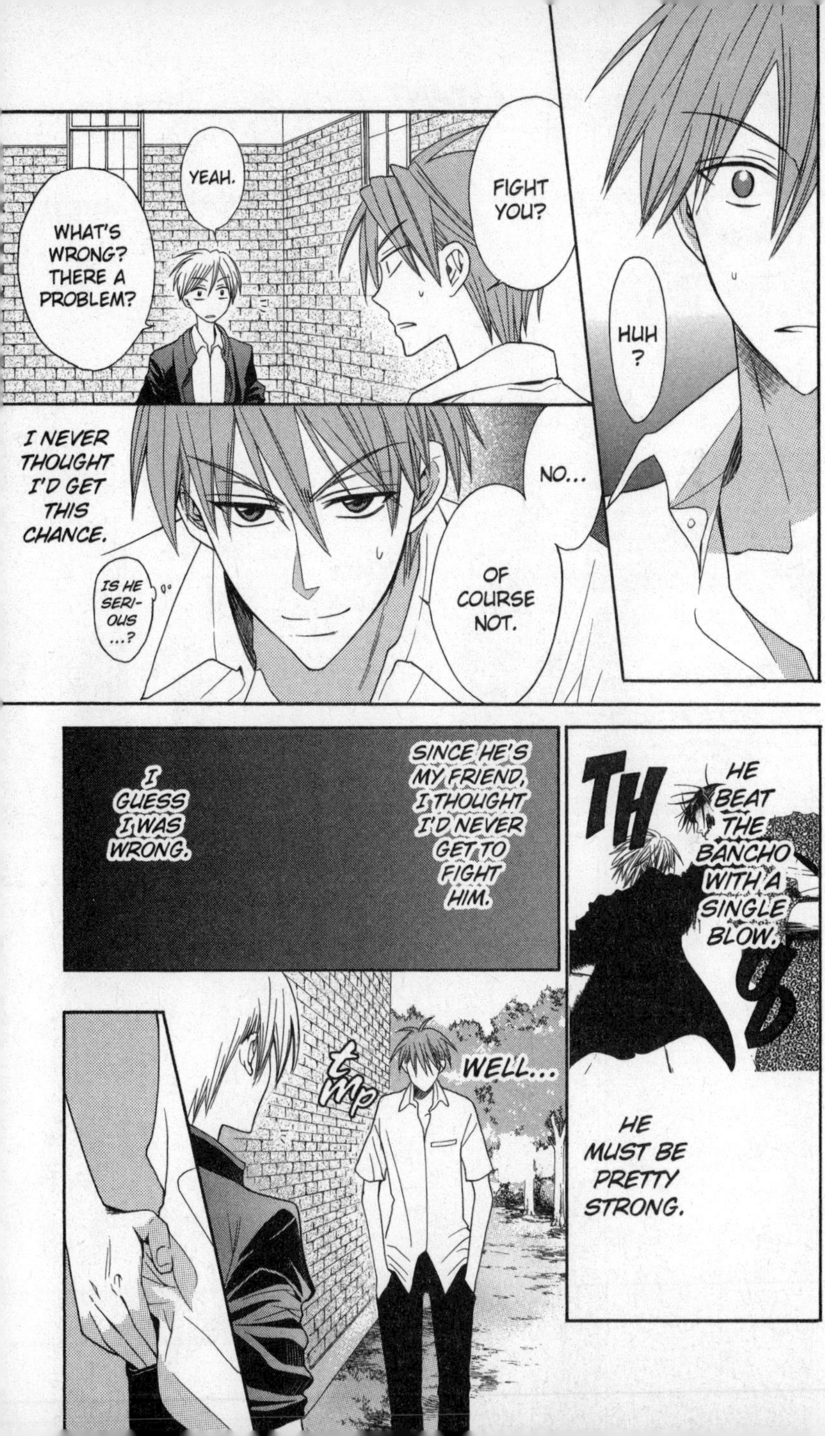
HUH?
FIGHT YOU?
YEAH.
WHAT'S WRONG? THERE A PROBLEM?
NO...
OF COURSE NOT.
I NEVER THOUGHT I'D GET THIS CHANCE.
IS HE SERIOUS...?
THUD
HE BEAT THE BANCHO WITH A SINGLE BLOW.
HE MUST BE PRETTY STRONG.
SINCE HE'S MY FRIEND, I THOUGHT I'D NEVER GET TO FIGHT HIM.
I GUESS I WAS WRONG.
WELL...
tmp

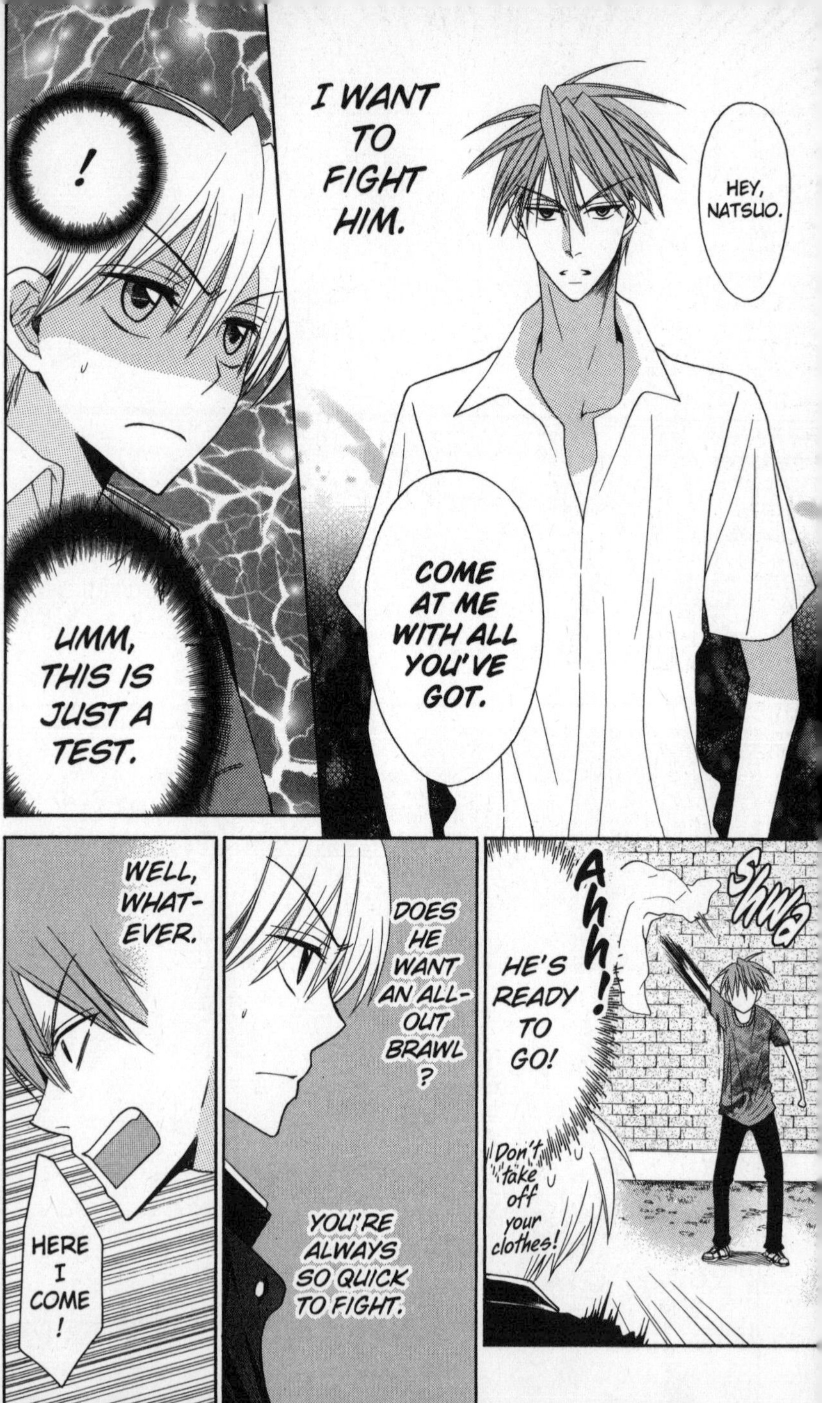
HEY, NATSUO.
I WANT TO FIGHT HIM.
COME AT ME WITH ALL YOU'VE GOT.
!
UMM, THIS IS JUST A TEST.
Shwa
Ahh!
HE'S READY TO GO!
Don't take off your clothes!
DOES HE WANT AN ALL-OUT BRAWL?
YOU'RE ALWAYS SO QUICK TO FIGHT.
WELL, WHAT-EVER.
HERE I COME!

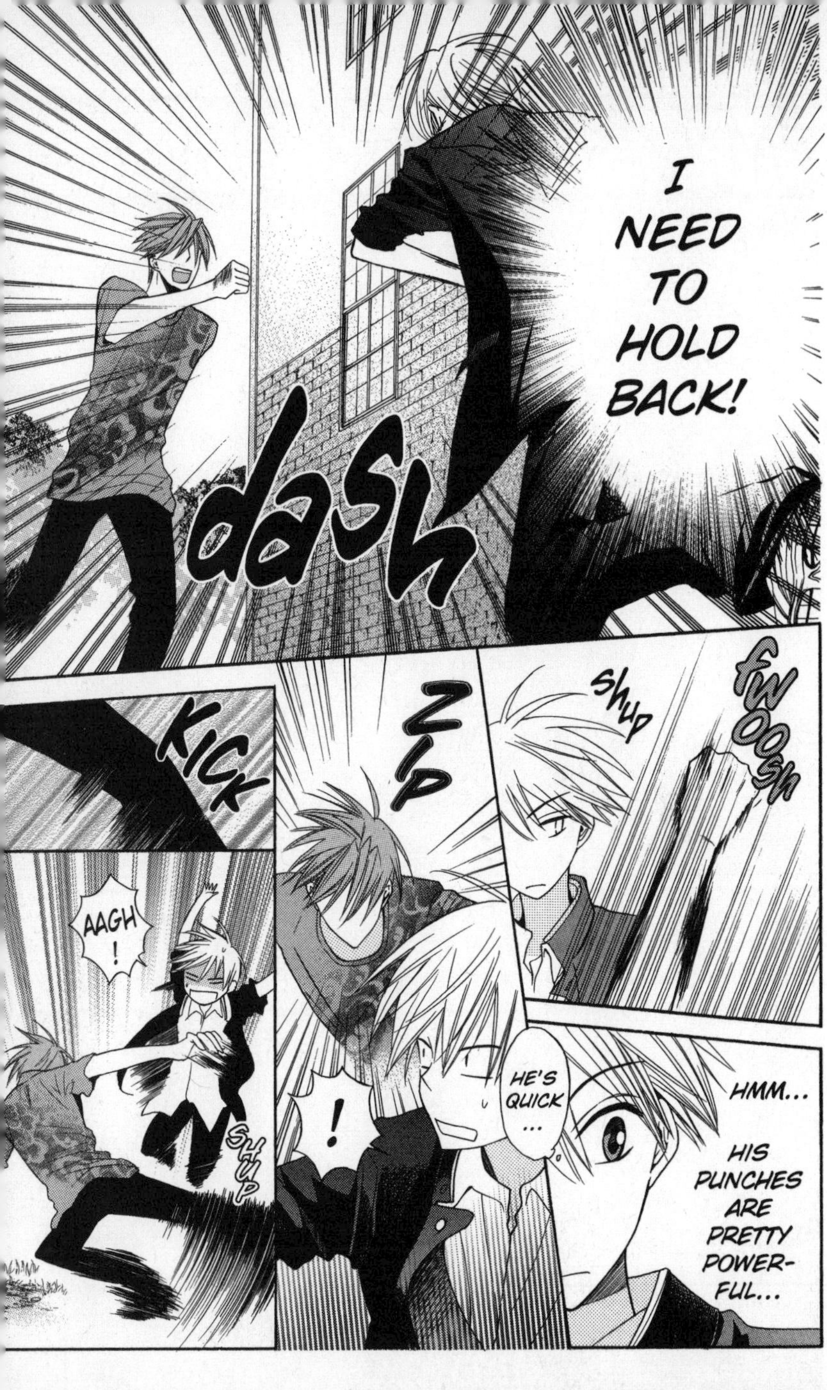
I NEED TO HOLD BACK!
dash
fwoosh
shup
HMM...
HIS PUNCHES ARE PRETTY POWER-FUL...
HE'S QUICK...
ZIP
!
KICK
AAGH!
SHUP

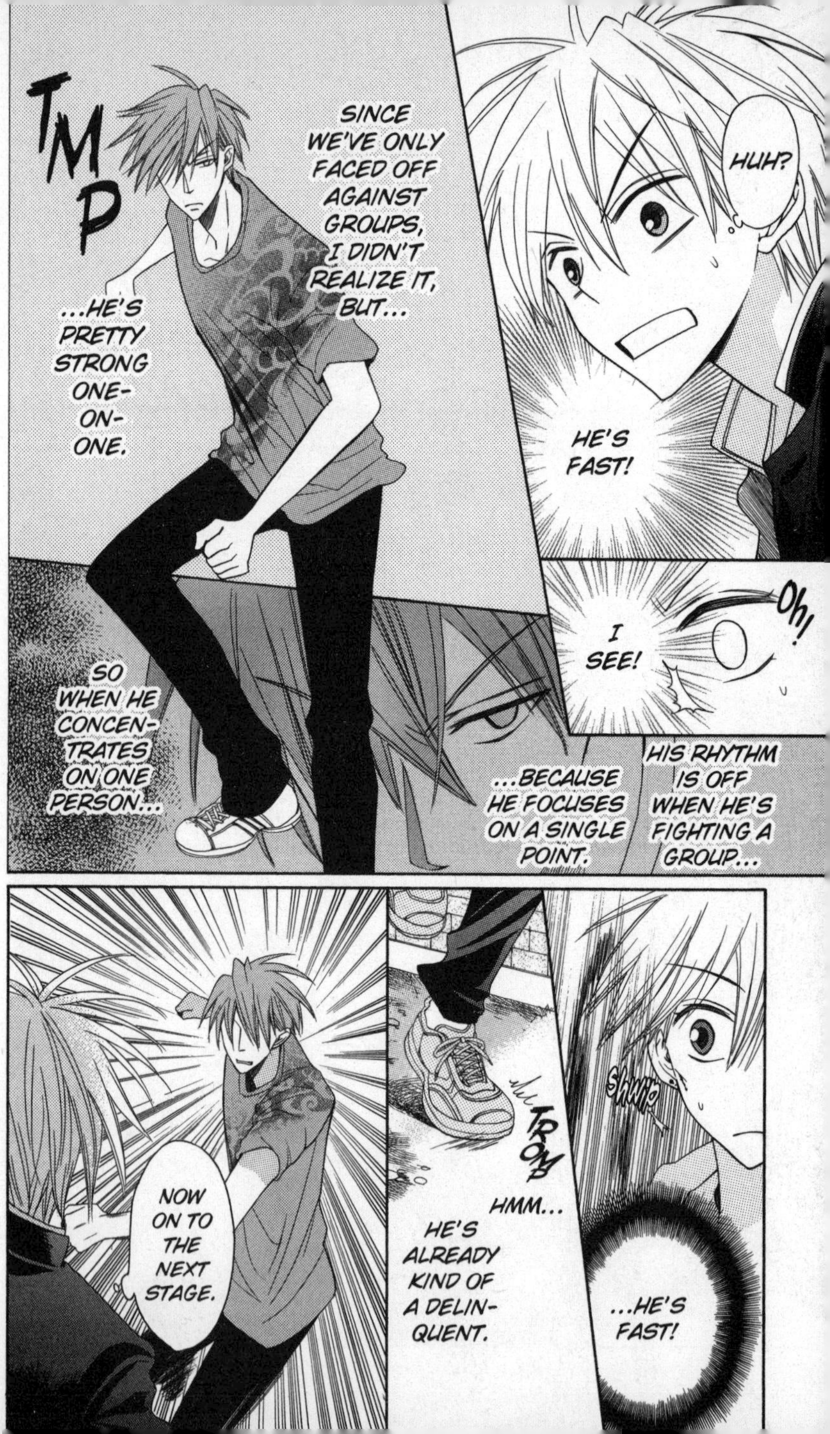
HUH?
HE'S FAST!
TMP
SINCE WE'VE ONLY FACED OFF AGAINST GROUPS, I DIDN'T REALIZE IT, BUT...
...HE'S PRETTY STRONG ONE-ON-ONE.
Oh!
I SEE!
HIS RHYTHM IS OFF WHEN HE'S FIGHTING A GROUP...
...BECAUSE HE FOCUSES ON A SINGLE POINT.
SO WHEN HE CONCENTRATES ON ONE PERSON...
SHWIP
...HE'S FAST!
TROMP
HMM... HE'S ALREADY KIND OF A DELINQUENT.
NOW ON TO THE NEXT STAGE.

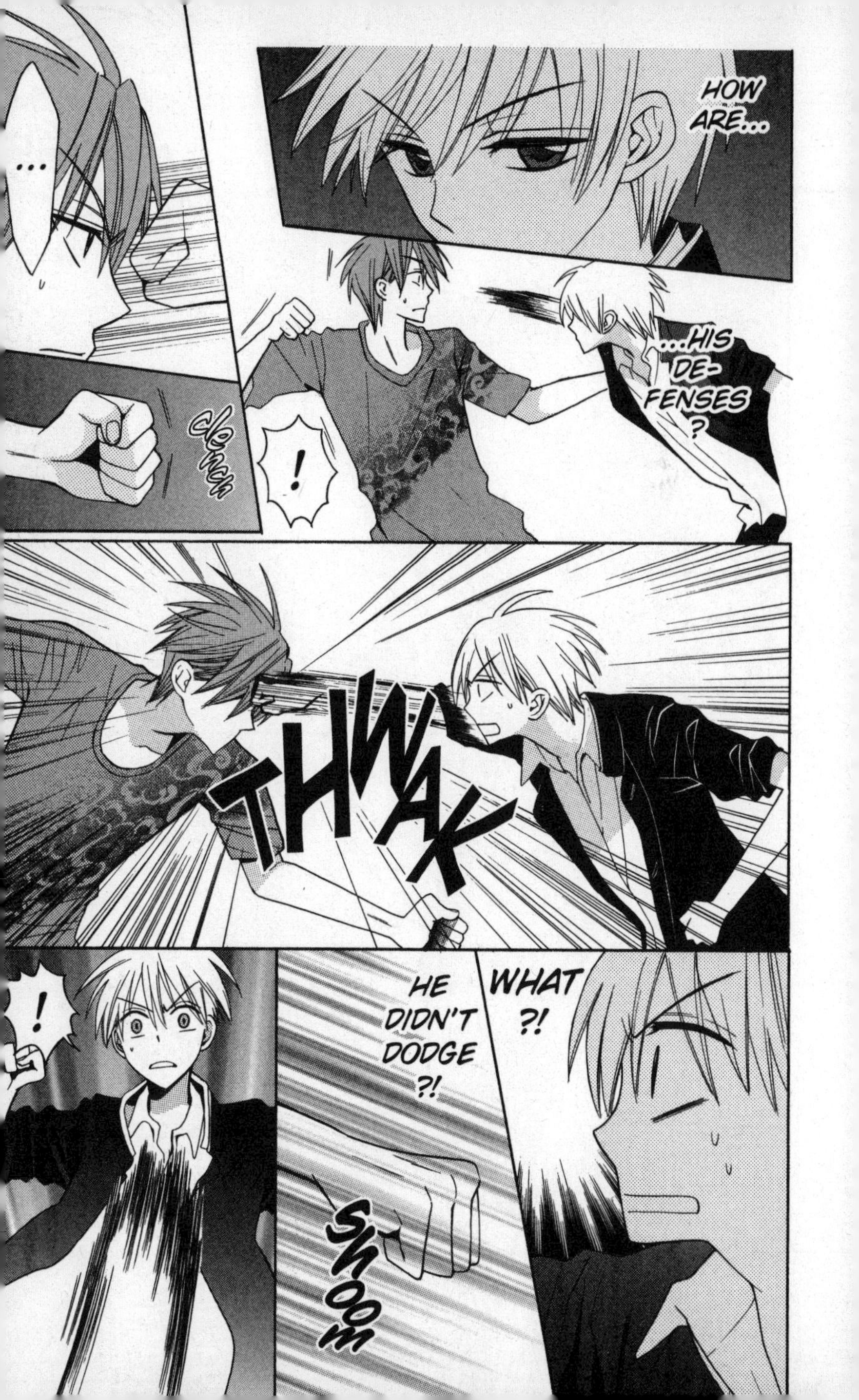
HOW ARE...
...HIS DE-FENSES?
!
...
clench
THWAK
WHAT?!
HE DIDN'T DODGE?!
SHOOM
!

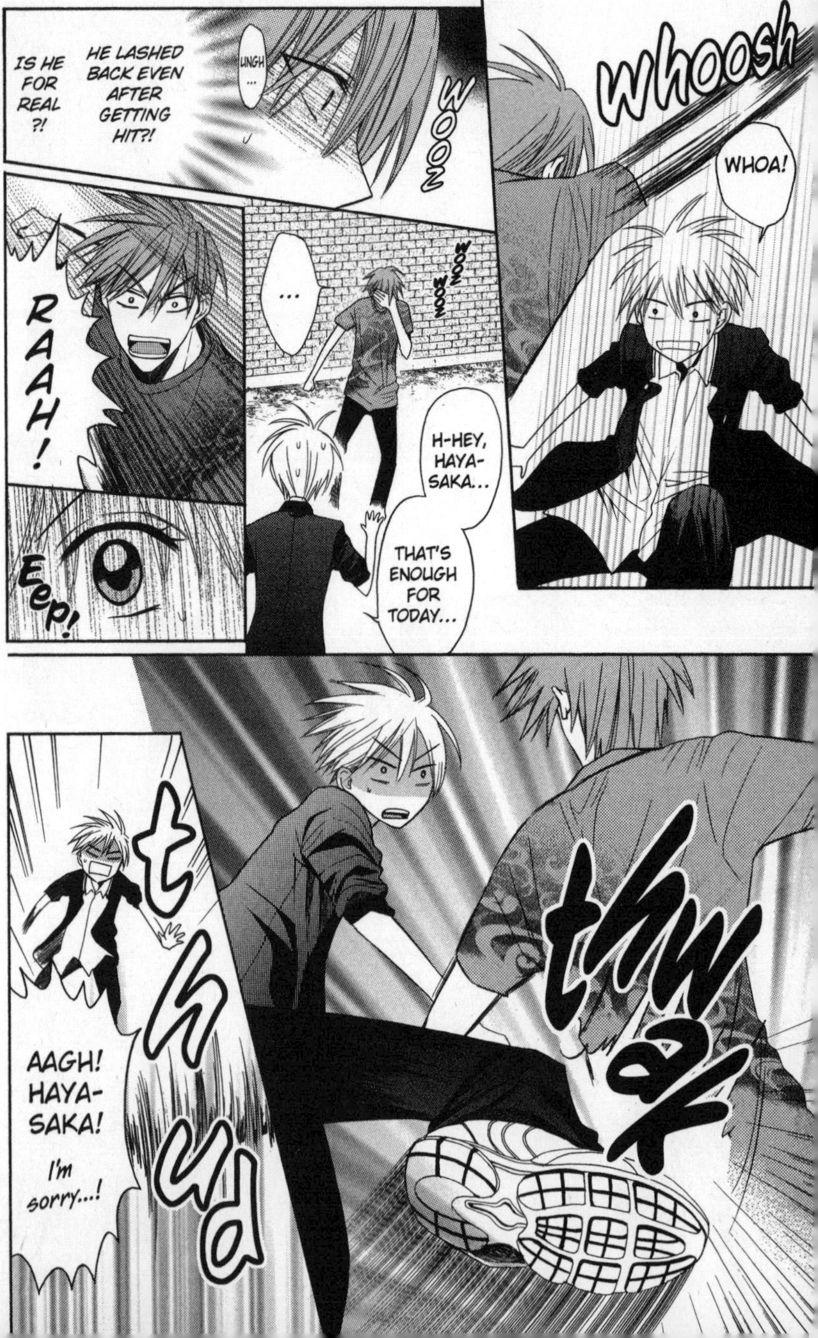
whoosh
WHOA!
UNGH...
WOOOZ
HE LASHED BACK EVEN AFTER GETTING HIT?!
IS HE FOR REAL?!
...
WOOZ WOOZ
H-HEY, HAYA-SAKA...
THAT'S ENOUGH FOR TODAY...
RAAAH!
Eep!
thwak
thud
AAGH! HAYA-SAKA!
I'm sorry...!

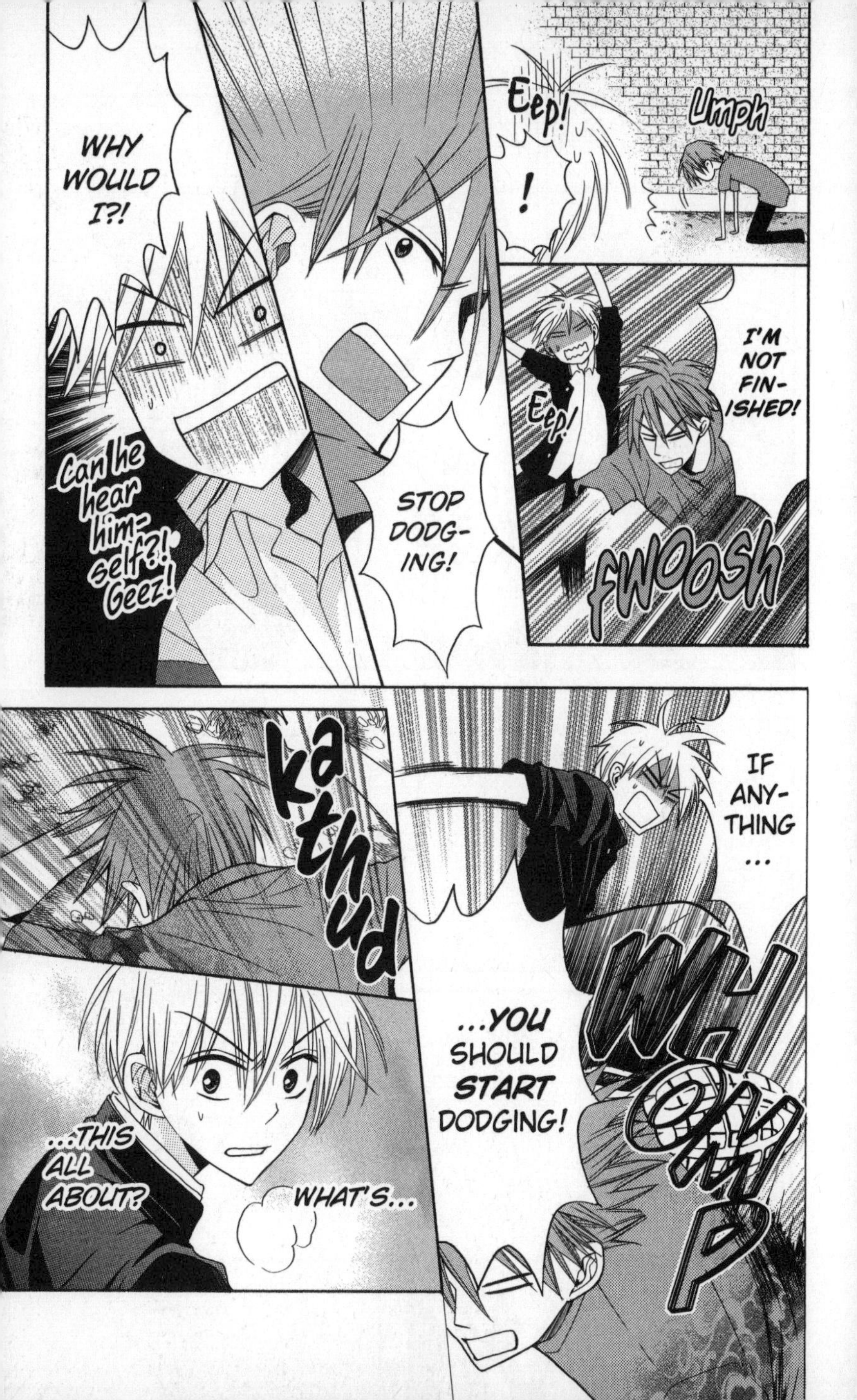
Umph
Eep!
!
I'M NOT FIN-ISHED!
Eep!
FWOOSH
STOP DODG-ING!
WHY WOULD I?!
Can he hear him-self?! Geez!
IF ANY-THING...
...YOU SHOULD START DODGING!
WHOMP
kathud
WHAT'S...
...THIS ALL ABOUT?

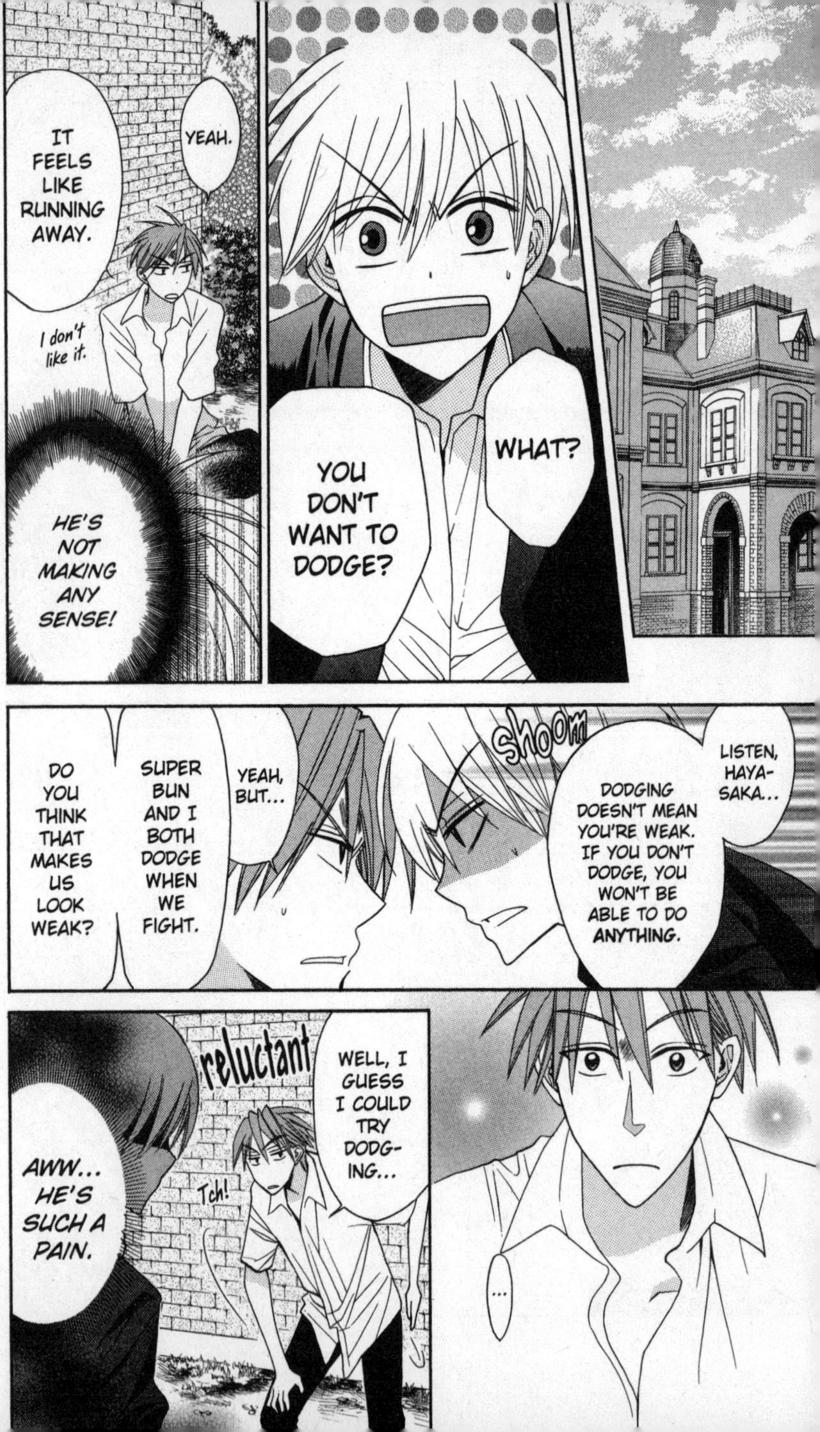
WHAT?
YOU DON'T WANT TO DODGE?
YEAH.
IT FEELS LIKE RUNNING AWAY.
I don't like it.
HE'S NOT MAKING ANY SENSE!
LISTEN, HAYA-SAKA...
shoom
DODGING DOESN'T MEAN YOU'RE WEAK. IF YOU DON'T DODGE, YOU WON'T BE ABLE TO DO ANYTHING.
YEAH, BUT...
SUPER BUN AND I BOTH DODGE WHEN WE FIGHT.
DO YOU THINK THAT MAKES US LOOK WEAK?
...
WELL, I GUESS I COULD TRY DODG-ING...
reluctant
Tch!
AWW... HE'S SUCH A PAIN.

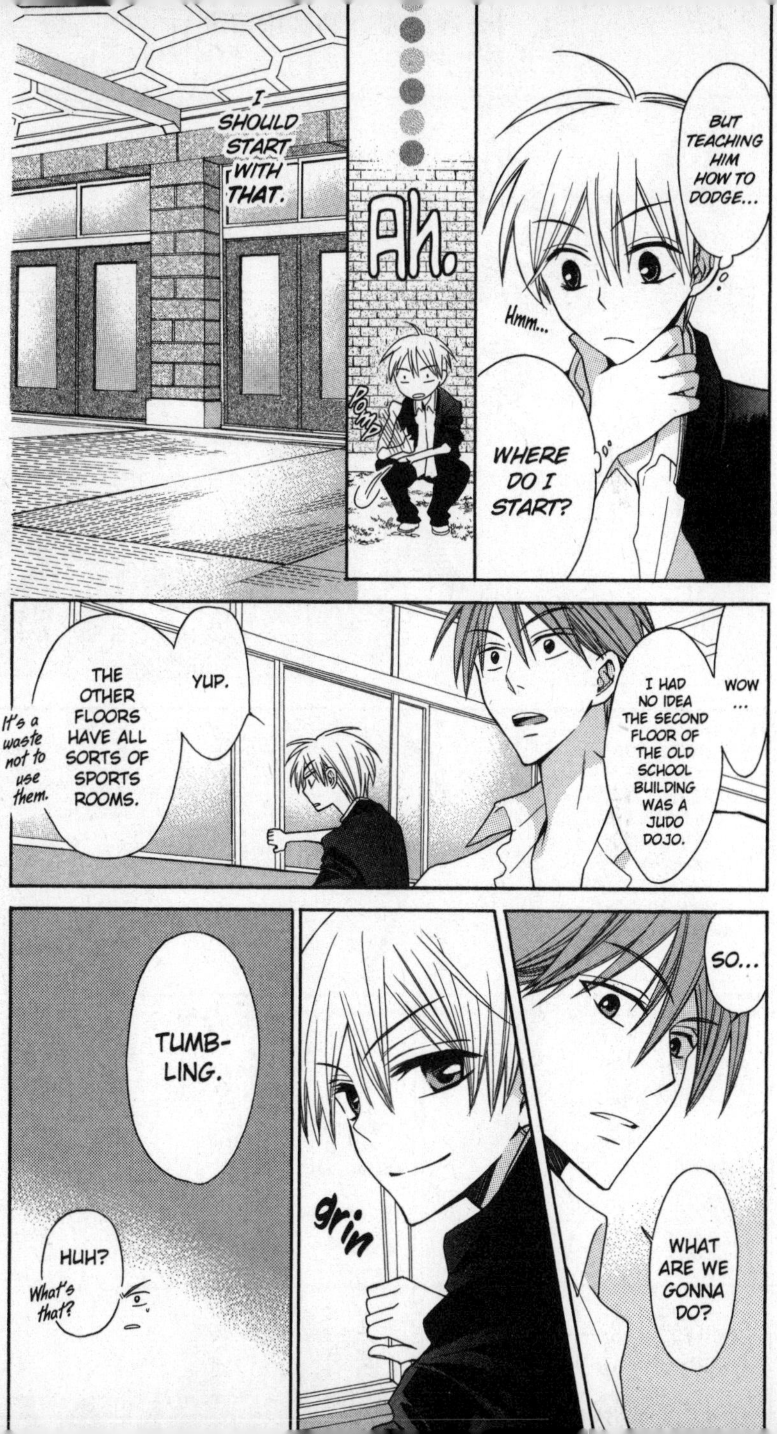
BUT TEACHING HIM HOW TO DODGE...
Hmm...
WHERE DO I START?
Ah.
Pomp
I SHOULD START WITH THAT.
WOW...
I HAD NO IDEA THE SECOND FLOOR OF THE OLD SCHOOL BUILDING WAS A JUDO DOJO.
YUP.
THE OTHER FLOORS HAVE ALL SORTS OF SPORTS ROOMS.
It's a waste not to use them.
SO...
WHAT ARE WE GONNA DO?
grin
TUMB-LING.
HUH?
What's that?

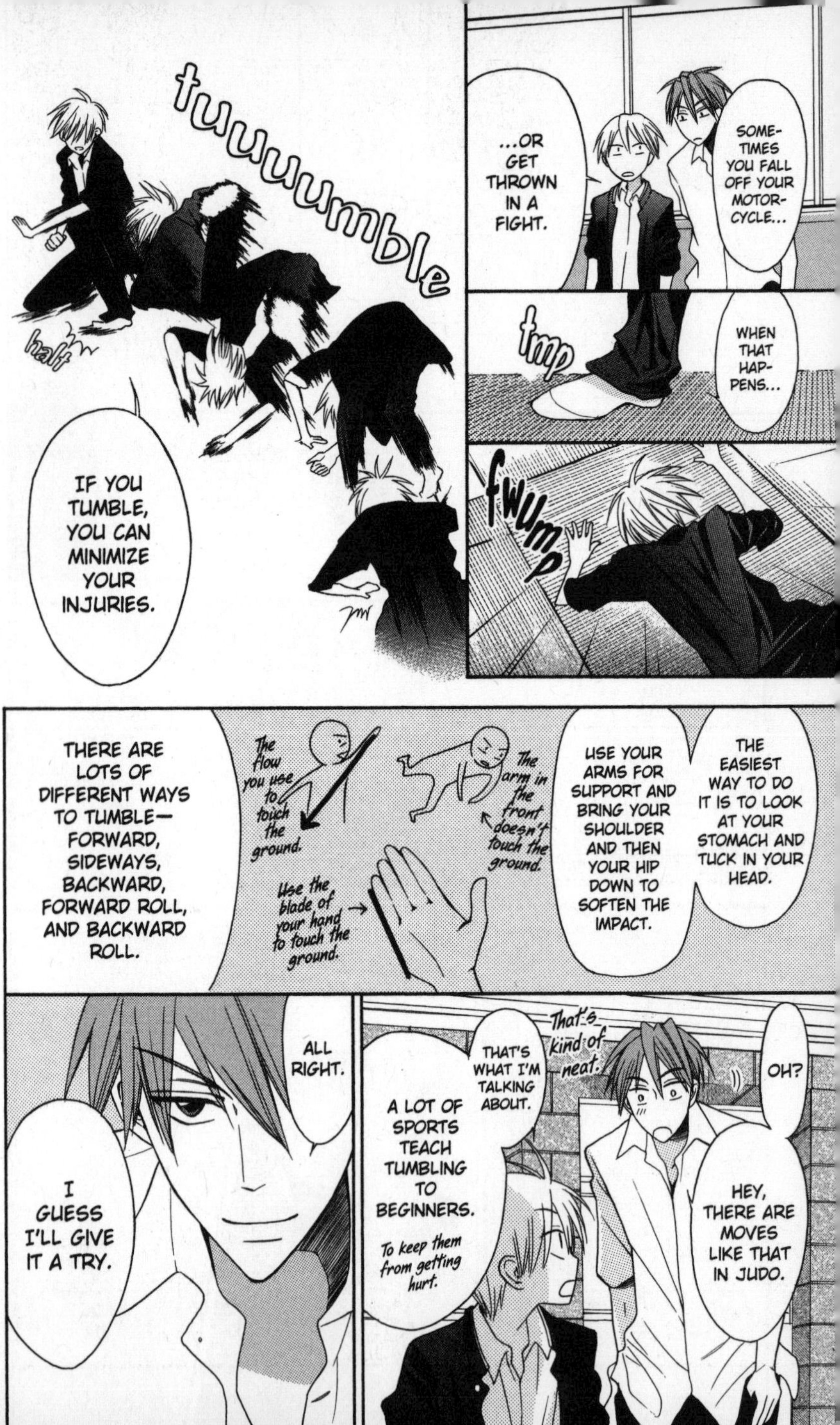
SOMETIMES YOU FALL OFF YOUR MOTORCYCLE...
...OR GET THROWN IN A FIGHT.
WHEN THAT HAPPENS...
tmp
fwump
tuuuumble
halt
IF YOU TUMBLE, YOU CAN MINIMIZE YOUR INJURIES.
THE EASIEST WAY TO DO IT IS TO LOOK AT YOUR STOMACH AND TUCK IN YOUR HEAD.
USE YOUR ARMS FOR SUPPORT AND BRING YOUR SHOULDER AND THEN YOUR HIP DOWN TO SOFTEN THE IMPACT.
The arm in the front doesn't touch the ground.
The flow you use to touch the ground.
Use the blade of your hand to touch the ground.
THERE ARE LOTS OF DIFFERENT WAYS TO TUMBLE—FORWARD, SIDEWAYS, BACKWARD, FORWARD ROLL, AND BACKWARD ROLL.
OH?
HEY, THERE ARE MOVES LIKE THAT IN JUDO.
That's kind of neat.
THAT'S WHAT I'M TALKING ABOUT.
A LOT OF SPORTS TEACH TUMBLING TO BEGINNERS.
To keep them from getting hurt.
ALL RIGHT.
I GUESS I'LL GIVE IT A TRY.

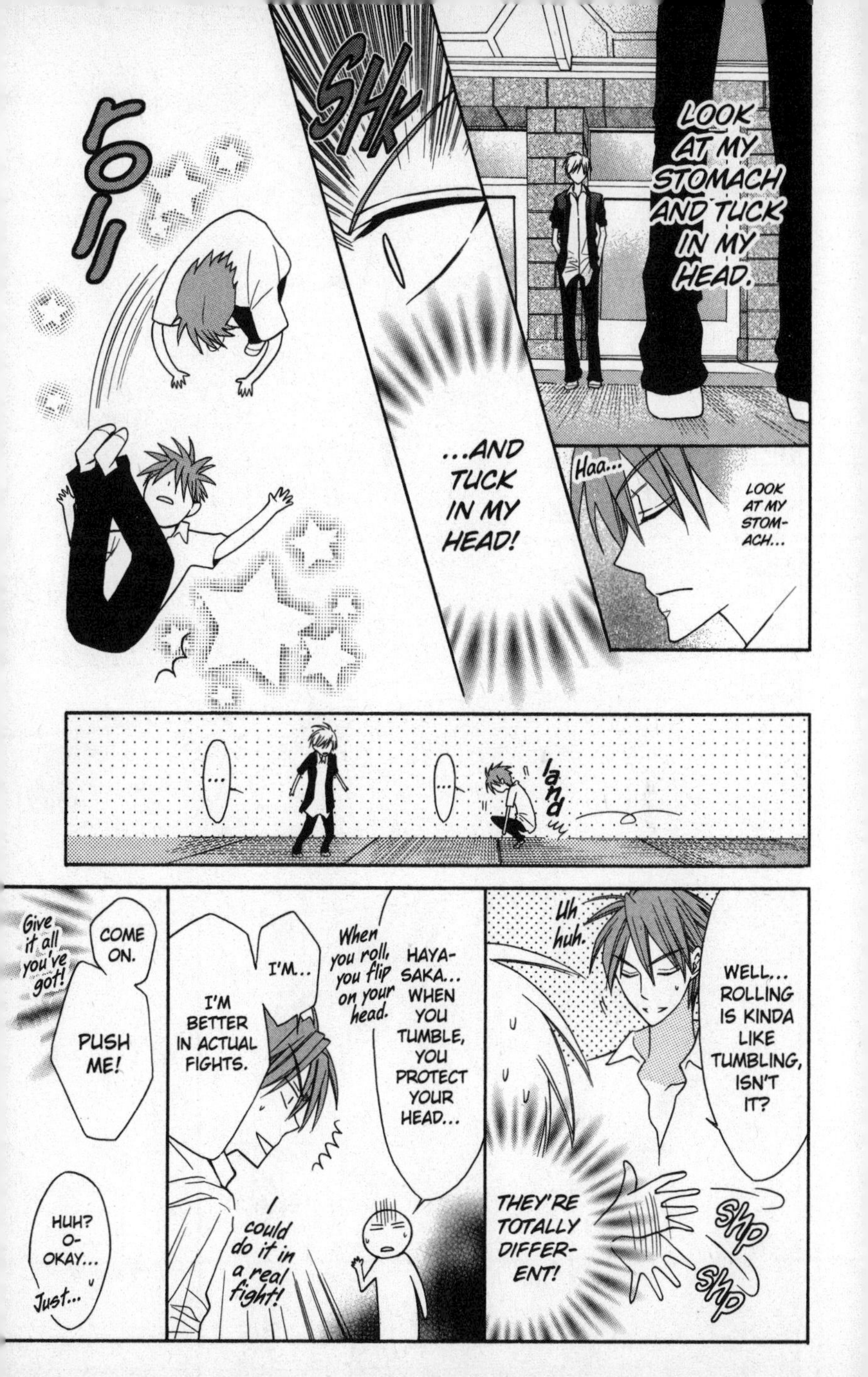
LOOK AT MY STOMACH AND TUCK IN MY HEAD.
Haa...
LOOK AT MY STOMACH...
SHK
...
...AND TUCK IN MY HEAD!
roll
...
...
land
Uh huh.
WELL... ROLLING IS KINDA LIKE TUMBLING, ISN'T IT?
THEY'RE TOTALLY DIFFERENT!
Shp
Shp
HAYA-SAKA... WHEN YOU TUMBLE, YOU PROTECT YOUR HEAD...
When you roll, you flip on your head.
I'M...
I'M BETTER IN ACTUAL FIGHTS.
I could do it in a real fight!
COME ON.
Give it all you've got!
PUSH ME!
HUH? O-OKAY...
Just...

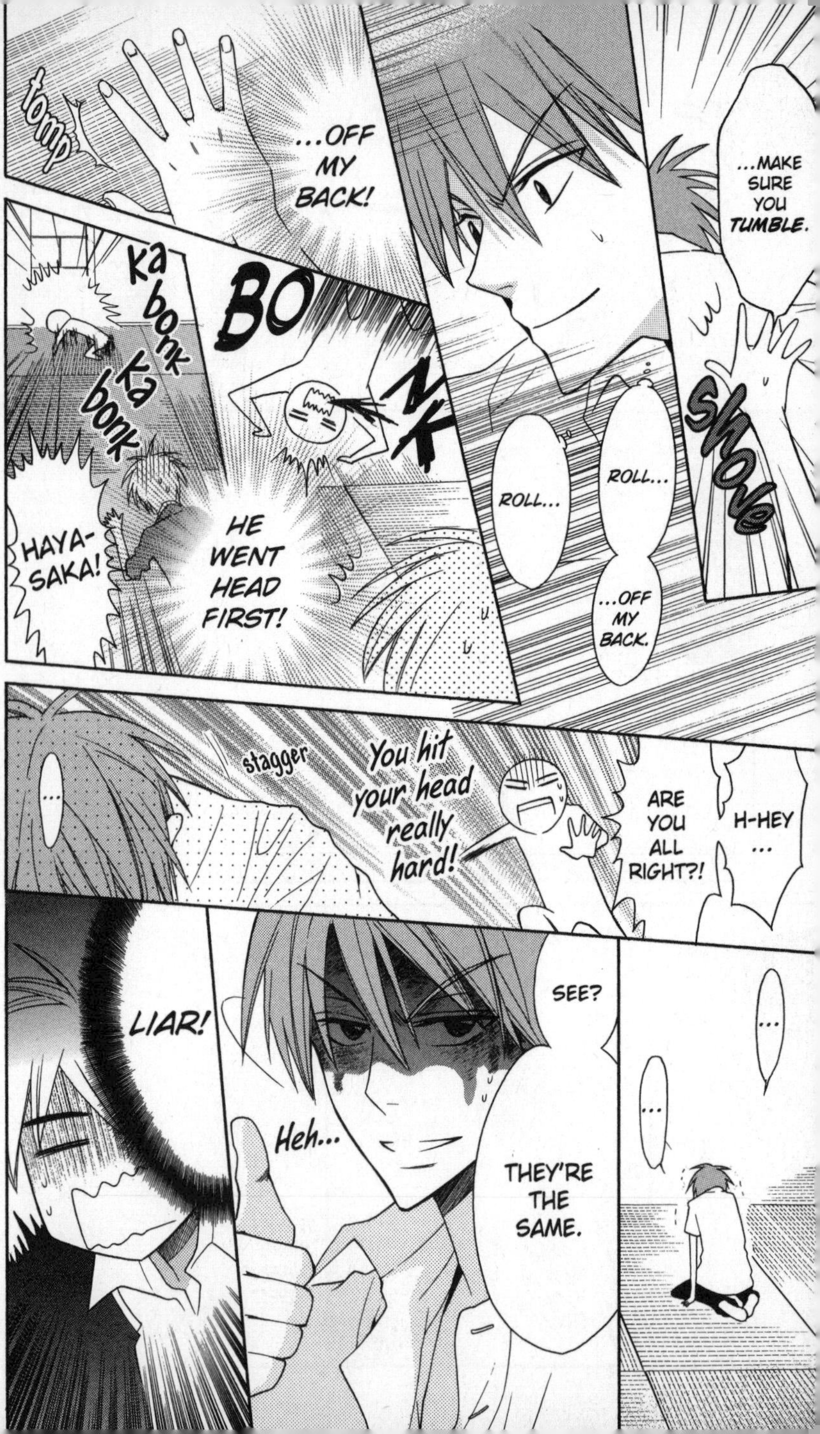
...MAKE SURE YOU *TUMBLE.*
shove
ROLL...
ROLL...
...OFF MY BACK.
...OFF MY BACK!
tomp
BONK
HE WENT HEAD FIRST!
ka bonk ka bonk
HAYA-SAKA!
H-HEY ...
ARE YOU ALL RIGHT?!
You hit your head really hard!
stagger
...
...
...
SEE?
THEY'RE THE SAME.
Heh...
LIAR!

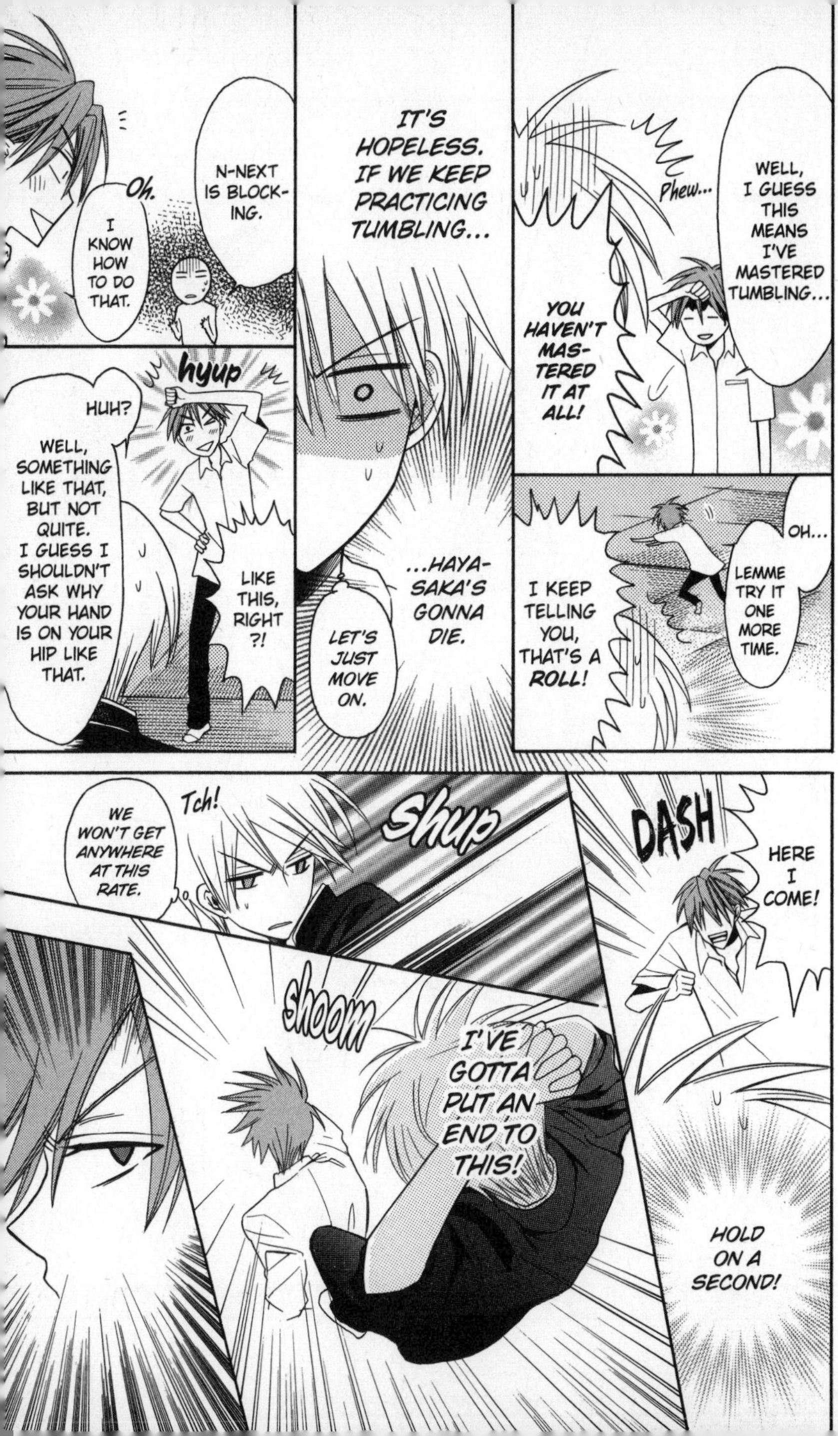
Phew...
WELL, I GUESS THIS MEANS I'VE MASTERED TUMBLING...
YOU HAVEN'T MAS-TERED IT AT ALL!
OH...
LEMME TRY IT ONE MORE TIME.
I KEEP TELLING YOU, THAT'S A ROLL!
IT'S HOPELESS. IF WE KEEP PRACTICING TUMBLING...
...HAYA-SAKA'S GONNA DIE.
LET'S JUST MOVE ON.
N-NEXT IS BLOCK-ING.
Oh.
I KNOW HOW TO DO THAT.
hyup
LIKE THIS, RIGHT?!
HUH?
WELL, SOMETHING LIKE THAT, BUT NOT QUITE. I GUESS I SHOULDN'T ASK WHY YOUR HAND IS ON YOUR HIP LIKE THAT.
DASH
HERE I COME!
HOLD ON A SECOND!
Tch!
WE WON'T GET ANYWHERE AT THIS RATE.
Shup
shoom
I'VE GOTTA PUT AN END TO THIS!

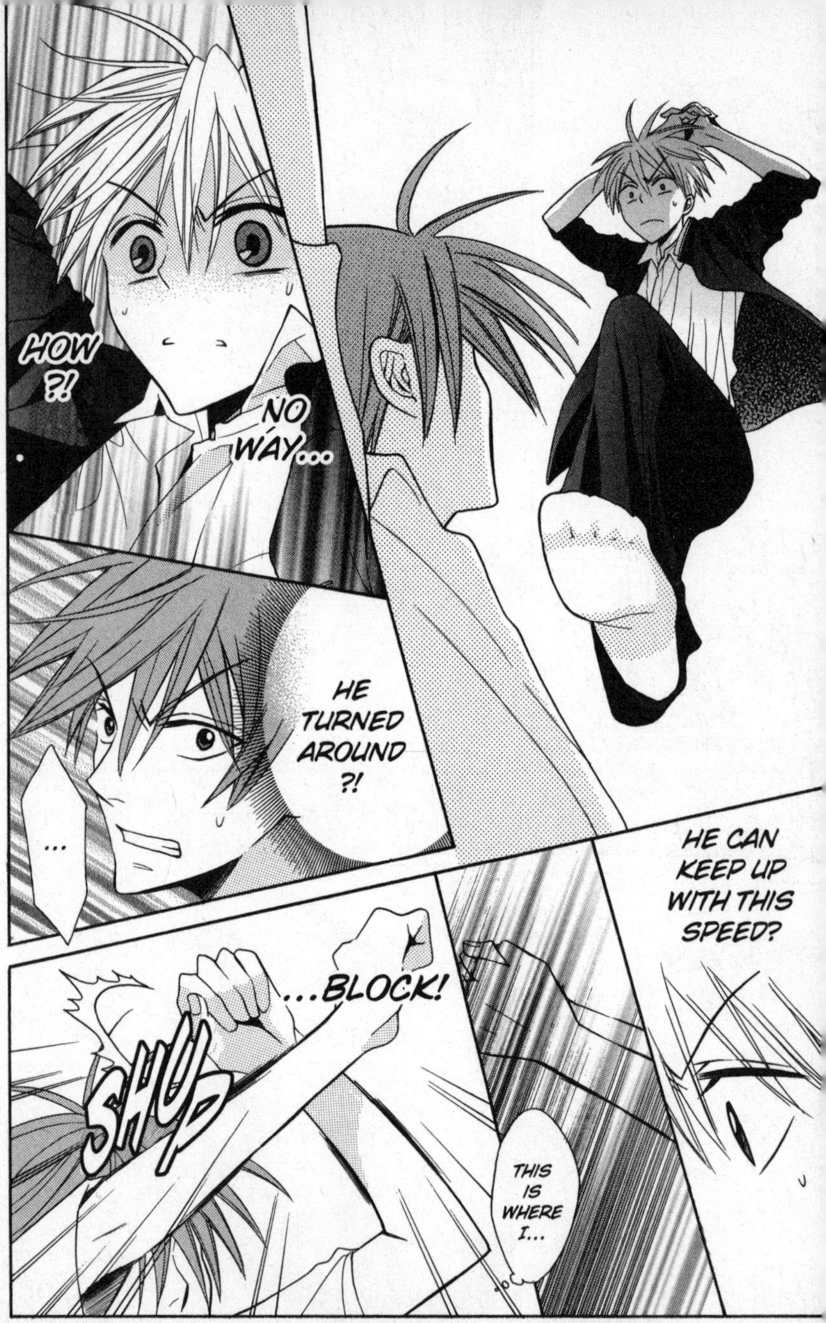
HE TURNED AROUND ?!
NO WAY...
HOW ?!
...
HE CAN KEEP UP WITH THIS SPEED?
THIS IS WHERE I...
...BLOCK!
SHU

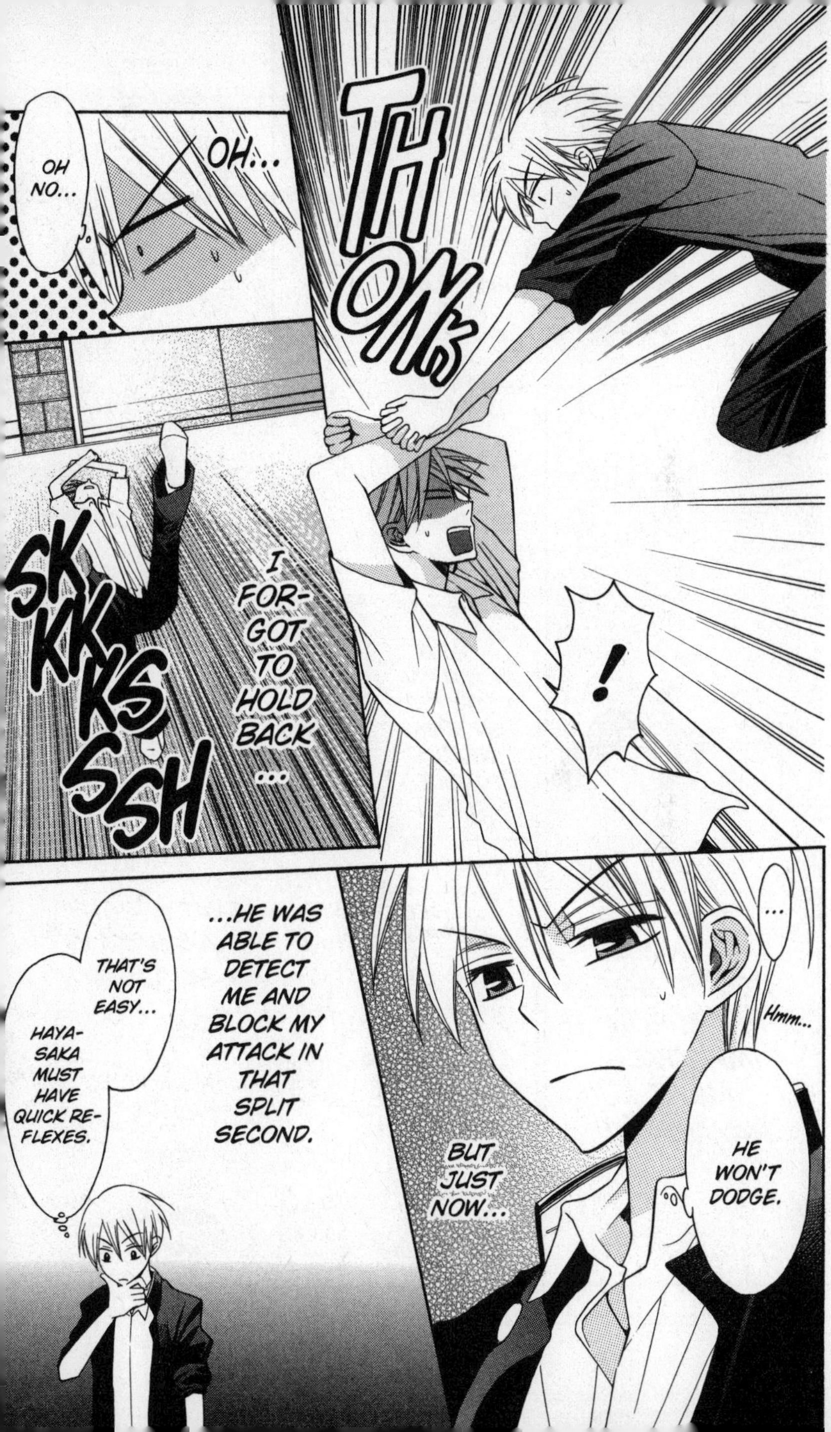
THONK
!
OH...
OH NO...
I FORGOT TO HOLD BACK...
SKKKSSSH
...
Hmm...
HE WON'T DODGE.
BUT JUST NOW...
...HE WAS ABLE TO DETECT ME AND BLOCK MY ATTACK IN THAT SPLIT SECOND.
THAT'S NOT EASY... HAYASAKA MUST HAVE QUICK REFLEXES.

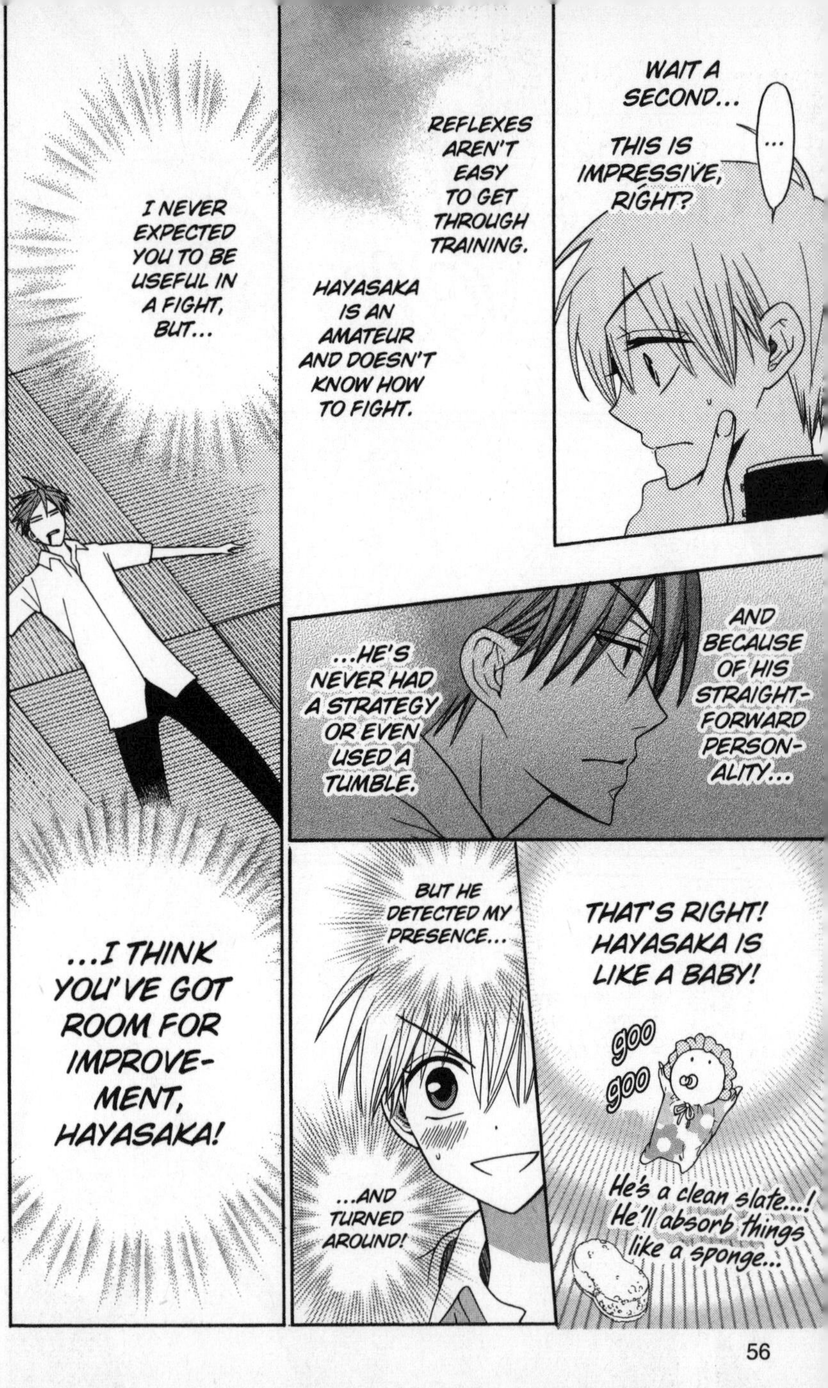
WAIT A SECOND...
THIS IS IMPRESSIVE, RIGHT?
...
REFLEXES AREN'T EASY TO GET THROUGH TRAINING.
HAYASAKA IS AN AMATEUR AND DOESN'T KNOW HOW TO FIGHT.
AND BECAUSE OF HIS STRAIGHT-FORWARD PERSON-ALITY...
...HE'S NEVER HAD A STRATEGY OR EVEN USED A TUMBLE.
BUT HE DETECTED MY PRESENCE...
...AND TURNED AROUND!
THAT'S RIGHT! HAYASAKA IS LIKE A BABY!
goo goo
He's a clean slate...! He'll absorb things like a sponge...
I NEVER EXPECTED YOU TO BE USEFUL IN A FIGHT, BUT...
...I THINK YOU'VE GOT ROOM FOR IMPROVE-MENT, HAYASAKA!

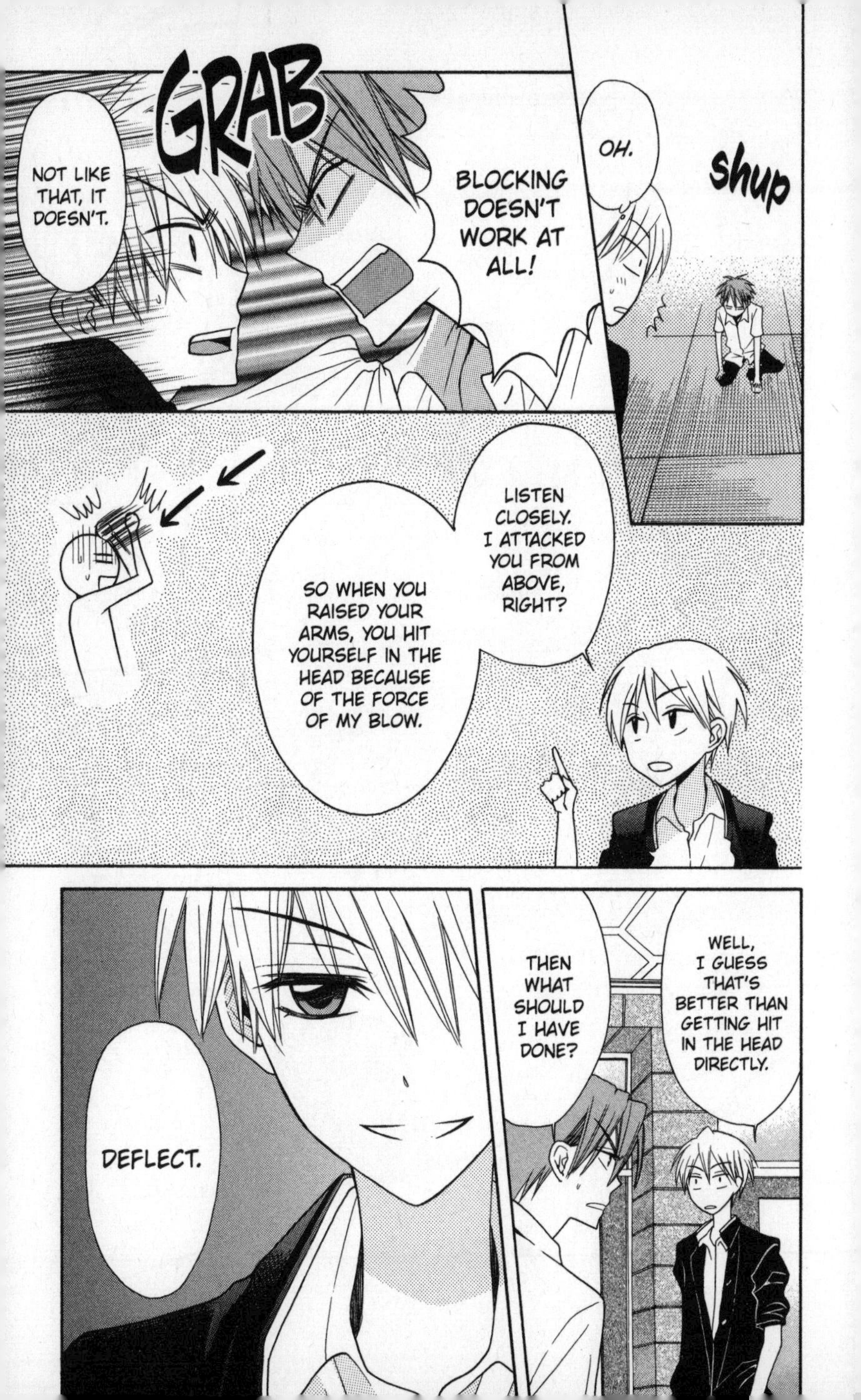
OH.
shup
BLOCKING DOESN'T WORK AT ALL!
GRAB
NOT LIKE THAT, IT DOESN'T.
LISTEN CLOSELY. I ATTACKED YOU FROM ABOVE, RIGHT?
SO WHEN YOU RAISED YOUR ARMS, YOU HIT YOURSELF IN THE HEAD BECAUSE OF THE FORCE OF MY BLOW.
WELL, I GUESS THAT'S BETTER THAN GETTING HIT IN THE HEAD DIRECTLY.
THEN WHAT SHOULD I HAVE DONE?
DEFLECT.

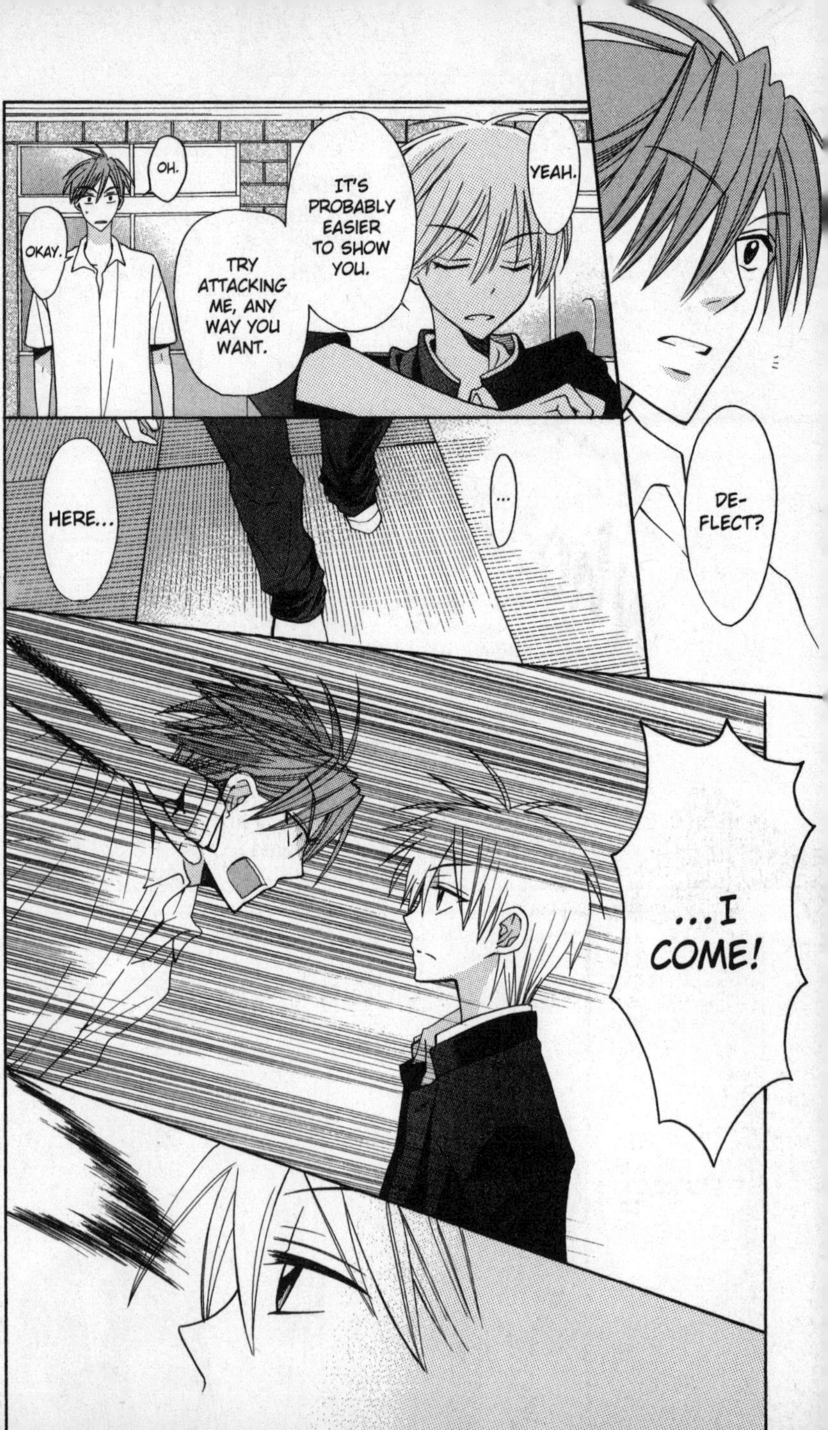
DE-FLECT?
YEAH.
IT'S PROBABLY EASIER TO SHOW YOU.
TRY ATTACKING ME, ANY WAY YOU WANT.
OH.
OKAY.
...
HERE...
...I COME!

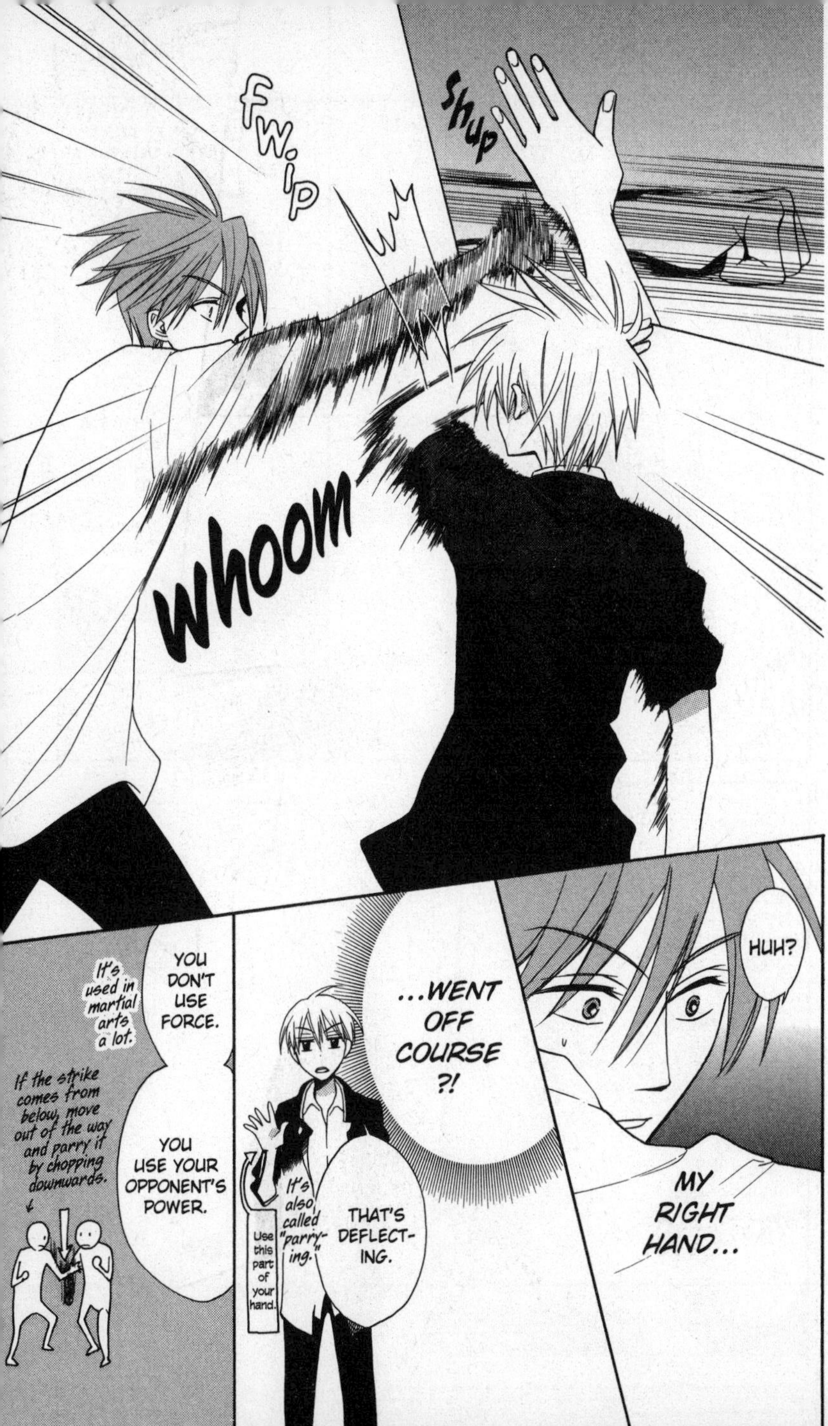
Shup
Fwip
whoom
HUH?
MY RIGHT HAND...
...WENT OFF COURSE?!
THAT'S DEFLECT-ING.
It's also called "parry-ing."
Use this part of your hand.
YOU DON'T USE FORCE.
It's used in martial arts a lot.
YOU USE YOUR OPPONENT'S POWER.
If the strike comes from below, move out of the way and parry it by chopping downwards.

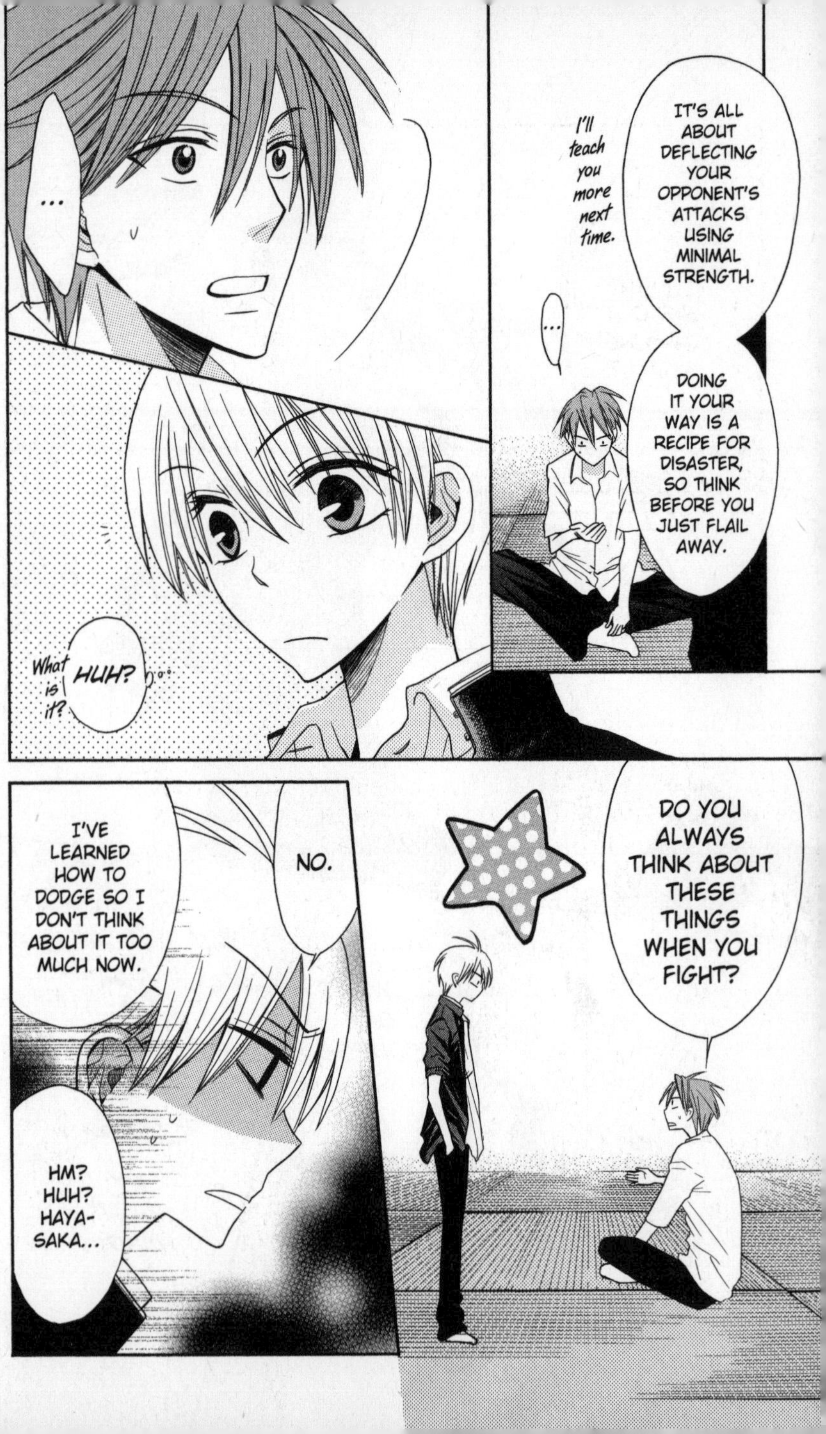
IT'S ALL ABOUT DEFLECTING YOUR OPPONENT'S ATTACKS USING MINIMAL STRENGTH.
I'll teach you more next time.
...
DOING IT YOUR WAY IS A RECIPE FOR DISASTER, SO THINK BEFORE YOU JUST FLAIL AWAY.
...
HUH?
What is it?
DO YOU ALWAYS THINK ABOUT THESE THINGS WHEN YOU FIGHT?
NO.
I'VE LEARNED HOW TO DODGE SO I DON'T THINK ABOUT IT TOO MUCH NOW.
HM? HUH? HAYA-SAKA...

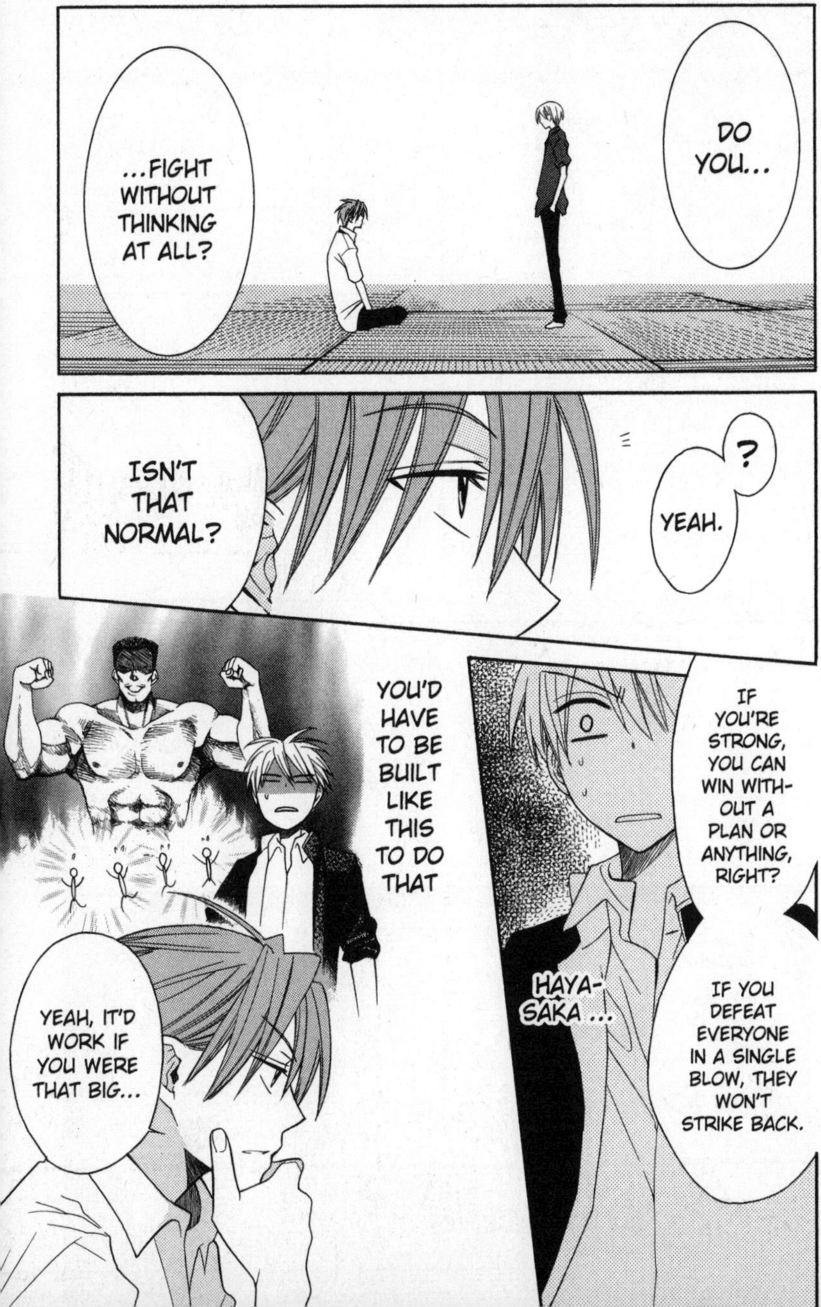
DO YOU...
...FIGHT WITHOUT THINKING AT ALL?
?
YEAH.
ISN'T THAT NORMAL?
IF YOU'RE STRONG, YOU CAN WIN WITH-OUT A PLAN OR ANYTHING, RIGHT?
HAYA-SAKA...
IF YOU DEFEAT EVERYONE IN A SINGLE BLOW, THEY WON'T STRIKE BACK.
YOU'D HAVE TO BE BUILT LIKE THIS TO DO THAT
YEAH, IT'D WORK IF YOU WERE THAT BIG...

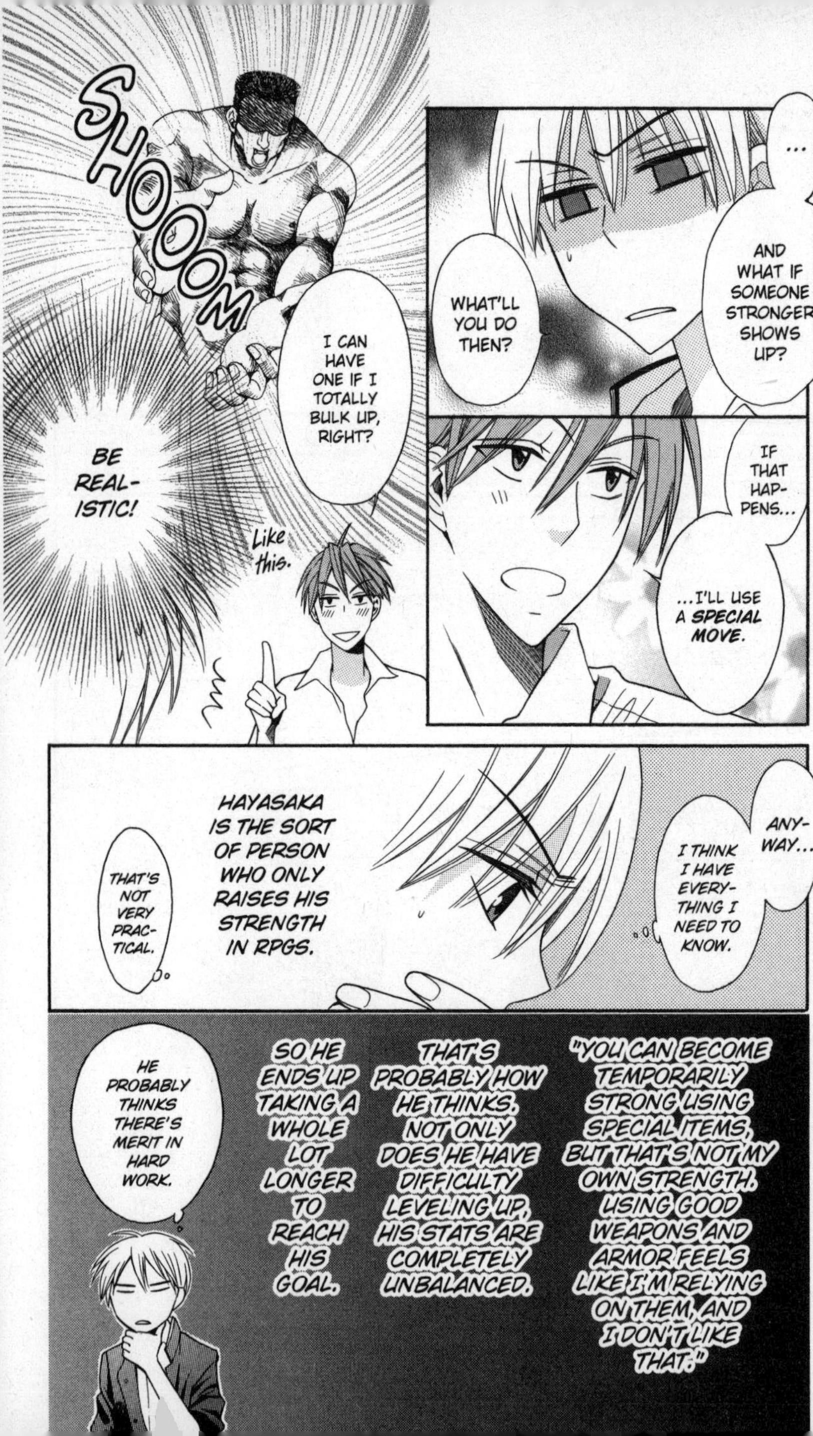
...
AND WHAT IF SOMEONE STRONGER SHOWS UP?
WHAT'LL YOU DO THEN?
IF THAT HAP-PENS...
...I'LL USE A *SPECIAL MOVE*.
I CAN HAVE ONE IF I TOTALLY BULK UP, RIGHT?
SHOOOOM
BE REAL-ISTIC!
Like this.
ANY-WAY...
I THINK I HAVE EVERY-THING I NEED TO KNOW.
HAYASAKA IS THE SORT OF PERSON WHO ONLY RAISES HIS STRENGTH IN RPGS.
THAT'S NOT VERY PRAC-TICAL.
"YOU CAN BECOME TEMPORARILY STRONG USING SPECIAL ITEMS, BUT THAT'S NOT MY OWN STRENGTH. USING GOOD WEAPONS AND ARMOR FEELS LIKE I'M RELYING ON THEM, AND I DON'T LIKE THAT."
THAT'S PROBABLY HOW HE THINKS. NOT ONLY DOES HE HAVE DIFFICULTY LEVELING UP, HIS STATS ARE COMPLETELY UNBALANCED.
SO HE ENDS UP TAKING A WHOLE LOT LONGER TO REACH HIS GOAL.
HE PROBABLY THINKS THERE'S MERIT IN HARD WORK.

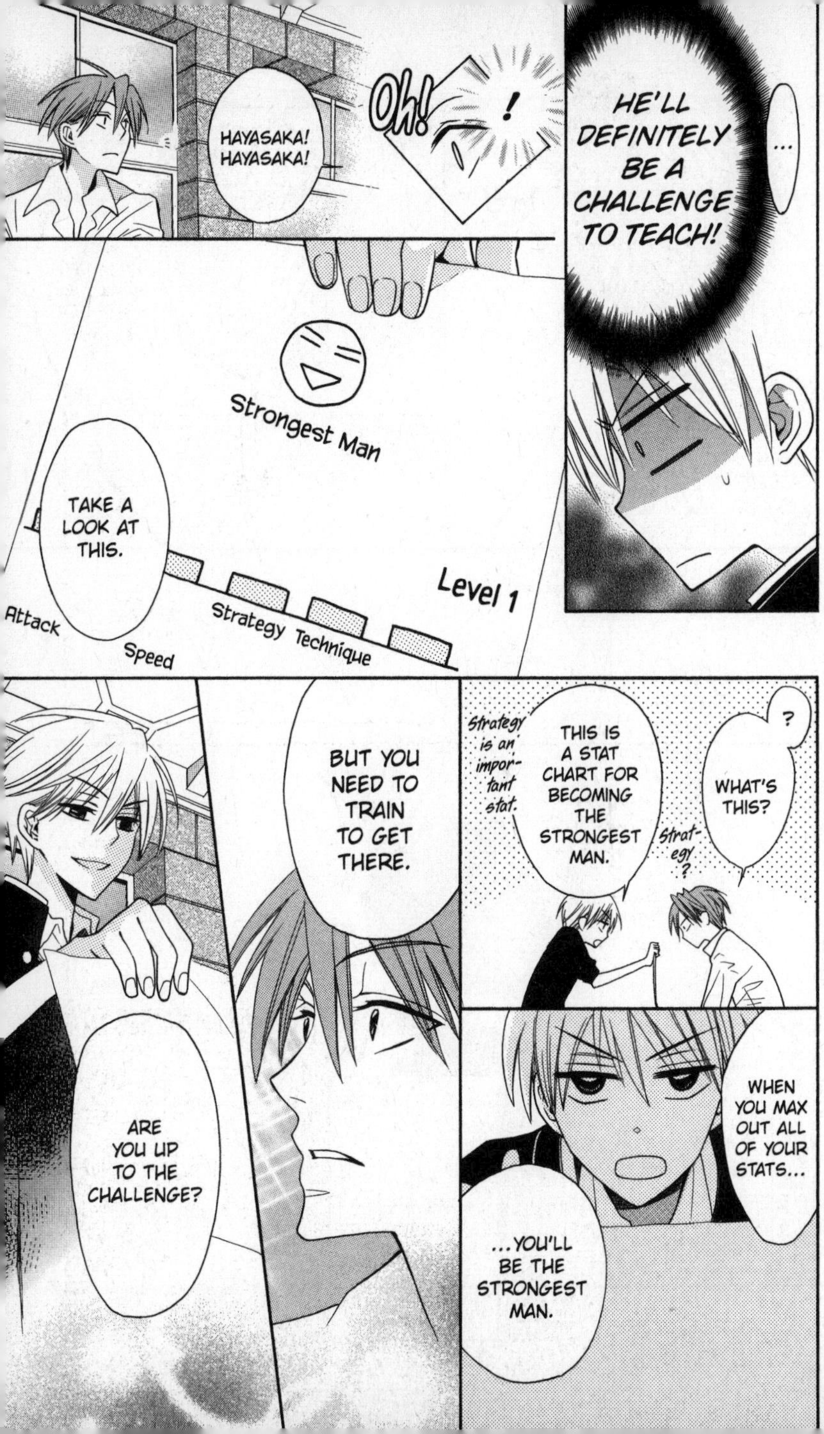
...
HE'LL DEFINITELY BE A CHALLENGE TO TEACH!
Oh!
!
HAYASAKA! HAYASAKA!
Strongest Man
Level 1
TAKE A LOOK AT THIS.
Attack
Speed
Strategy
Technique
?
WHAT'S THIS?
Strat-egy?
THIS IS A STAT CHART FOR BECOMING THE STRONGEST MAN.
Strategy is an impor-tant stat.
WHEN YOU MAX OUT ALL OF YOUR STATS...
...YOU'LL BE THE STRONGEST MAN.
BUT YOU NEED TO TRAIN TO GET THERE.
ARE YOU UP TO THE CHALLENGE?

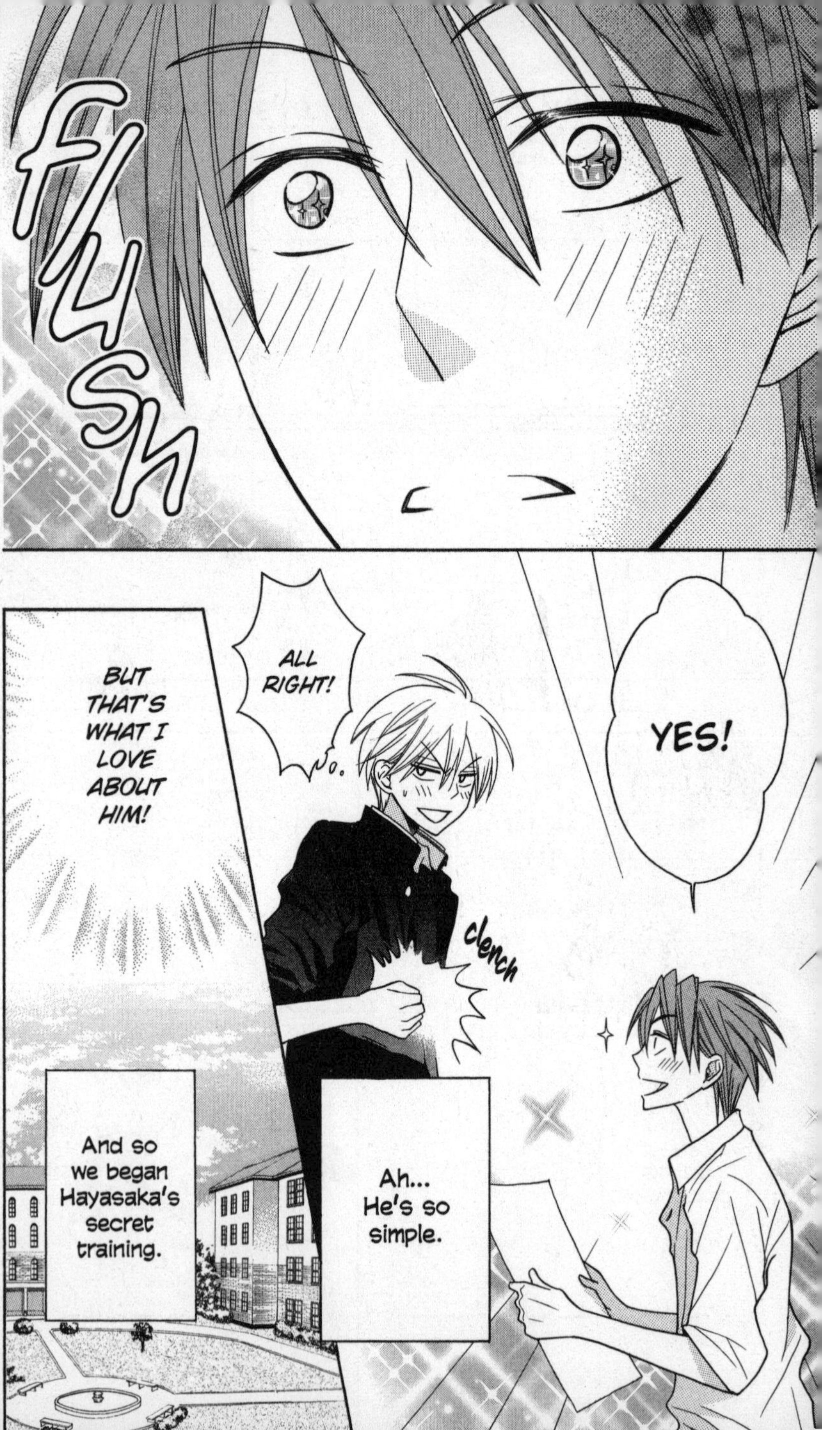
flush
YES!
ALL RIGHT!
clench
Ah... He's so simple.
BUT THAT'S WHAT I LOVE ABOUT HIM!
And so we began Hayasaka's secret training.

Let's Train! Part 1

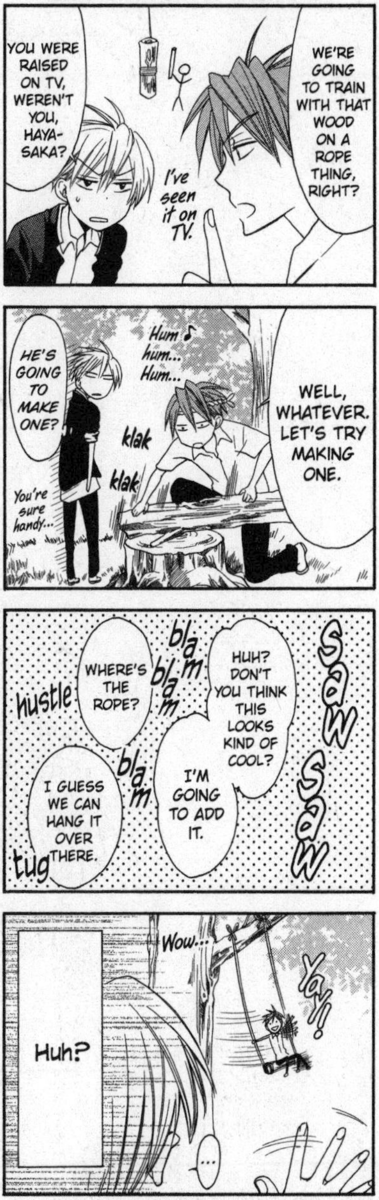
WE'RE GOING TO TRAIN WITH THAT WOOD ON A ROPE THING, RIGHT?
I've seen it on TV.
YOU WERE RAISED ON TV, WEREN'T YOU, HAYASAKA?
WELL, WHATEVER. LET'S TRY MAKING ONE.
Hum ♪ hum... Hum...
klak
klak
HE'S GOING TO MAKE ONE?
You're sure handy...
saw saw
HUH? DON'T YOU THINK THIS LOOKS KIND OF COOL?
blam blam blam blam
WHERE'S THE ROPE?
hustle
I'M GOING TO ADD IT.
I GUESS WE CAN HANG IT OVER THERE.
tug
Yay!
Wow...
Huh?
...

Let's Train! Part 2

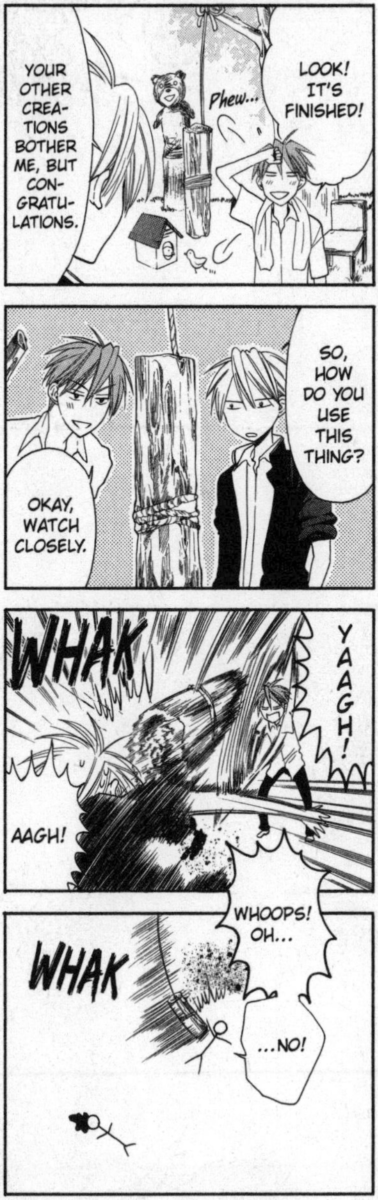
LOOK! IT'S FINISHED!
Phew...
YOUR OTHER CREATIONS BOTHER ME, BUT CONGRATULATIONS.
SO, HOW DO YOU USE THIS THING?
OKAY, WATCH CLOSELY.
YAAGH!
WHAK
AAGH!
WHOOPS! OH...
...NO!
WHAK

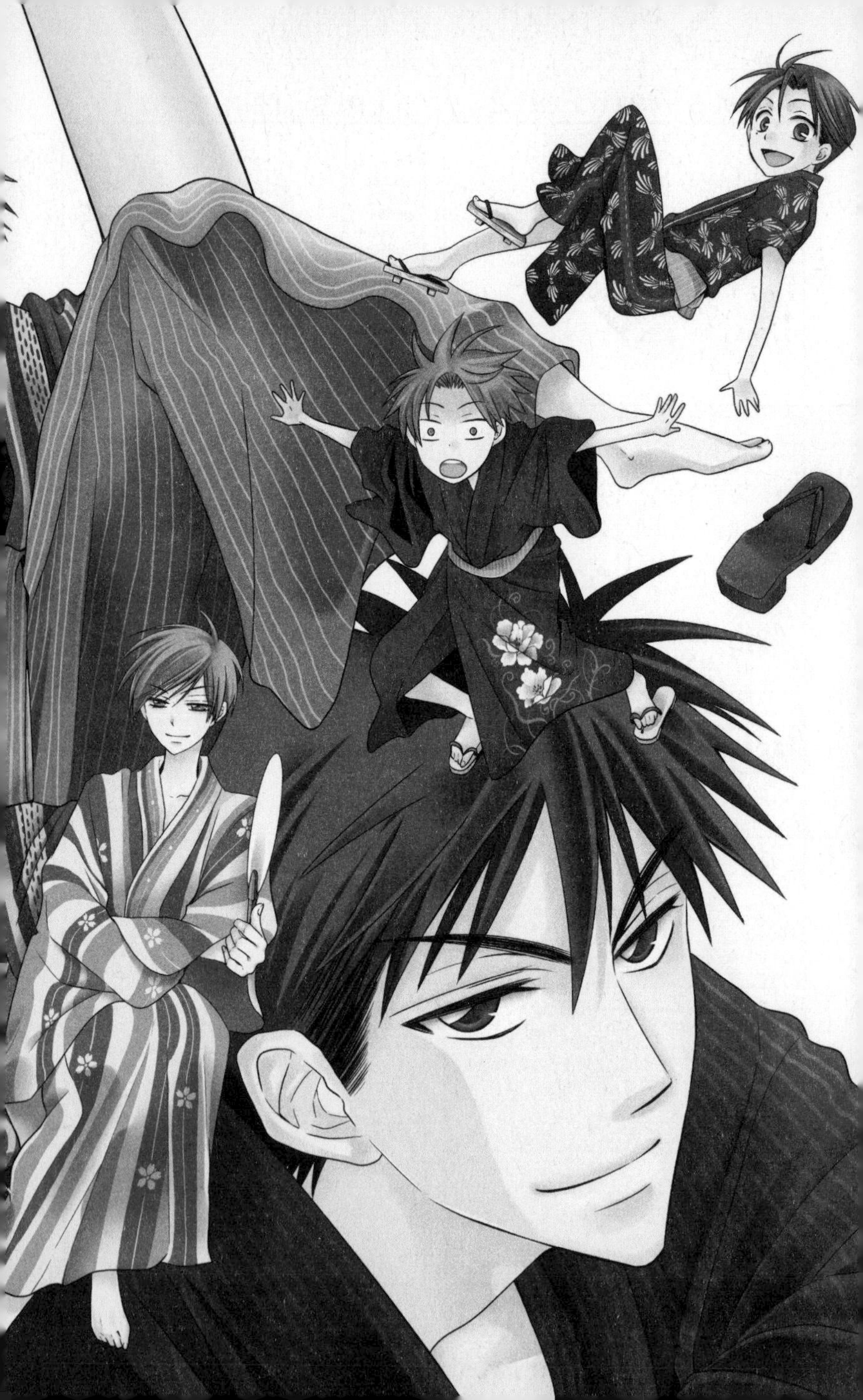

Chapter 20

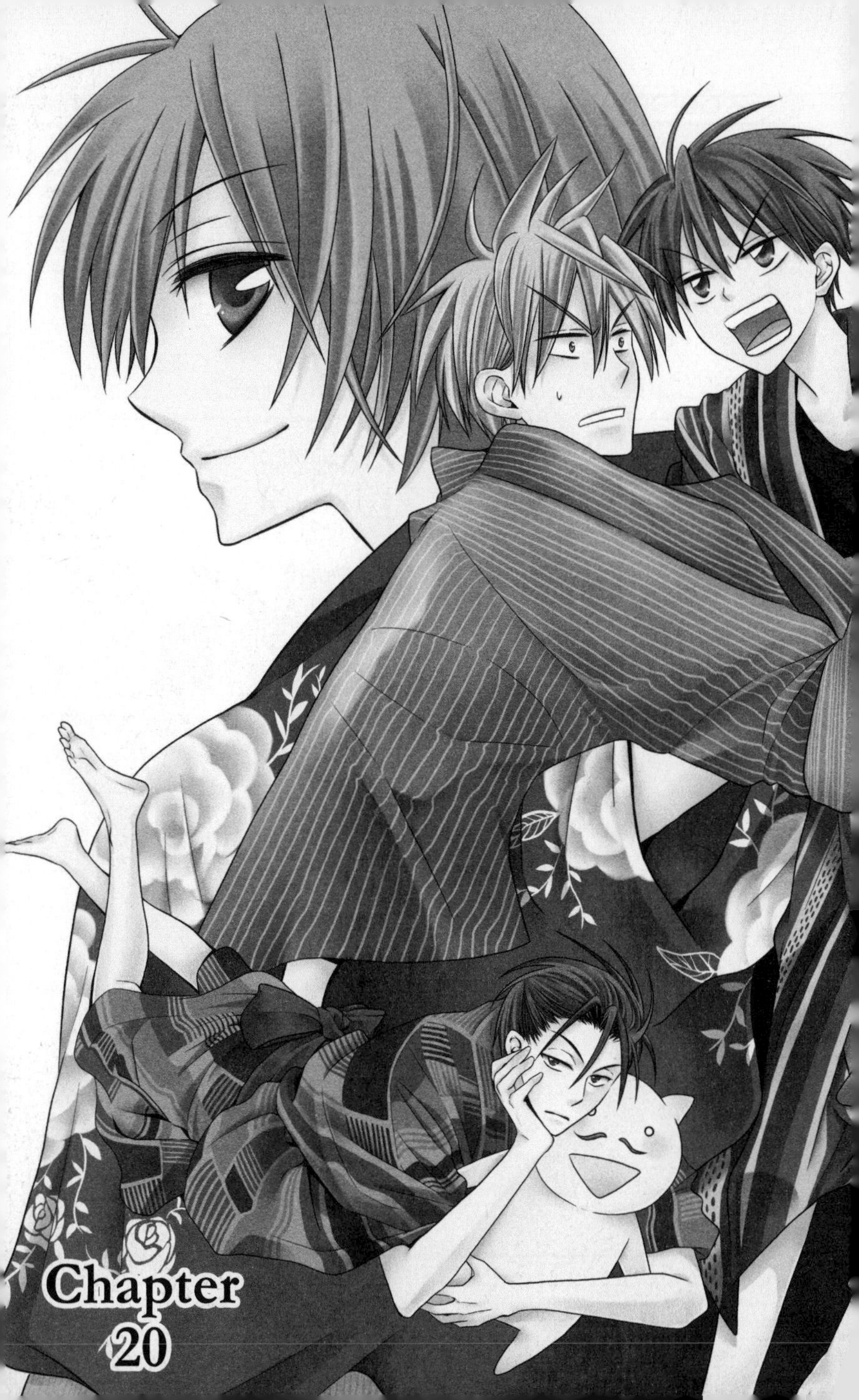

Teacher/Student Relationships

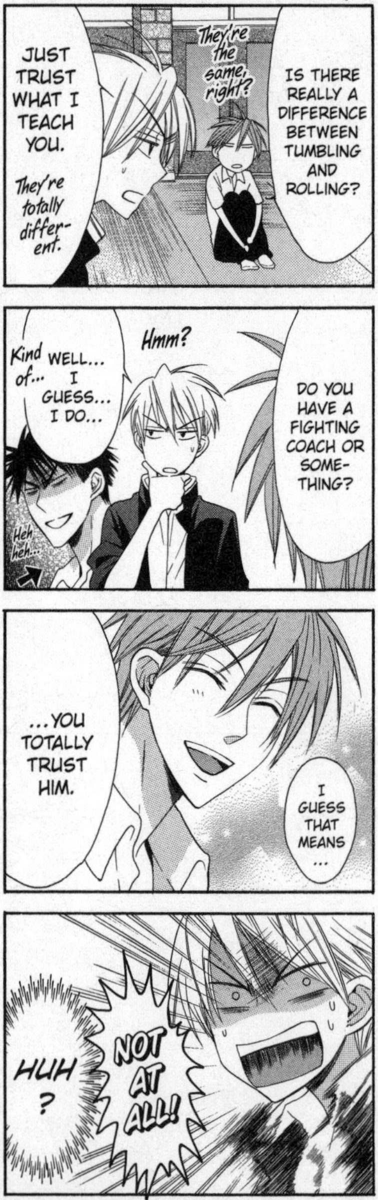

IS THERE REALLY A DIFFERENCE BETWEEN TUMBLING AND ROLLING?
They're the same, right?
JUST TRUST WHAT I TEACH YOU.
They're totally differ-ent.
DO YOU HAVE A FIGHTING COACH OR SOME-THING?
Hmm?
WELL... I GUESS... I DO...
Kind of...
Heh heh...
I GUESS THAT MEANS ...
...YOU TOTALLY TRUST HIM.
NOT AT ALL!
HUH ?

Before and After

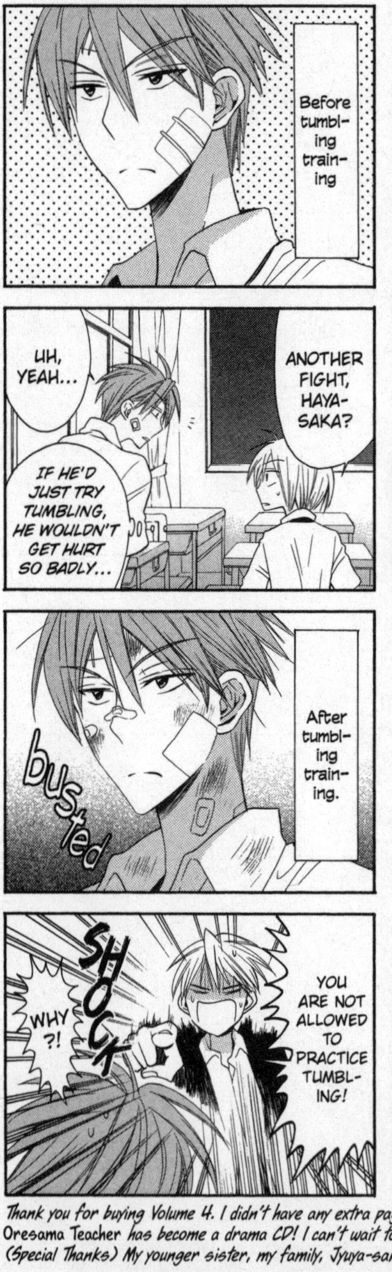

Before tumbl-ing train-ing
ANOTHER FIGHT, HAYA-SAKA?
UH, YEAH...
IF HE'D JUST TRY TUMBLING, HE WOULDN'T GET HURT SO BADLY...
After tumbl-ing train-ing.
busted
YOU ARE NOT ALLOWED TO PRACTICE TUMBL-ING!
SHOCK
WHY ?!

Thank you for buying Volume 4. I didn't have any extra pages this time, so I'm writing in the margin. Oh yeah! Oresama Teacher has become a drama CD! I can't wait to see the finished product!
(Special Thanks) My younger sister, my family, Jyuya-san, Shiina-san, Pochi-san, my editor.

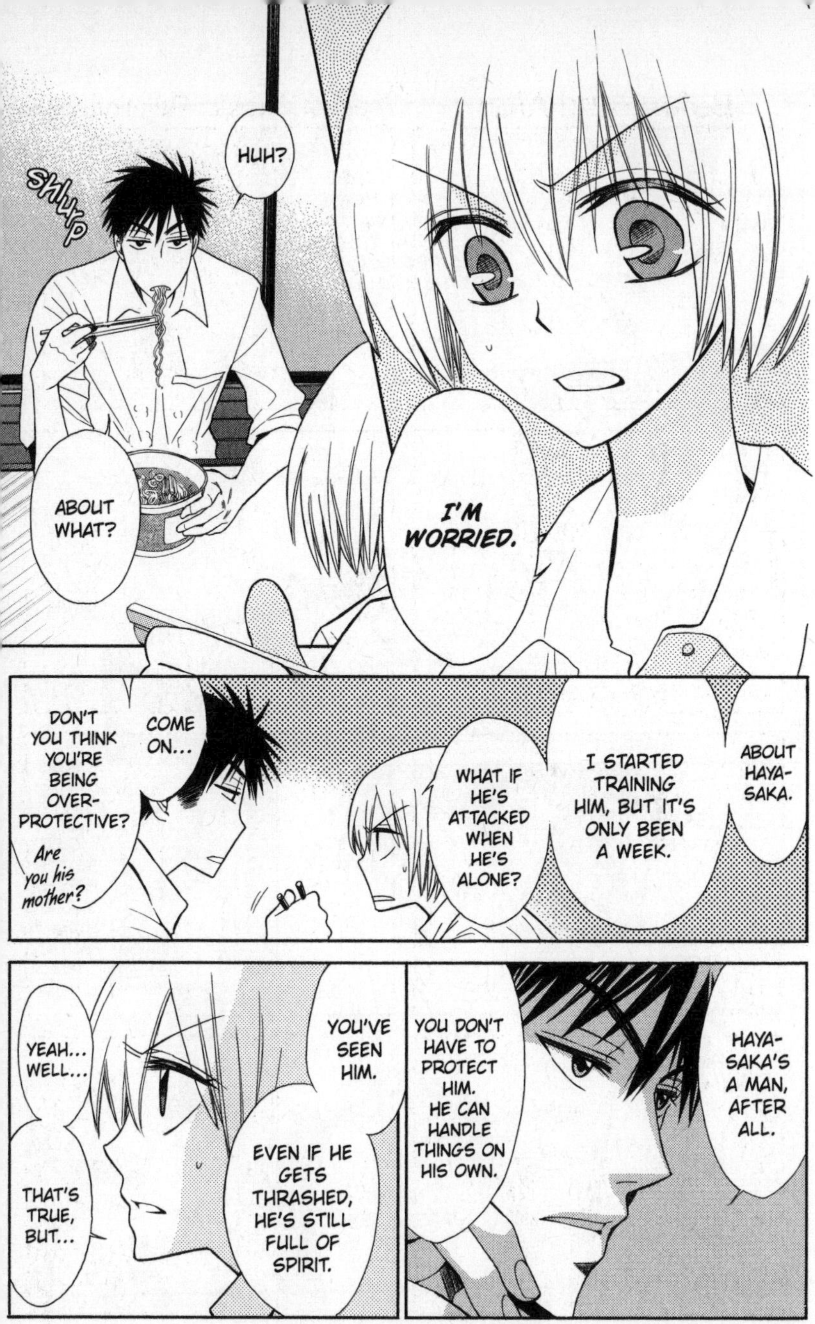
I'M WORRIED.
SHLUP
HUH?
ABOUT WHAT?
ABOUT HAYA-SAKA.
I STARTED TRAINING HIM, BUT IT'S ONLY BEEN A WEEK.
WHAT IF HE'S ATTACKED WHEN HE'S ALONE?
COME ON...
DON'T YOU THINK YOU'RE BEING OVER-PROTECTIVE?
Are you his mother?
HAYA-SAKA'S A MAN, AFTER ALL.
YOU DON'T HAVE TO PROTECT HIM. HE CAN HANDLE THINGS ON HIS OWN.
YOU'VE SEEN HIM.
EVEN IF HE GETS THRASHED, HE'S STILL FULL OF SPIRIT.
YEAH... WELL...
THAT'S TRUE, BUT...

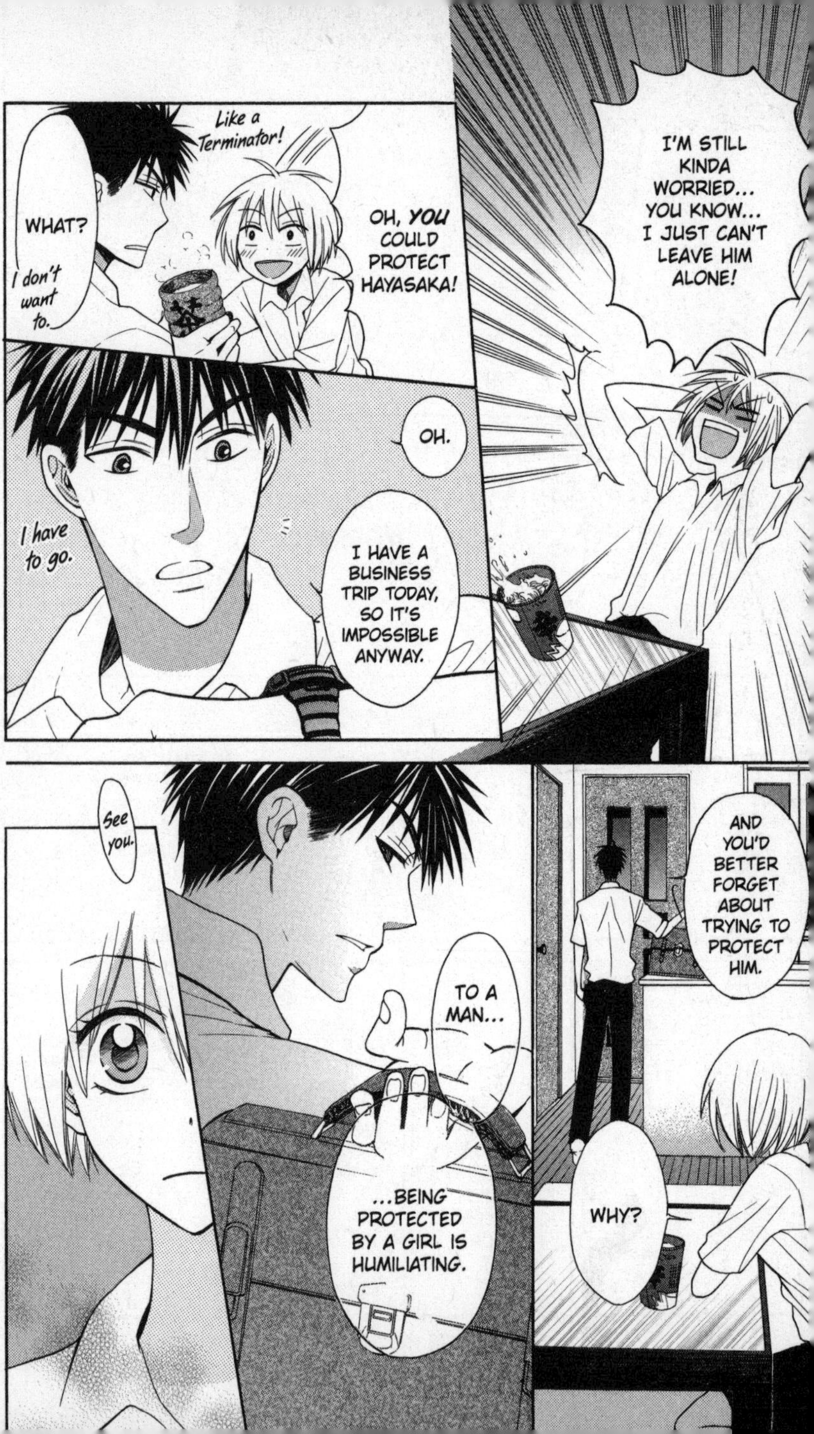
I'M STILL KINDA WORRIED... YOU KNOW... I JUST CAN'T LEAVE HIM ALONE!
OH, *YOU* COULD PROTECT HAYASAKA!
Like a Terminator!
WHAT?
I don't want to.
OH.
I HAVE A BUSINESS TRIP TODAY, SO IT'S IMPOSSIBLE ANYWAY.
I have to go.
AND YOU'D BETTER FORGET ABOUT TRYING TO PROTECT HIM.
WHY?
TO A MAN...
...BEING PROTECTED BY A GIRL IS HUMILIATING.
See you.

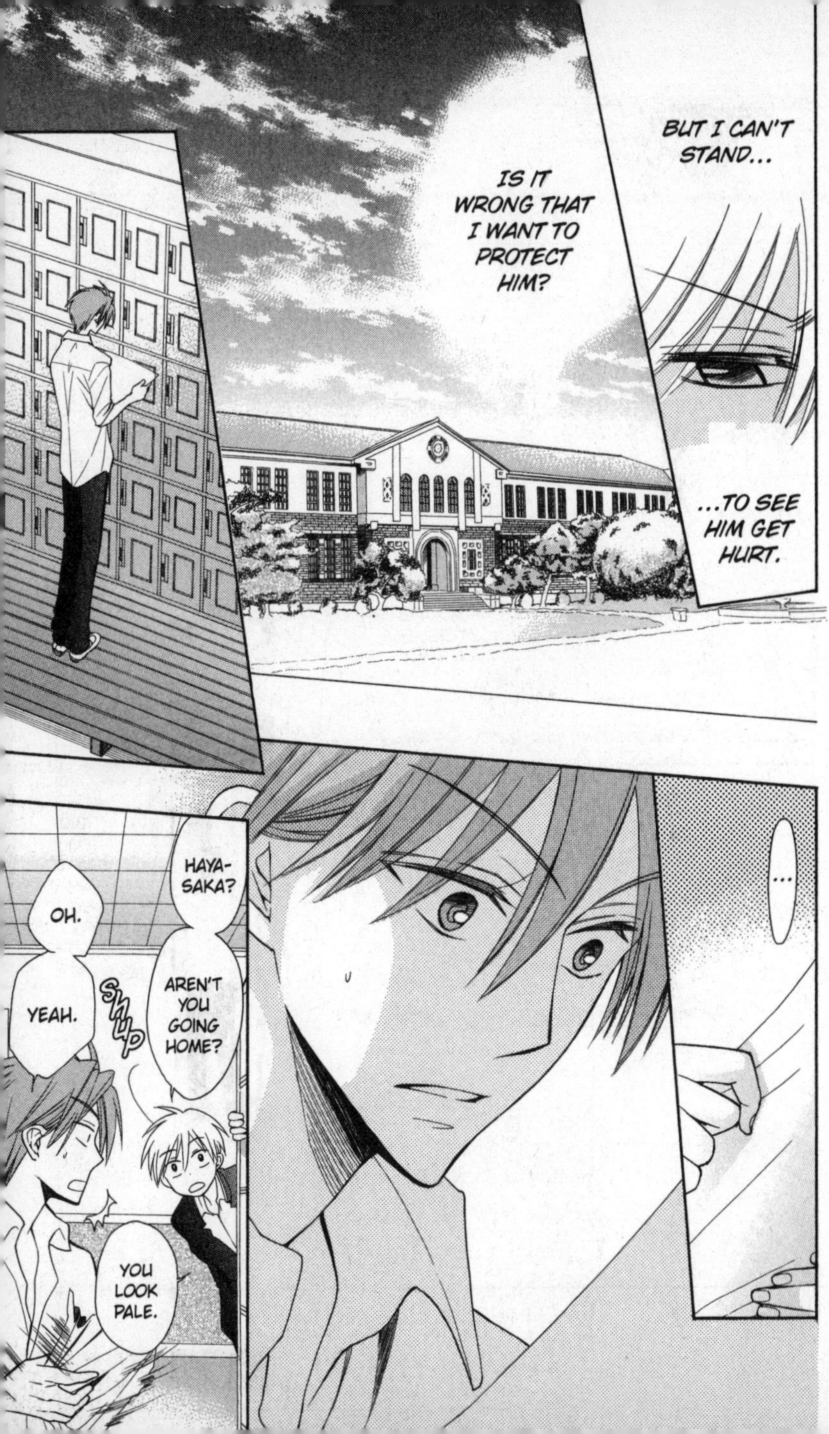

BUT I CAN'T STAND...
...TO SEE HIM GET HURT.
IS IT WRONG THAT I WANT TO PROTECT HIM?
...
HAYA-SAKA?
OH.
AREN'T YOU GOING HOME?
YEAH.
SHUP
YOU LOOK PALE.

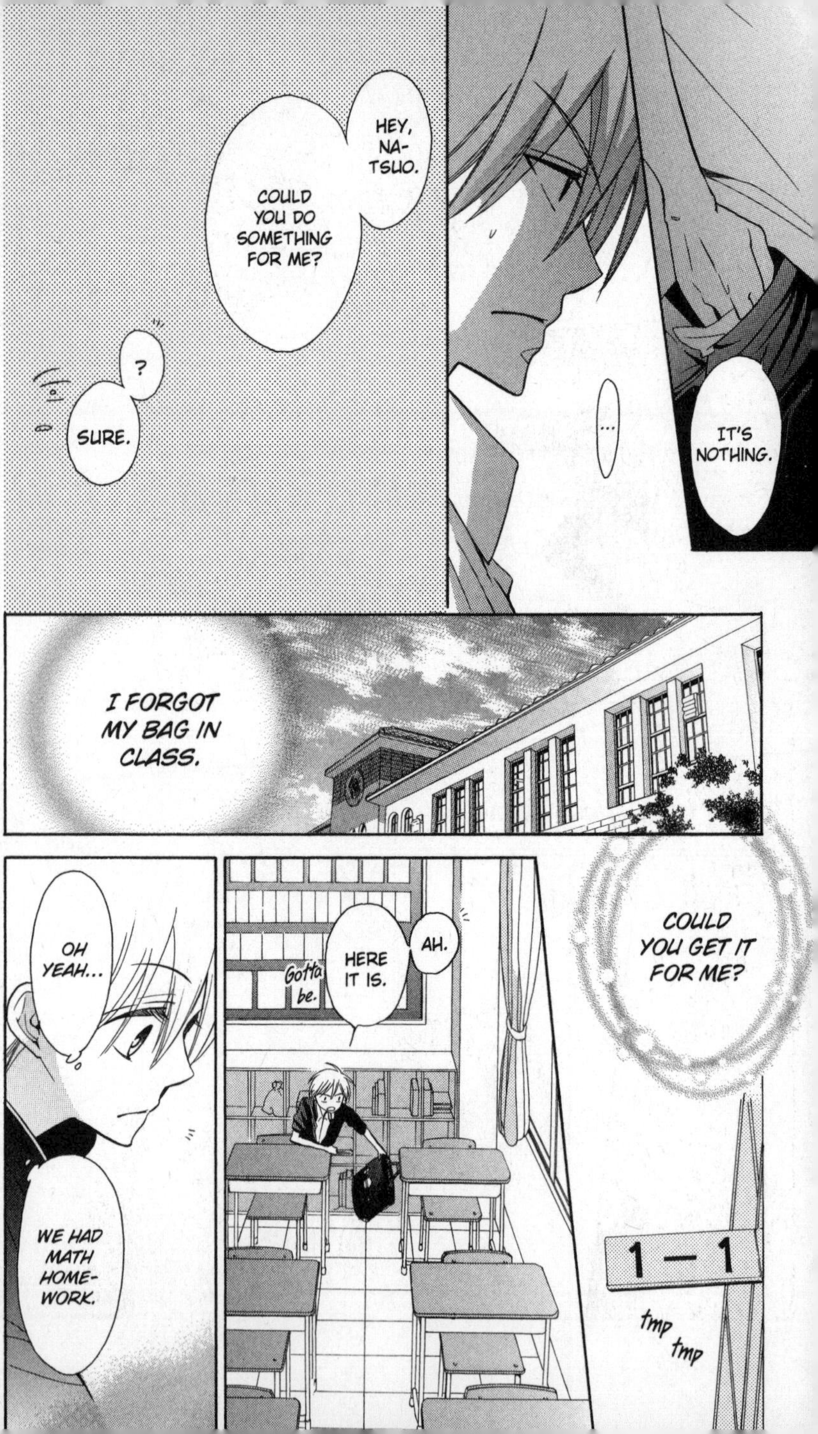
IT'S NOTHING.
...
HEY, NA-TSUO.
COULD YOU DO SOMETHING FOR ME?
?
SURE.
I FORGOT MY BAG IN CLASS.
COULD YOU GET IT FOR ME?
1 — 1
tmp tmp
AH.
HERE IT IS.
Gotta be.
OH YEAH...
WE HAD MATH HOME-WORK.

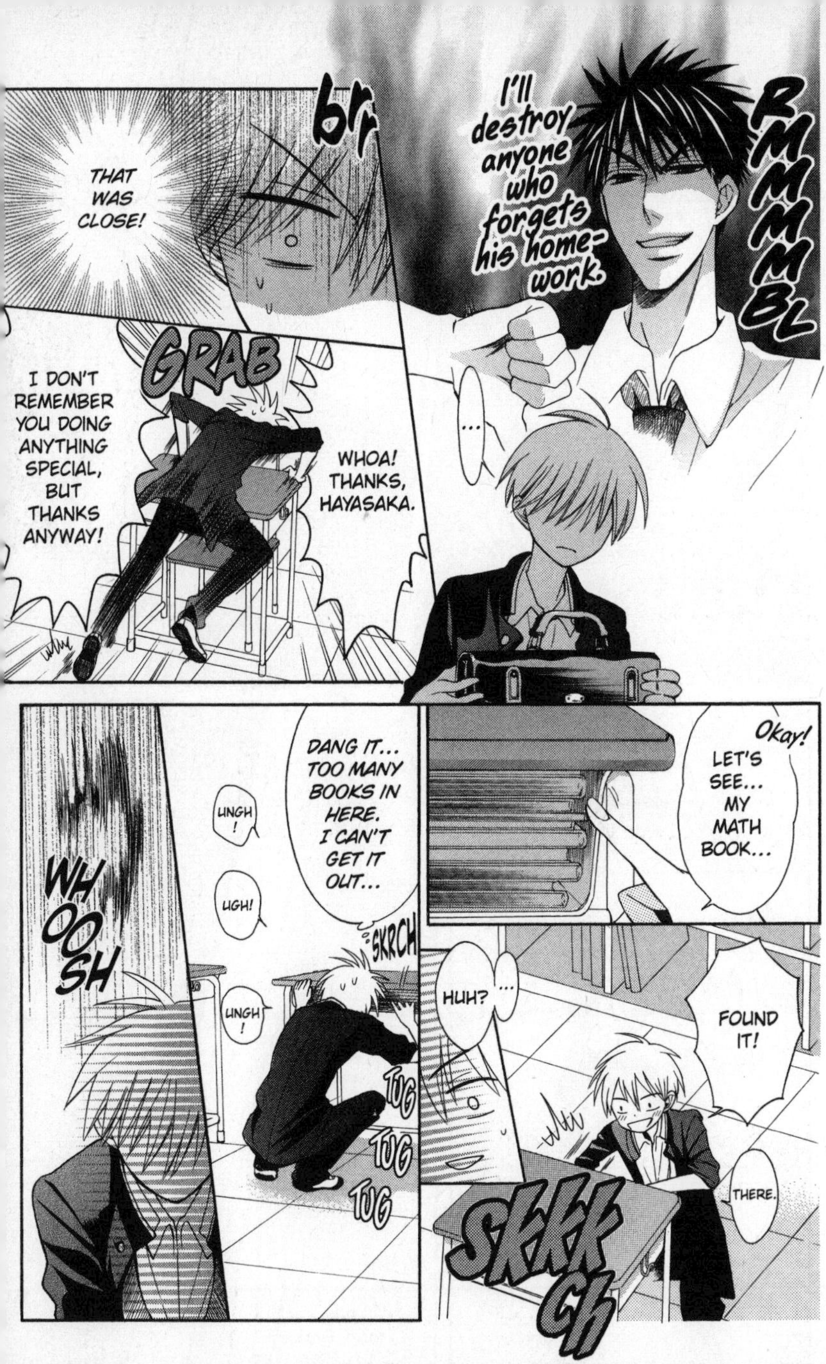
RMMMMBL
I'll destroy anyone who forgets his home-work.
...
brr
THAT WAS CLOSE!
GRAB
WHOA! THANKS, HAYASAKA.
I DON'T REMEMBER YOU DOING ANYTHING SPECIAL, BUT THANKS ANYWAY!
Okay!
LET'S SEE... MY MATH BOOK...
FOUND IT!
THERE.
SKKKCH
HUH?
...
DANG IT... TOO MANY BOOKS IN HERE. I CAN'T GET IT OUT...
UNGH!
UGH!
SKRCH
UNGH!
TUG
TUG
TUG
WHOOSH

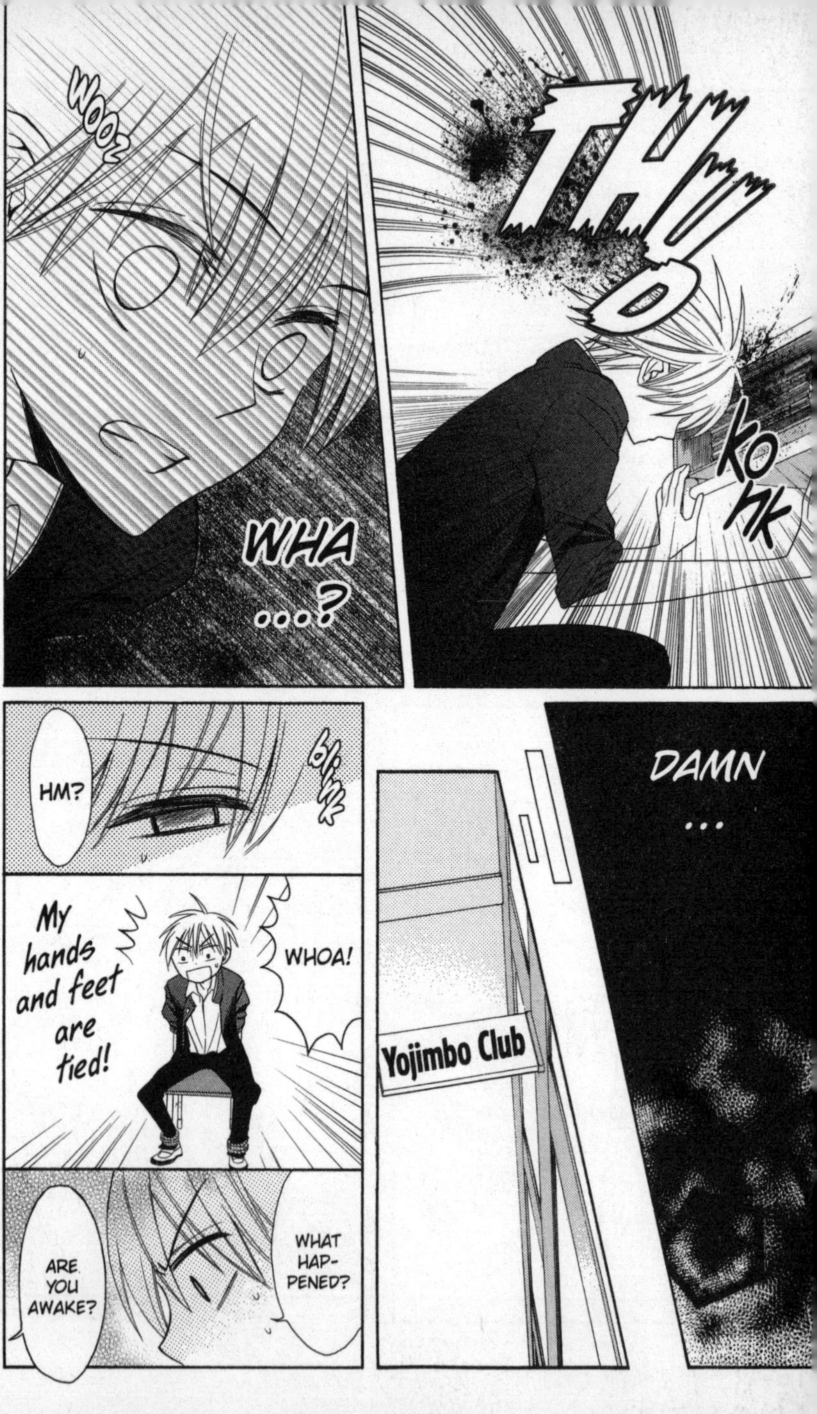
THUD
konk
WOOZ
WHA...?
DAMN...
Yojimbo Club
blink
HM?
WHOA!
My hands and feet are tied!
WHAT HAP-PENED?
ARE YOU AWAKE?

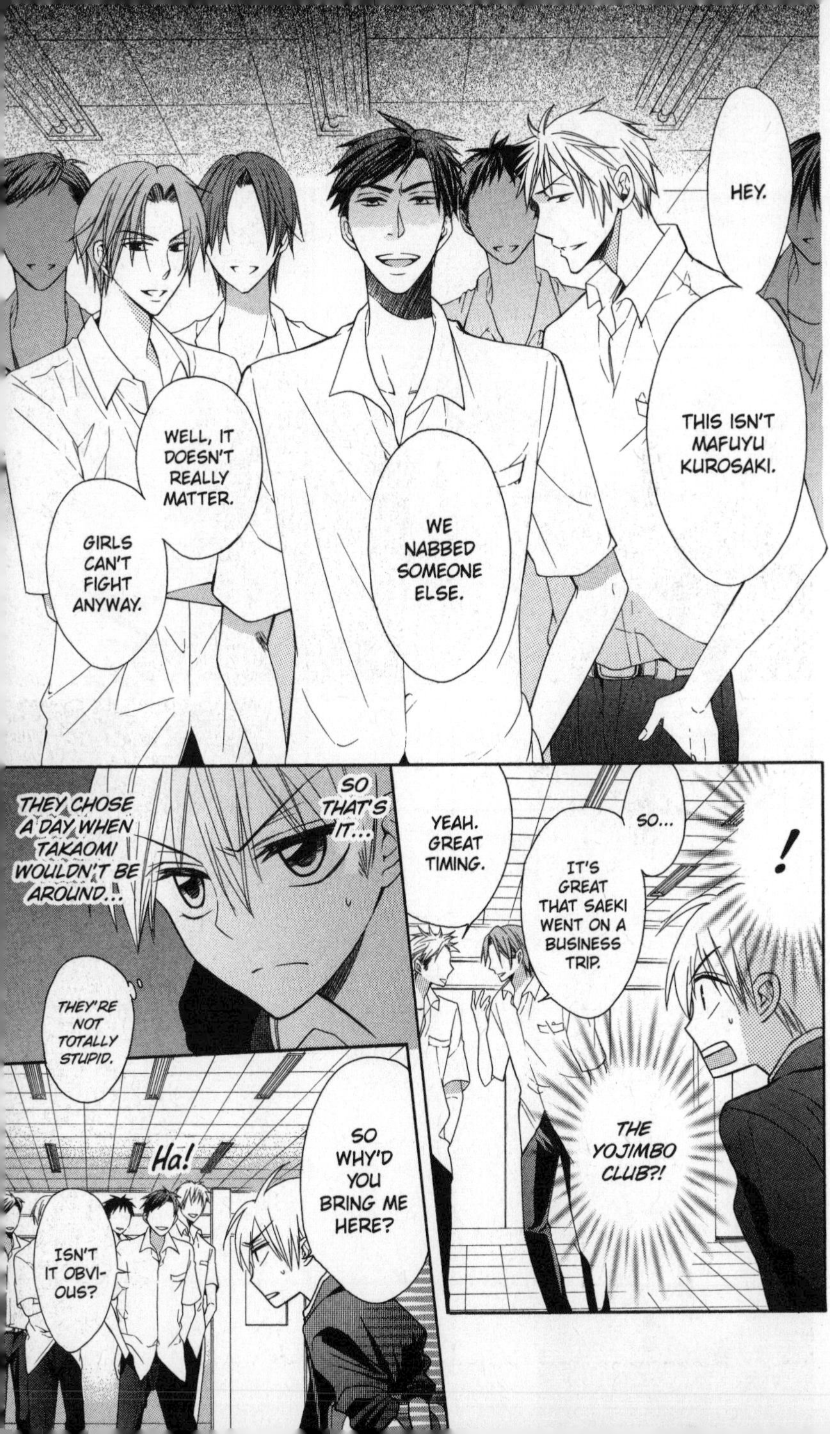
HEY.
THIS ISN'T MAFUYU KUROSAKI.
WE NABBED SOMEONE ELSE.
WELL, IT DOESN'T REALLY MATTER.
GIRLS CAN'T FIGHT ANYWAY.
!
SO...
IT'S GREAT THAT SAEKI WENT ON A BUSINESS TRIP.
YEAH. GREAT TIMING.
THE YOJIMBO CLUB?!
SO THAT'S IT...
THEY CHOSE A DAY WHEN TAKAOMI WOULDN'T BE AROUND...
THEY'RE NOT TOTALLY STUPID.
SO WHY'D YOU BRING ME HERE?
Ha!
ISN'T IT OBVIOUS?

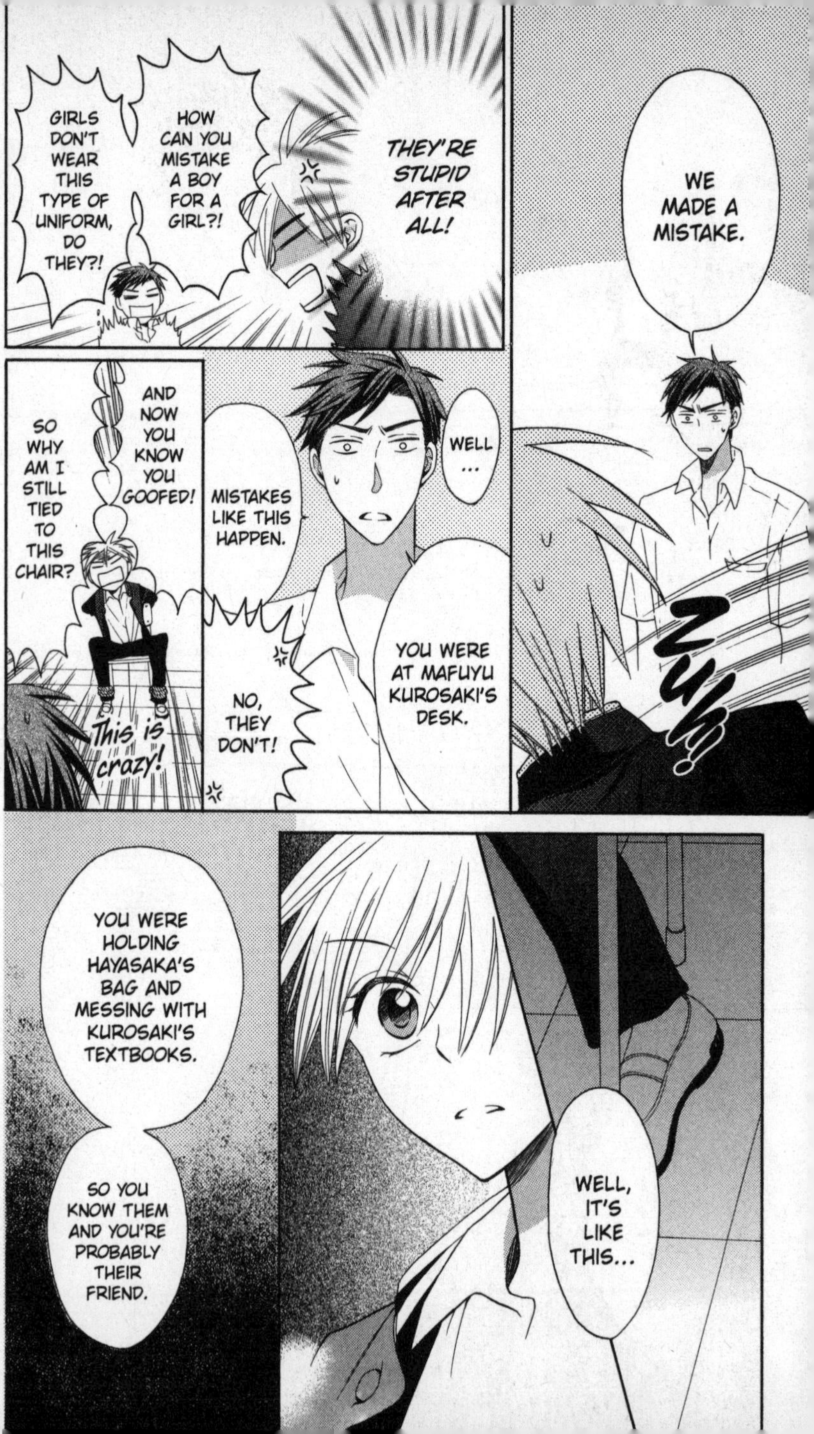
WE MADE A MISTAKE.
ZUN!!
THEY'RE STUPID AFTER ALL!
HOW CAN YOU MISTAKE A BOY FOR A GIRL?!
GIRLS DON'T WEAR THIS TYPE OF UNIFORM, DO THEY?!
WELL...
MISTAKES LIKE THIS HAPPEN.
YOU WERE AT MAFUYU KUROSAKI'S DESK.
NO, THEY DON'T!
AND NOW YOU KNOW YOU GOOFED!
SO WHY AM I STILL TIED TO THIS CHAIR?
This is crazy!
WELL, IT'S LIKE THIS...
YOU WERE HOLDING HAYASAKA'S BAG AND MESSING WITH KUROSAKI'S TEXTBOOKS.
SO YOU KNOW THEM AND YOU'RE PROBABLY THEIR FRIEND.

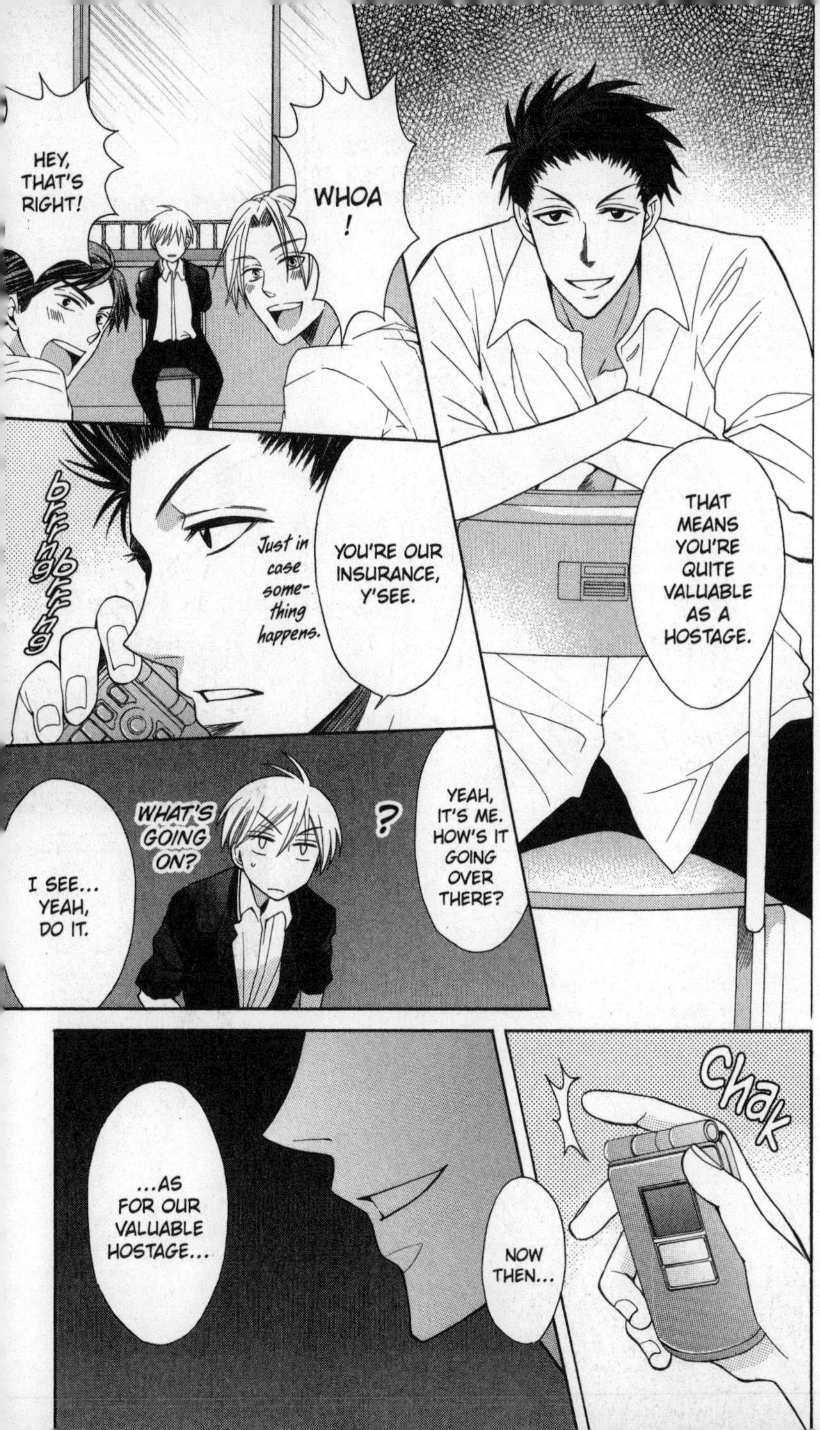
THAT MEANS YOU'RE QUITE VALUABLE AS A HOSTAGE.
WHOA!
HEY, THAT'S RIGHT!
brrring brrring
YOU'RE OUR INSURANCE, Y'SEE.
Just in case something happens.
YEAH, IT'S ME. HOW'S IT GOING OVER THERE?
?
WHAT'S GOING ON?
I SEE... YEAH, DO IT.
Chak
NOW THEN...
...AS FOR OUR VALUABLE HOSTAGE...

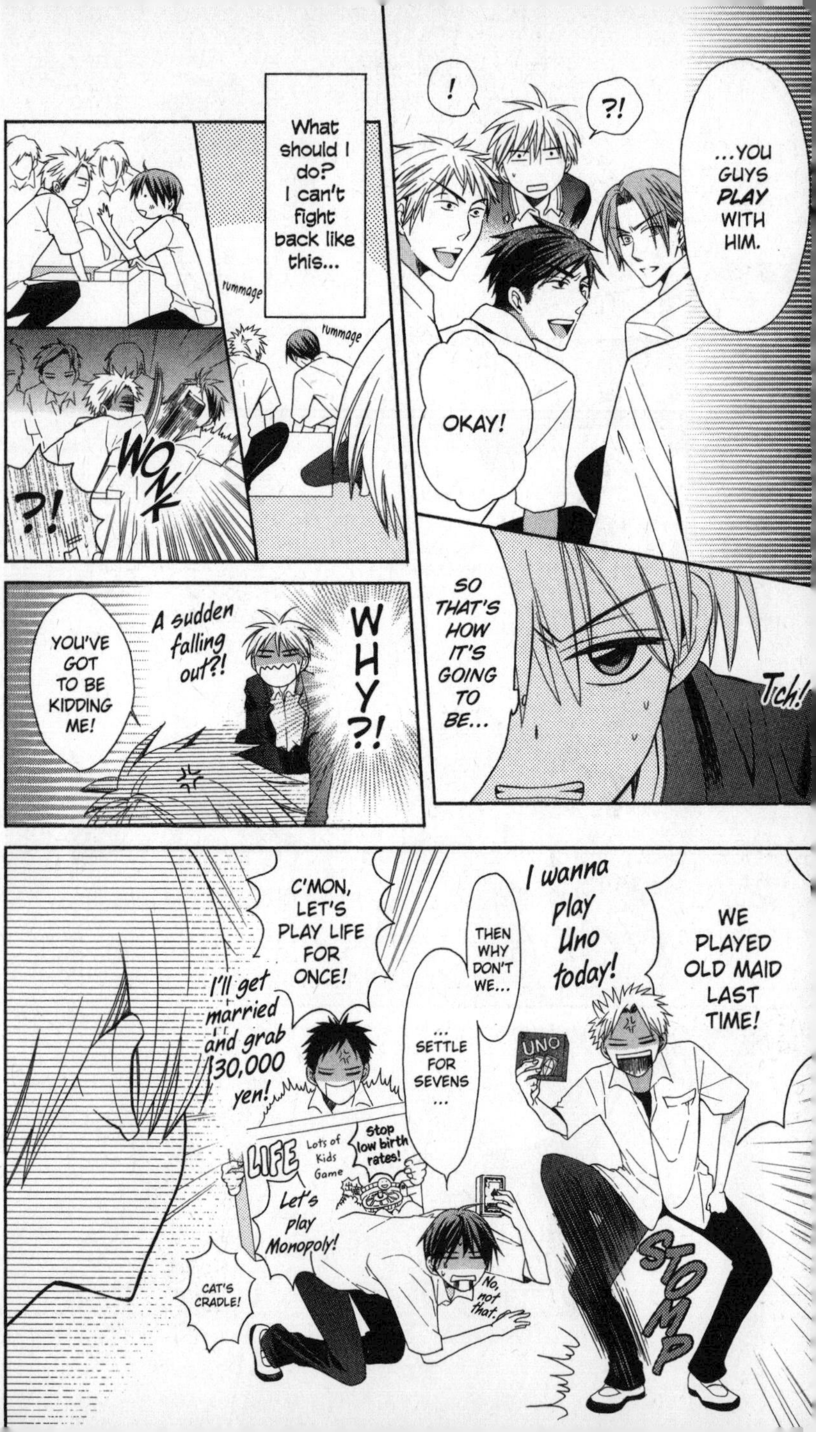

...YOU GUYS PLAY WITH HIM.
?!
!
OKAY!
What should I do? I can't fight back like this...
rummage
rummage
WONK
?!
Tch!
SO THAT'S HOW IT'S GOING TO BE...
WHY?!
A sudden falling out?!
YOU'VE GOT TO BE KIDDING ME!
WE PLAYED OLD MAID LAST TIME!
I wanna play Uno today!
UNO
THEN WHY DON'T WE...
... SETTLE FOR SEVENS ...
C'MON, LET'S PLAY LIFE FOR ONCE!
I'll get married and grab 30,000 yen!
Stop low birth rates!
LIFE
Lots of Kids Game
Let's play Monopoly!
No, not that.
CAT'S CRADLE!
STOMP

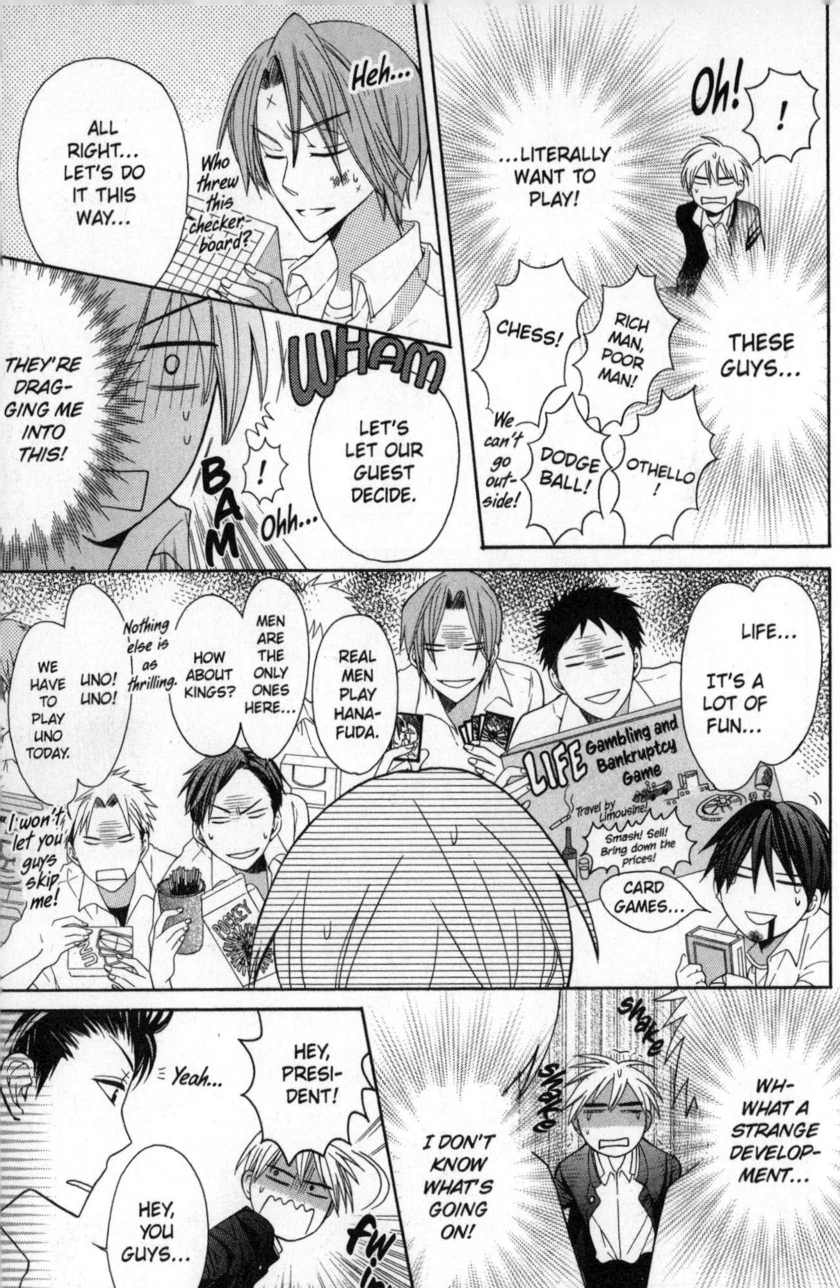

Oh!
!
...LITERALLY WANT TO PLAY!
THESE GUYS...
RICH MAN, POOR MAN!
CHESS!
OTHELLO!
DODGE BALL!
We can't go out-side!
Heh...
ALL RIGHT... LET'S DO IT THIS WAY...
Who threw this checker-board?
WHAM
LET'S LET OUR GUEST DECIDE.
BAM
!
Ohh...
THEY'RE DRAG-GING ME INTO THIS!
LIFE...
IT'S A LOT OF FUN...
LIFE Gambling and Bankruptcy Game
Travel by Limousine!
Smash! Sell! Bring down the prices!
CARD GAMES...
REAL MEN PLAY HANA-FUDA.
MEN ARE THE ONLY ONES HERE...
HOW ABOUT KINGS?
Nothing else is as thrilling.
UNO! UNO!
WE HAVE TO PLAY UNO TODAY.
I won't let you guys skip me!
POCKEY
WH-WHAT A STRANGE DEVELOP-MENT...
shake
shake
I DON'T KNOW WHAT'S GOING ON!
HEY, PRESI-DENT!
Yeah...
fwip!
HEY, YOU GUYS...

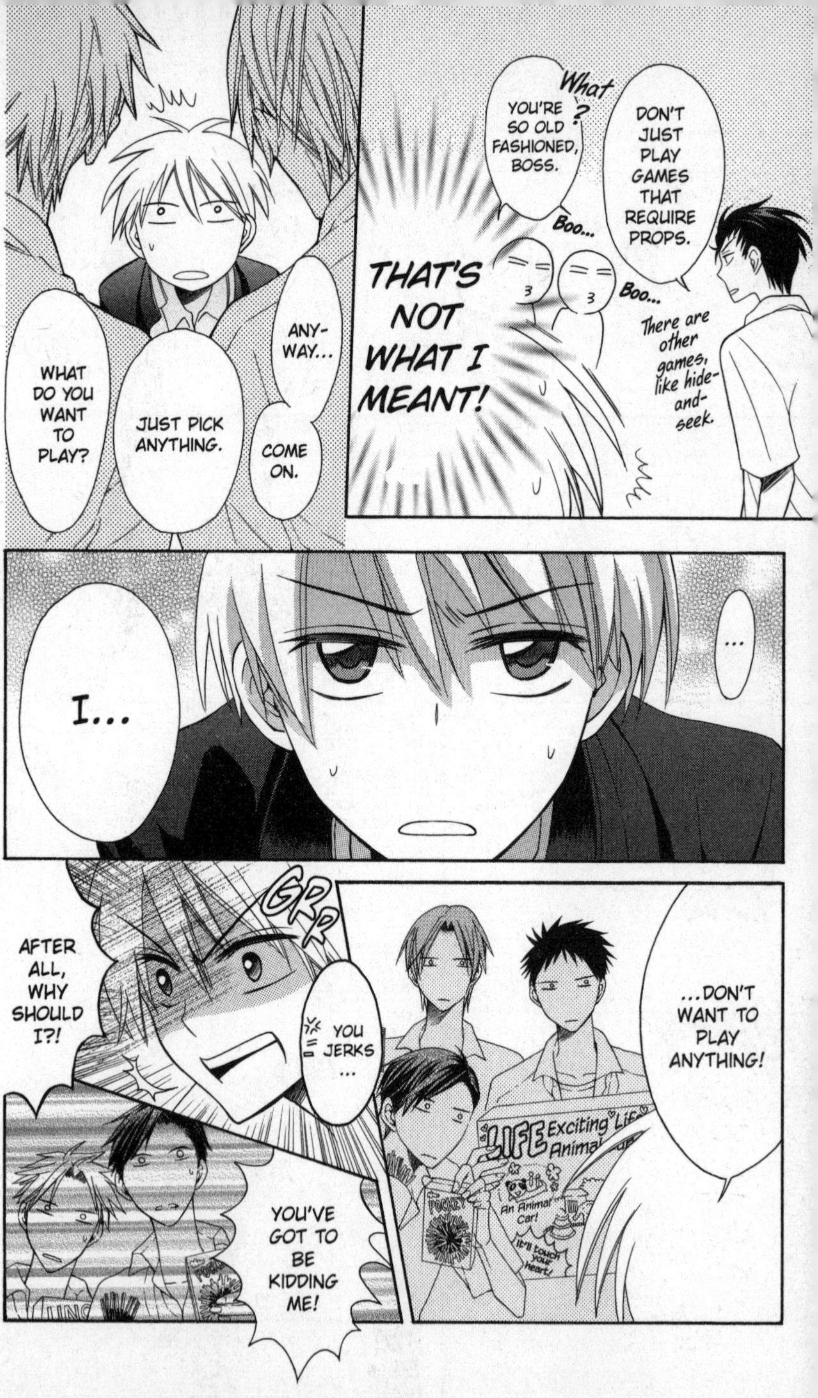
DON'T JUST PLAY GAMES THAT REQUIRE PROPS.
What ?
YOU'RE SO OLD FASHIONED, BOSS.
Boo...
Boo...
There are other games, like hide-and-seek.
THAT'S NOT WHAT I MEANT!
ANY-WAY...
COME ON.
JUST PICK ANYTHING.
WHAT DO YOU WANT TO PLAY?
...
I...
...DON'T WANT TO PLAY ANYTHING!
LIFE
An Animal Car!
It'll touch your heart!
POCKY
GRR
YOU JERKS...
AFTER ALL, WHY SHOULD I?!
YOU'VE GOT TO BE KIDDING ME!

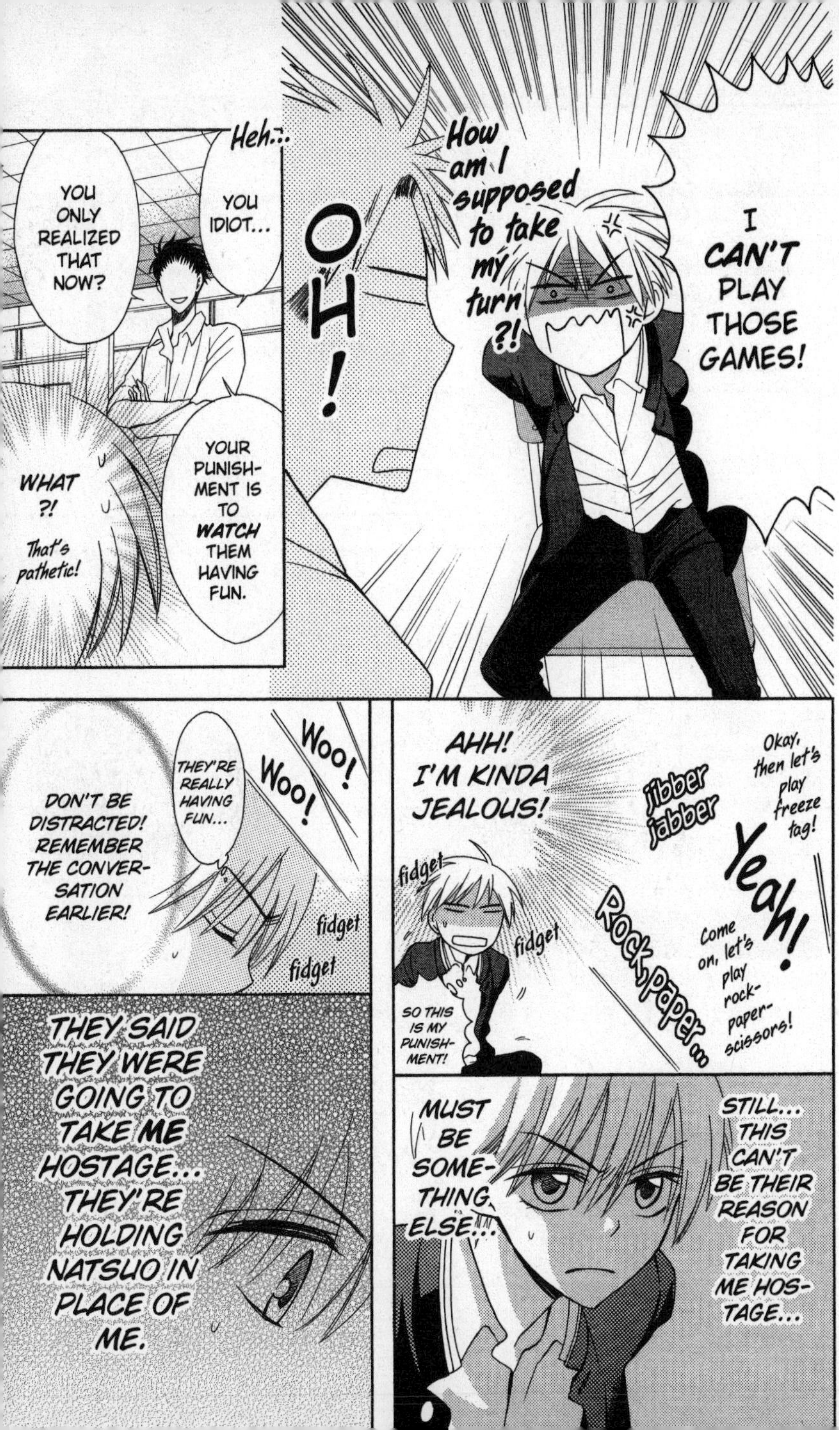
I CAN'T PLAY THOSE GAMES!
How am I supposed to take my turn?!
OH!
Heh...
YOU IDIOT...
YOU ONLY REALIZED THAT NOW?
YOUR PUNISHMENT IS TO WATCH THEM HAVING FUN.
WHAT?!
That's pathetic!
Okay, then let's play freeze tag!
Yeah!
jibber jabber
AHH! I'M KINDA JEALOUS!
Come on, let's play rock-paper-scissors!
Rock, paper...
fidget
fidget
SO THIS IS MY PUNISHMENT!
Woo!
Woo!
THEY'RE REALLY HAVING FUN...
DON'T BE DISTRACTED! REMEMBER THE CONVERSATION EARLIER!
fidget
fidget
STILL... THIS CAN'T BE THEIR REASON FOR TAKING ME HOSTAGE...
MUST BE SOMETHING ELSE...
THEY SAID THEY WERE GOING TO TAKE ME HOSTAGE... THEY'RE HOLDING NATSUO IN PLACE OF ME.

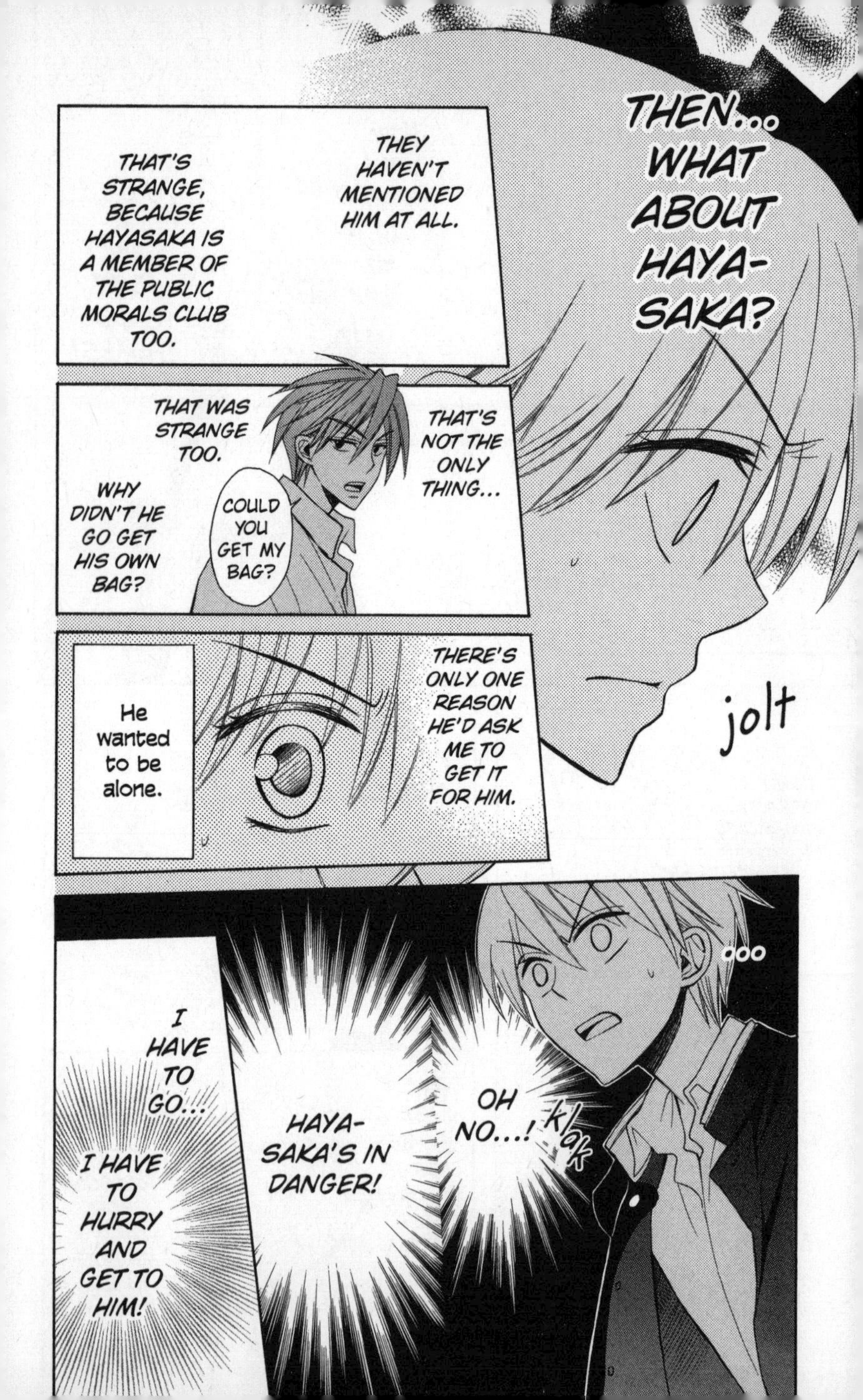

THEN... WHAT ABOUT HAYA-SAKA?
jolt
THEY HAVEN'T MENTIONED HIM AT ALL.
THAT'S STRANGE, BECAUSE HAYASAKA IS A MEMBER OF THE PUBLIC MORALS CLUB TOO.
THAT'S NOT THE ONLY THING...
THAT WAS STRANGE TOO.
COULD YOU GET MY BAG?
WHY DIDN'T HE GO GET HIS OWN BAG?
THERE'S ONLY ONE REASON HE'D ASK ME TO GET IT FOR HIM.
He wanted to be alone.
ooo
klak
OH NO...!
HAYA-SAKA'S IN DANGER!
I HAVE TO GO...
I HAVE TO HURRY AND GET TO HIM!

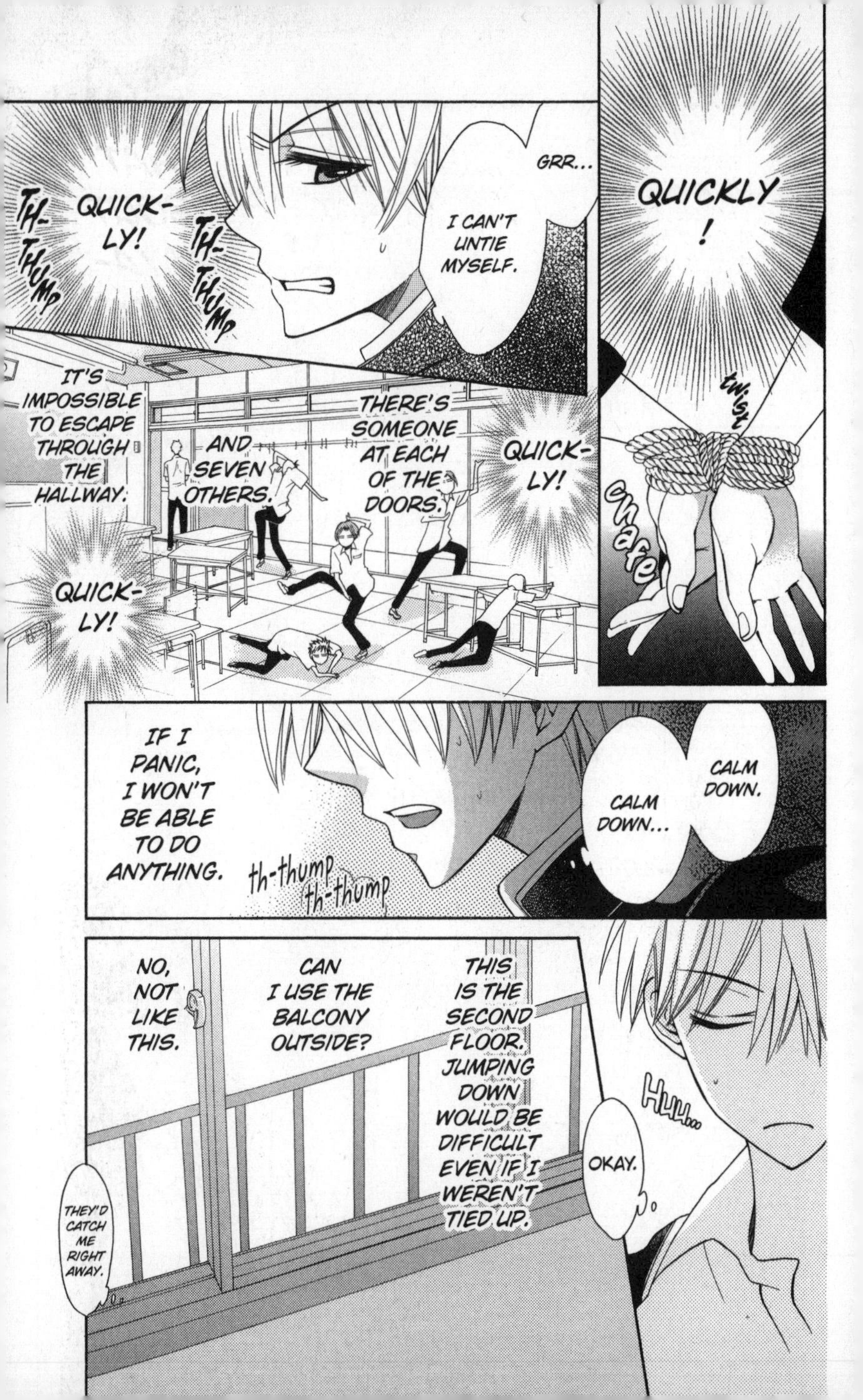
QUICKLY !
twist
GRR...
I CAN'T UNTIE MYSELF.
TH-THUMP
QUICK-LY!
TH-THUMP
QUICK-LY!
THERE'S SOMEONE AT EACH OF THE DOORS.
AND SEVEN OTHERS.
IT'S IMPOSSIBLE TO ESCAPE THROUGH THE HALLWAY.
QUICK-LY!
CALM DOWN.
CALM DOWN...
th-thump th-thump
IF I PANIC, I WON'T BE ABLE TO DO ANYTHING.
HUU...
OKAY.
THIS IS THE SECOND FLOOR. JUMPING DOWN WOULD BE DIFFICULT EVEN IF I WEREN'T TIED UP.
CAN I USE THE BALCONY OUTSIDE?
NO, NOT LIKE THIS.
THEY'D CATCH ME RIGHT AWAY.

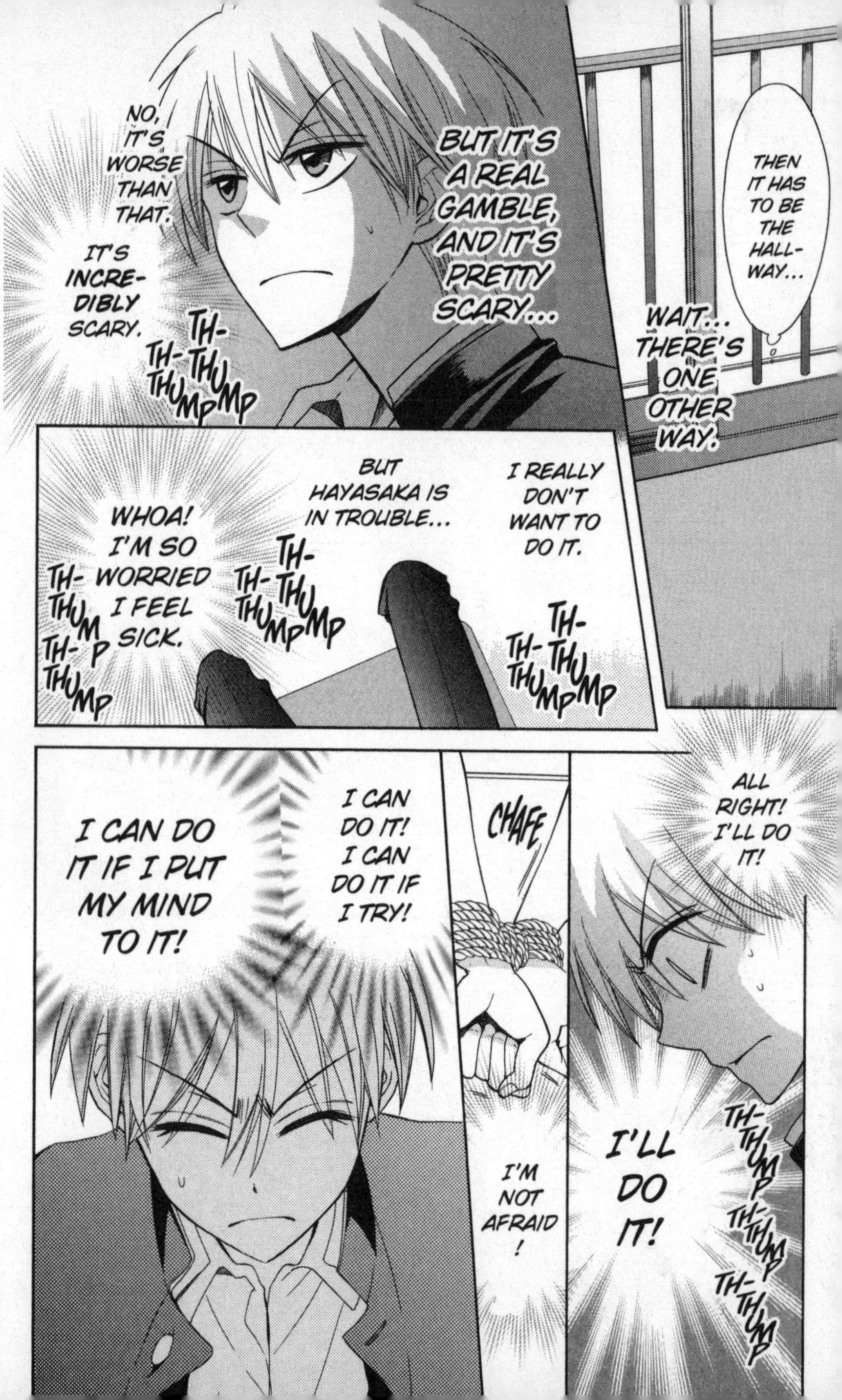
THEN IT HAS TO BE THE HALL-WAY...
WAIT... THERE'S ONE OTHER WAY.
BUT IT'S A REAL GAMBLE, AND IT'S PRETTY SCARY...
NO, IT'S WORSE THAN THAT.
IT'S INCRE-DIBLY SCARY.
TH-TH-THUMP THUMP
I REALLY DON'T WANT TO DO IT.
TH-TH-THUMP THUMP
BUT HAYASAKA IS IN TROUBLE...
TH-TH-THUMP THUMP
WHOA! I'M SO WORRIED I FEEL SICK.
TH-THUMP TH-THUMP
ALL RIGHT! I'LL DO IT!
TH-THUMP TH-THUMP TH-THUMP
I'LL DO IT!
I'M NOT AFRAID!
CHAFE
I CAN DO IT! I CAN DO IT IF I TRY!
I CAN DO IT IF I PUT MY MIND TO IT!

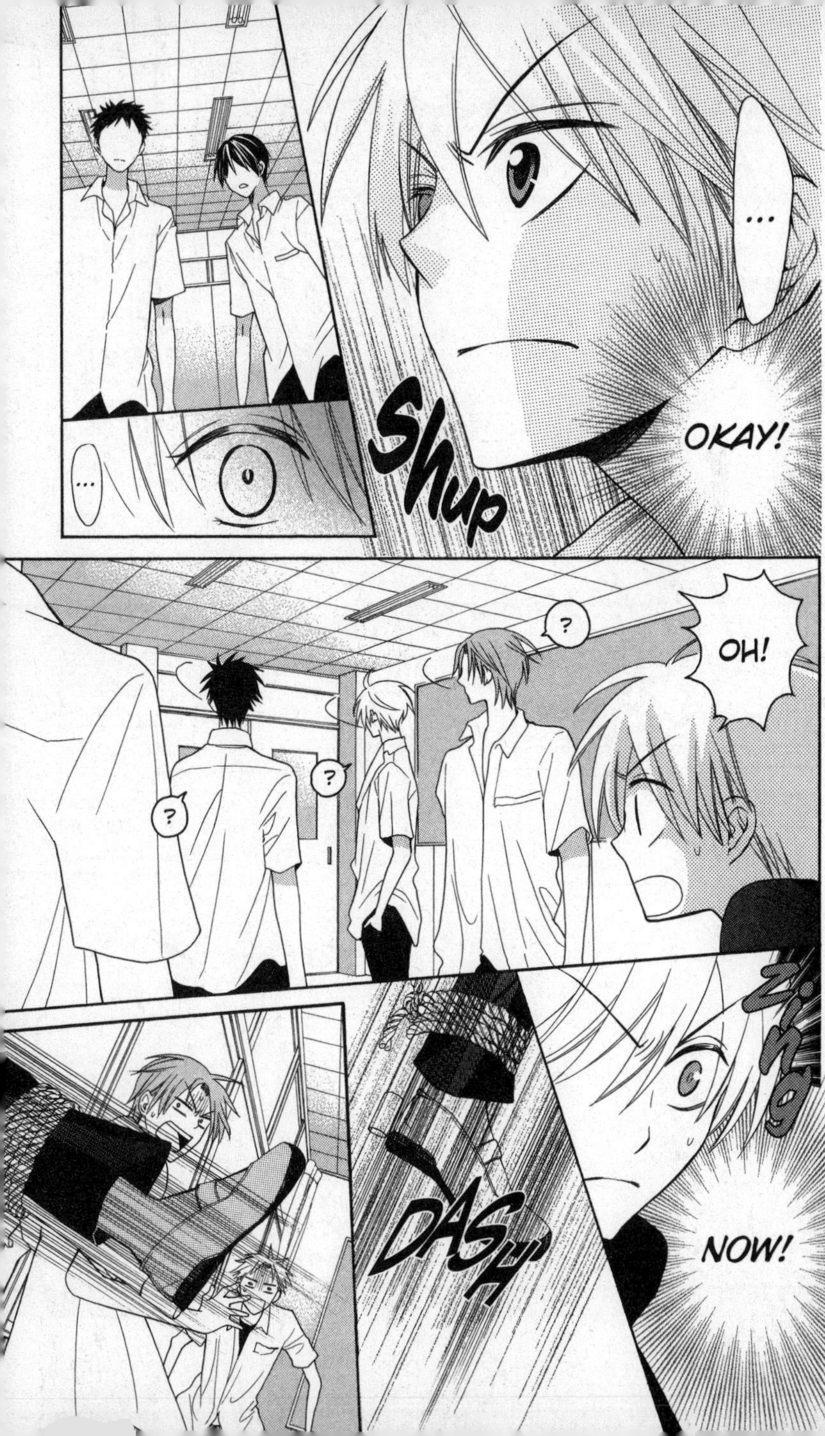
...
OKAY!
Shup
...
OH!
?
?
?
Zing
NOW!
DASH

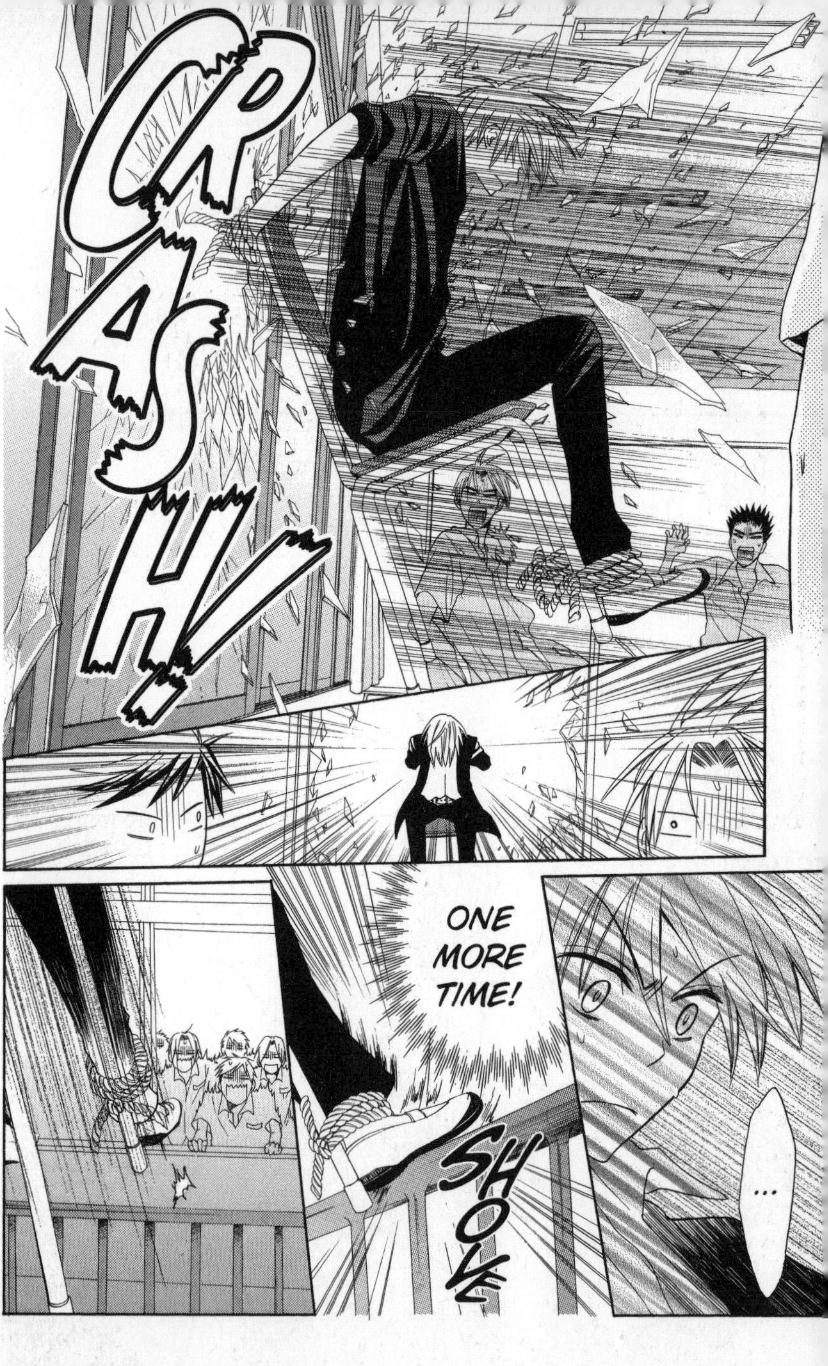
CRASH!
...
ONE MORE TIME!
SHOVE

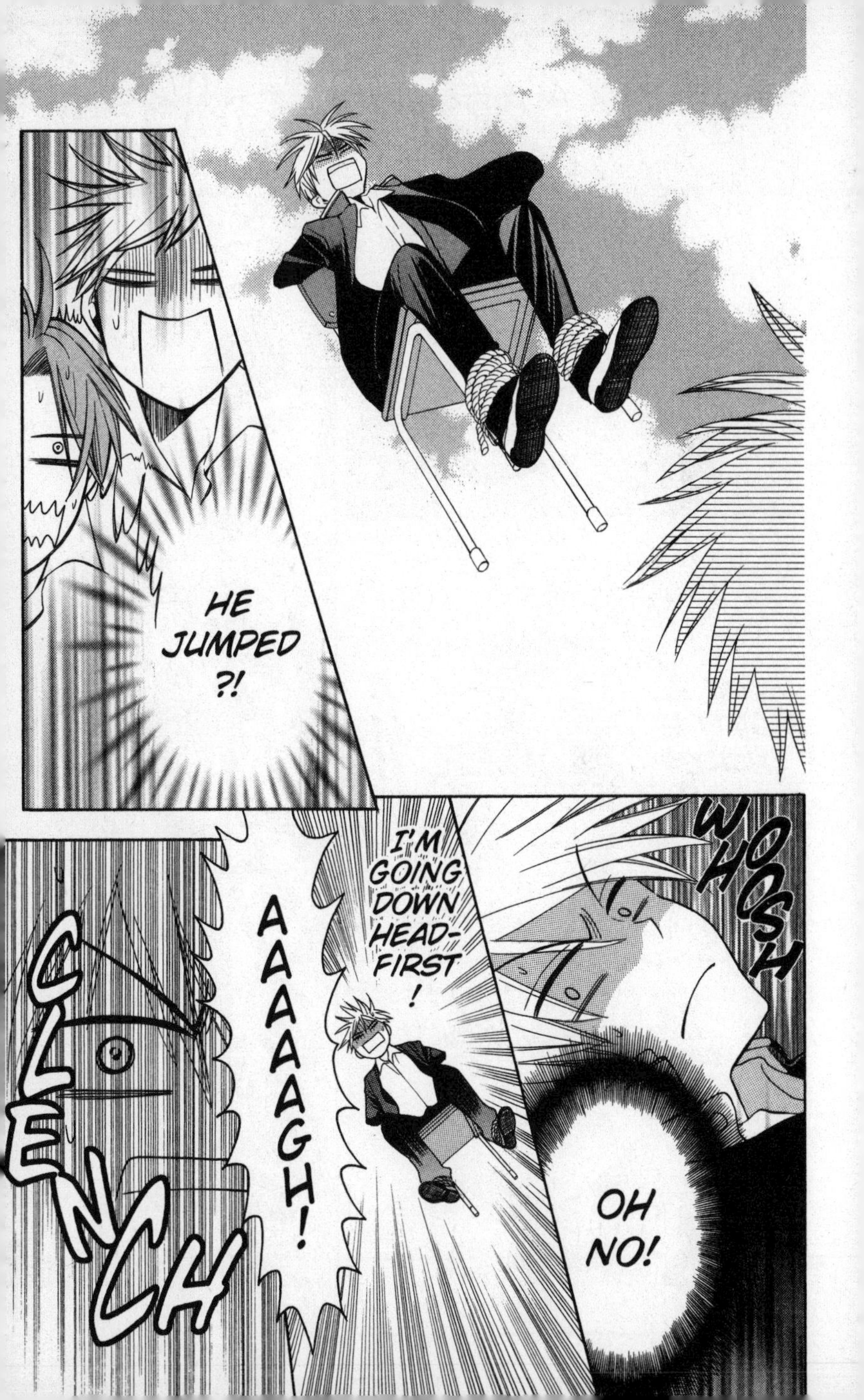
HE JUMPED ?!
WHOOSH
OH NO!
I'M GOING DOWN HEAD-FIRST!
AAAAAGH!
CLENCH

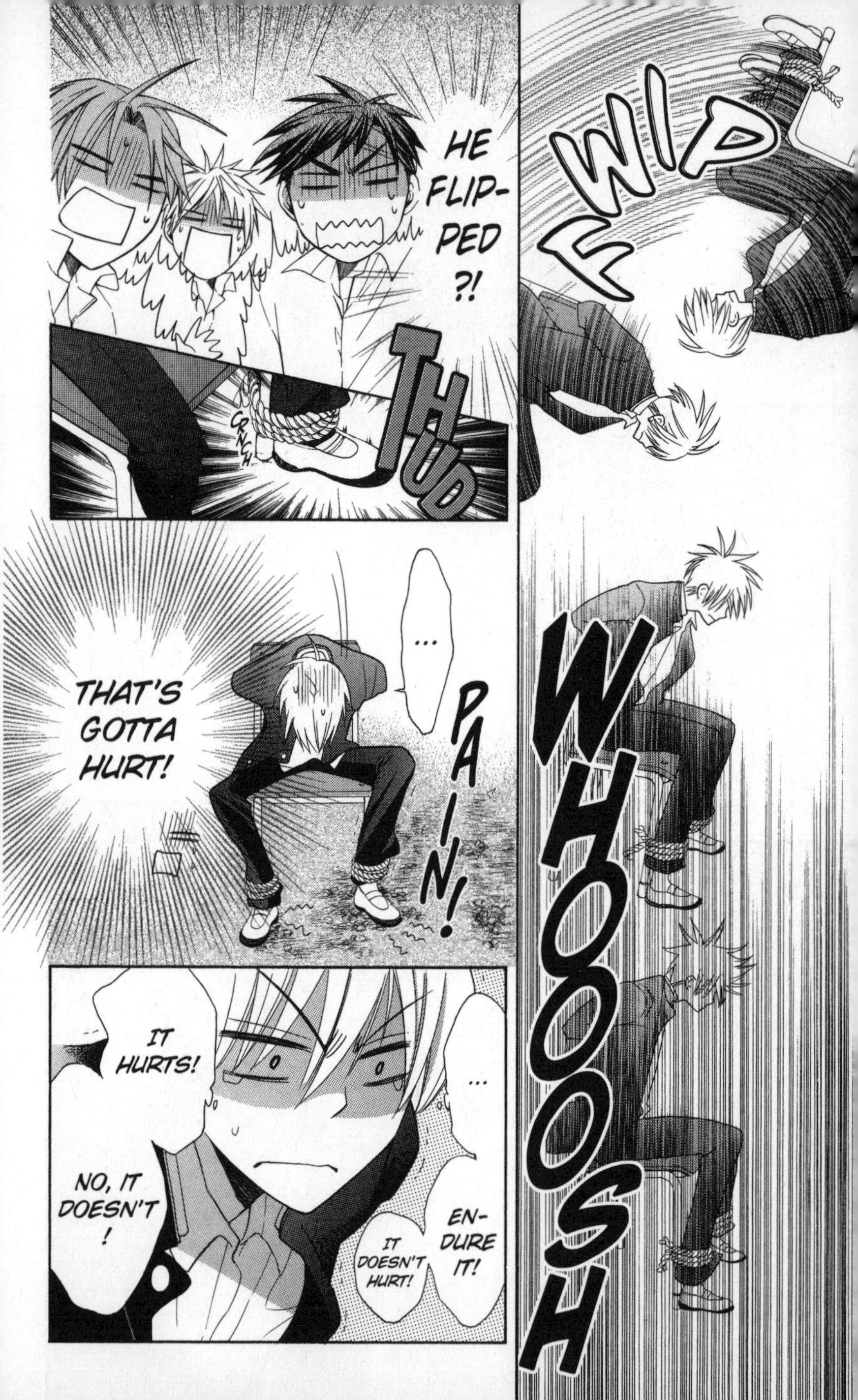

WIP
HE FLIPPED?!
THUD
CRNCH
WHOOSH
...
PAIN!
THAT'S GOTTA HURT!
...
ENDURE IT!
IT DOESN'T HURT!
IT HURTS!
NO, IT DOESN'T!

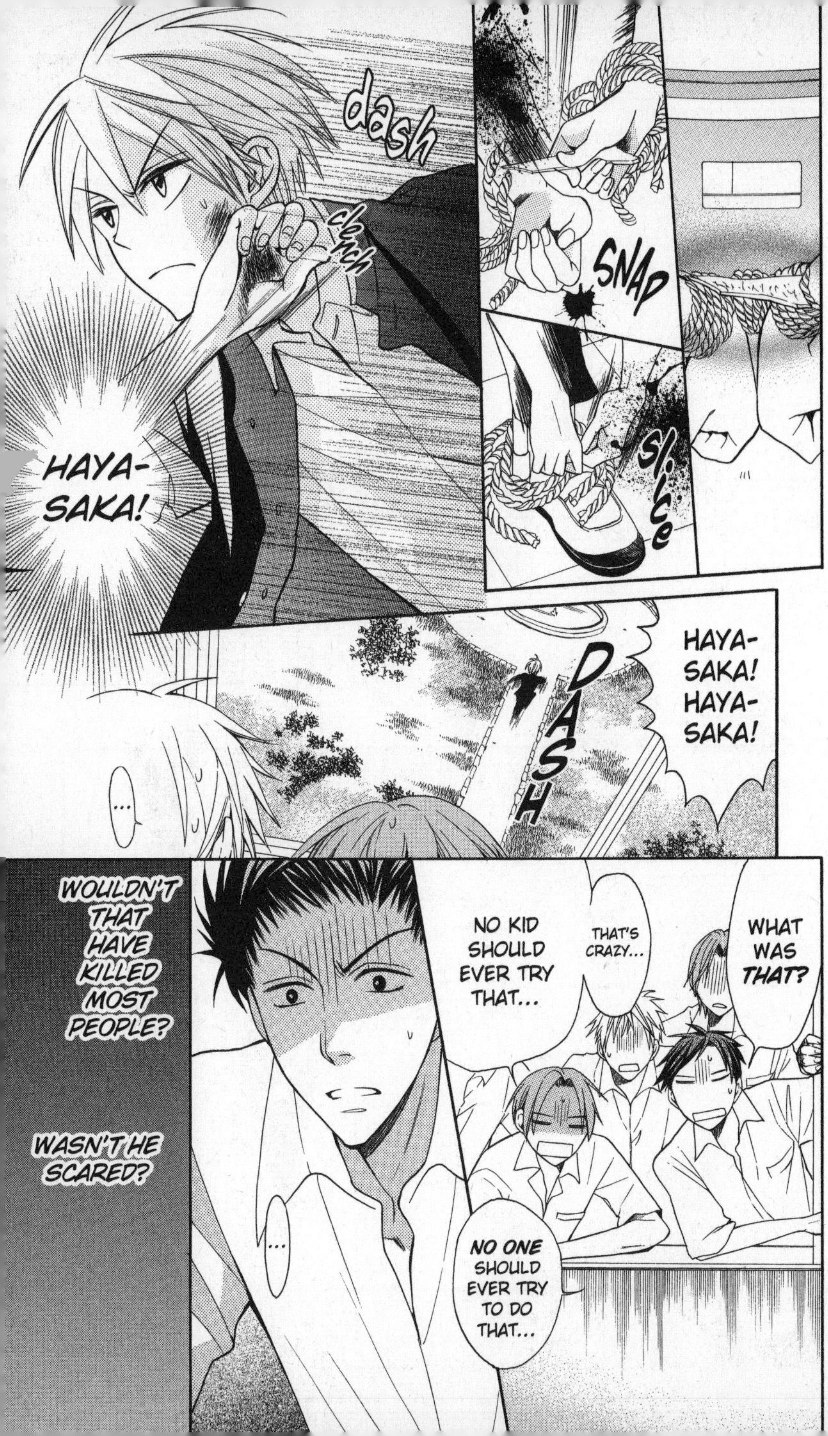
SNAP
slice
dash
clench
HAYA-SAKA!
HAYA-SAKA! HAYA-SAKA!
DASH
...
WHAT WAS THAT?
THAT'S CRAZY...
NO KID SHOULD EVER TRY THAT...
NO ONE SHOULD EVER TRY TO DO THAT...
...
WOULDN'T THAT HAVE KILLED MOST PEOPLE?
WASN'T HE SCARED?

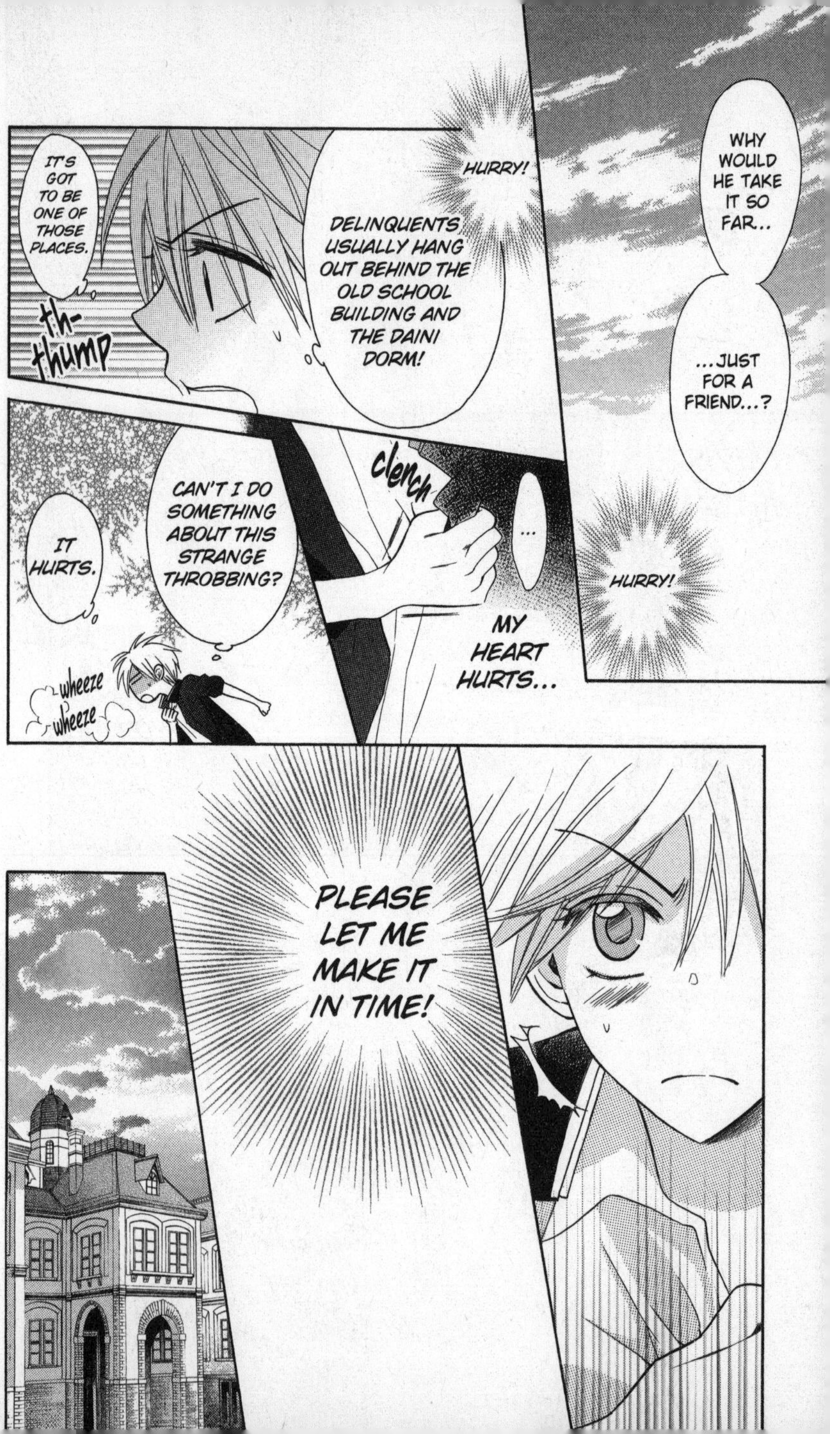
WHY WOULD HE TAKE IT SO FAR...
...JUST FOR A FRIEND...?
HURRY!
HURRY!
DELINQUENTS USUALLY HANG OUT BEHIND THE OLD SCHOOL BUILDING AND THE DAINI DORM!
IT'S GOT TO BE ONE OF THOSE PLACES.
th-thump
clench
...
MY HEART HURTS...
CAN'T I DO SOMETHING ABOUT THIS STRANGE THROBBING?
IT HURTS.
wheeze wheeze
PLEASE LET ME MAKE IT IN TIME!

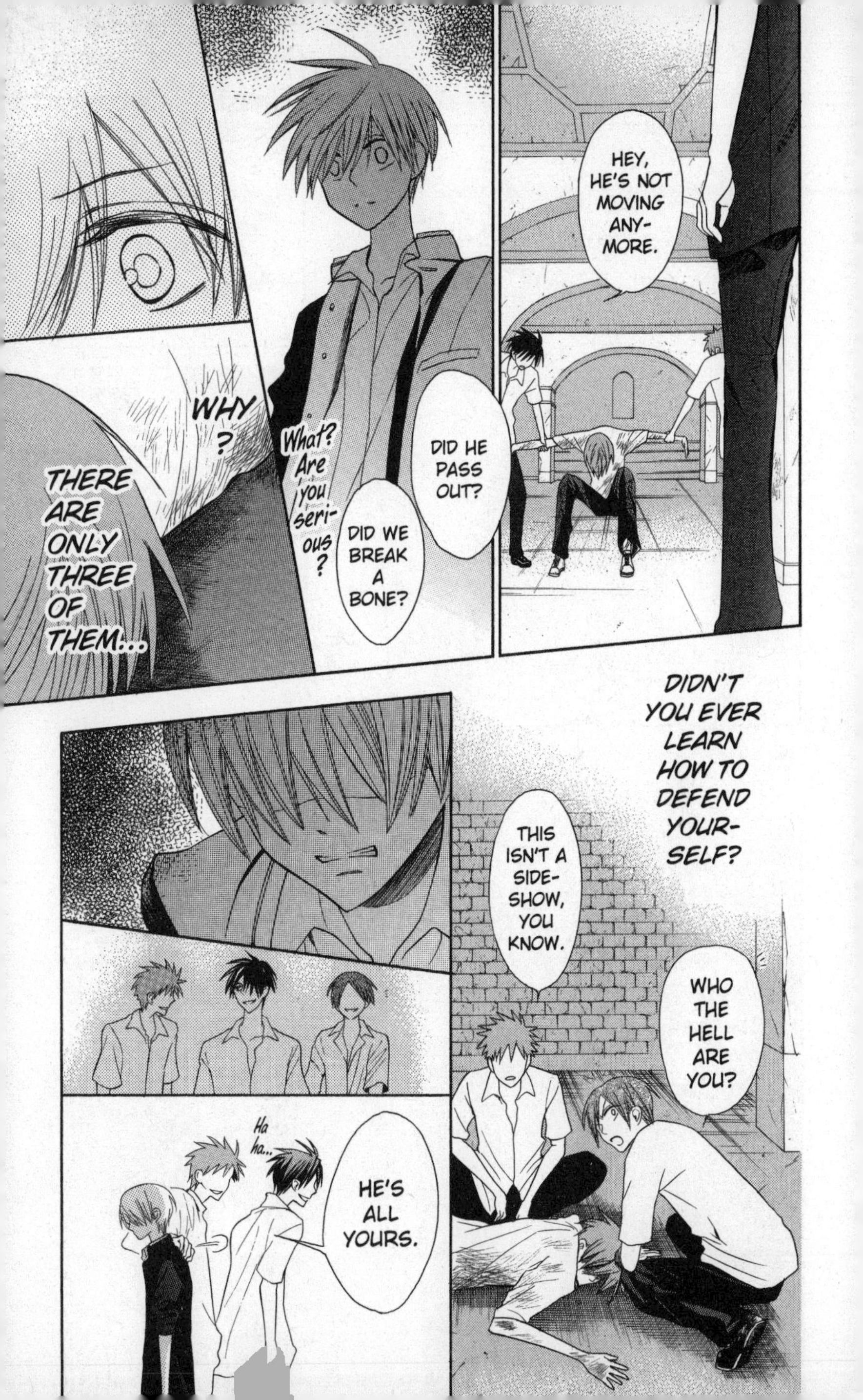
HEY, HE'S NOT MOVING ANYMORE.
DID HE PASS OUT?
DID WE BREAK A BONE?
What? Are you serious?
WHY?
THERE ARE ONLY THREE OF THEM...
DIDN'T YOU EVER LEARN HOW TO DEFEND YOURSELF?
THIS ISN'T A SIDESHOW, YOU KNOW.
WHO THE HELL ARE YOU?
Ha ha...
HE'S ALL YOURS.

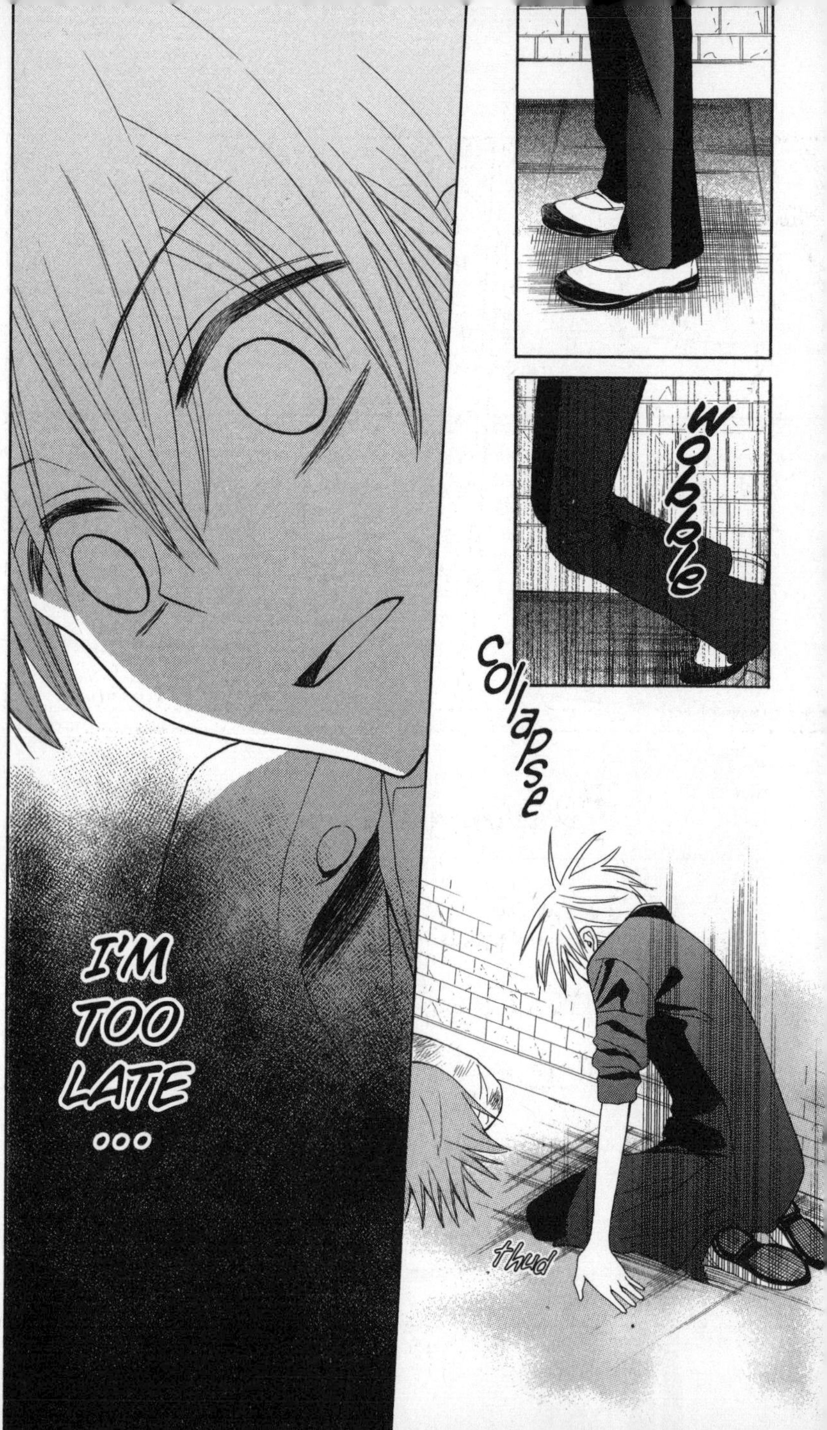
wobble
collapse
thud
I'M TOO LATE...

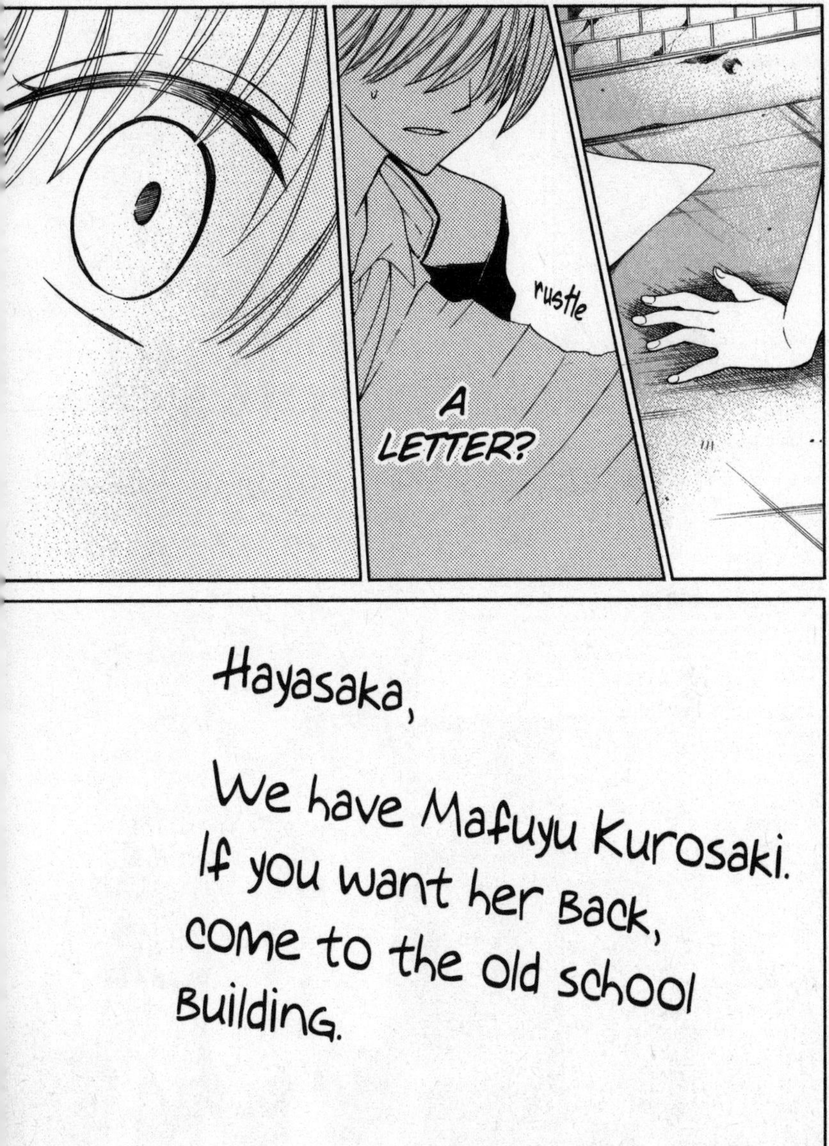
rustle
A LETTER?
Hayasaka,
We have Mafuyu Kurosaki. If you want her Back, come to the old school Building.

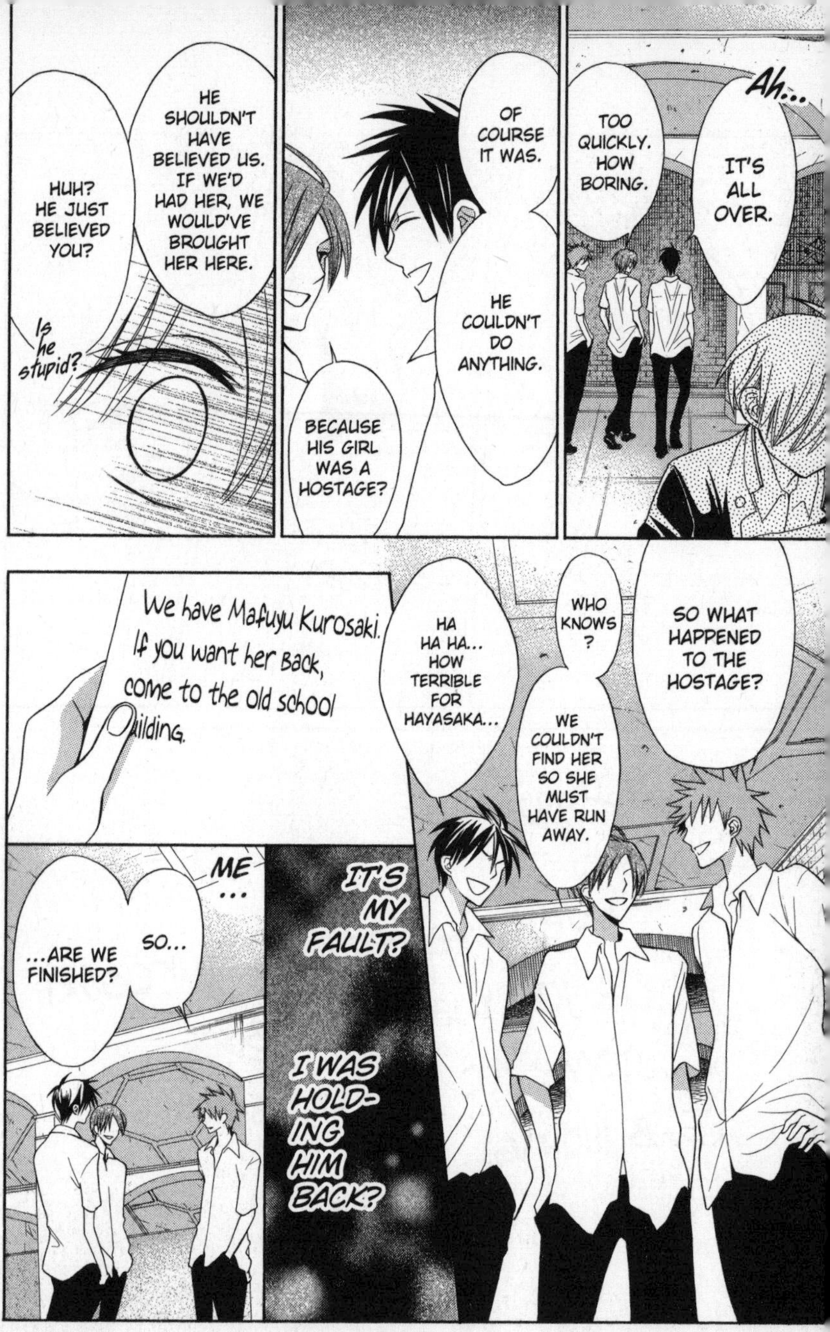
Ah...
IT'S ALL OVER.
TOO QUICKLY. HOW BORING.
OF COURSE IT WAS.
HE COULDN'T DO ANYTHING.
BECAUSE HIS GIRL WAS A HOSTAGE?
HE SHOULDN'T HAVE BELIEVED US. IF WE'D HAD HER, WE WOULD'VE BROUGHT HER HERE.
HUH? HE JUST BELIEVED YOU?
Is he stupid?
SO WHAT HAPPENED TO THE HOSTAGE?
WHO KNOWS?
WE COULDN'T FIND HER SO SHE MUST HAVE RUN AWAY.
HA HA HA... HOW TERRIBLE FOR HAYASAKA...
We have Mafuyu Kurosaki. If you want her back, come to the old school building.
IT'S MY FAULT?
I WAS HOLDING HIM BACK?
ME...
SO...
...ARE WE FINISHED?

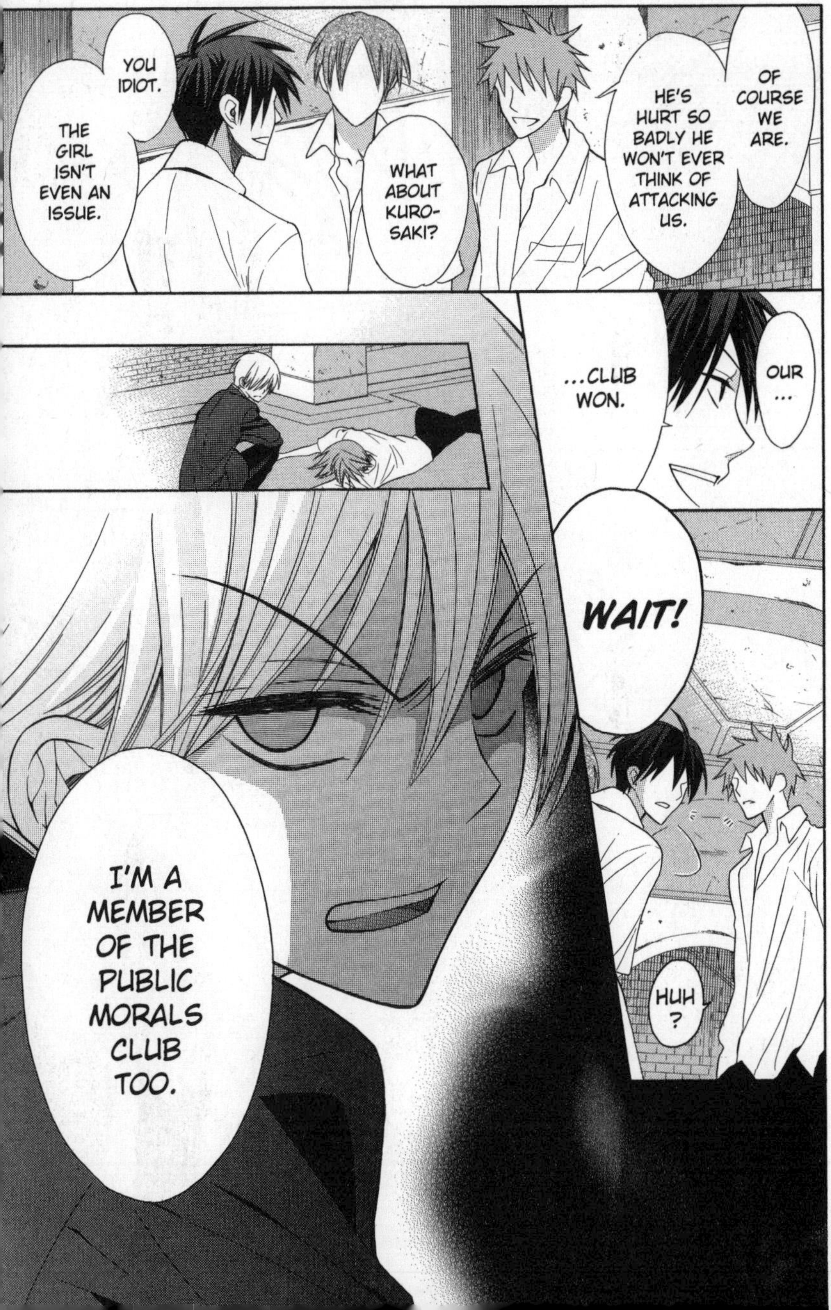
OF COURSE WE ARE.
HE'S HURT SO BADLY HE WON'T EVER THINK OF ATTACKING US.
WHAT ABOUT KURO-SAKI?
YOU IDIOT.
THE GIRL ISN'T EVEN AN ISSUE.
OUR...
...CLUB WON.
WAIT!
HUH?
I'M A MEMBER OF THE PUBLIC MORALS CLUB TOO.

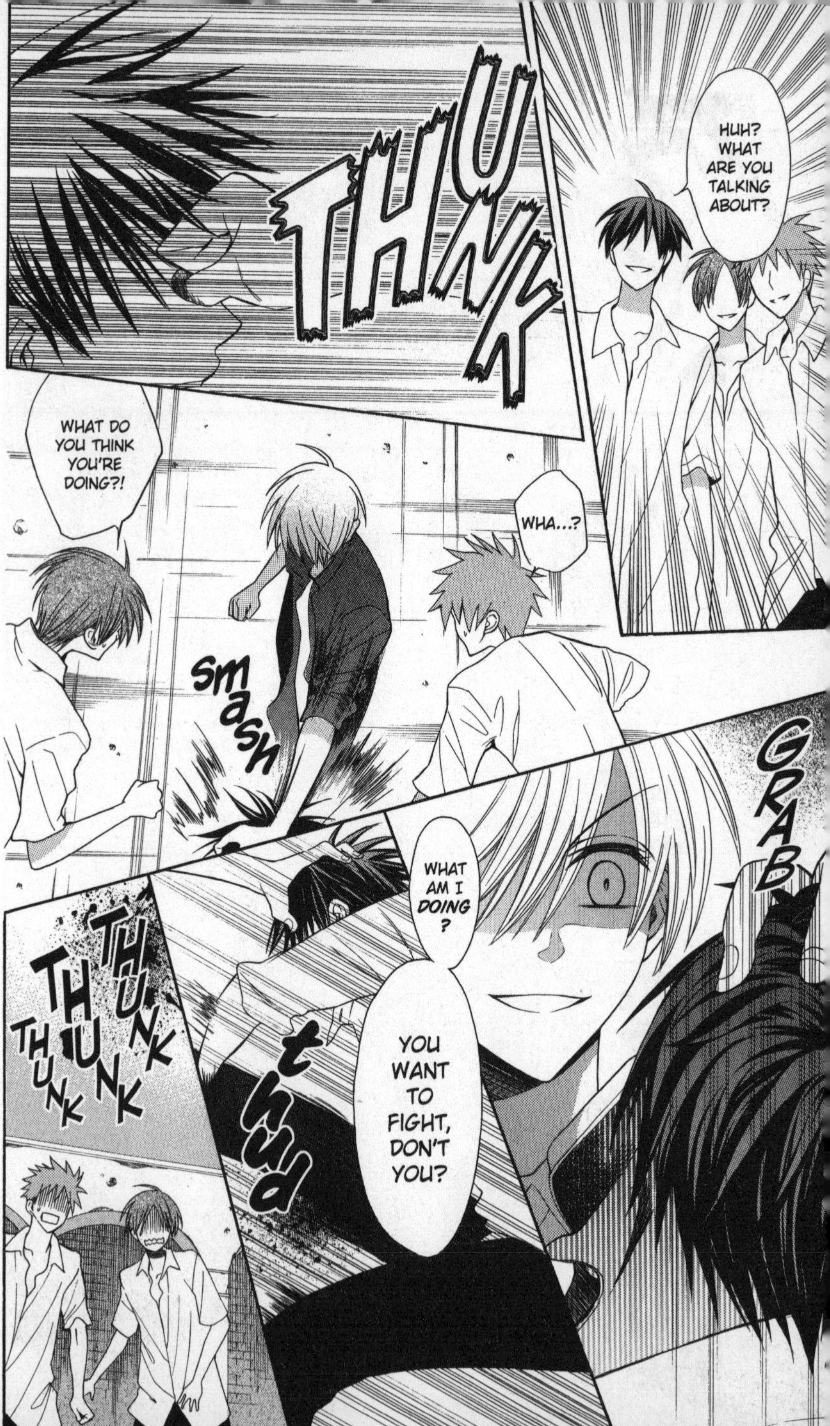
HUH? WHAT ARE YOU TALKING ABOUT?
THUNK
WHA...?
WHAT DO YOU THINK YOU'RE DOING?!
SMASH
GRAB
WHAT AM I *DOING*?
YOU WANT TO FIGHT, DON'T YOU?
thud
THUNK
THUNK
THUNK

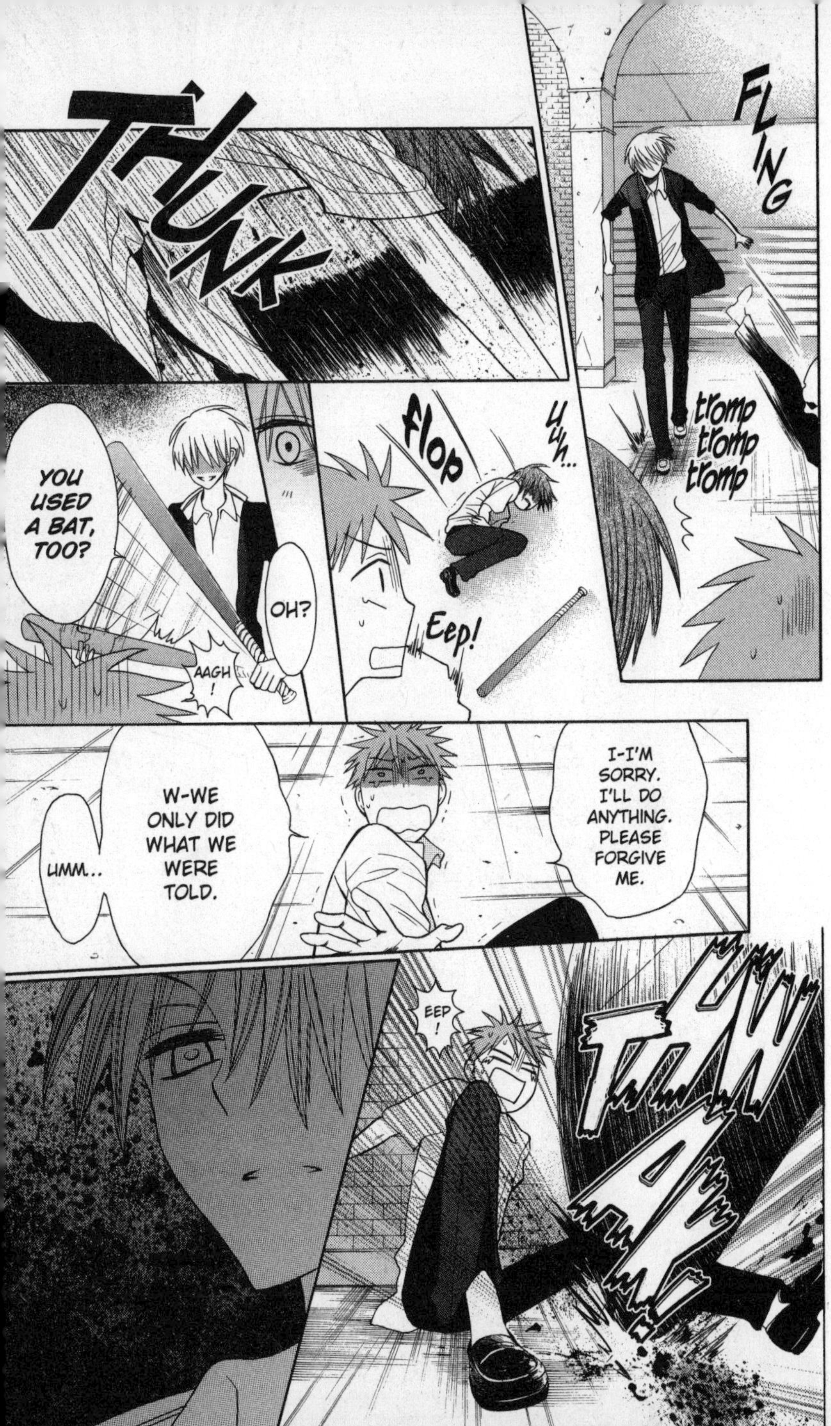
FLING
tromp tromp tromp
THUNK
flop
Uuh...
Eep!
OH?
YOU USED A BAT, TOO?
AAGH!
I-I'M SORRY. I'LL DO ANYTHING. PLEASE FORGIVE ME.
W-WE ONLY DID WHAT WE WERE TOLD.
UMM...
TWAA
EEP!

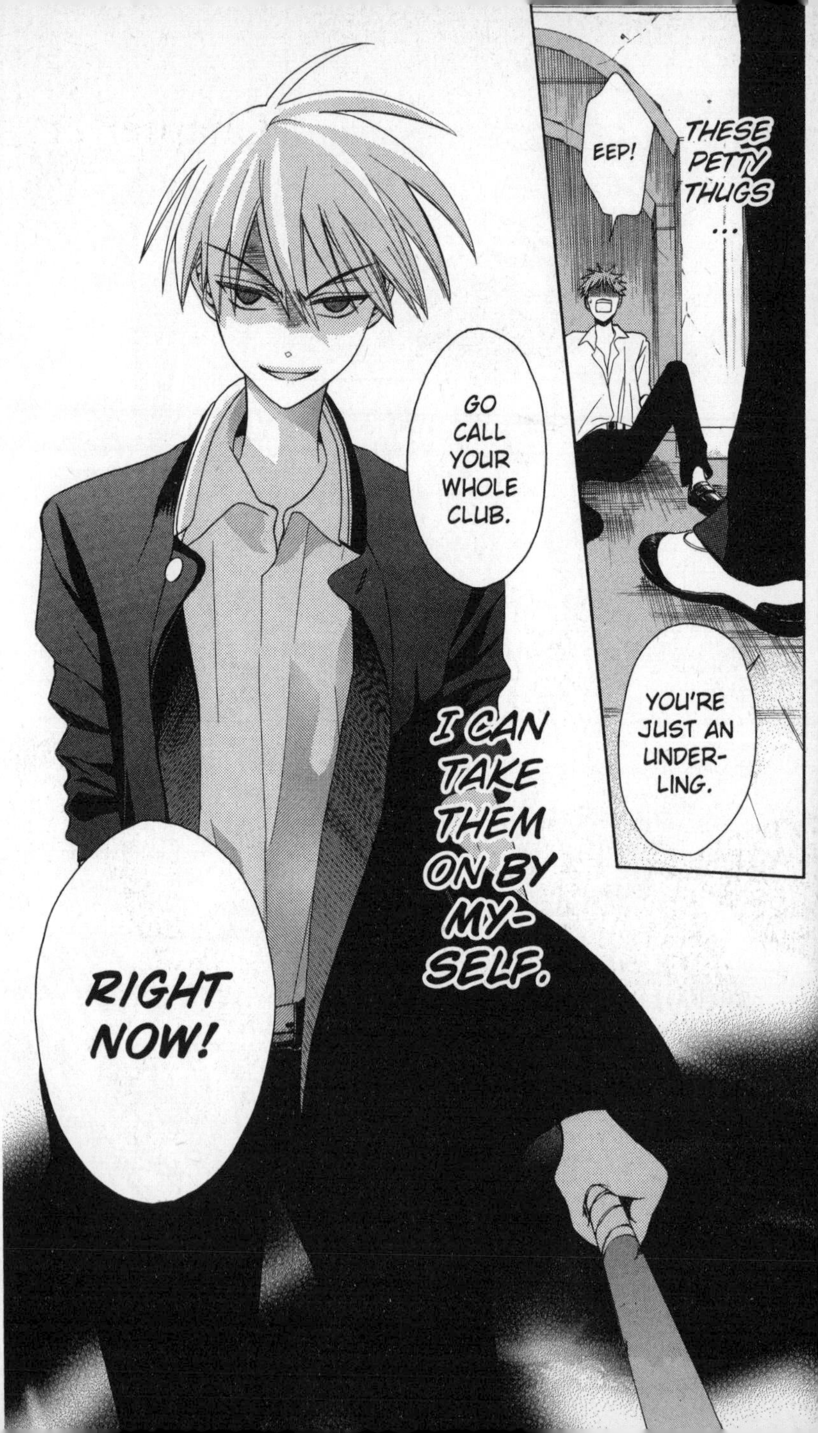
THESE PETTY THUGS...
EEP!
YOU'RE JUST AN UNDERLING.
GO CALL YOUR WHOLE CLUB.
I CAN TAKE THEM ON BY MYSELF.
RIGHT NOW!

Chapter 21

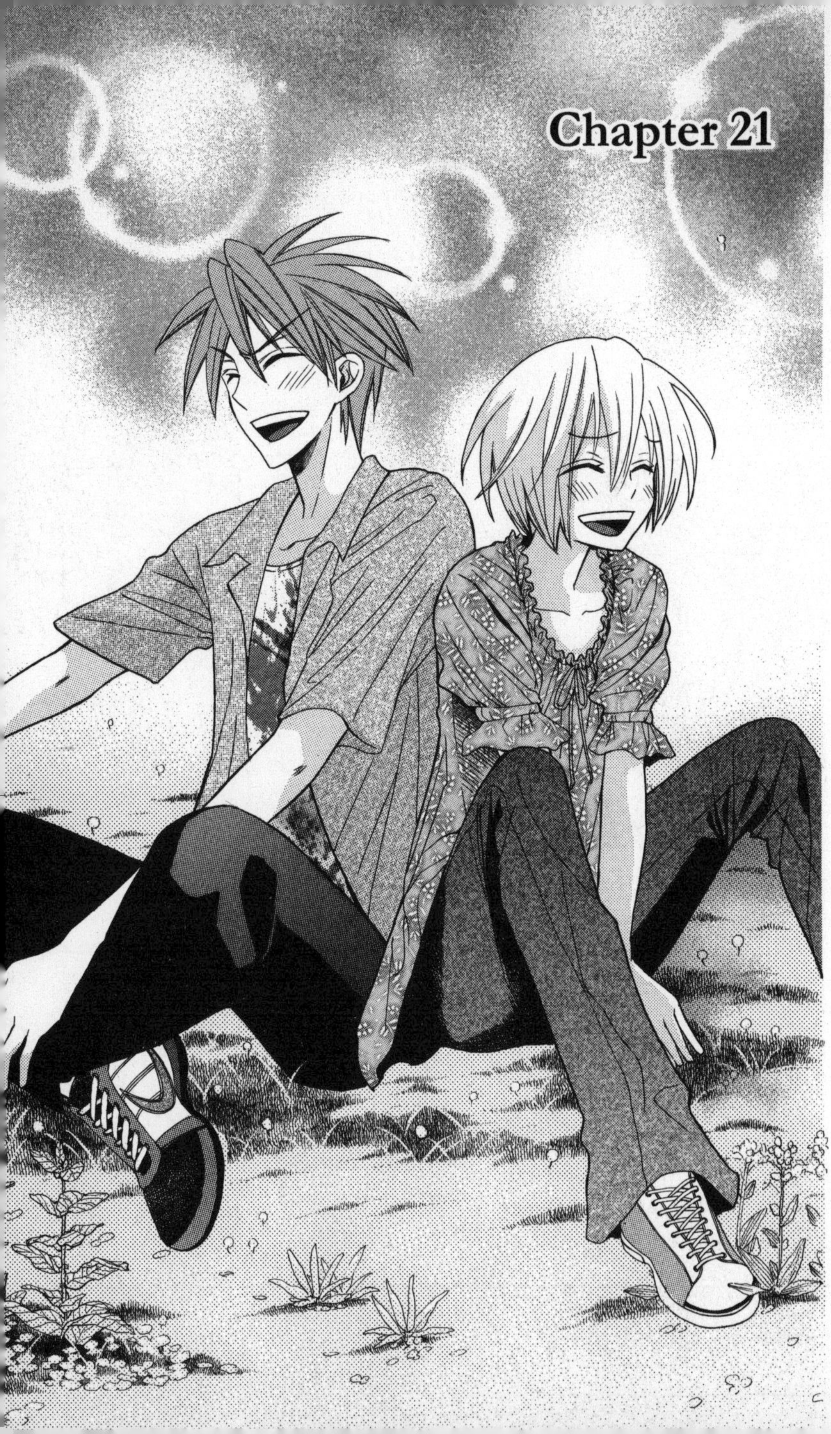

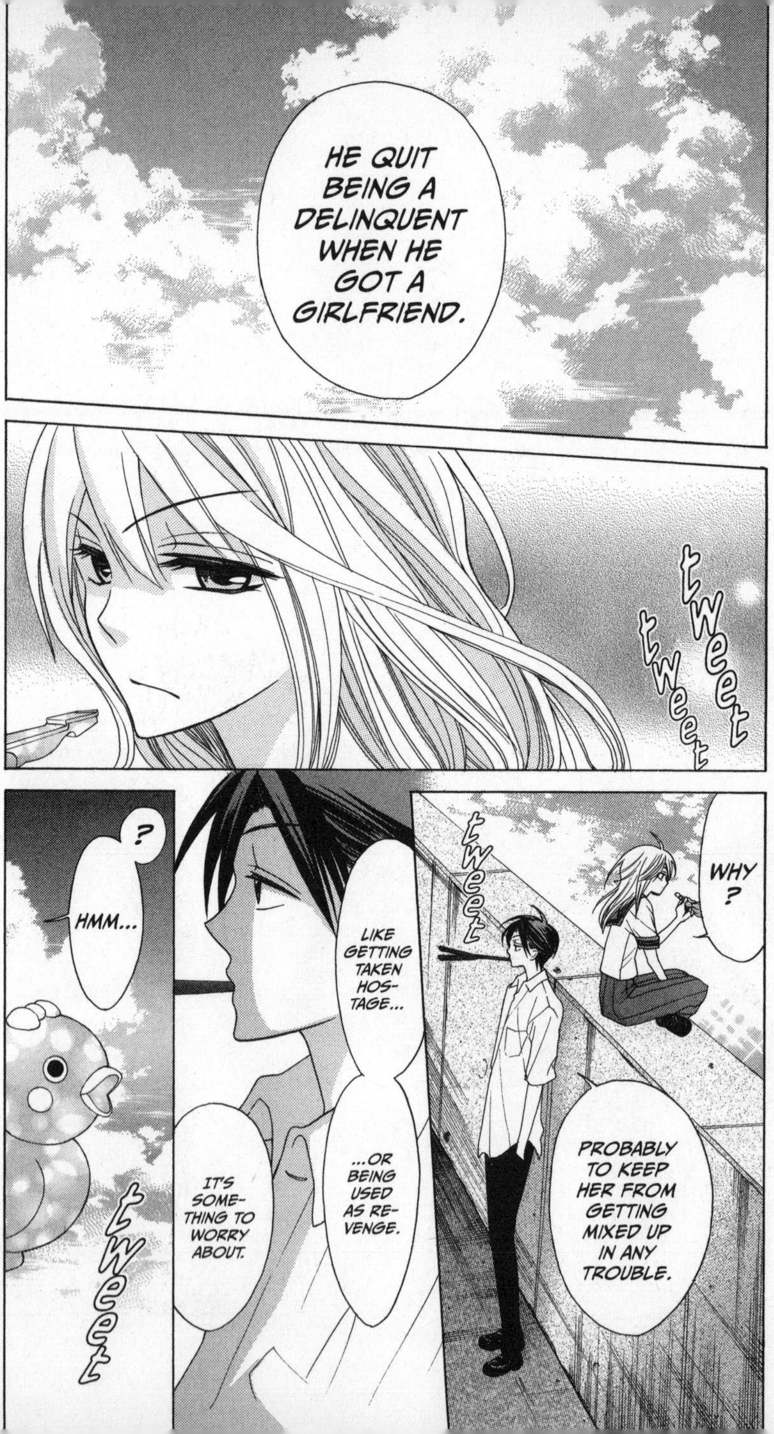
HE QUIT BEING A DELINQUENT WHEN HE GOT A GIRLFRIEND.
tweet
tweet
WHY?
tweet
PROBABLY TO KEEP HER FROM GETTING MIXED UP IN ANY TROUBLE.
LIKE GETTING TAKEN HOS-TAGE...
...OR BEING USED AS RE-VENGE.
IT'S SOME-THING TO WORRY ABOUT.
?
HMM...
tweet

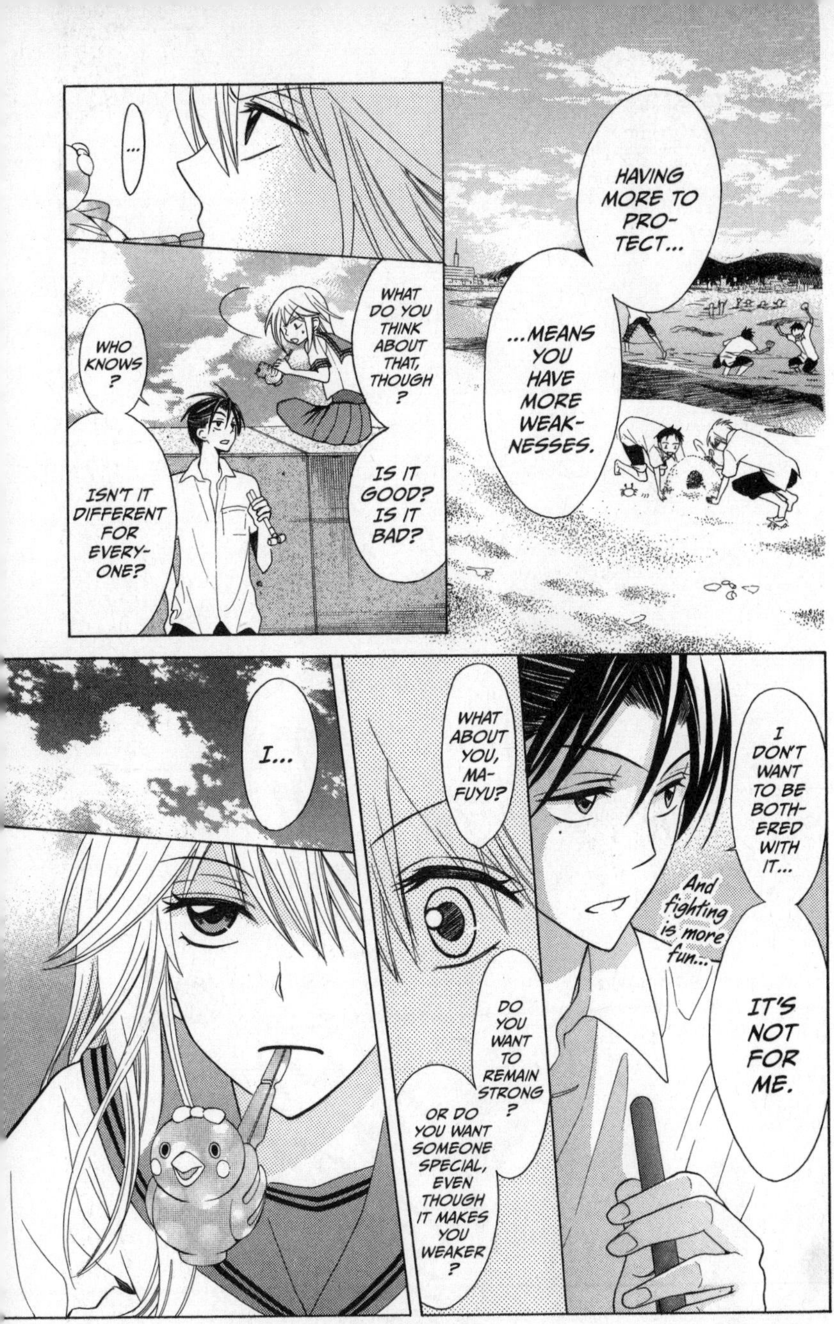
HAVING MORE TO PRO-TECT...
...MEANS YOU HAVE MORE WEAK-NESSES.
...
WHAT DO YOU THINK ABOUT THAT, THOUGH?
IS IT GOOD? IS IT BAD?
WHO KNOWS?
ISN'T IT DIFFERENT FOR EVERY-ONE?
I DON'T WANT TO BE BOTH-ERED WITH IT...
And fighting is more fun...
IT'S NOT FOR ME.
WHAT ABOUT YOU, MA-FUYU?
DO YOU WANT TO REMAIN STRONG?
OR DO YOU WANT SOMEONE SPECIAL, EVEN THOUGH IT MAKES YOU WEAKER?
I...

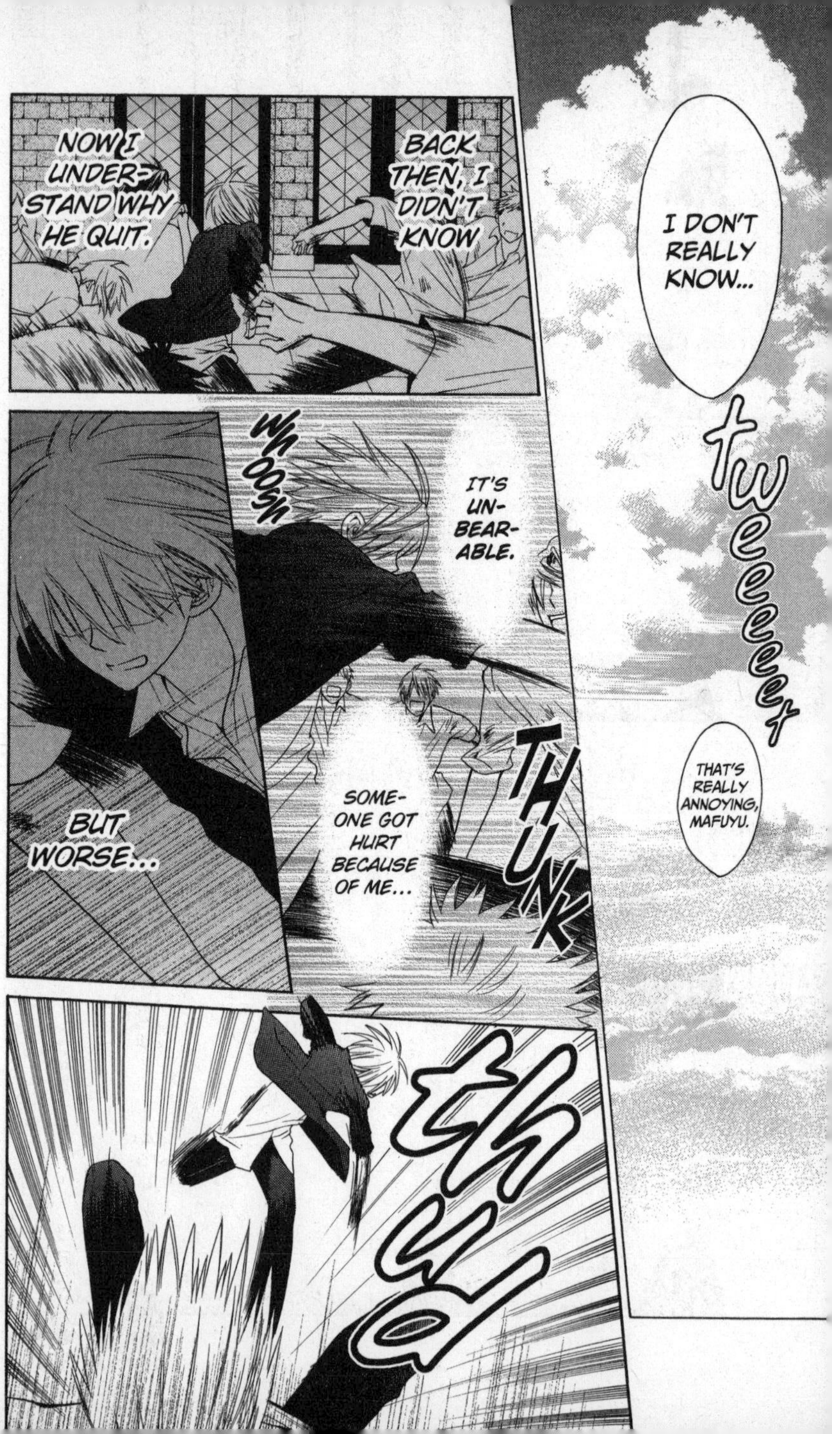
I DON'T REALLY KNOW...
tweeeeet
THAT'S REALLY ANNOYING, MAFUYU.
BACK THEN, I DIDN'T KNOW
NOW I UNDER-STAND WHY HE QUIT.
WHOOSH!!
IT'S UN-BEAR-ABLE.
THUNK
SOME-ONE GOT HURT BECAUSE OF ME...
BUT WORSE...
thhud

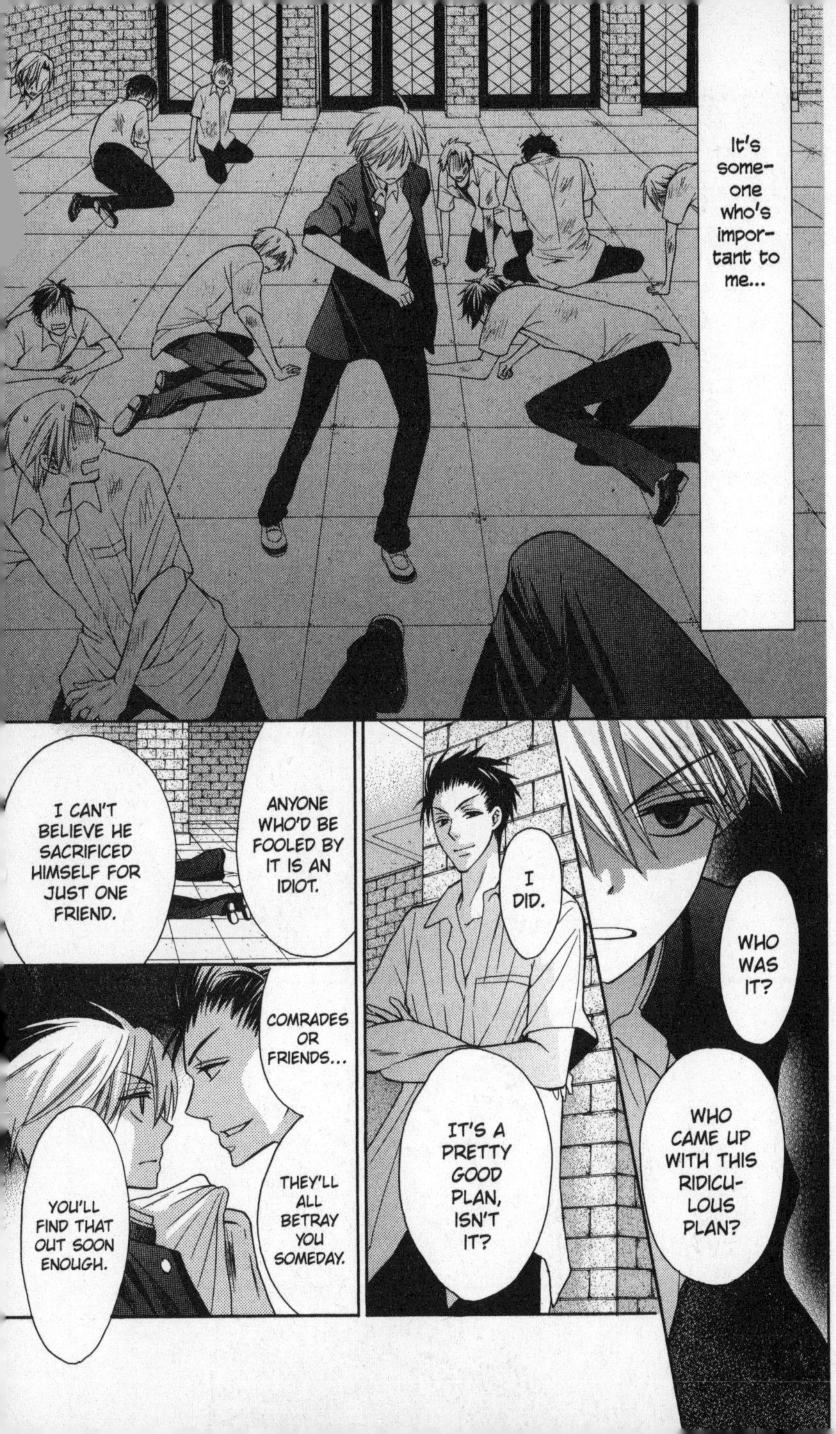
It's someone who's important to me...
WHO WAS IT?
WHO CAME UP WITH THIS RIDICULOUS PLAN?
I DID.
IT'S A PRETTY GOOD PLAN, ISN'T IT?
ANYONE WHO'D BE FOOLED BY IT IS AN IDIOT.
I CAN'T BELIEVE HE SACRIFICED HIMSELF FOR JUST ONE FRIEND.
COMRADES OR FRIENDS...
THEY'LL ALL BETRAY YOU SOMEDAY.
YOU'LL FIND THAT OUT SOON ENOUGH.

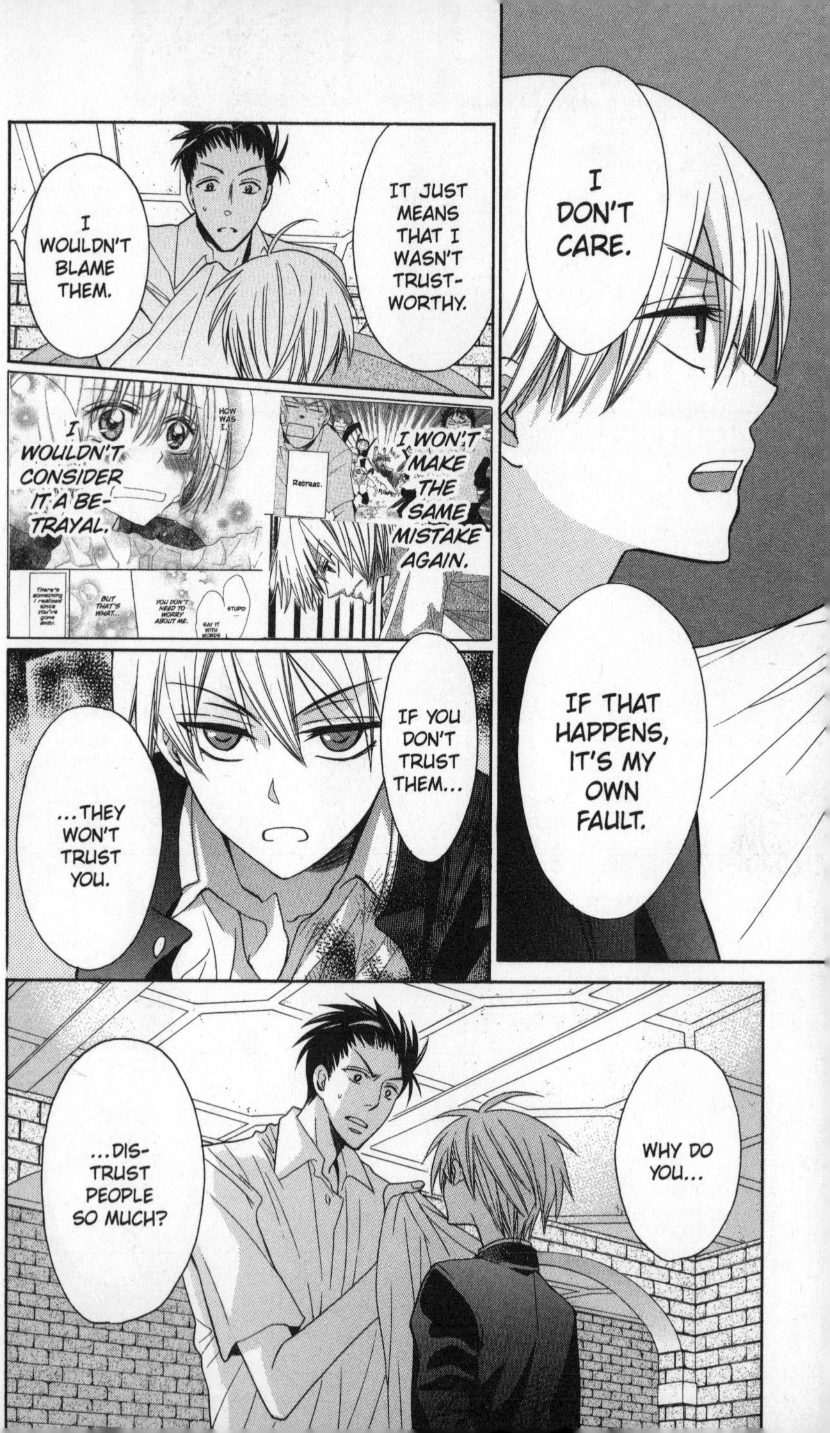
I DON'T CARE.
IF THAT HAPPENS, IT'S MY OWN FAULT.
IT JUST MEANS THAT I WASN'T TRUST-WORTHY.
I WOULDN'T BLAME THEM.
Retreat.
I WON'T MAKE THE SAME MISTAKE AGAIN.
HOW WAS I...
I WOULDN'T CONSIDER IT A BE-TRAYAL.
STUPID ...
SAY IT WITH WORDS
YOU DON'T NEED TO WORRY ABOUT ME.
BUT THAT'S WHAT...
There's something I realized since you've gone away.
IF YOU DON'T TRUST THEM...
...THEY WON'T TRUST YOU.
WHY DO YOU...
...DIS-TRUST PEOPLE SO MUCH?

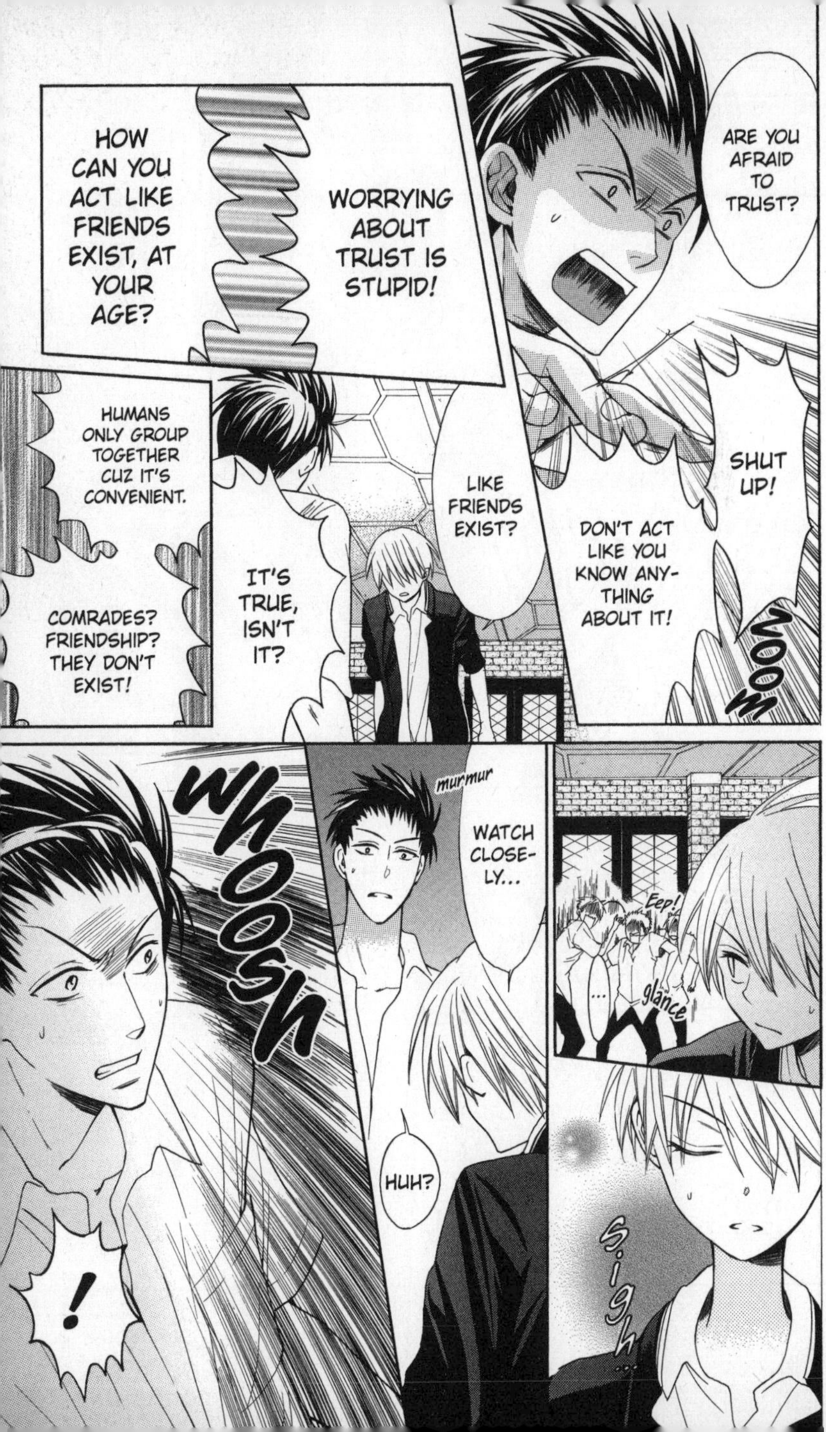
ARE YOU AFRAID TO TRUST?
SHUT UP!
DON'T ACT LIKE YOU KNOW ANY-THING ABOUT IT!
VOOM
WORRYING ABOUT TRUST IS STUPID!
HOW CAN YOU ACT LIKE FRIENDS EXIST, AT YOUR AGE?
LIKE FRIENDS EXIST?
IT'S TRUE, ISN'T IT?
HUMANS ONLY GROUP TOGETHER CUZ IT'S CONVENIENT.
COMRADES? FRIENDSHIP? THEY DON'T EXIST!
Eep!
...
glance
sigh...
murmur
WATCH CLOSE-LY...
HUH?
WHOOSH
!

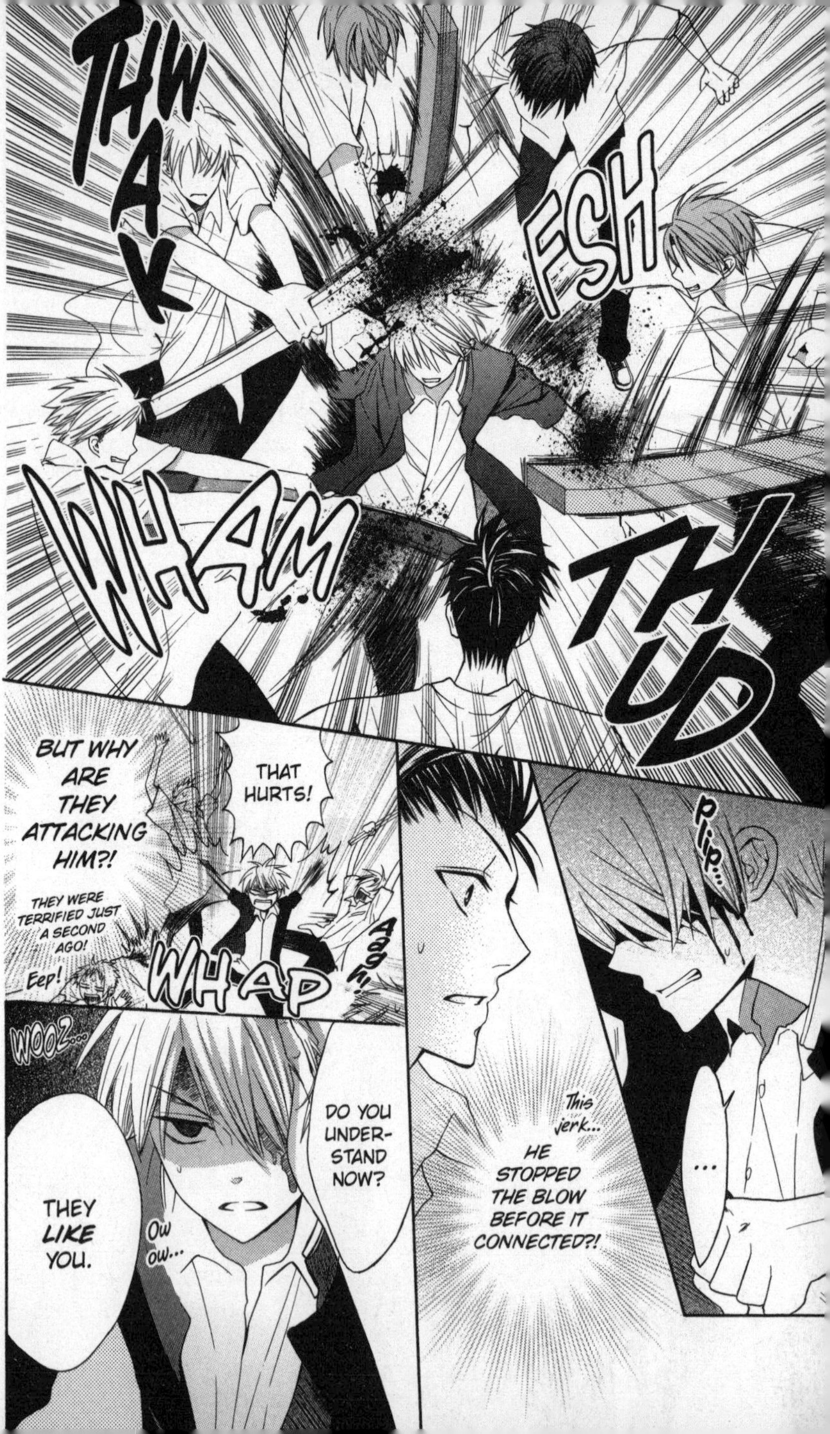
THWAK
FSH
WHAM
THUD
Plip...
This jerk...
HE STOPPED THE BLOW BEFORE IT CONNECTED?!
...
THAT HURTS!
BUT WHY ARE THEY ATTACKING HIM?!
THEY WERE TERRIFIED JUST A SECOND AGO!
Aagh!
WHAP
Eep!
WOOZ...
DO YOU UNDER-STAND NOW?
Ow ow...
THEY LIKE YOU.

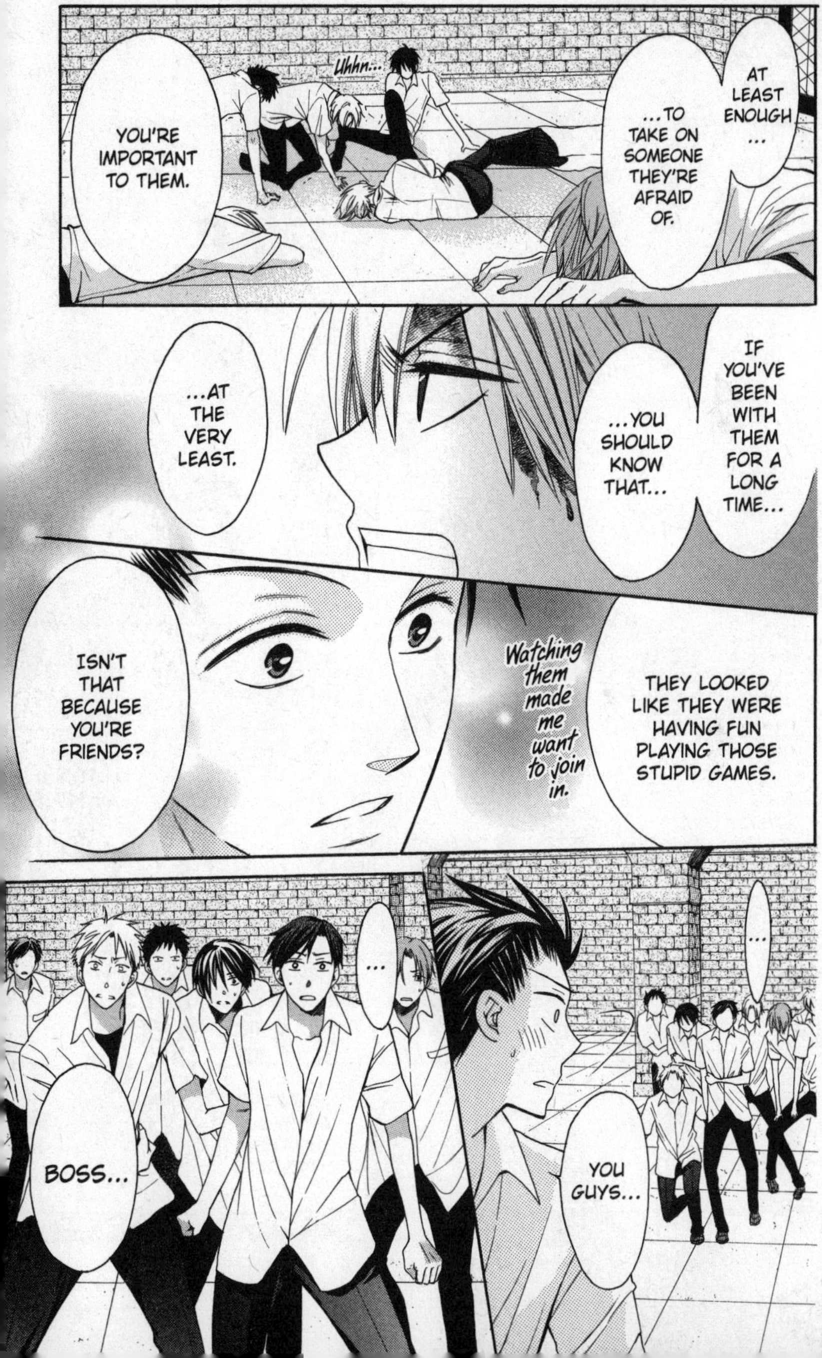
AT LEAST ENOUGH...
...TO TAKE ON SOMEONE THEY'RE AFRAID OF.
Uhhn...
YOU'RE IMPORTANT TO THEM.
IF YOU'VE BEEN WITH THEM FOR A LONG TIME...
...YOU SHOULD KNOW THAT...
...AT THE VERY LEAST.
THEY LOOKED LIKE THEY WERE HAVING FUN PLAYING THOSE STUPID GAMES.
Watching them made me want to join in.
ISN'T THAT BECAUSE YOU'RE FRIENDS?
...
YOU GUYS...
...
BOSS...

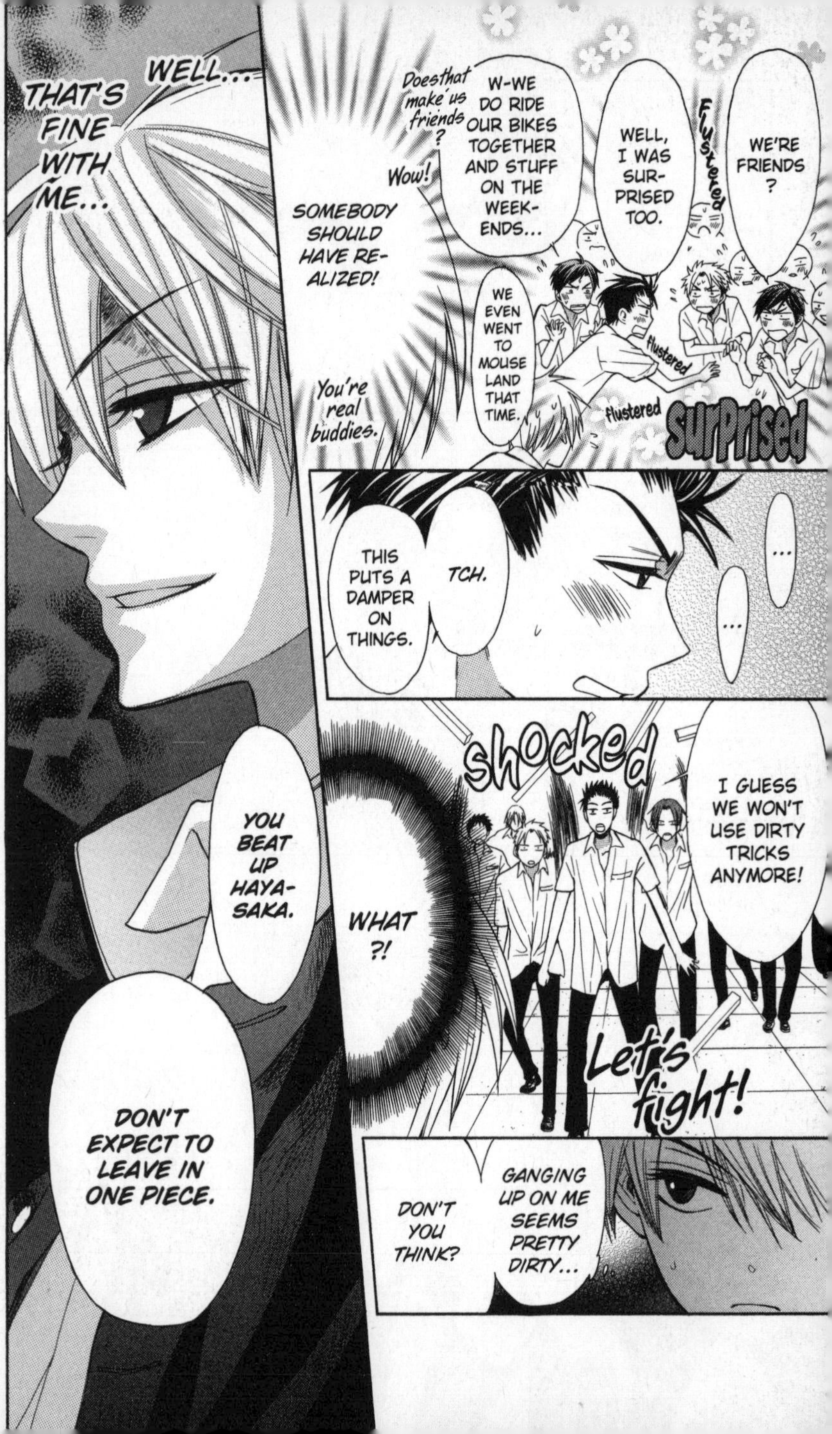
WE'RE FRIENDS?
WELL, I WAS SUR-PRISED TOO.
Flustered
W-WE DO RIDE OUR BIKES TOGETHER AND STUFF ON THE WEEK-ENDS...
Doesthat make us friends?
Wow!
WE EVEN WENT TO MOUSE LAND THAT TIME.
flustered
flustered
SurPrised
SOMEBODY SHOULD HAVE RE-ALIZED!
You're real buddies.
...
...
TCH.
THIS PUTS A DAMPER ON THINGS.
I GUESS WE WON'T USE DIRTY TRICKS ANYMORE!
shocked
Let's fight!
WHAT?!
GANGING UP ON ME SEEMS PRETTY DIRTY...
DON'T YOU THINK?
WELL...
THAT'S FINE WITH ME...
YOU BEAT UP HAYA-SAKA.
DON'T EXPECT TO LEAVE IN ONE PIECE.

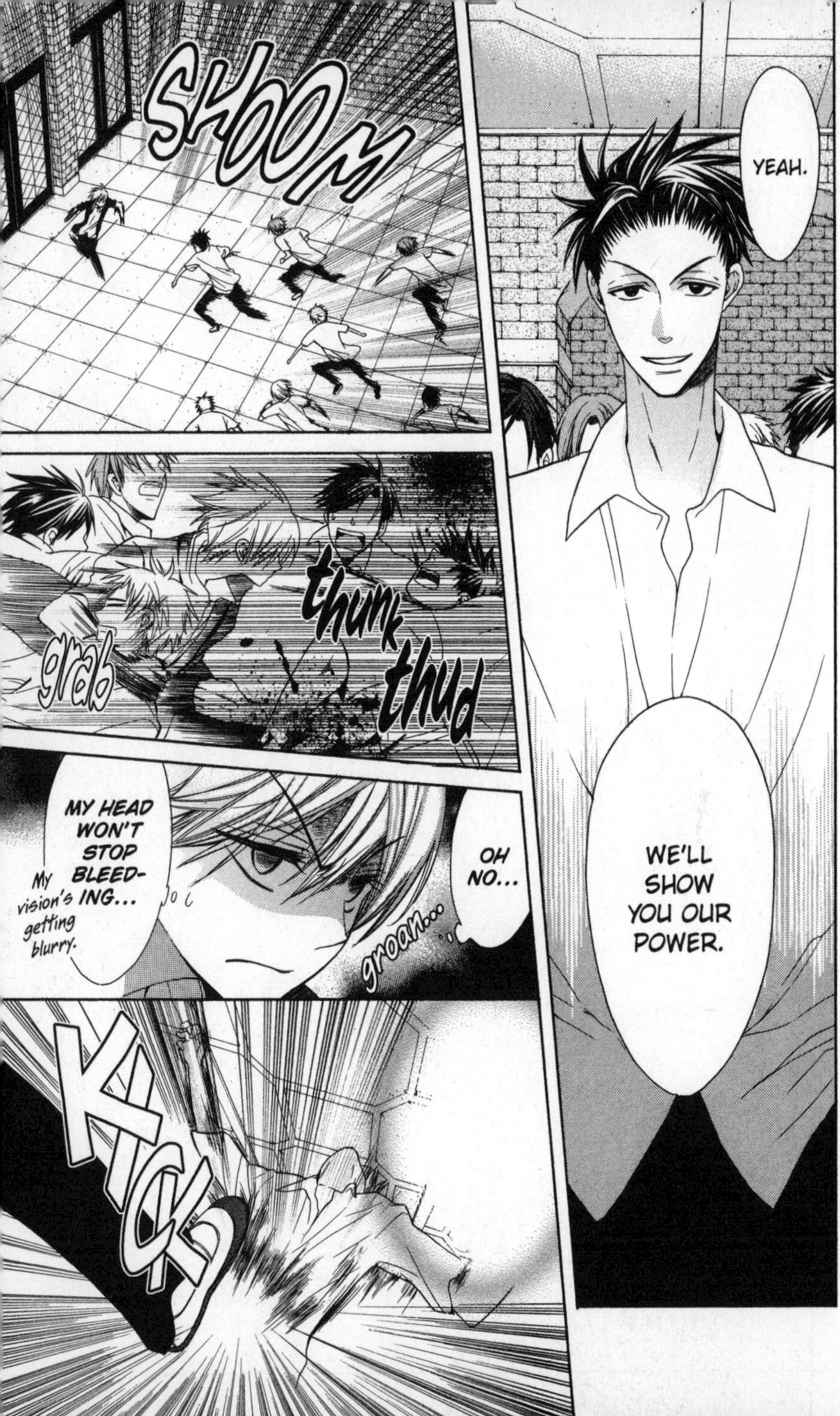
YEAH.
WE'LL SHOW YOU OUR POWER.
SHOOM
thunk
thud
grab
OH NO...
groan...
MY HEAD WON'T STOP BLEEDING...
My vision's getting blurry.
KICK

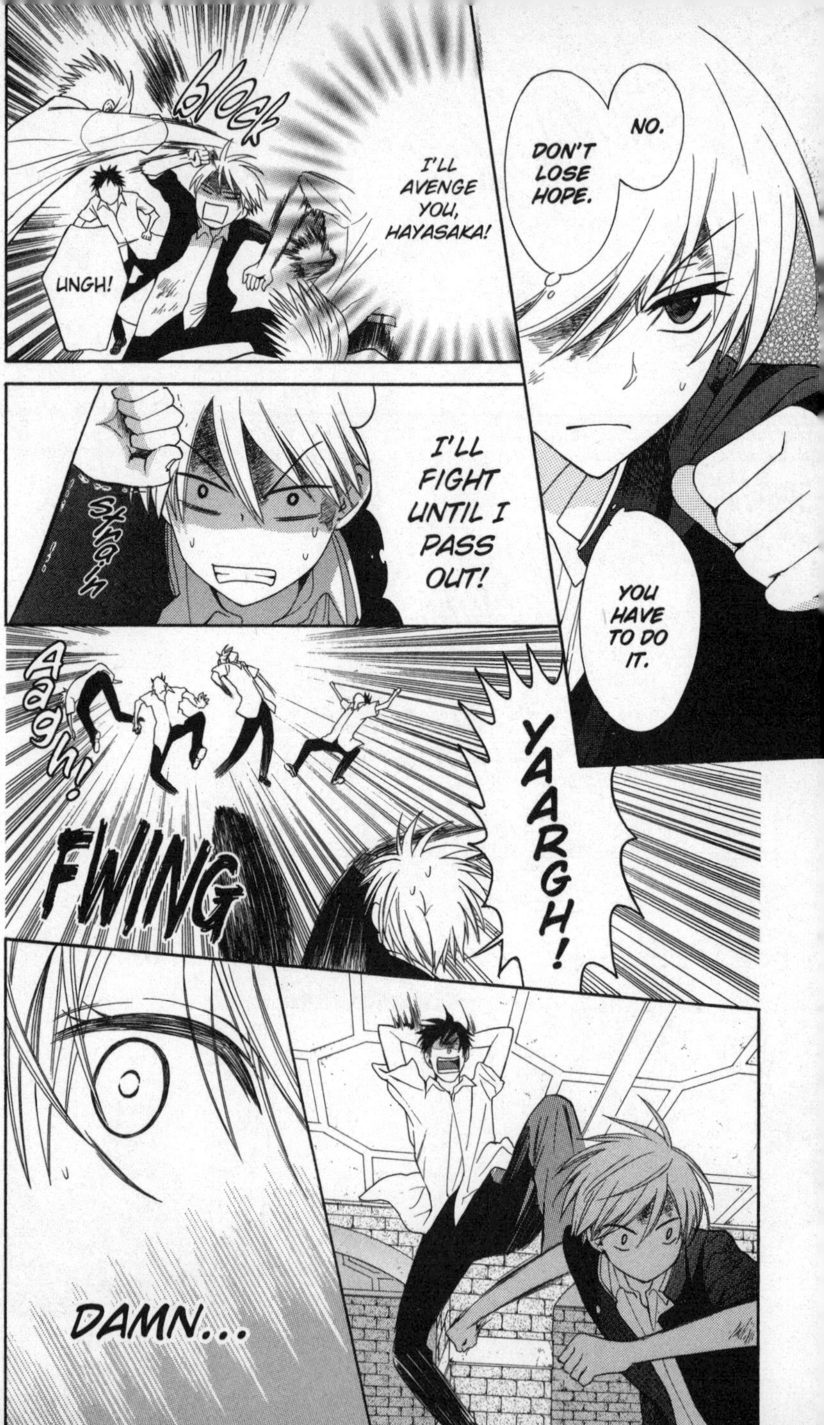
NO.
DON'T LOSE HOPE.
YOU HAVE TO DO IT.
block
I'LL AVENGE YOU, HAYASAKA!
UNGH!
I'LL FIGHT UNTIL I PASS OUT!
strain
YAARGH!
Aagh!
FWING
DAMN...

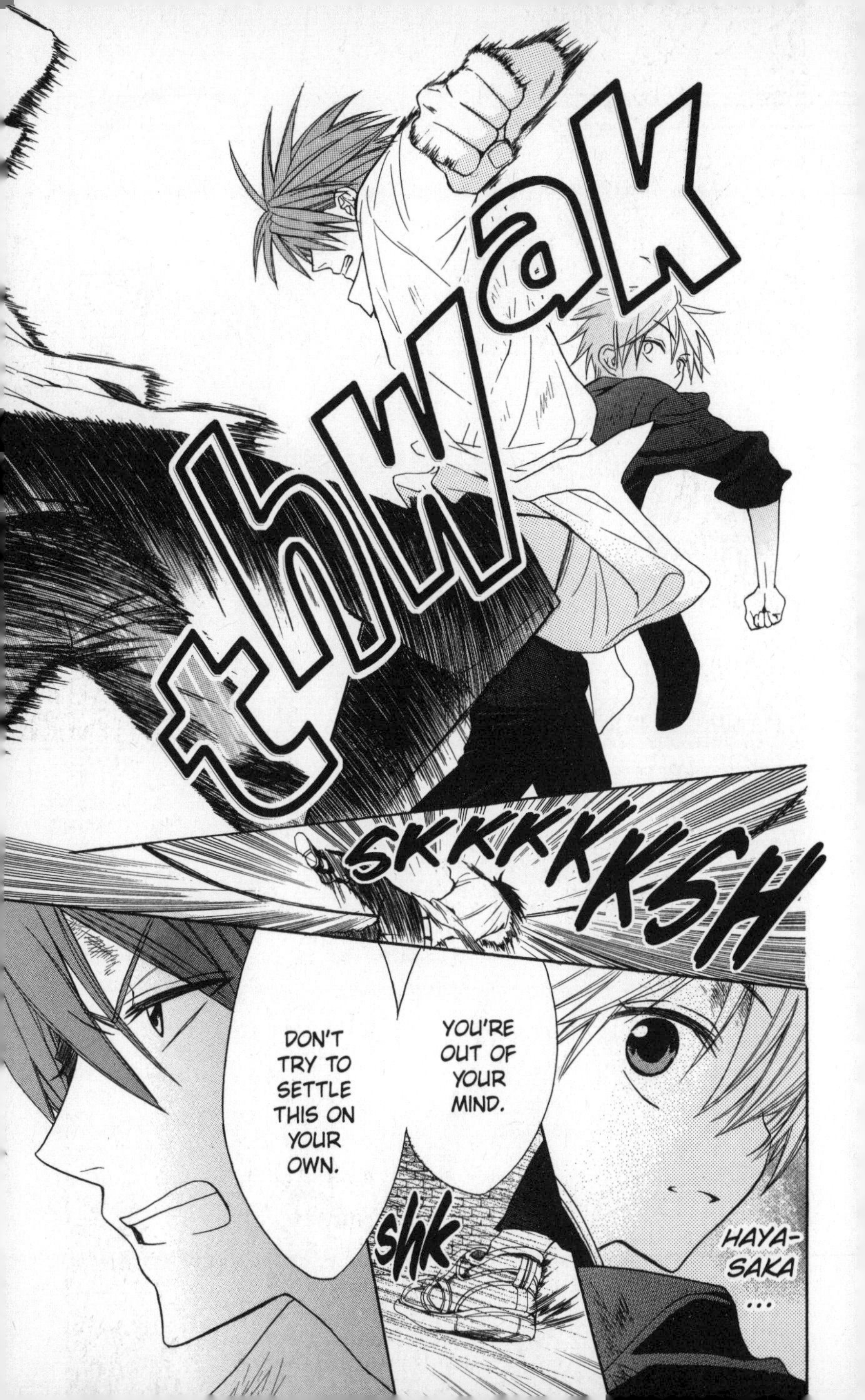
thwak
SKKKKKSH
HAYA-SAKA ...
YOU'RE OUT OF YOUR MIND.
DON'T TRY TO SETTLE THIS ON YOUR OWN.
shk

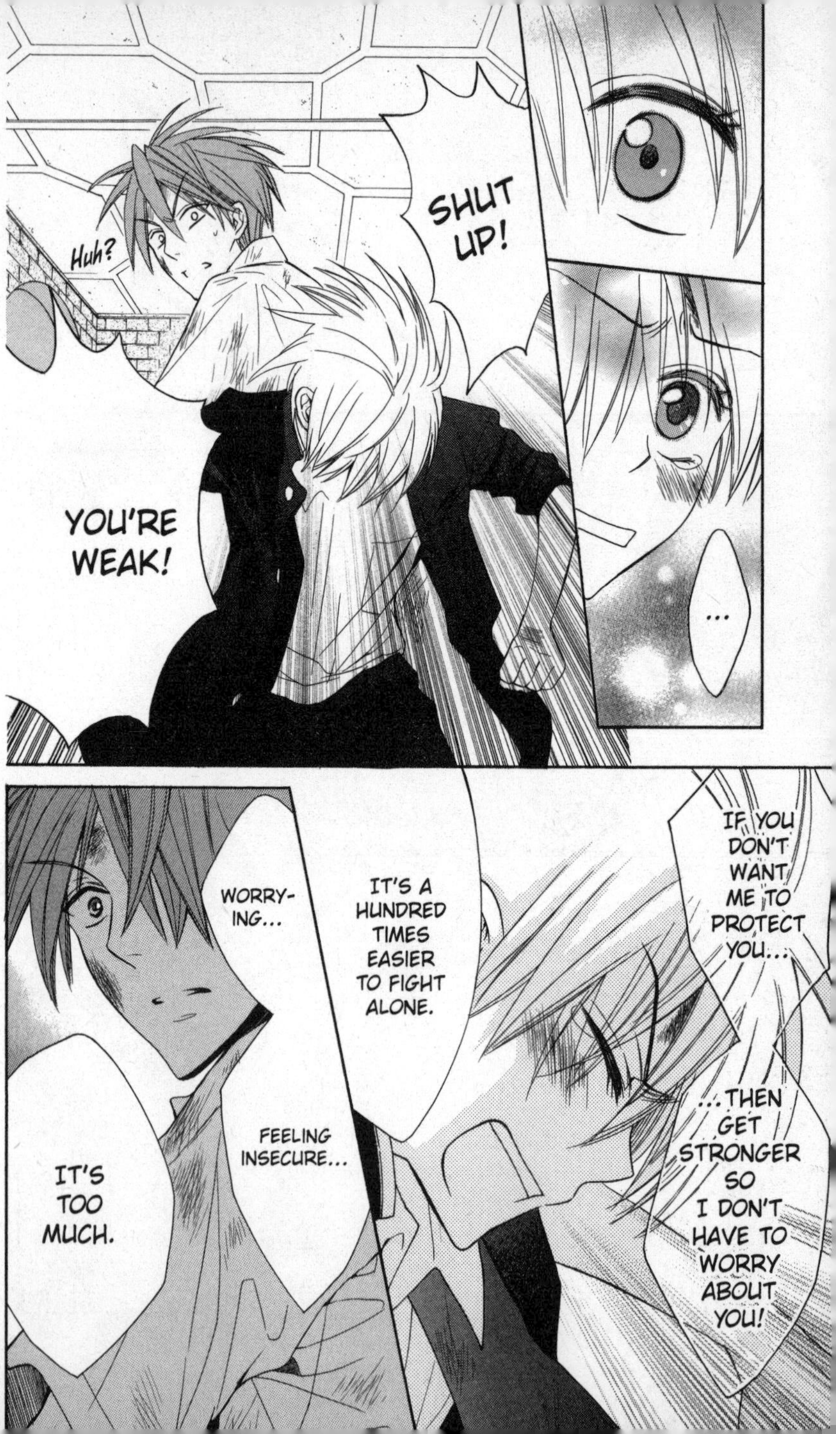
...
SHUT UP!
Huh?
YOU'RE WEAK!
IF YOU DON'T WANT ME TO PROTECT YOU...
...THEN GET STRONGER SO I DON'T HAVE TO WORRY ABOUT YOU!
IT'S A HUNDRED TIMES EASIER TO FIGHT ALONE.
WORRY-ING...
FEELING INSECURE...
IT'S TOO MUCH.

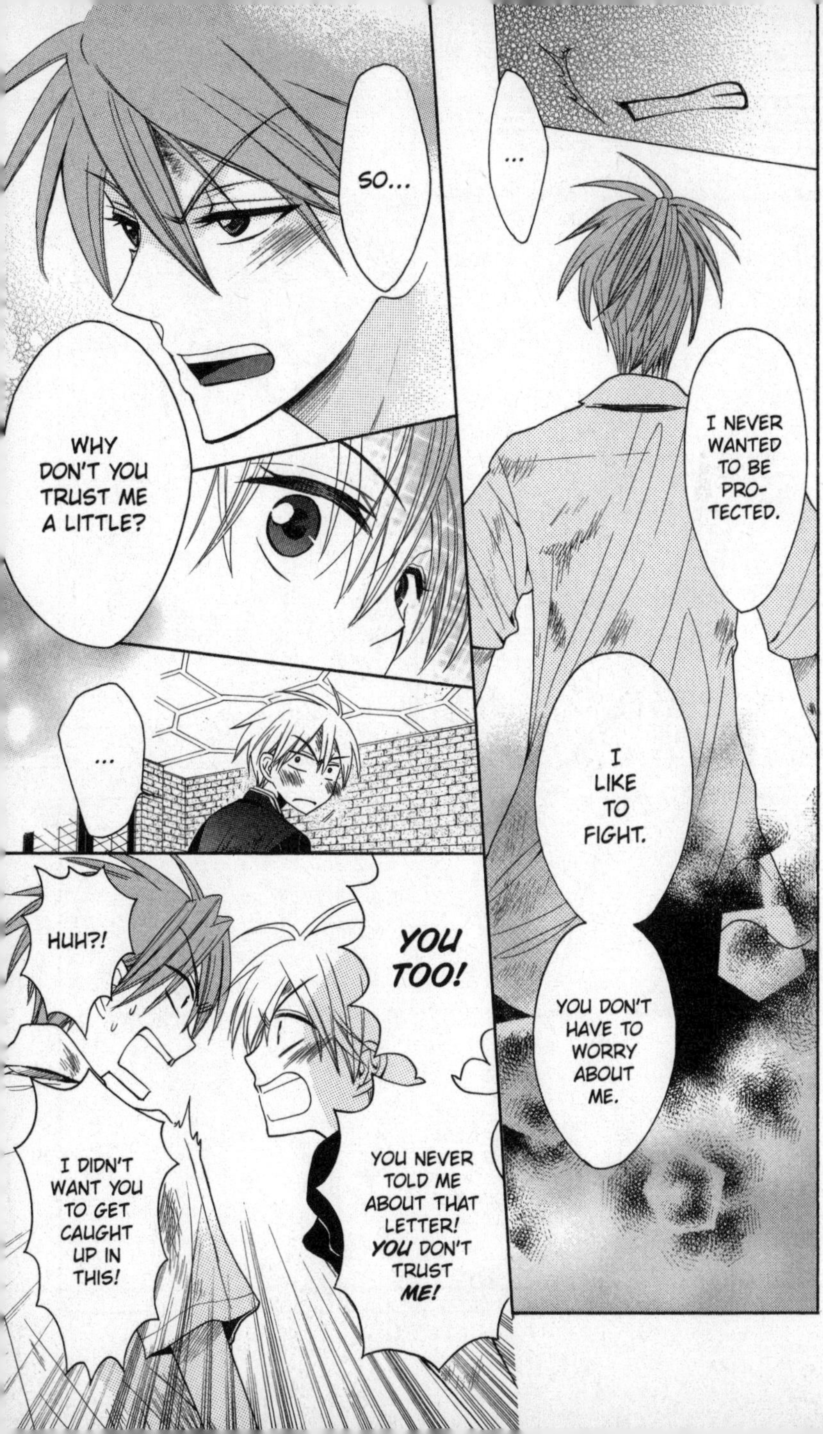
...
SO...
WHY DON'T YOU TRUST ME A LITTLE?
...
I NEVER WANTED TO BE PRO-TECTED.
I LIKE TO FIGHT.
YOU DON'T HAVE TO WORRY ABOUT ME.
YOU TOO!
YOU NEVER TOLD ME ABOUT THAT LETTER! ***YOU*** DON'T TRUST ***ME!***
HUH?!
I DIDN'T WANT YOU TO GET CAUGHT UP IN THIS!

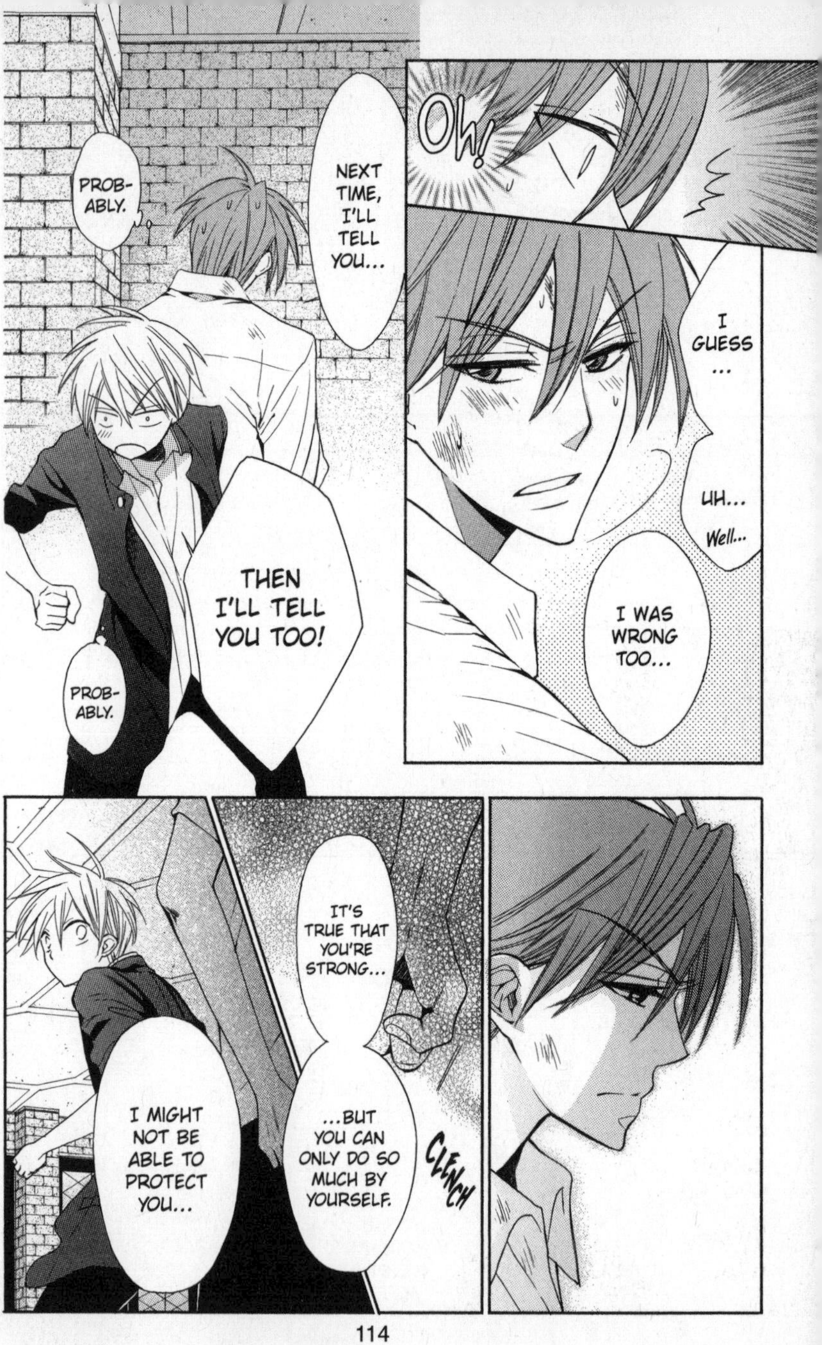
OH!
I GUESS...
UH...
Well...
I WAS WRONG TOO...
NEXT TIME, I'LL TELL YOU...
PROB-ABLY.
THEN I'LL TELL YOU TOO!
PROB-ABLY.
IT'S TRUE THAT YOU'RE STRONG...
...BUT YOU CAN ONLY DO SO MUCH BY YOURSELF.
CLENCH
I MIGHT NOT BE ABLE TO PROTECT YOU...

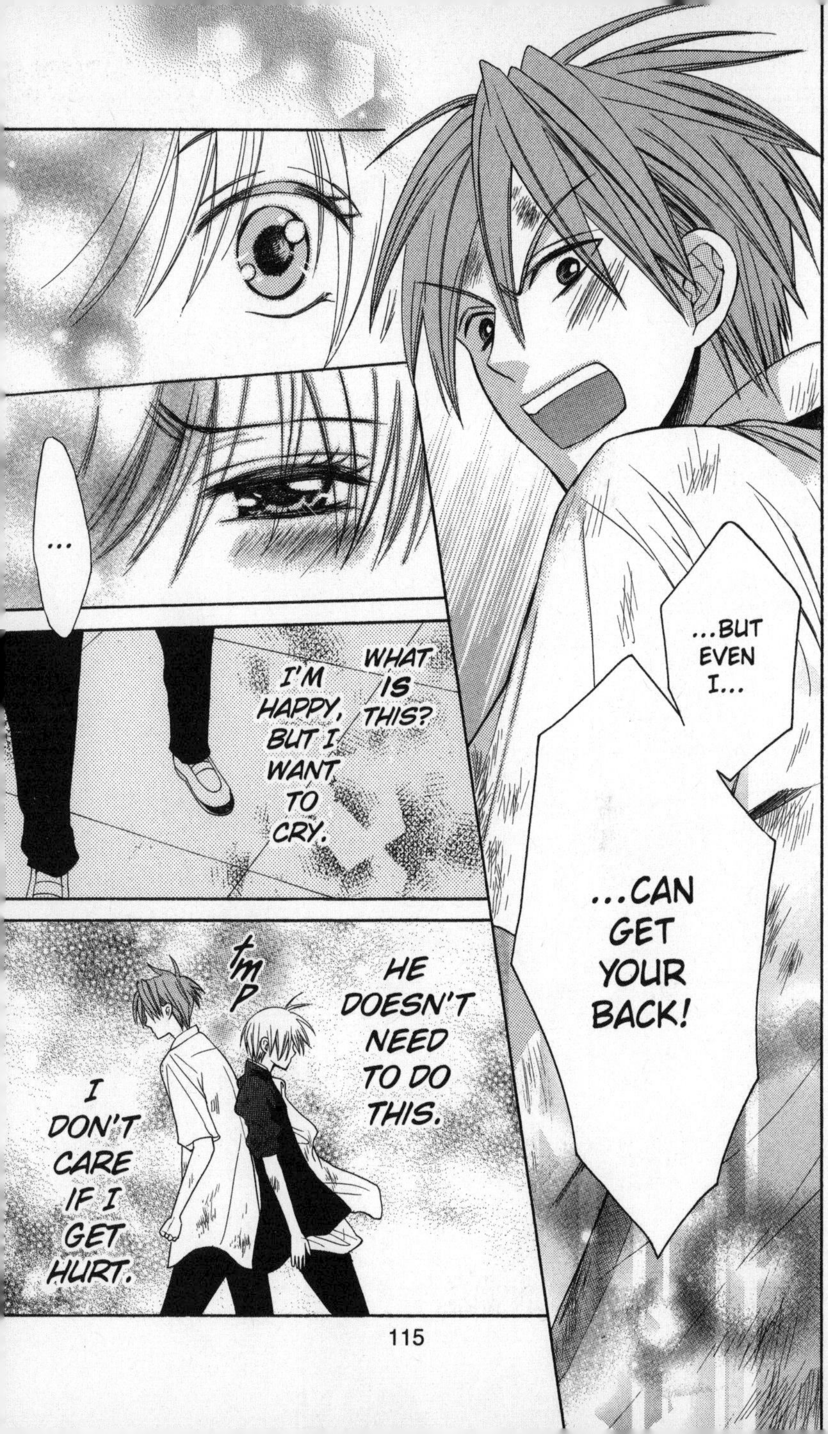
...BUT EVEN I...
...CAN GET YOUR BACK!
...
WHAT IS THIS?
I'M HAPPY, BUT I WANT TO CRY.
tmp
HE DOESN'T NEED TO DO THIS.
I DON'T CARE IF I GET HURT.

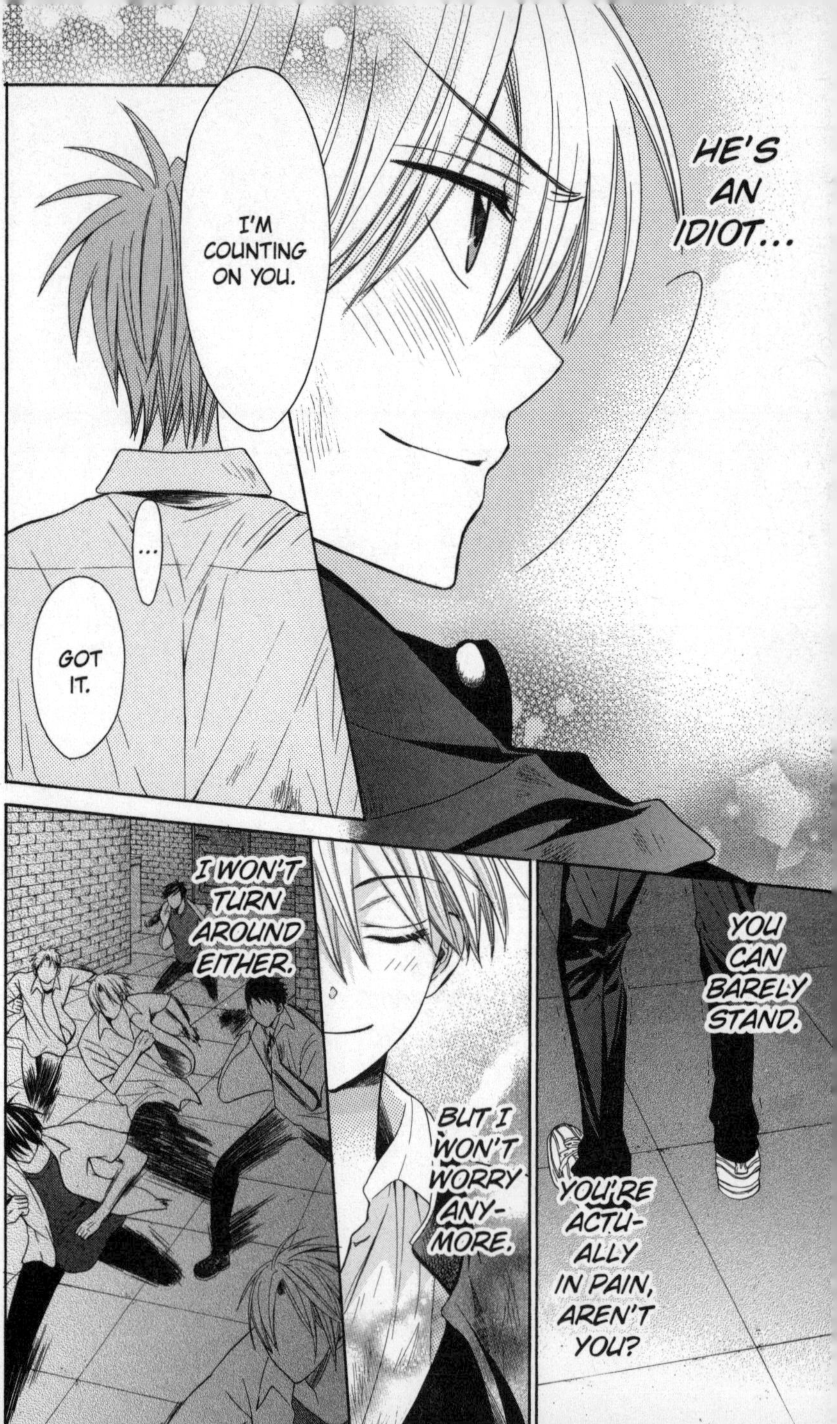
HE'S AN IDIOT...
I'M COUNTING ON YOU.
...
GOT IT.
YOU CAN BARELY STAND.
YOU'RE ACTU-ALLY IN PAIN, AREN'T YOU?
BUT I WON'T WORRY ANY-MORE.
I WON'T TURN AROUND EITHER.

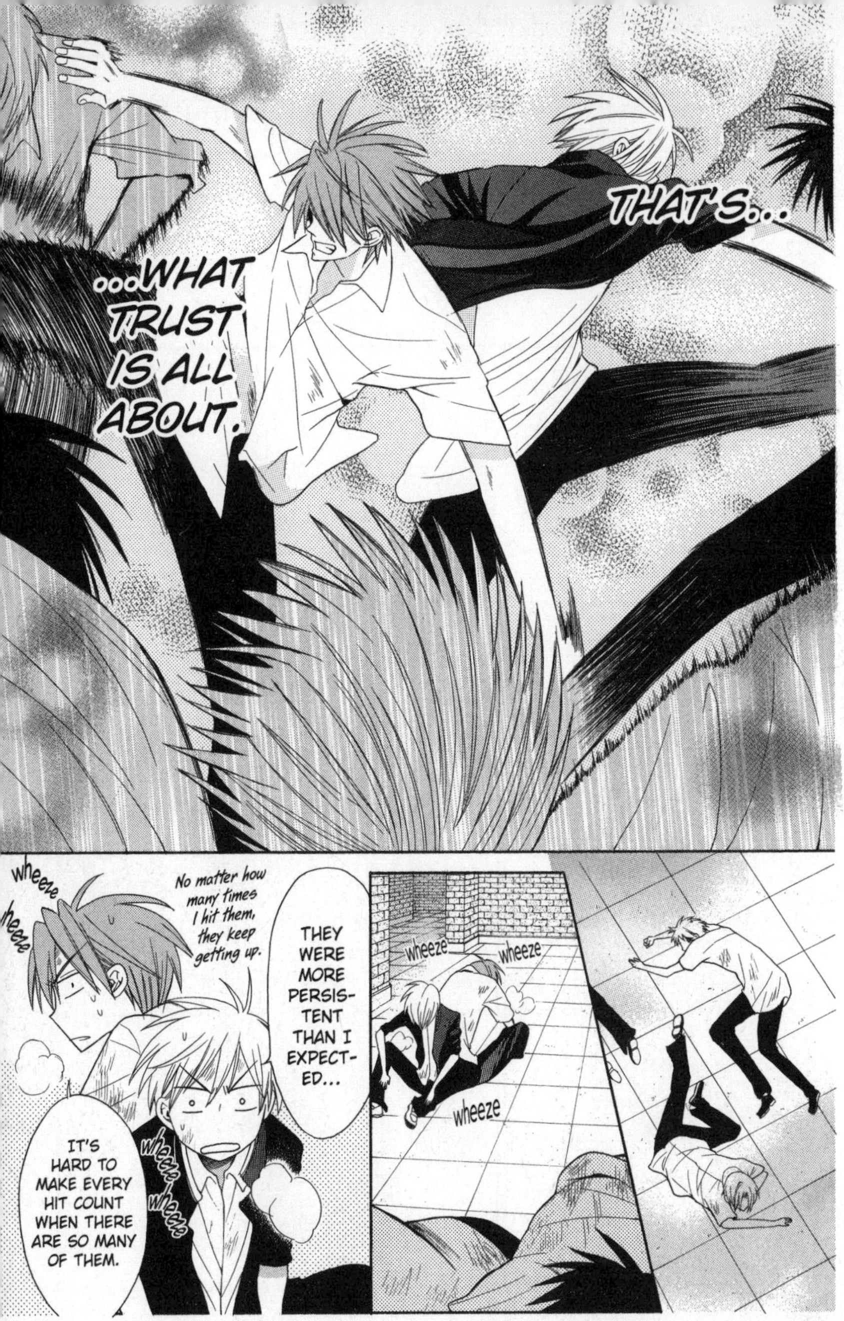
THAT'S...
...WHAT TRUST IS ALL ABOUT.
wheeze
wheeze
wheeze
THEY WERE MORE PERSIS-TENT THAN I EXPECT-ED...
No matter how many times I hit them, they keep getting up.
wheeze
wheeze
IT'S HARD TO MAKE EVERY HIT COUNT WHEN THERE ARE SO MANY OF THEM.
wheeze
wheeze

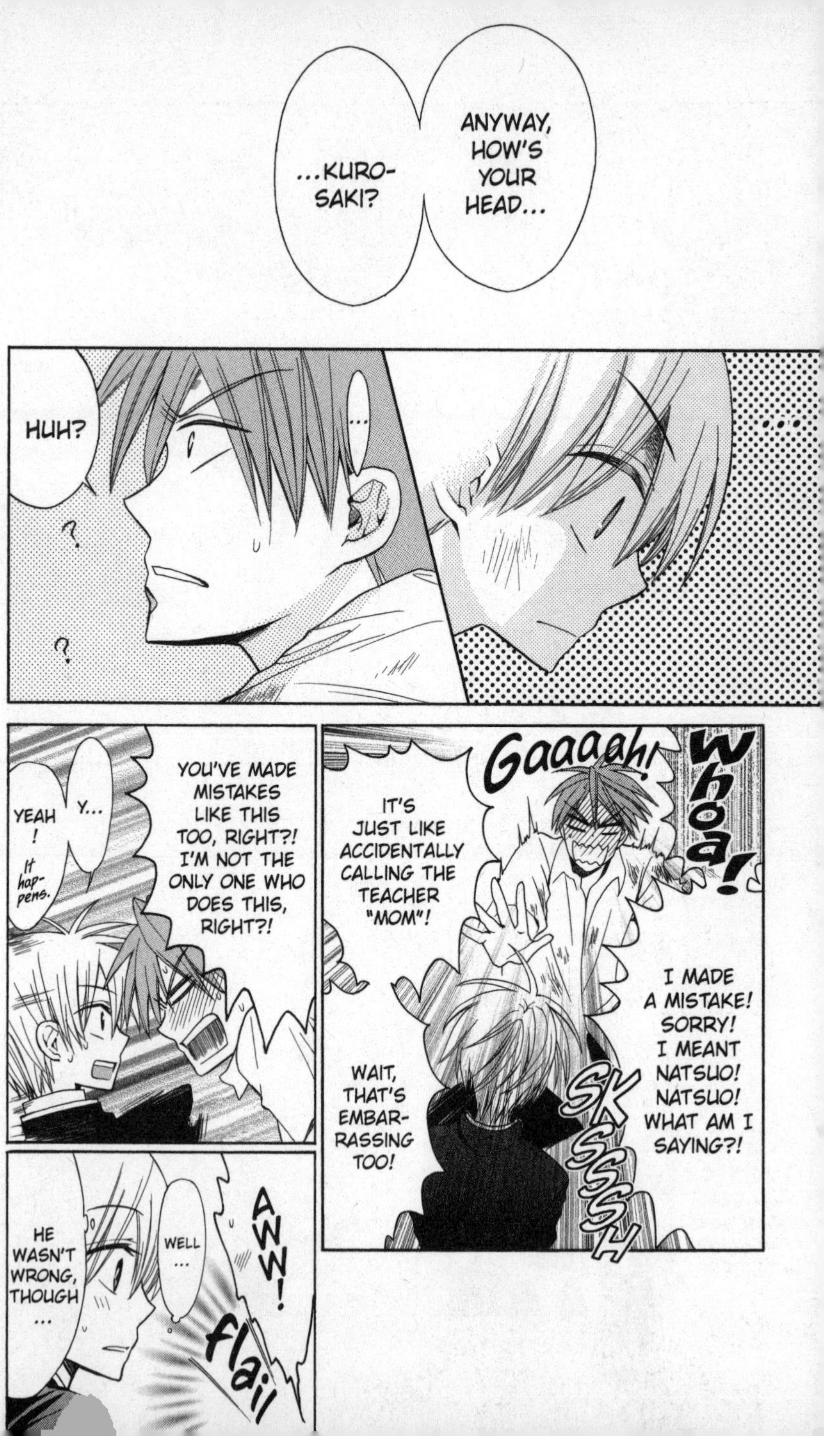

ANYWAY, HOW'S YOUR HEAD...
...KURO-SAKI?
...
...
HUH?
Whoa!
Gaaaah!
IT'S JUST LIKE ACCIDENTALLY CALLING THE TEACHER "MOM"!
I MADE A MISTAKE! SORRY! I MEANT NATSUO! NATSUO! WHAT AM I SAYING?!
SKSSSH
WAIT, THAT'S EMBARRASSING TOO!
YOU'VE MADE MISTAKES LIKE THIS TOO, RIGHT?! I'M NOT THE ONLY ONE WHO DOES THIS, RIGHT?!
Y...
YEAH! It happens.
AWW!
flail
WELL...
HE WASN'T WRONG, THOUGH...

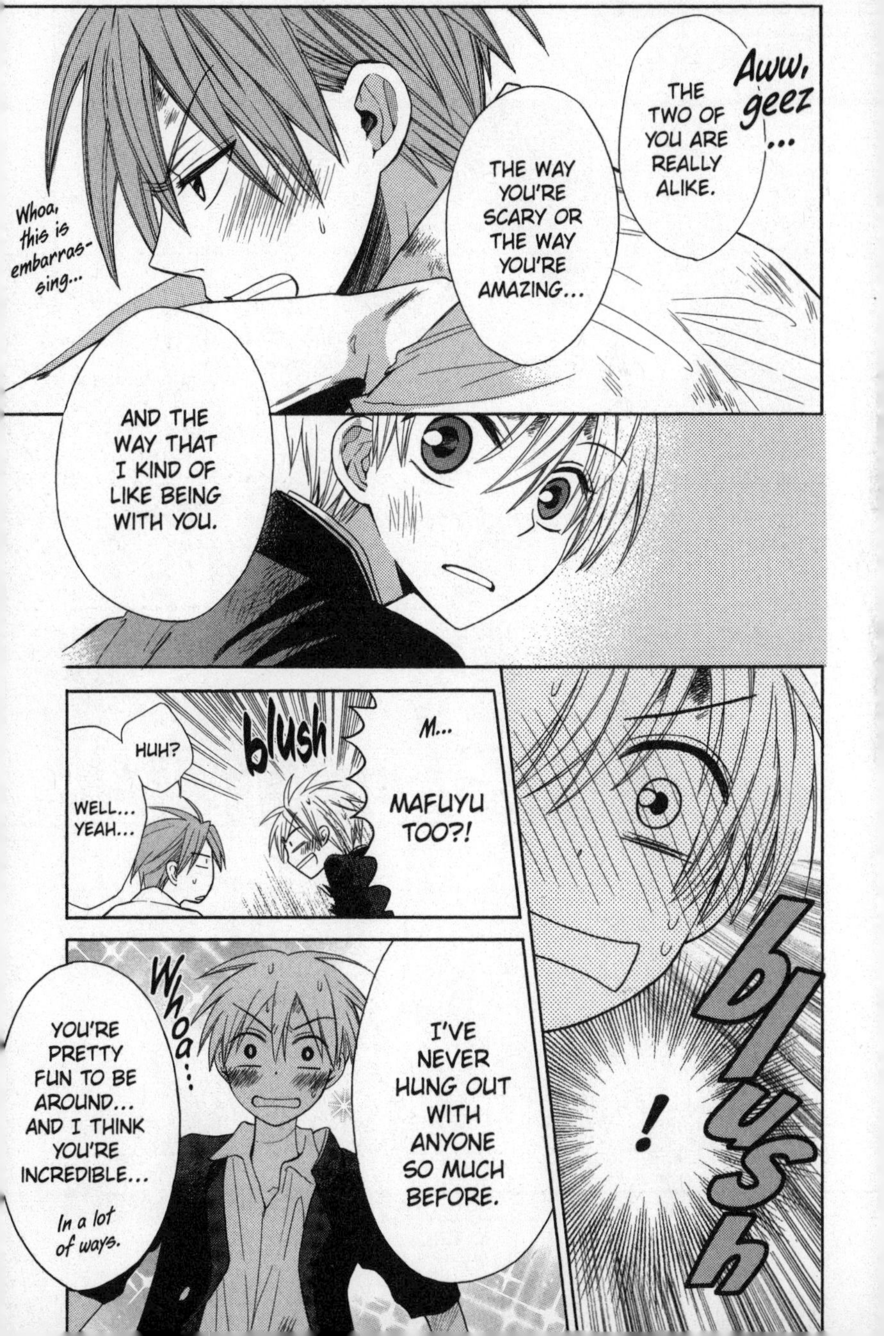
Aww, geez...
THE TWO OF YOU ARE REALLY ALIKE.
THE WAY YOU'RE SCARY OR THE WAY YOU'RE AMAZING...
Whoa, this is embarras-sing...
AND THE WAY THAT I KIND OF LIKE BEING WITH YOU.
!
blush
M...
MAFUYU TOO?!
blush
HUH?
WELL... YEAH...
I'VE NEVER HUNG OUT WITH ANYONE SO MUCH BEFORE.
Whoa...
YOU'RE PRETTY FUN TO BE AROUND... AND I THINK YOU'RE INCREDIBLE...
In a lot of ways.

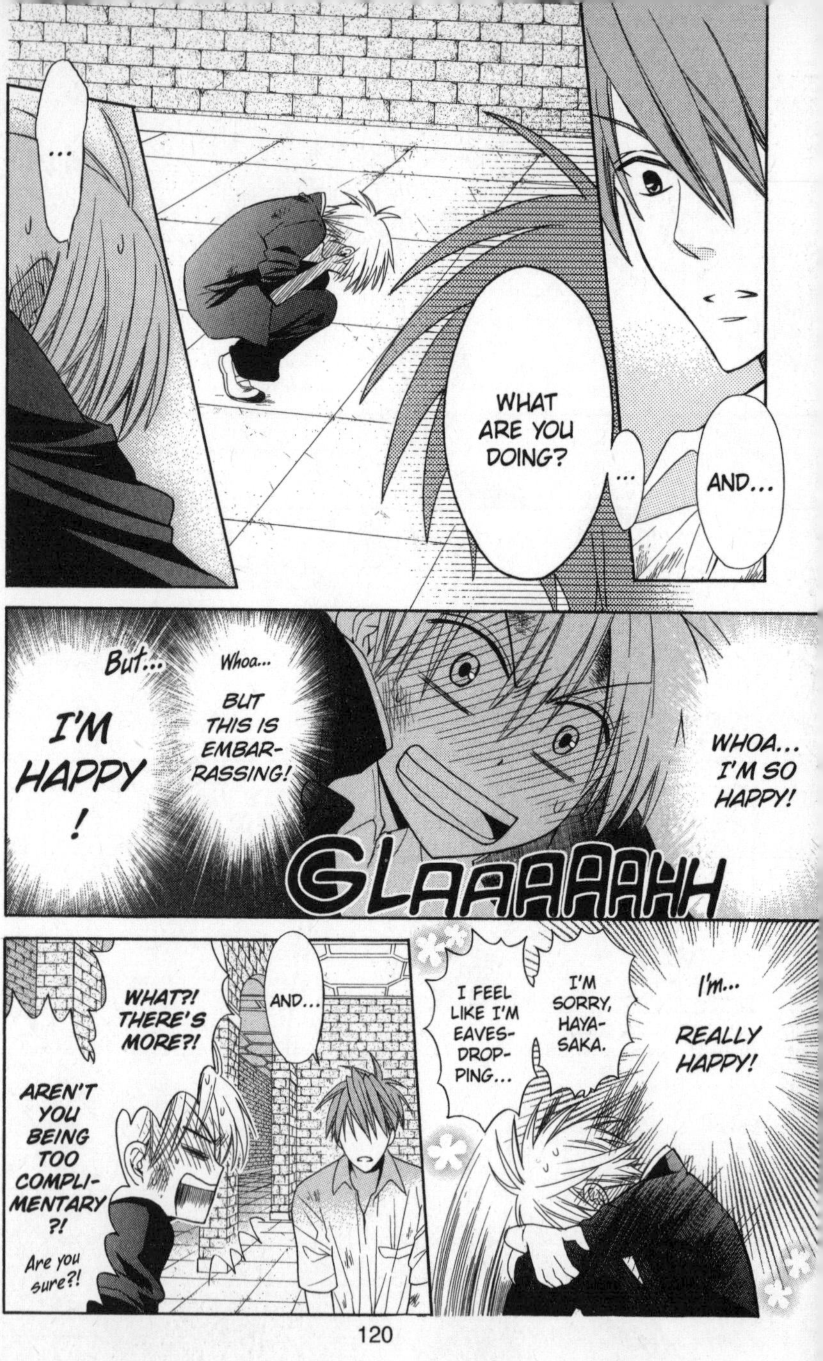
AND...
...
WHAT ARE YOU DOING?
...
WHOA... I'M SO HAPPY!
GLAAAAAHH
Whoa...
BUT THIS IS EMBARRASSING!
But...
I'M HAPPY!
I'm...
REALLY HAPPY!
I'M SORRY, HAYASAKA.
I FEEL LIKE I'M EAVESDROPPING...
AND...
WHAT?! THERE'S MORE?!
AREN'T YOU BEING TOO COMPLIMENTARY?!
Are you sure?!

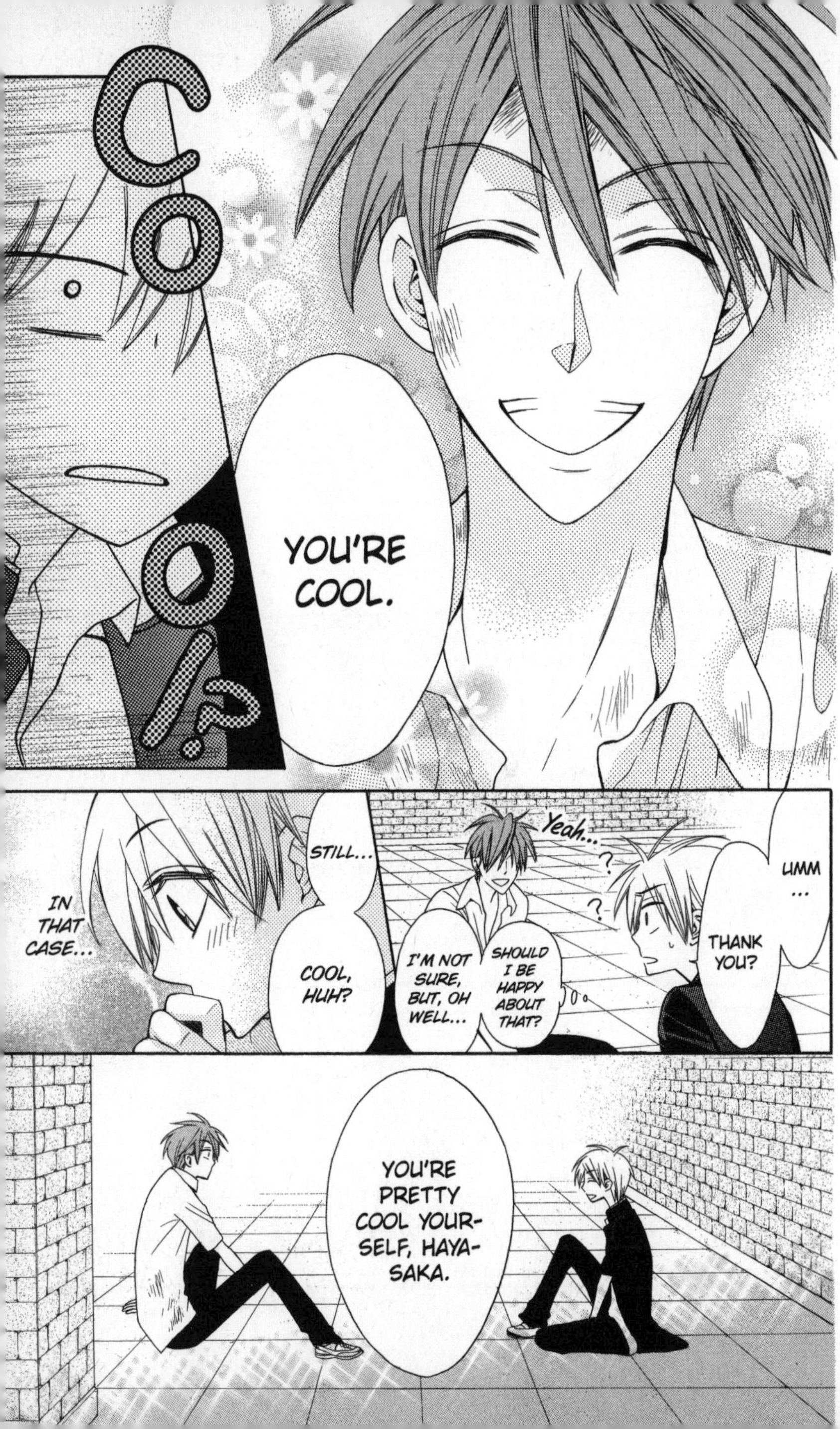
YOU'RE COOL.
COOL?!
UMM ... THANK YOU?
Yeah...
SHOULD I BE HAPPY ABOUT THAT?
I'M NOT SURE, BUT, OH WELL...
STILL... COOL, HUH?
IN THAT CASE...
YOU'RE PRETTY COOL YOURSELF, HAYASAKA.

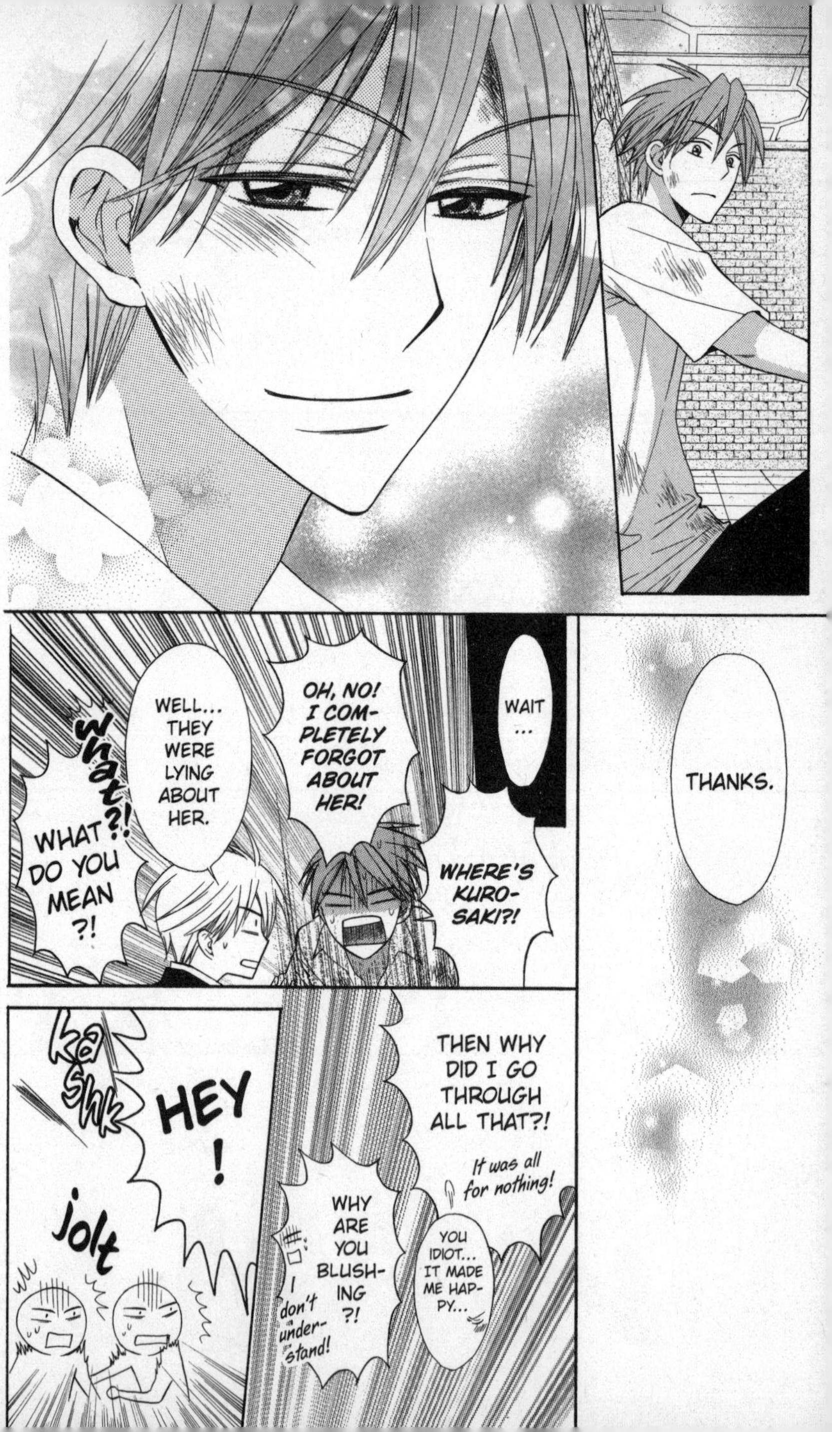
THANKS.
WAIT ...
WHERE'S KURO-SAKI?!
OH, NO! I COM-PLETELY FORGOT ABOUT HER!
WELL... THEY WERE LYING ABOUT HER.
what?!
WHAT DO YOU MEAN ?!
THEN WHY DID I GO THROUGH ALL THAT?!
It was all for nothing!
YOU IDIOT... IT MADE ME HAP-PY...
WHY ARE YOU BLUSH-ING ?!
I don't under-stand!
kashk
HEY !
jolt

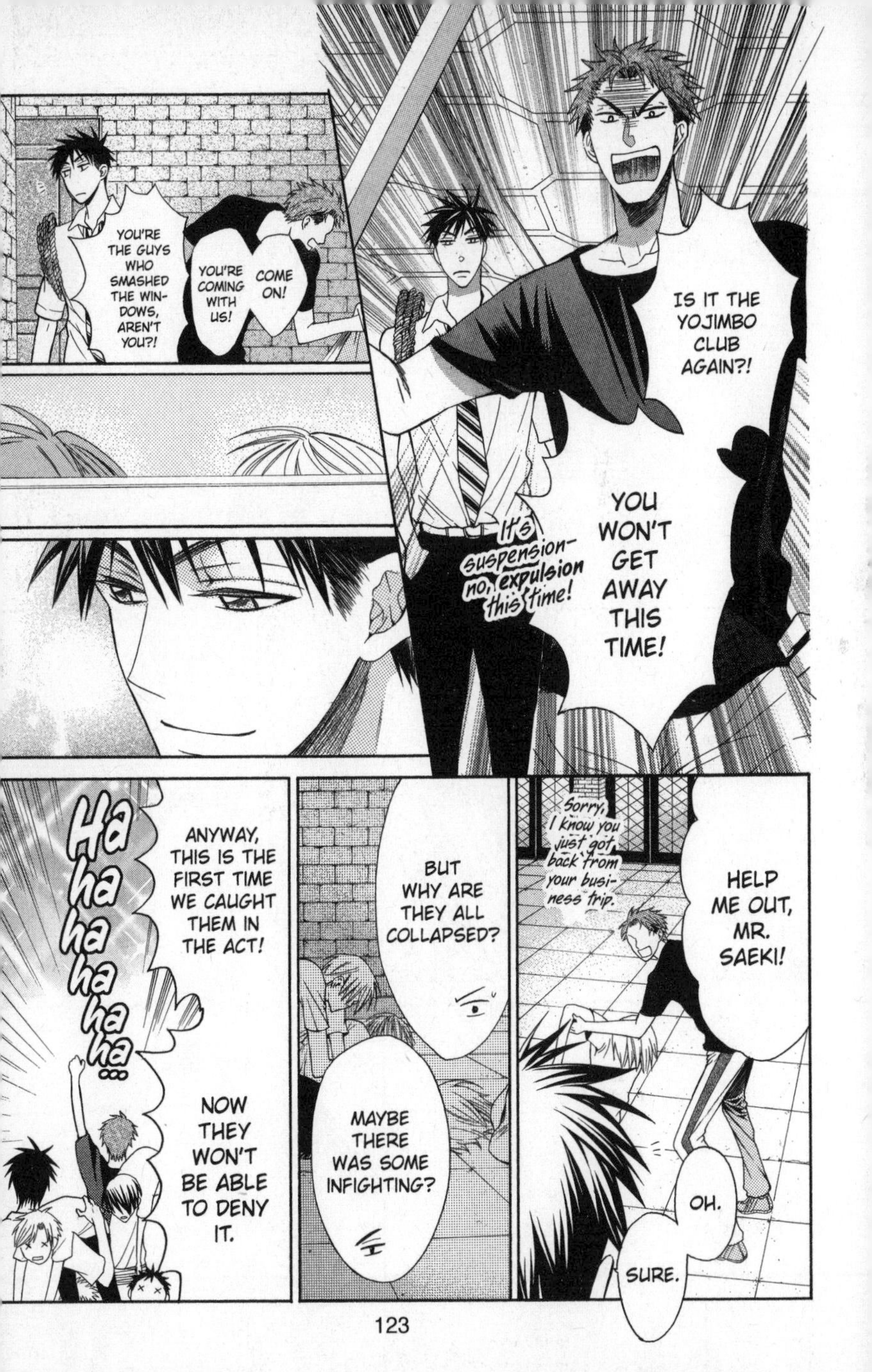
IS IT THE YOJIMBO CLUB AGAIN?!
YOU WON'T GET AWAY THIS TIME!
It's suspension-no, expulsion this time!
COME ON!
YOU'RE COMING WITH US!
YOU'RE THE GUYS WHO SMASHED THE WIN-DOWS, AREN'T YOU?!
HELP ME OUT, MR. SAEKI!
Sorry, I know you just got back from your busi-ness trip.
OH.
SURE.
BUT WHY ARE THEY ALL COLLAPSED?
MAYBE THERE WAS SOME INFIGHTING?
Ha ha ha ha ha ha...
ANYWAY, THIS IS THE FIRST TIME WE CAUGHT THEM IN THE ACT!
NOW THEY WON'T BE ABLE TO DENY IT.

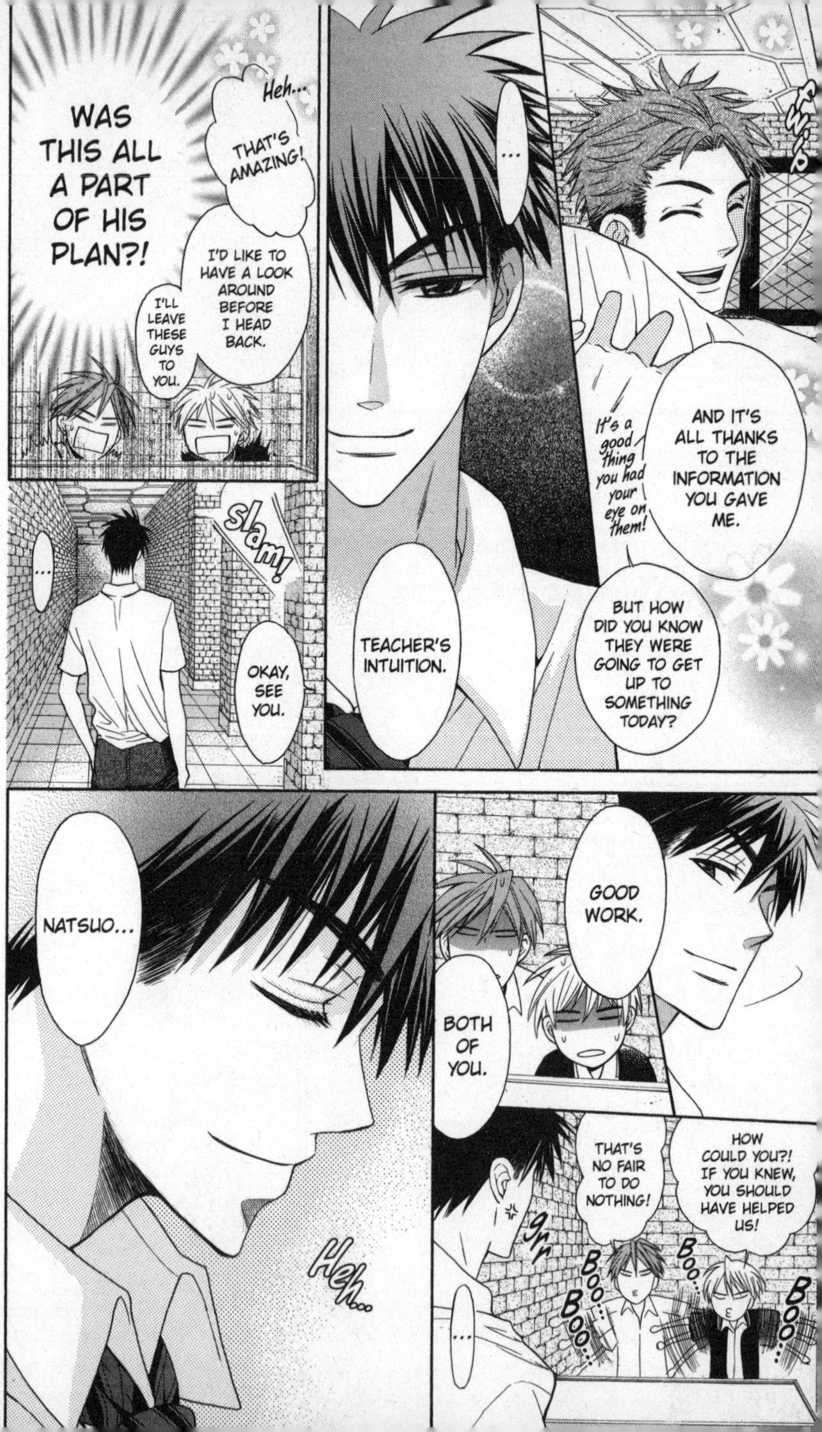
AND IT'S ALL THANKS TO THE INFORMATION YOU GAVE ME.
It's a good thing you had your eye on them!
BUT HOW DID YOU KNOW THEY WERE GOING TO GET UP TO SOMETHING TODAY?
...
TEACHER'S INTUITION.
Heh...
THAT'S AMAZING!
I'D LIKE TO HAVE A LOOK AROUND BEFORE I HEAD BACK.
I'LL LEAVE THESE GUYS TO YOU.
WAS THIS ALL A PART OF HIS PLAN?!
slam!
OKAY, SEE YOU.
...
GOOD WORK.
BOTH OF YOU.
HOW COULD YOU?! IF YOU KNEW, YOU SHOULD HAVE HELPED US!
THAT'S NO FAIR TO DO NOTHING!
grr
Boo... Boo...
Boo... Boo...
...
NATSUO...
Heh...

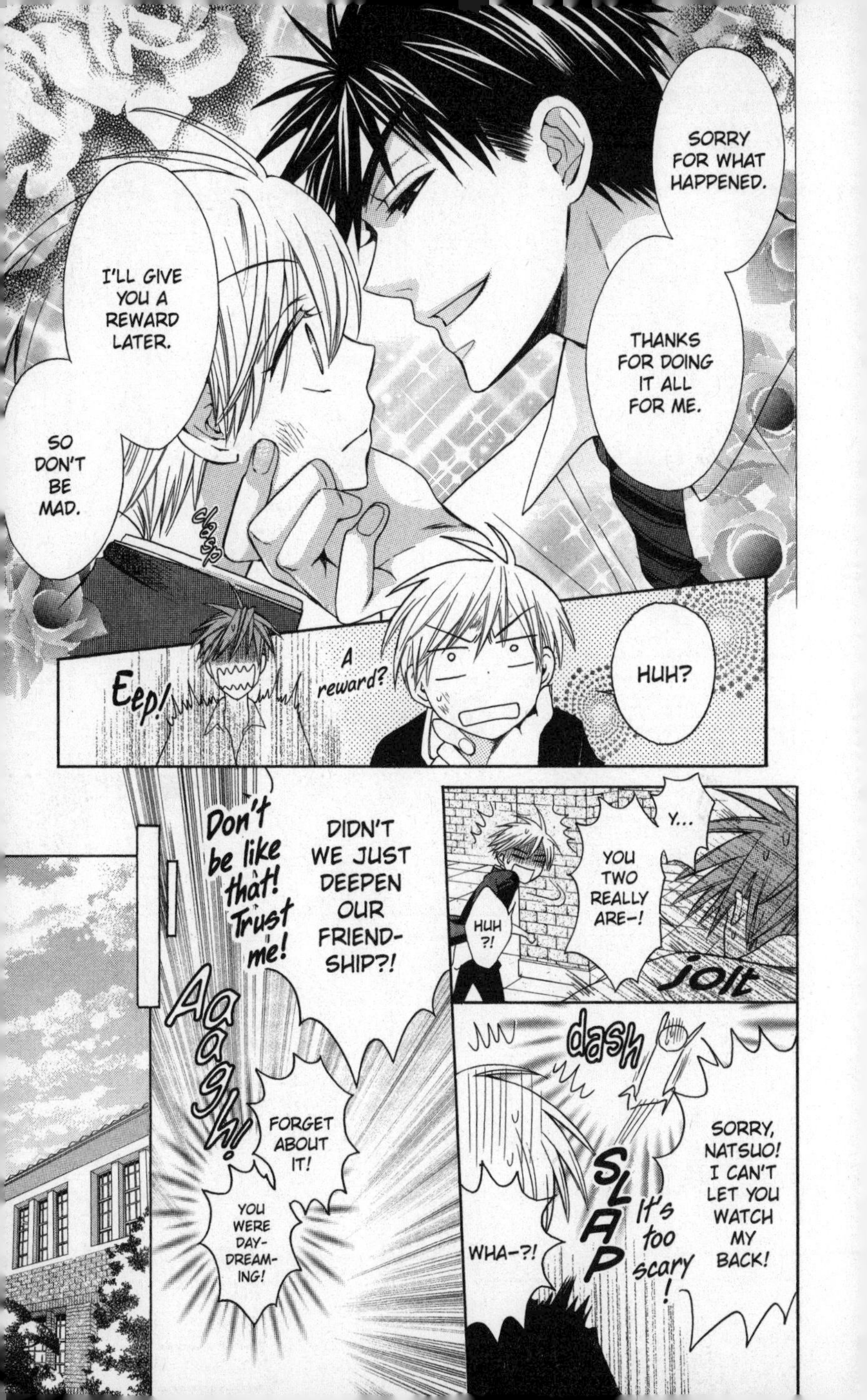
SORRY FOR WHAT HAPPENED.
THANKS FOR DOING IT ALL FOR ME.
I'LL GIVE YOU A REWARD LATER.
SO DON'T BE MAD.
clasp
HUH?
A reward?
Eep!
Y...
YOU TWO REALLY ARE-!
jolt
HUH ?!
dash
SORRY, NATSUO! I CAN'T LET YOU WATCH MY BACK!
SLAP
It's too scary!
WHA-?!
DIDN'T WE JUST DEEPEN OUR FRIEND-SHIP?!
Don't be like that! Trust me!
Aaagh!
FORGET ABOUT IT!
YOU WERE DAY-DREAM-ING!

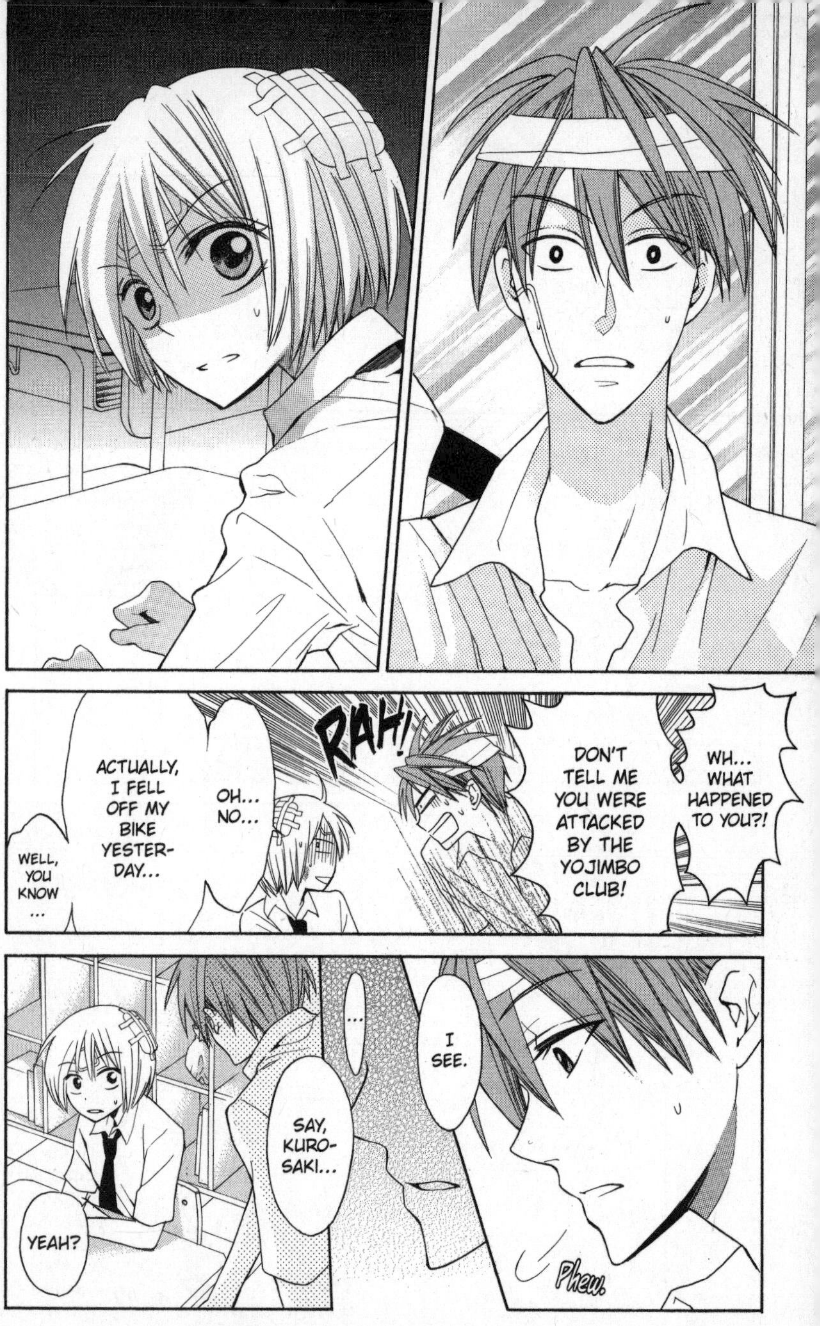

WH... WHAT HAPPENED TO YOU?!
DON'T TELL ME YOU WERE ATTACKED BY THE YOJIMBO CLUB!
RAH!
OH... NO...
WELL, YOU KNOW ...
ACTUALLY, I FELL OFF MY BIKE YESTER-DAY...
I SEE.
Phew.
...
SAY, KURO-SAKI...
YEAH?

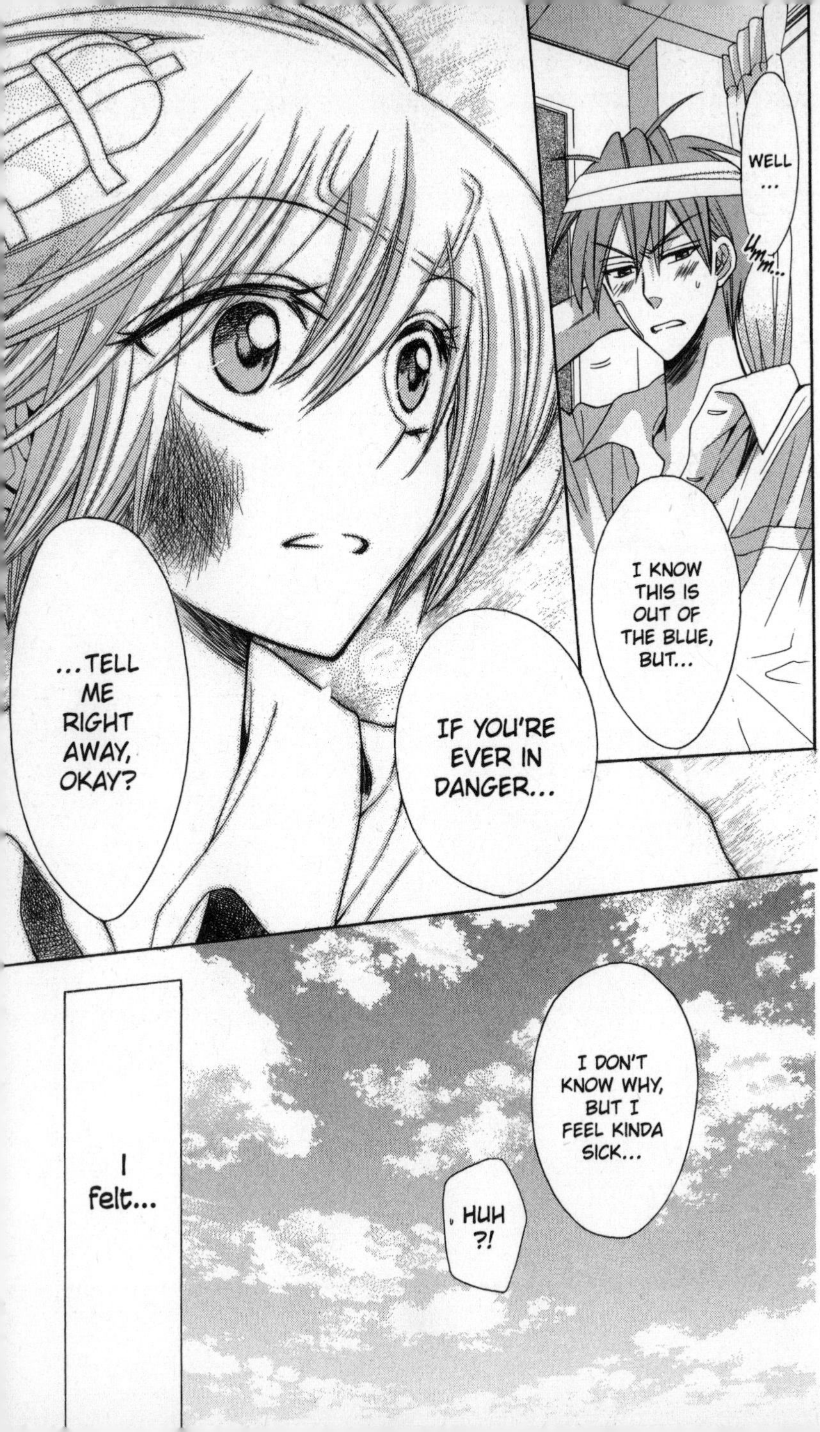
WELL...
Umm...
I KNOW THIS IS OUT OF THE BLUE, BUT...
IF YOU'RE EVER IN DANGER...
...TELL ME RIGHT AWAY, OKAY?
I DON'T KNOW WHY, BUT I FEEL KINDA SICK...
HUH?!
I felt...

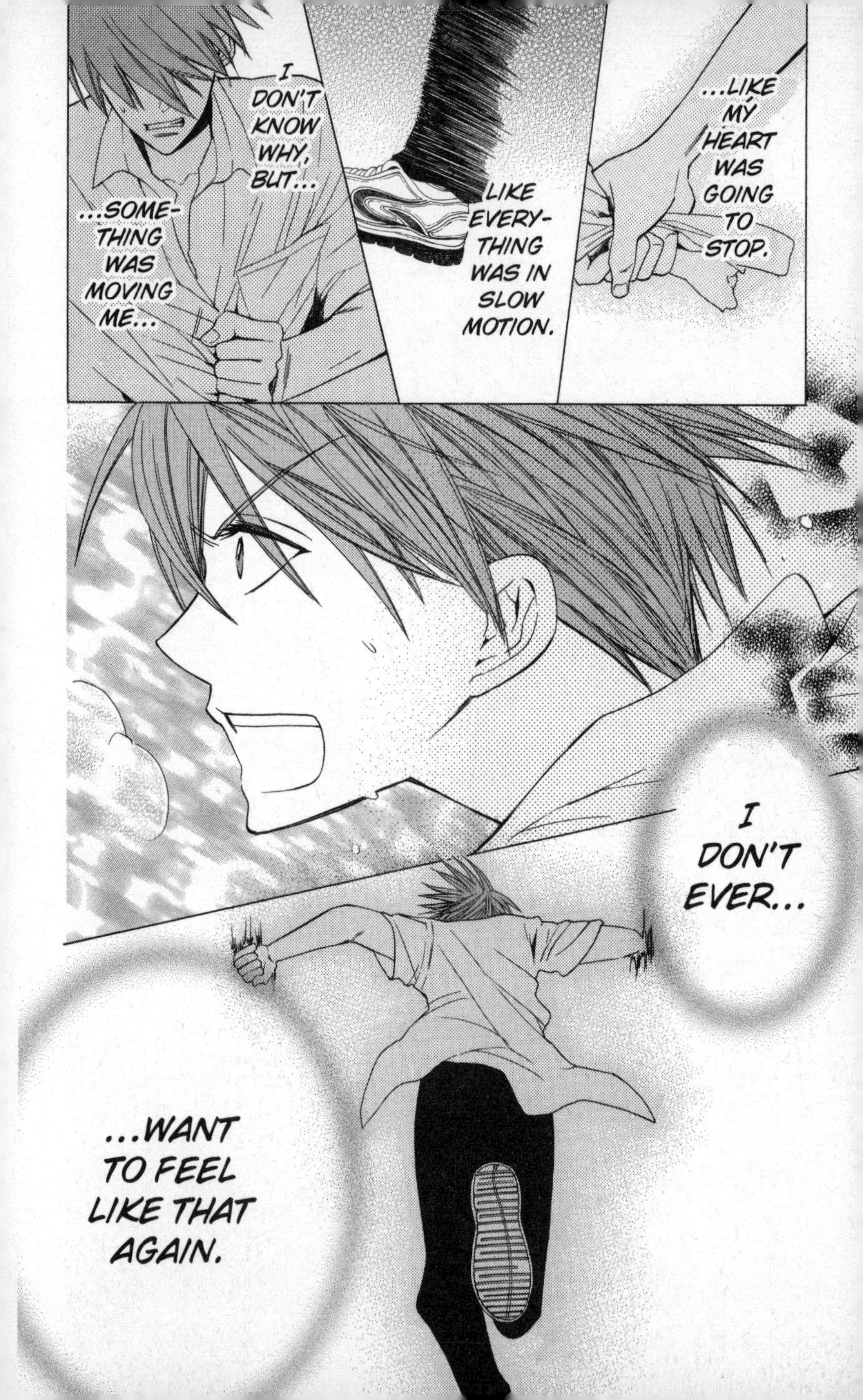
...LIKE MY HEART WAS GOING TO STOP.
LIKE EVERYTHING WAS IN SLOW MOTION.
I DON'T KNOW WHY, BUT...
...SOMETHING WAS MOVING ME...
I DON'T EVER...
...WANT TO FEEL LIKE THAT AGAIN.

Men's
MAIZON
How to Look Great In Ropes!
"Men's Maizon"
22
When Kindness Isn't Enough
The Sweetest Pain
Our Must-have List!
Where to buy away from prying eyes
Uncomplicate Your Cravings
Be a Drama King
A Flair for Bare!
Magnificent dancing on the Autumn Avenues
Special Feature
Holidays for Men
Recapture that youthful insouciance! • My Ennui Life
Fiction: My Strawberry Dumpling Happiness
Special Gift! Men's MAIZON Original Black Tights from Yuto Maizono

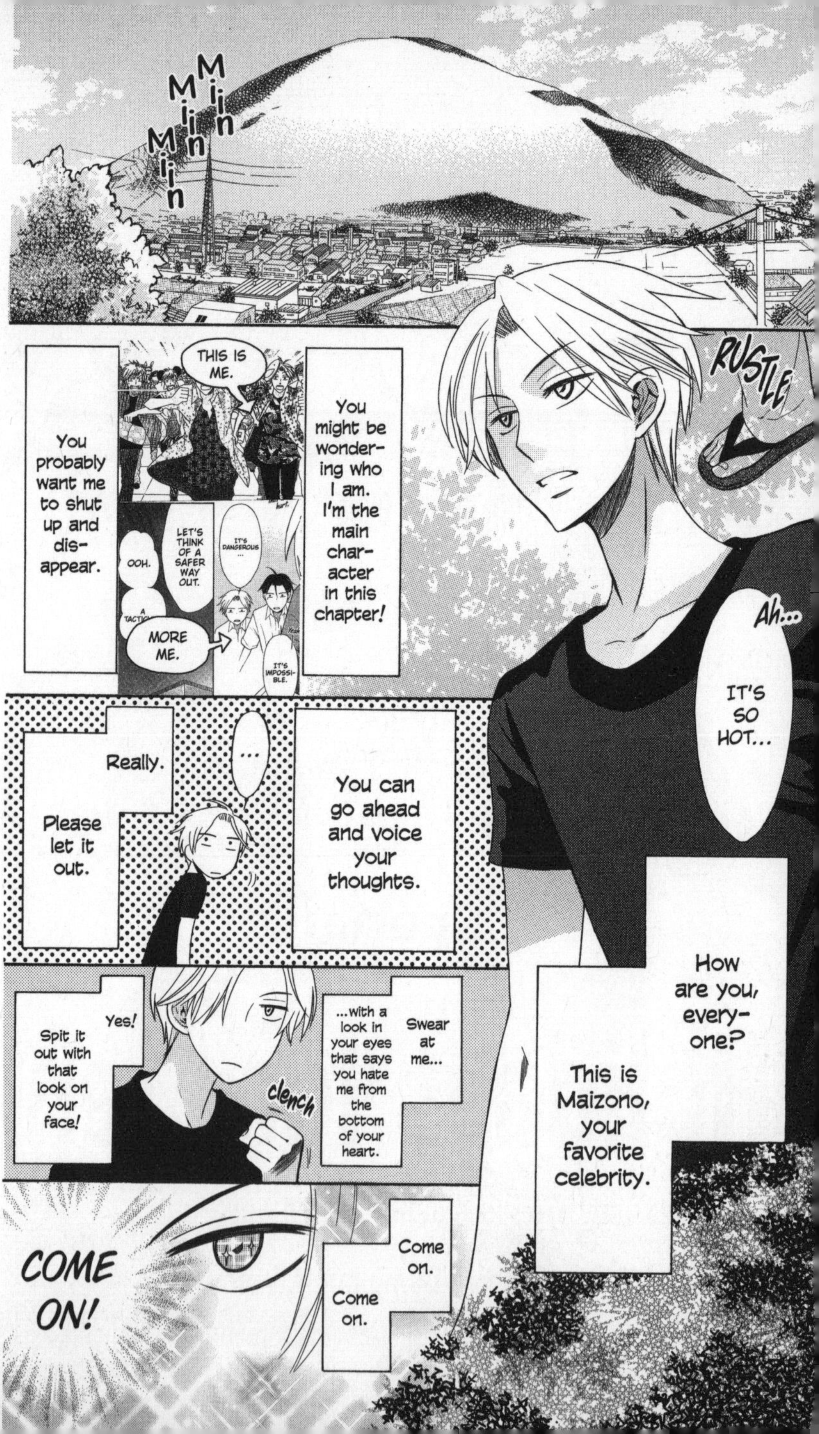
Miin Miin Miin
RUSTLE
Ah...
IT'S SO HOT...
How are you, everyone?
This is Maizono, your favorite celebrity.
You might be wondering who I am. I'm the main character in this chapter!
THIS IS ME.
IT'S DANGEROUS...
LET'S THINK OF A SAFER WAY OUT.
OOH.
IT'S IMPOSSIBLE.
MORE ME.
You probably want me to shut up and disappear.
You can go ahead and voice your thoughts.
...
Really.
Please let it out.
Swear at me...
...with a look in your eyes that says you hate me from the bottom of your heart.
clench
Yes!
Spit it out with that look on your face!
Come on.
Come on.
COME ON!

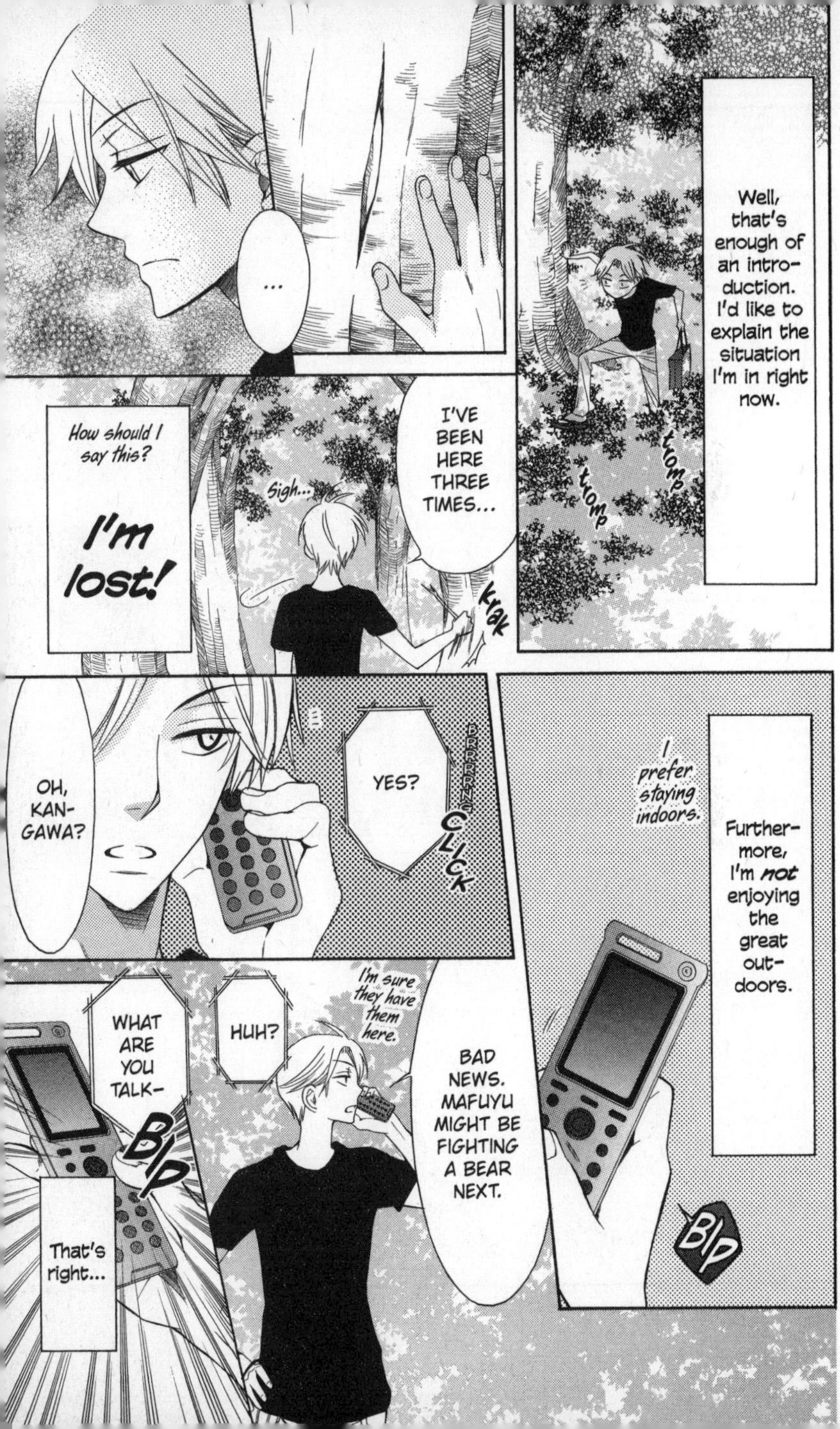

Well, that's enough of an introduction. I'd like to explain the situation I'm in right now.
tromp
tromp
...
I'VE BEEN HERE THREE TIMES...
Sigh...
krak
How should I say this?
I'm lost!
Furthermore, I'm *not* enjoying the great outdoors.
I prefer staying indoors.
BAD NEWS. MAFUYU MIGHT BE FIGHTING A BEAR NEXT.
BIP
BRRRRING
CLICK
YES?
OH, KAN-GAWA?
I'm sure they have them here.
HUH?
WHAT ARE YOU TALK-
BIP
That's right...

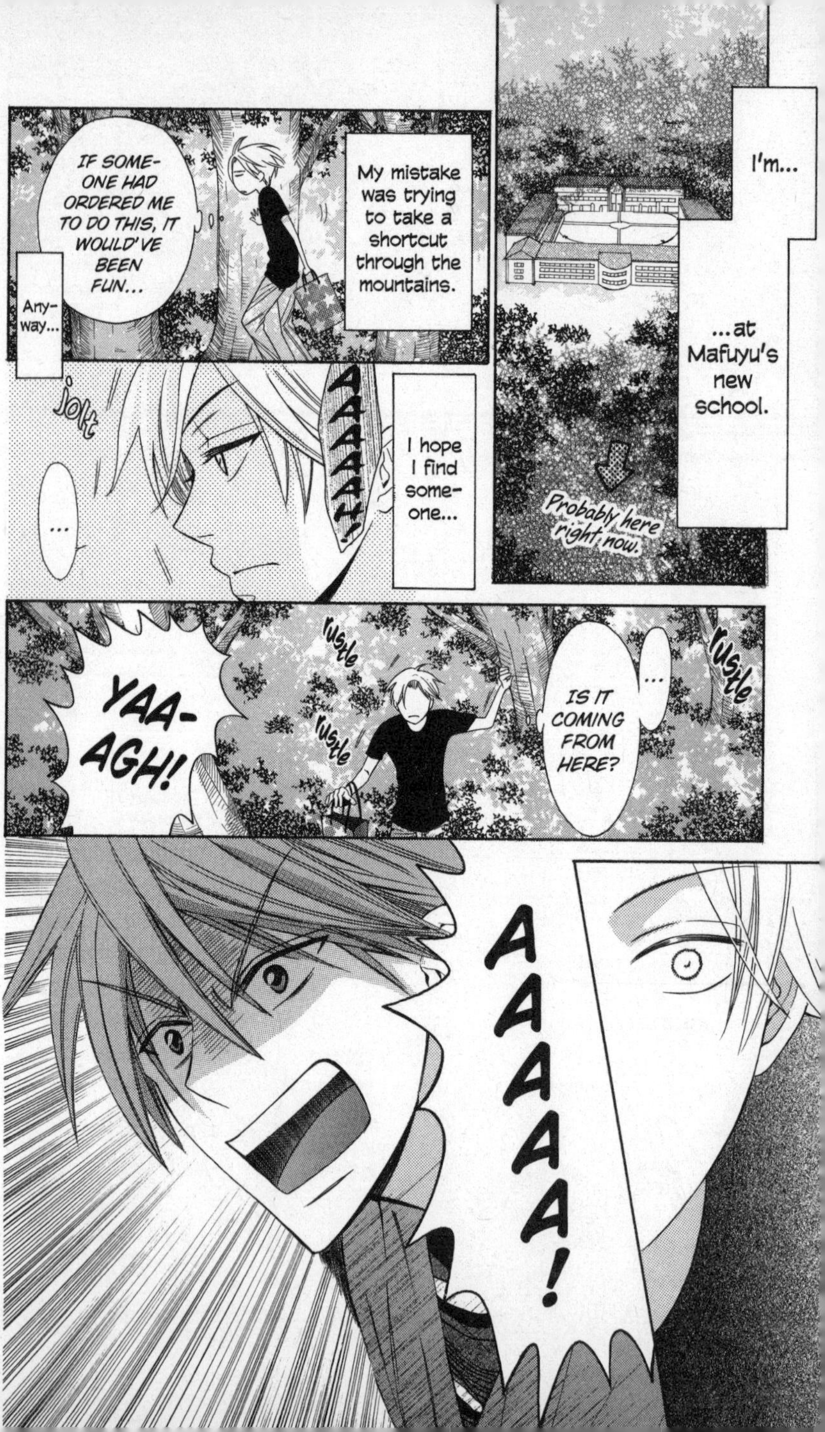
I'm...
...at Mafuyu's new school.
Probably here right now.
My mistake was trying to take a shortcut through the mountains.
IF SOME-ONE HAD ORDERED ME TO DO THIS, IT WOULD'VE BEEN FUN...
Any-way...
I hope I find some-one...
AAAAAH!
jolt
...
rustle
...
IS IT COMING FROM HERE?
rustle
rustle
YAA-AGH!
AAAAAA!

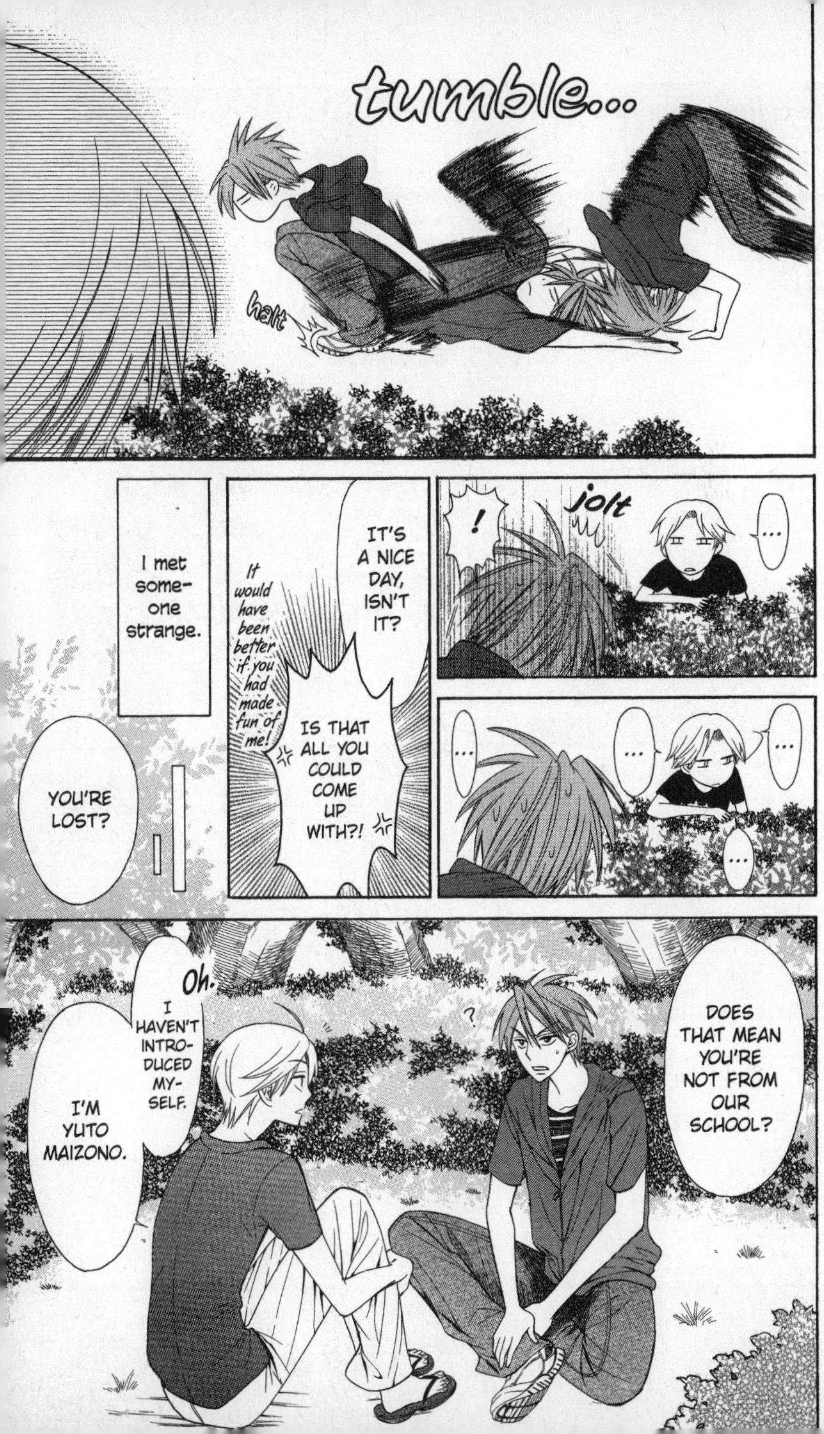
tumble...
halt
...
jolt
!
...
...
...
...
IT'S A NICE DAY, ISN'T IT?
It would have been better if you had made fun of me!
IS THAT ALL YOU COULD COME UP WITH?!
I met some-one strange.
YOU'RE LOST?
DOES THAT MEAN YOU'RE NOT FROM OUR SCHOOL?
?
Oh.
I HAVEN'T INTRO-DUCED MY-SELF.
I'M YUTO MAIZONO.

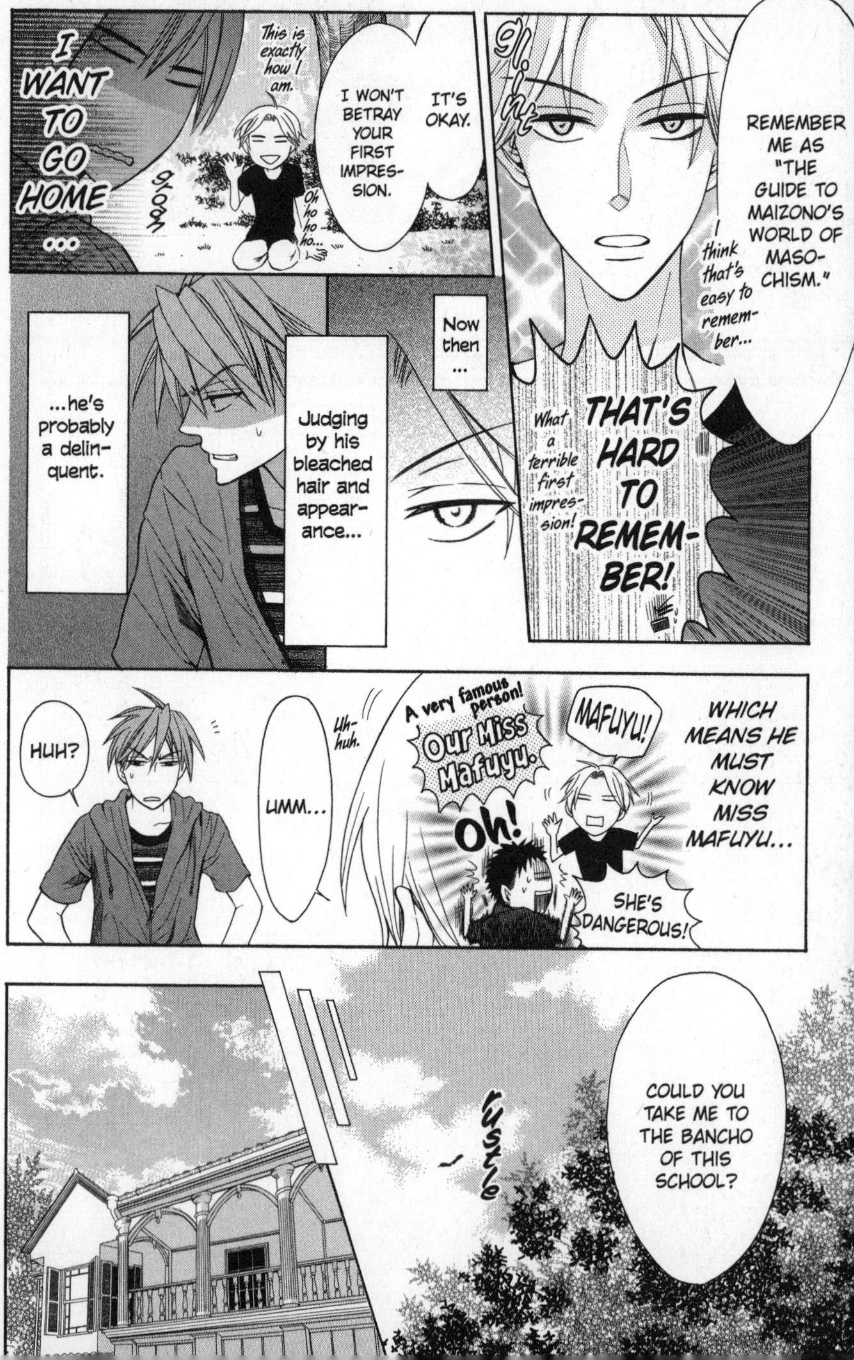
REMEMBER ME AS "THE GUIDE TO MAIZONO'S WORLD OF MASOCHISM."
glint
I think that's easy to remember...
IT'S OKAY.
I WON'T BETRAY YOUR FIRST IMPRESSION.
This is exactly how I am.
Oh ho ho ho...
groan
I WANT TO GO HOME...
THAT'S HARD TO REMEMBER!
What a terrible first impression!
Now then...
Judging by his bleached hair and appearance...
...he's probably a delinquent.
WHICH MEANS HE MUST KNOW MISS MAFUYU...
MAFUYU!
A very famous person!
Our Miss Mafuyu.
Oh!
SHE'S DANGEROUS!
Uh-huh.
UMM...
HUH?
COULD YOU TAKE ME TO THE BANCHO OF THIS SCHOOL?
rustle

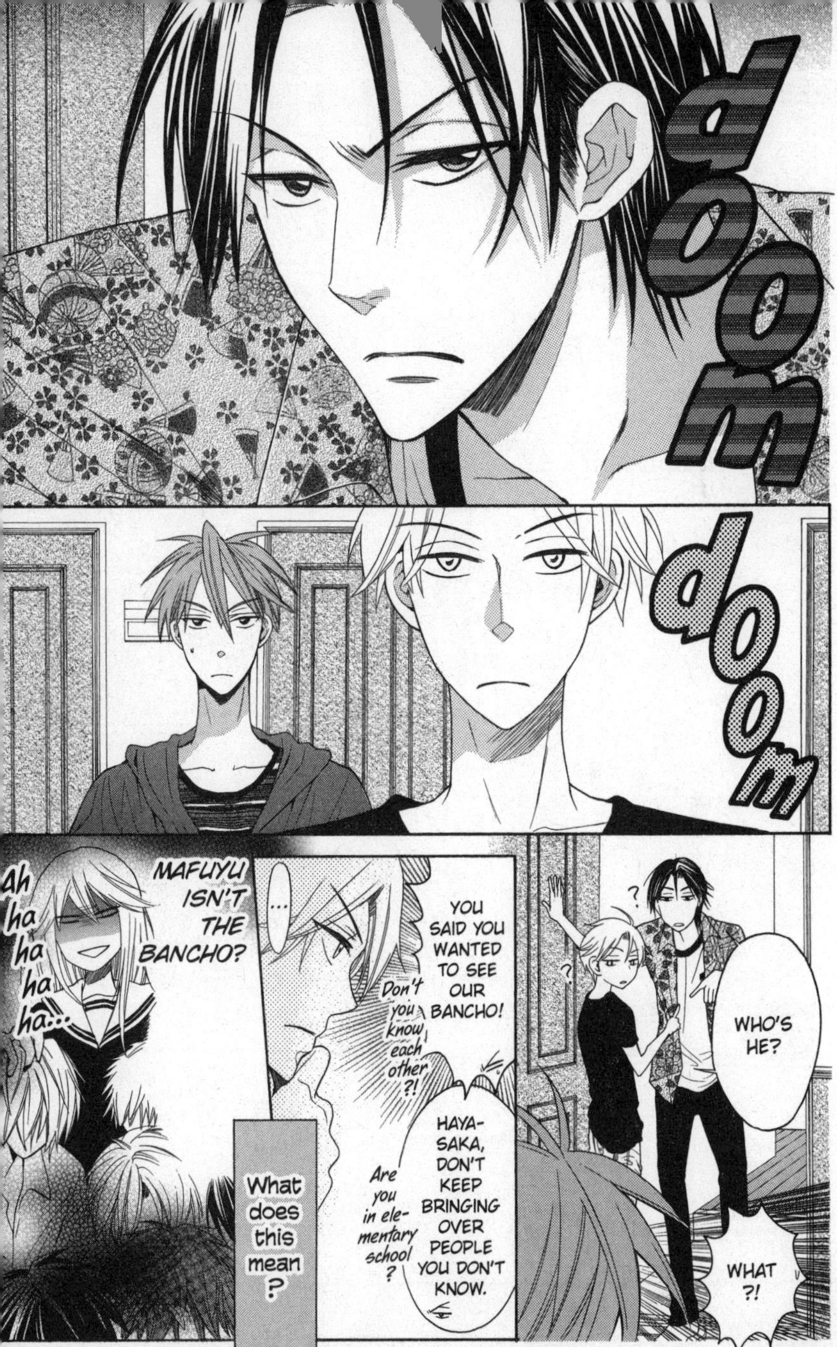
doom
dooom
WHO'S HE?
WHAT?!
YOU SAID YOU WANTED TO SEE OUR BANCHO!
Don't you know each other?!
...
HAYA-SAKA, DON'T KEEP BRINGING OVER PEOPLE YOU DON'T KNOW.
Are you in ele-mentary school?
What does this mean?
MAFUYU ISN'T THE BANCHO?
Ah ha ha ha ha...

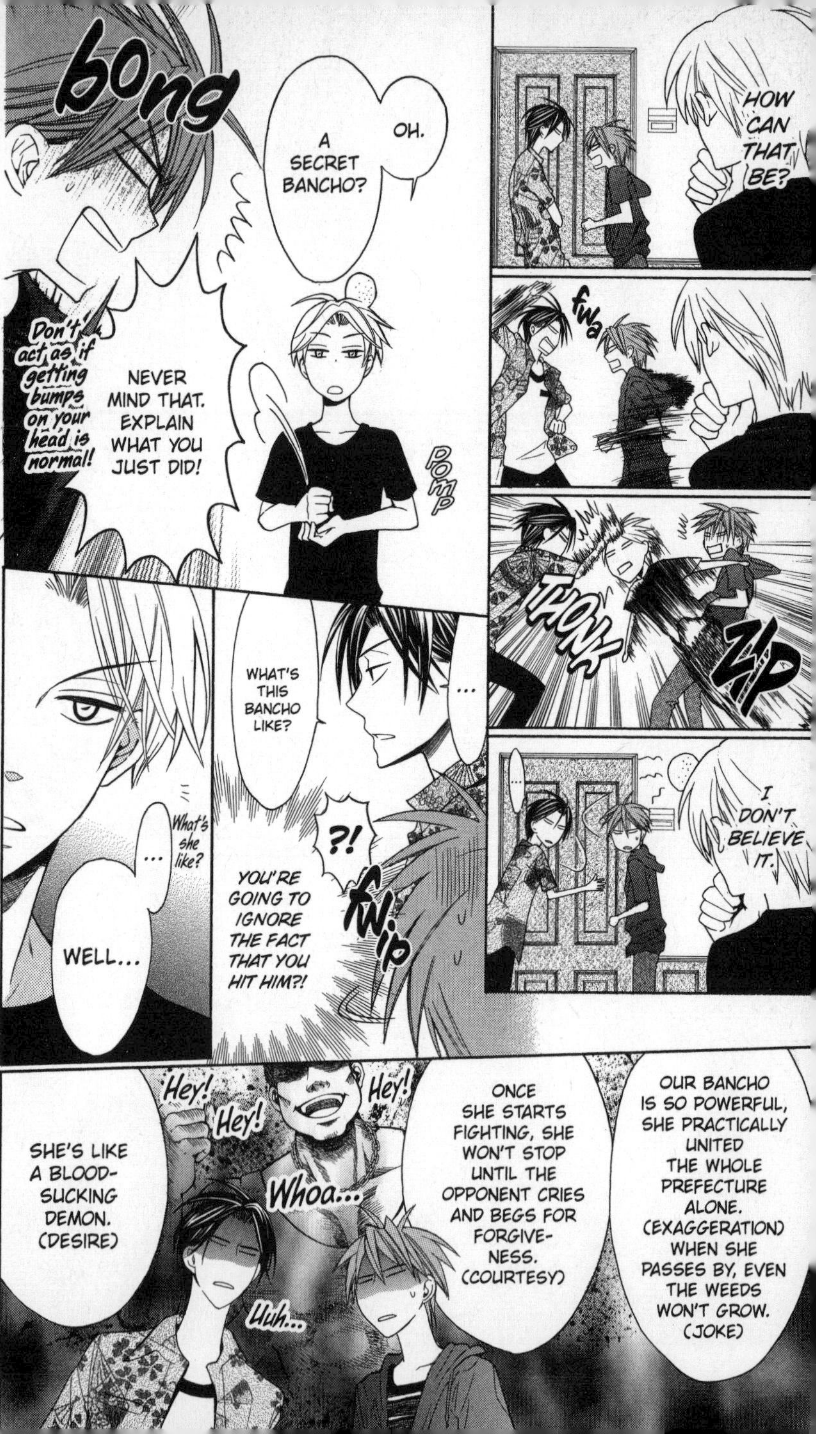
HOW CAN THAT BE?
fwa
THONK
ZIP
...
I DON'T BELIEVE IT.
OH.
A SECRET BANCHO?
bong
NEVER MIND THAT. EXPLAIN WHAT YOU JUST DID!
Don't act as if getting bumps on your head is normal!
pomp
...
WHAT'S THIS BANCHO LIKE?
?!
YOU'RE GOING TO IGNORE THE FACT THAT YOU HIT HIM?!
fwip
What's she like?
...
WELL...
OUR BANCHO IS SO POWERFUL, SHE PRACTICALLY UNITED THE WHOLE PREFECTURE ALONE. (EXAGGERATION) WHEN SHE PASSES BY, EVEN THE WEEDS WON'T GROW. (JOKE)
ONCE SHE STARTS FIGHTING, SHE WON'T STOP UNTIL THE OPPONENT CRIES AND BEGS FOR FORGIVE-NESS. (COURTESY)
Hey!
Hey!
Hey!
Whoa...
SHE'S LIKE A BLOOD-SUCKING DEMON. (DESIRE)
Uuh...

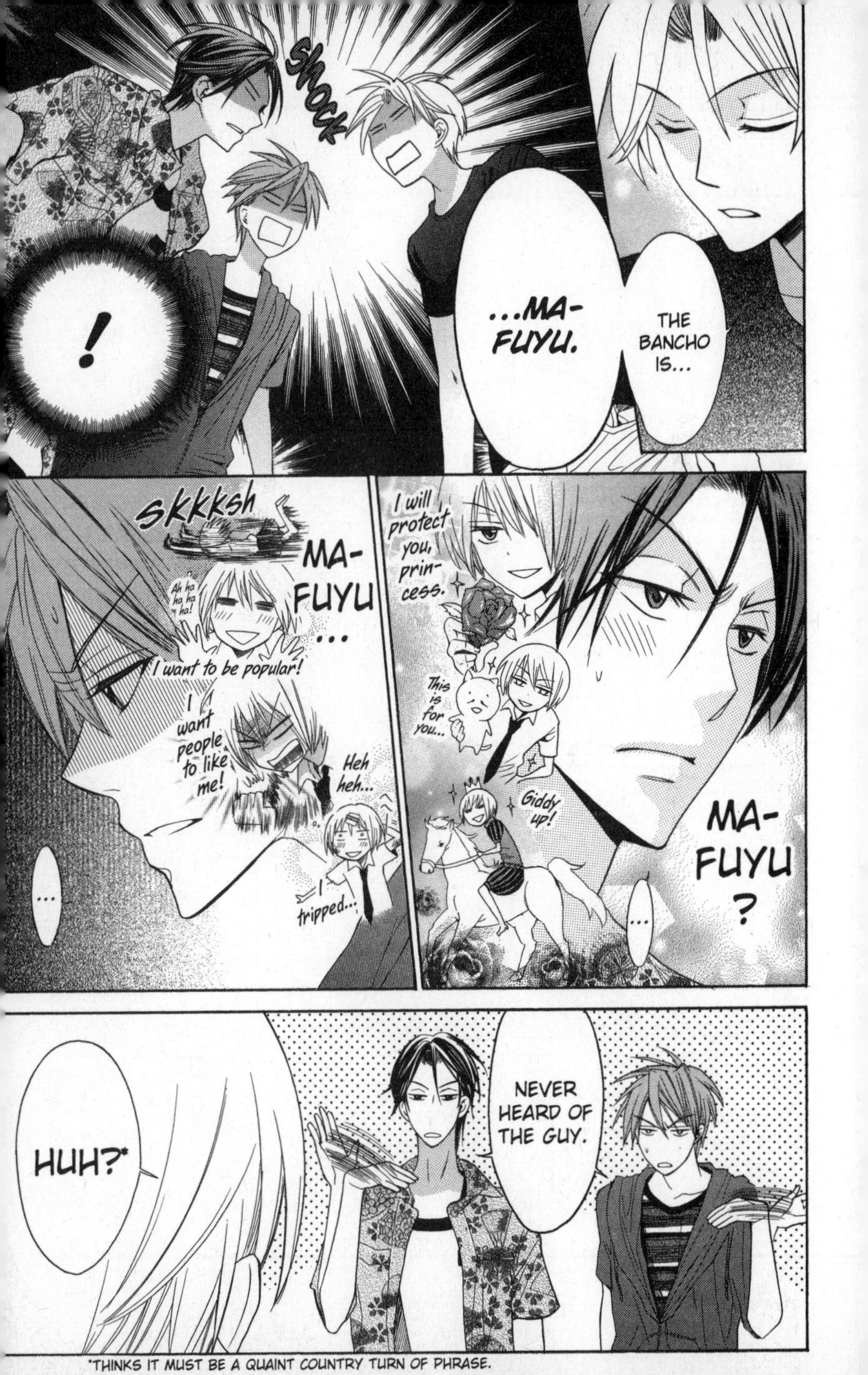
THE BANCHO IS...
...MA-FUYU.
SHOCK
!
MA-FUYU?
...
I will protect you, princess.
This is for you...
Giddy up!
SKKKSH
MA-FUYU...
Ah ha ha ha ha!
I want to be popular!
I want people to like me!
Heh heh...
I tripped...
...
NEVER HEARD OF THE GUY.
HUH?*

*THINKS IT MUST BE A QUAINT COUNTRY TURN OF PHRASE.

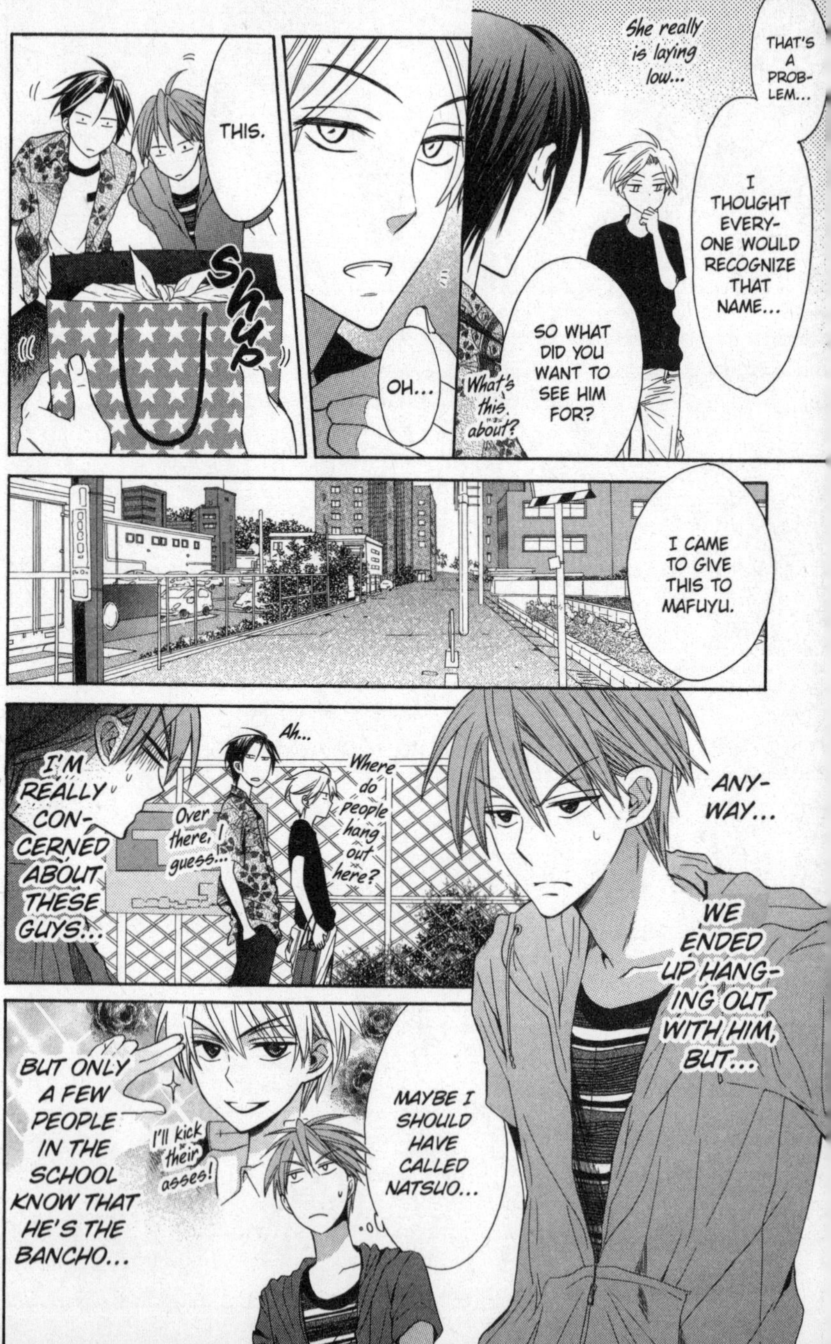
THAT'S A PROBLEM...
She really is laying low...
I THOUGHT EVERYONE WOULD RECOGNIZE THAT NAME...
SO WHAT DID YOU WANT TO SEE HIM FOR?
What's this about?
OH...
THIS.
SHUP
I CAME TO GIVE THIS TO MAFUYU.
ANYWAY...
WE ENDED UP HANGING OUT WITH HIM, BUT...
Ah...
Where do people hang out here?
Over there, I guess...
I'M REALLY CONCERNED ABOUT THESE GUYS...
MAYBE I SHOULD HAVE CALLED NATSUO...
BUT ONLY A FEW PEOPLE IN THE SCHOOL KNOW THAT HE'S THE BANCHO...
I'll kick their asses!

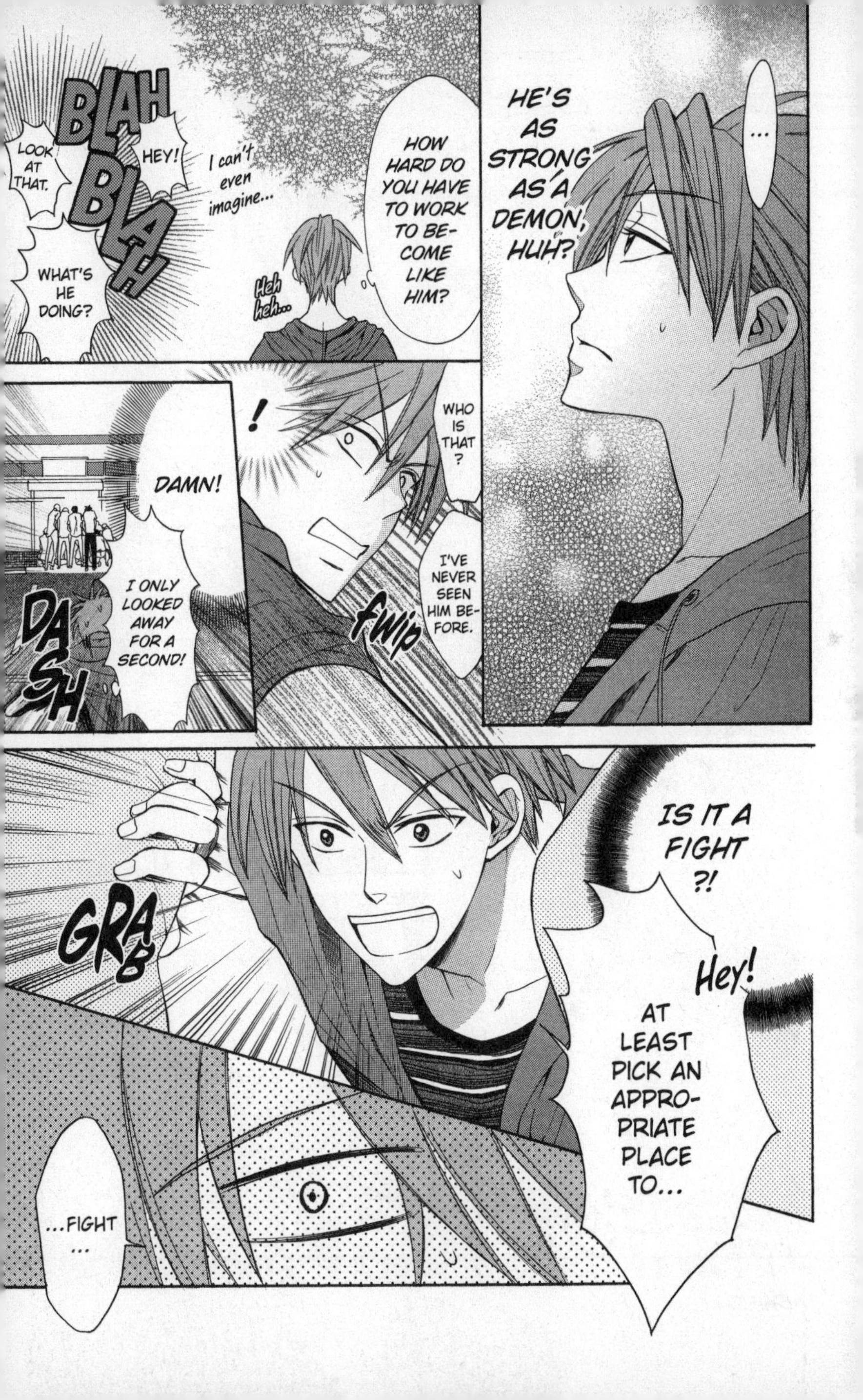
...
HE'S AS STRONG AS A DEMON, HUH?
HOW HARD DO YOU HAVE TO WORK TO BE-COME LIKE HIM?
I can't even imagine...
Heh heh...
HEY!
BLAH BLAH
LOOK AT THAT.
WHAT'S HE DOING?
!
WHO IS THAT?
I'VE NEVER SEEN HIM BE-FORE.
fwip
DAMN!
I ONLY LOOKED AWAY FOR A SECOND!
DASH
IS IT A FIGHT?!
Hey!
AT LEAST PICK AN APPRO-PRIATE PLACE TO...
GRAB
...FIGHT...

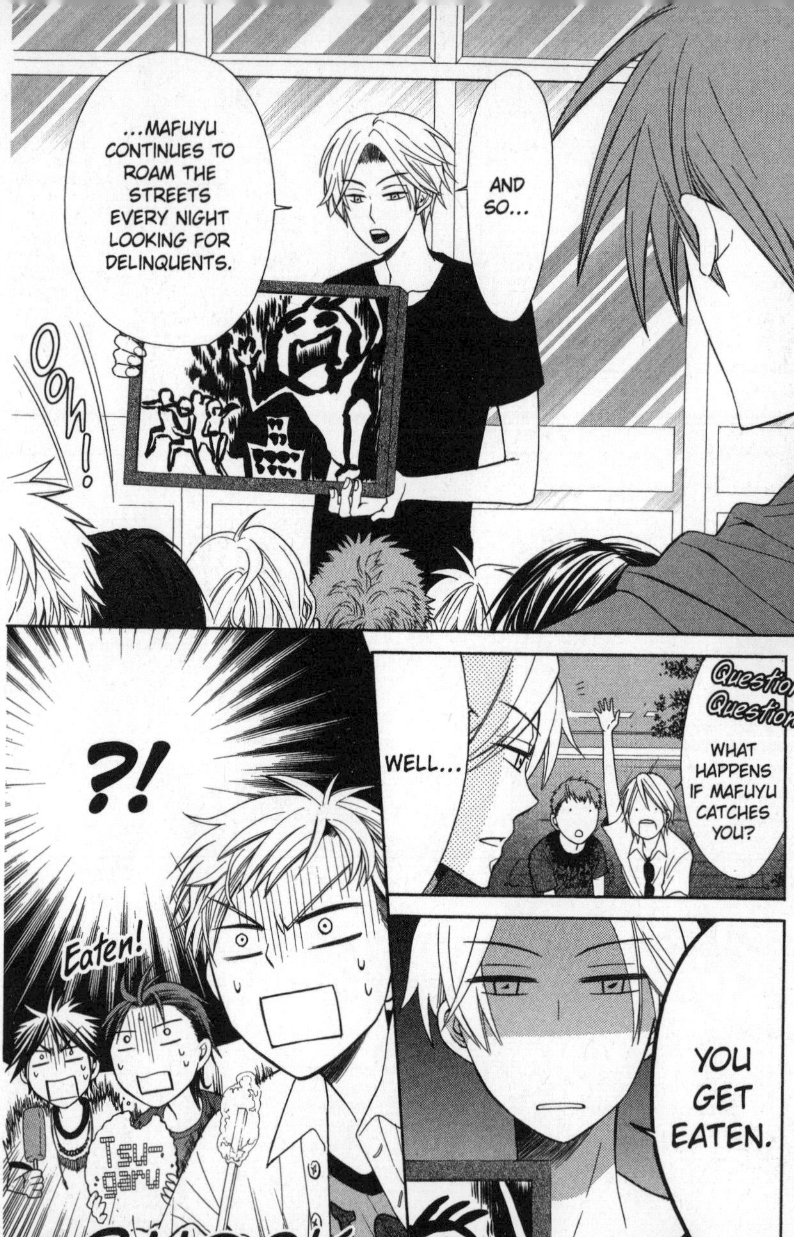

AND SO...
...MAFUYU CONTINUES TO ROAM THE STREETS EVERY NIGHT LOOKING FOR DELINQUENTS.
OOM!
Question! Question!
WHAT HAPPENS IF MAFUYU CATCHES YOU?
WELL...
YOU GET EATEN.
?!
Eaten!
Tsu-garu
SHOCK

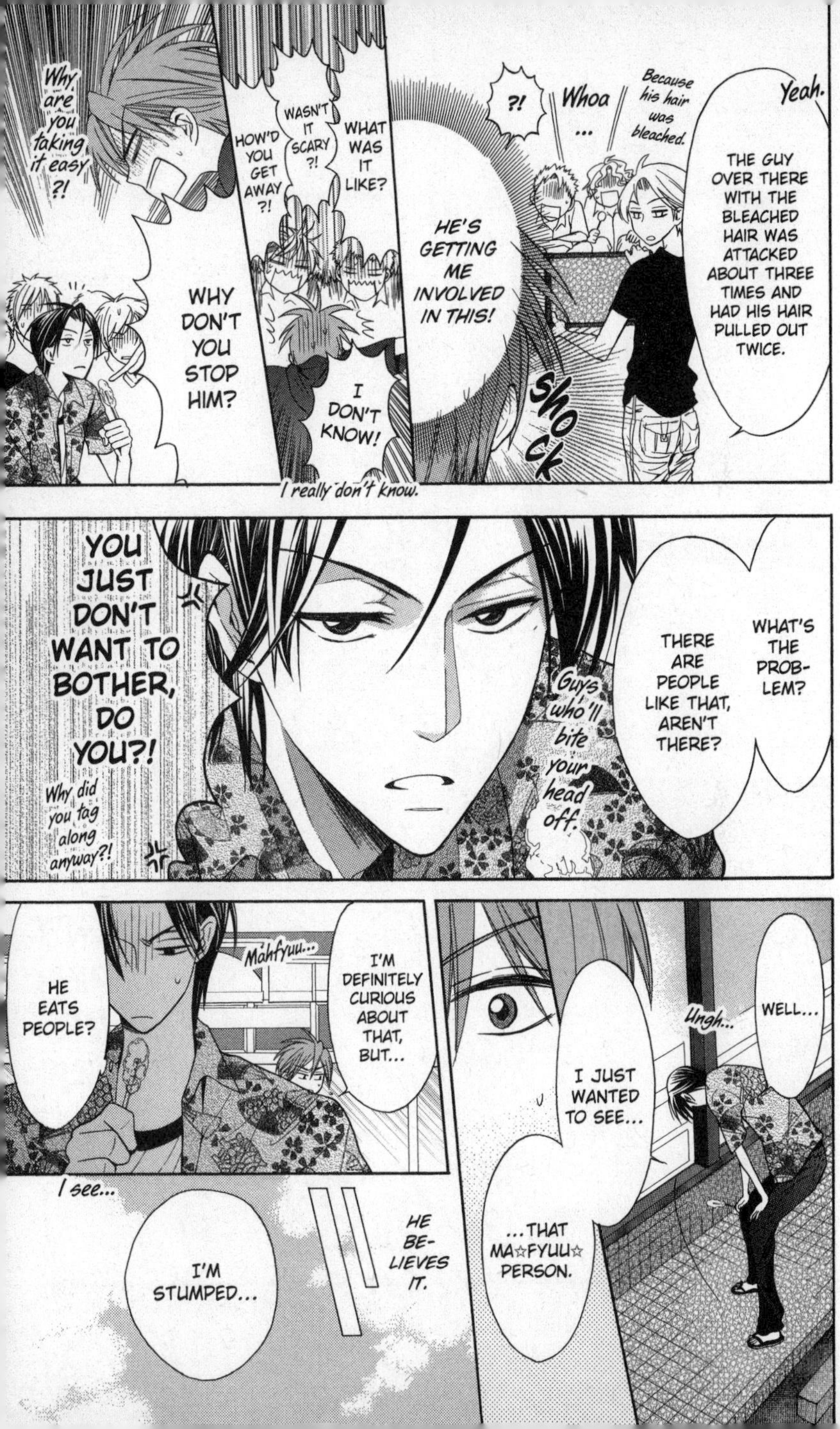
Yeah.
THE GUY OVER THERE WITH THE BLEACHED HAIR WAS ATTACKED ABOUT THREE TIMES AND HAD HIS HAIR PULLED OUT TWICE.
Because his hair was bleached.
Whoa...
?!
HE'S GETTING ME INVOLVED IN THIS!
SHOCK
WHAT WAS IT LIKE?
WASN'T IT SCARY?!
HOW'D YOU GET AWAY?!
I DON'T KNOW!
I really don't know.
Why are you taking it easy?!
WHY DON'T YOU STOP HIM?
WHAT'S THE PROB-LEM?
THERE ARE PEOPLE LIKE THAT, AREN'T THERE?
Guys who'll bite your head off.
YOU JUST DON'T WANT TO BOTHER, DO YOU?!
Why did you tag along anyway?!
WELL...
Ungh...
I JUST WANTED TO SEE...
...THAT MA☆FYUU☆ PERSON.
I'M DEFINITELY CURIOUS ABOUT THAT, BUT...
Mahfyuu...
HE EATS PEOPLE?
HE BE-LIEVES IT.
I'M STUMPED...
I see...

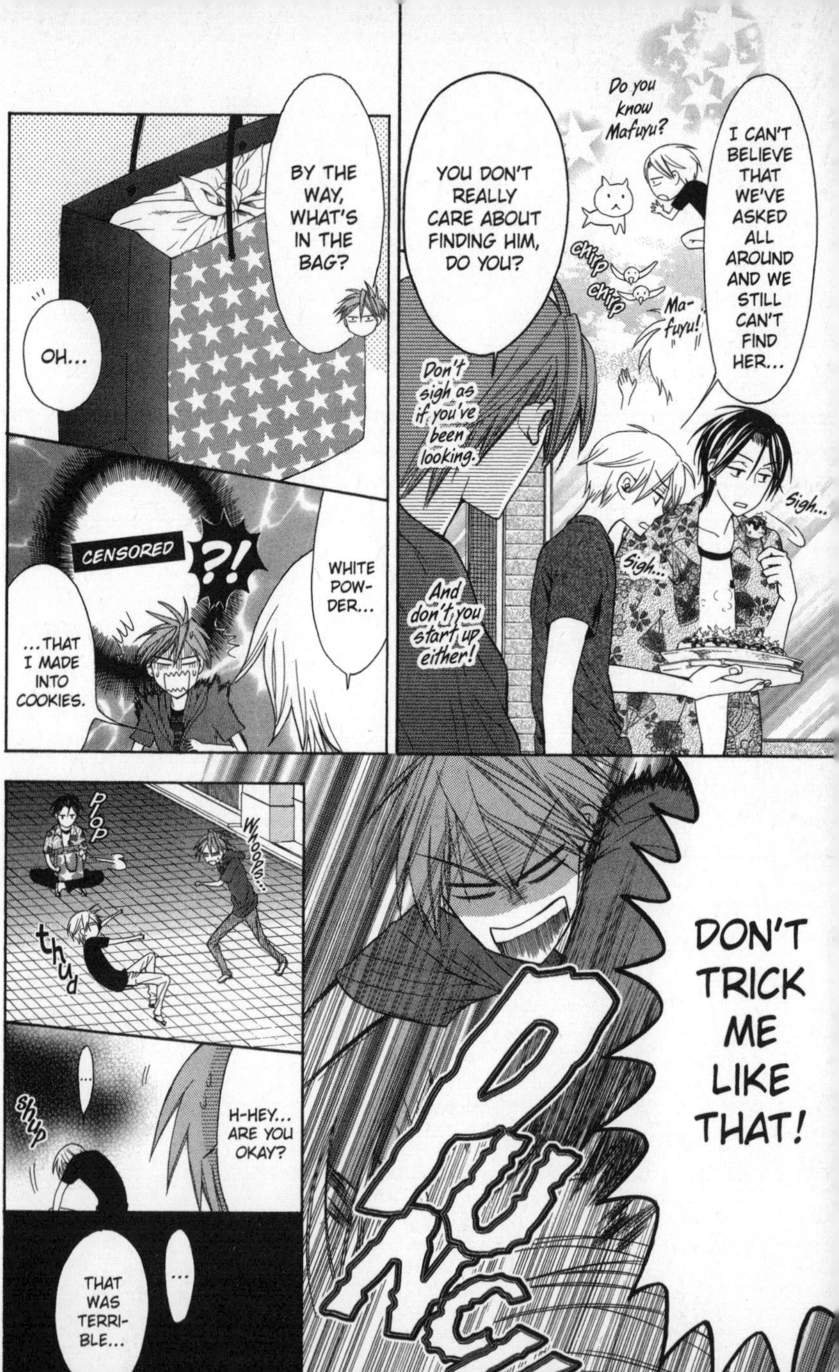
Do you know Mafuyu?
I CAN'T BELIEVE THAT WE'VE ASKED ALL AROUND AND WE STILL CAN'T FIND HER...
chirp chirp
Ma-fuyu!
YOU DON'T REALLY CARE ABOUT FINDING HIM, DO YOU?
Sigh...
Sigh...
Don't sigh as if you've been looking.
And don't you start up either!
BY THE WAY, WHAT'S IN THE BAG?
OH...
WHITE POW-DER...
CENSORED
?!
...THAT I MADE INTO COOKIES.
DON'T TRICK ME LIKE THAT!
PUNCH!
PLOP
Whoops...
thud
...
shup
H-HEY... ARE YOU OKAY?
...
THAT WAS TERRI-BLE...

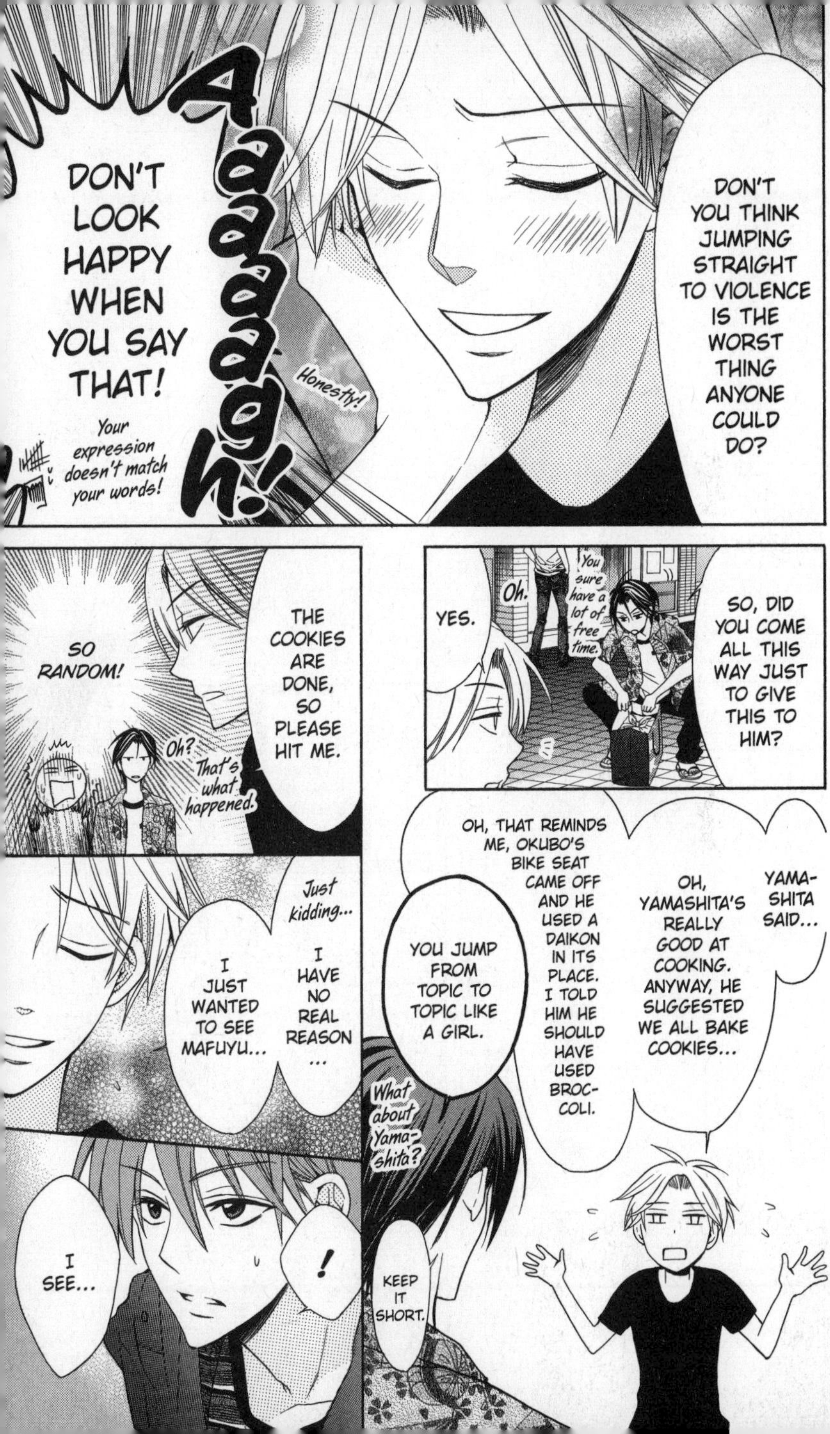
DON'T YOU THINK JUMPING STRAIGHT TO VIOLENCE IS THE WORST THING ANYONE COULD DO?
Honestly!
Aaaaaagh!
DON'T LOOK HAPPY WHEN YOU SAY THAT!
Your expression doesn't match your words!
SO, DID YOU COME ALL THIS WAY JUST TO GIVE THIS TO HIM?
You sure have a lot of free time.
Oh.
YES.
THE COOKIES ARE DONE, SO PLEASE HIT ME.
SO RANDOM!
Oh?
That's what happened.
YAMASHITA SAID...
OH, YAMASHITA'S REALLY GOOD AT COOKING. ANYWAY, HE SUGGESTED WE ALL BAKE COOKIES...
OH, THAT REMINDS ME, OKUBO'S BIKE SEAT CAME OFF AND HE USED A DAIKON IN ITS PLACE. I TOLD HIM HE SHOULD HAVE USED BROCCOLI.
YOU JUMP FROM TOPIC TO TOPIC LIKE A GIRL.
What about Yamashita?
KEEP IT SHORT.
Just kidding...
I HAVE NO REAL REASON...
I JUST WANTED TO SEE MAFUYU...
!
I SEE...

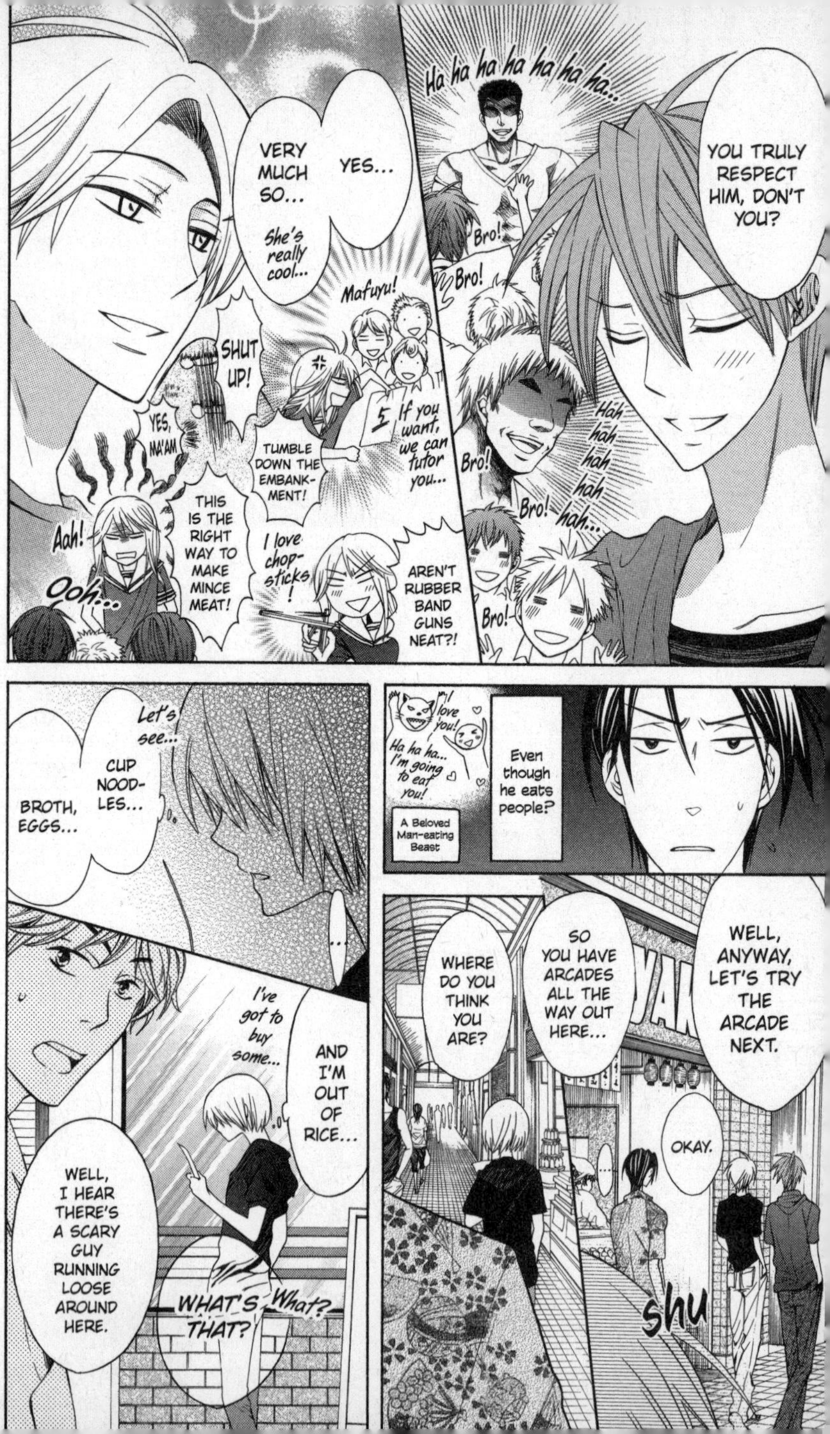
YOU TRULY RESPECT HIM, DON'T YOU?
Ha ha ha ha ha ha ha...
Bro!
Bro!
Hah hah hah hah hah...
Bro!
Bro!
Bro!
YES...
VERY MUCH SO...
She's really cool...
Mafuyu!
SHUT UP!
If you want, we can tutor you...
5
YES, MA'AM
TUMBLE DOWN THE EMBANKMENT!
THIS IS THE RIGHT WAY TO MAKE MINCE MEAT!
Aah!
Ooh...
I love chopsticks!
AREN'T RUBBER BAND GUNS NEAT?!
Even though he eats people?
I love you!
Ha ha ha... I'm going to eat you!
A Beloved Man-eating Beast
Let's see...
CUP NOODLES...
BROTH, EGGS...
WELL, ANYWAY, LET'S TRY THE ARCADE NEXT.
OKAY.
SO YOU HAVE ARCADES ALL THE WAY OUT HERE...
WHERE DO YOU THINK YOU ARE?
...
Shu
...
AND I'M OUT OF RICE...
I've got to buy some...
WELL, I HEAR THERE'S A SCARY GUY RUNNING LOOSE AROUND HERE.
What?
WHAT'S THAT?

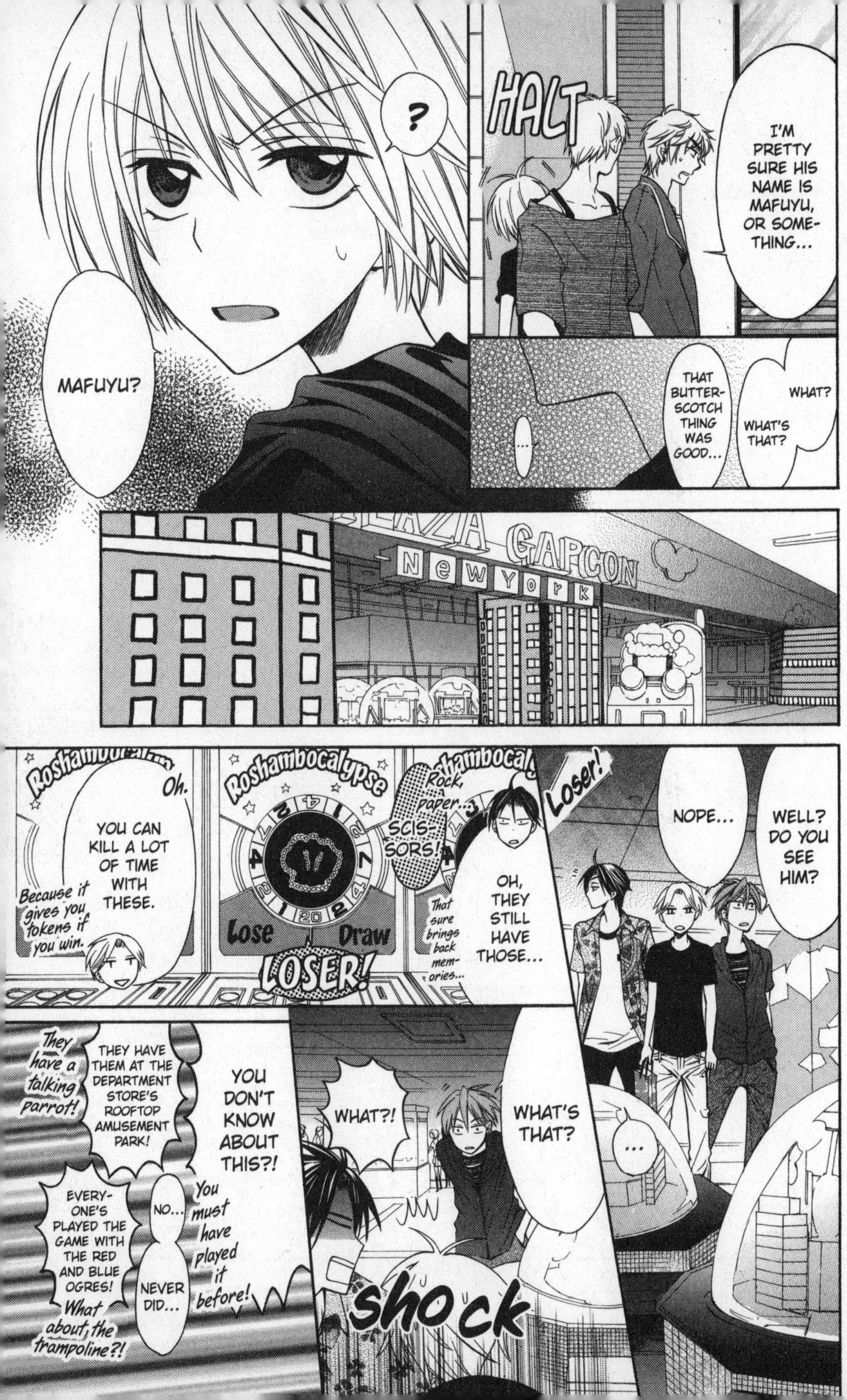
HALT
I'M PRETTY SURE HIS NAME IS MAFUYU, OR SOMETHING...
WHAT?
WHAT'S THAT?
THAT BUTTERSCOTCH THING WAS GOOD...
...
?
MAFUYU?
GAPCON
New York
WELL? DO YOU SEE HIM?
NOPE...
Loser!
Roshambocalypse
Rock, paper...
SCISSORS!
OH, THEY STILL HAVE THOSE...
That sure brings back memories...
Lose
Draw
Oh.
YOU CAN KILL A LOT OF TIME WITH THESE.
Because it gives you tokens if you win.
LOSER!
WHAT'S THAT?
...
WHAT?!
YOU DON'T KNOW ABOUT THIS?!
THEY HAVE THEM AT THE DEPARTMENT STORE'S ROOFTOP AMUSEMENT PARK!
They have a talking parrot!
You must have played it before!
NO...
NEVER DID...
EVERYONE'S PLAYED THE GAME WITH THE RED AND BLUE OGRES!
What about the trampoline?!
shock

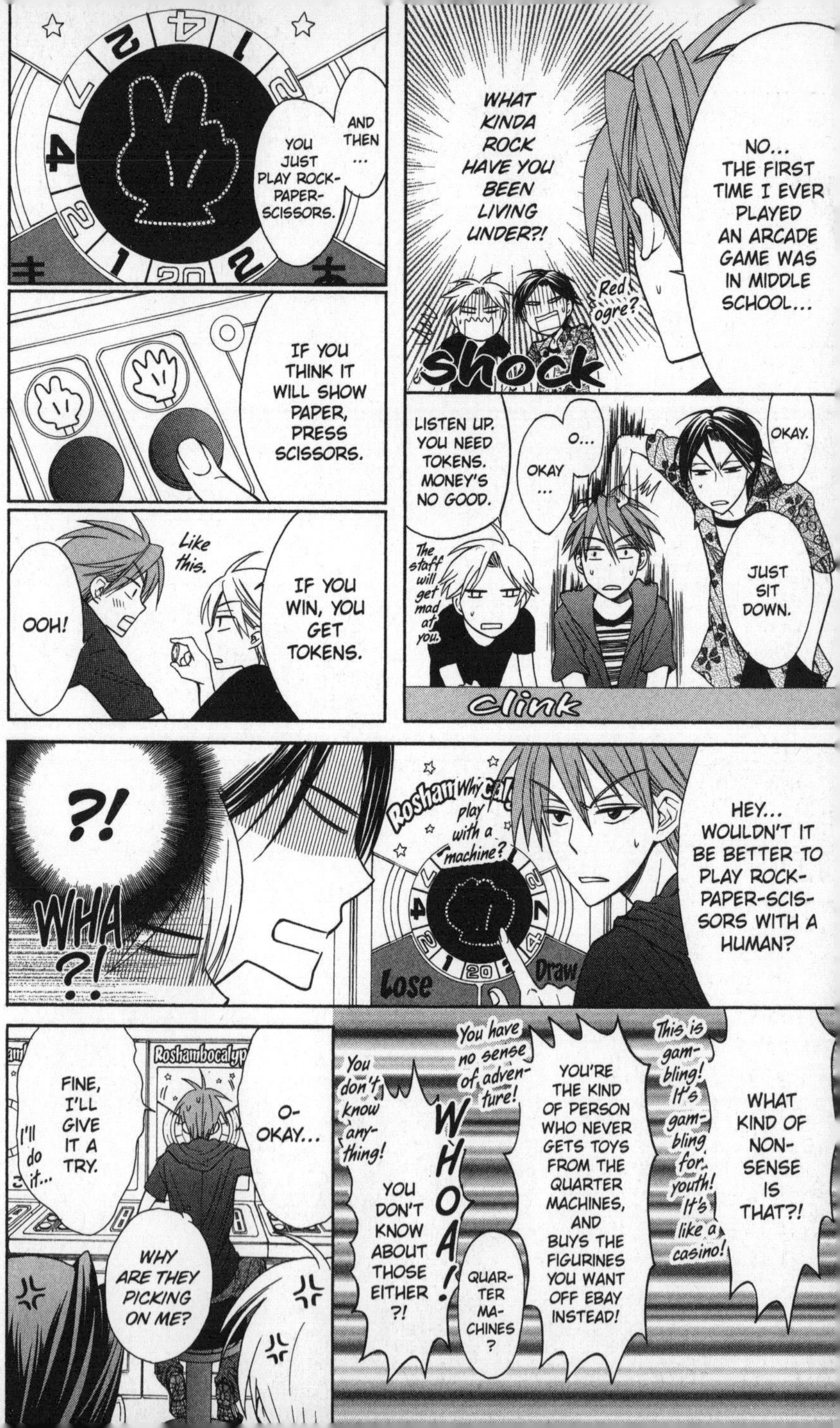
NO... THE FIRST TIME I EVER PLAYED AN ARCADE GAME WAS IN MIDDLE SCHOOL...
WHAT KINDA ROCK HAVE YOU BEEN LIVING UNDER?!
Red ogre?
shock
OKAY.
O... OKAY...
LISTEN UP. YOU NEED TOKENS. MONEY'S NO GOOD.
JUST SIT DOWN.
The staff will get mad at you.
clink
AND THEN...
YOU JUST PLAY ROCK-PAPER-SCISSORS.
IF YOU THINK IT WILL SHOW PAPER, PRESS SCISSORS.
IF YOU WIN, YOU GET TOKENS.
Like this.
OOH!
HEY... WOULDN'T IT BE BETTER TO PLAY ROCK-PAPER-SCISSORS WITH A HUMAN?
Why play with a machine?
Rosham
Draw
Lose
?!
WHA ?!
WHAT KIND OF NON-SENSE IS THAT?!
This is gambling! It's gambling for youth! It's like a casino!
YOU'RE THE KIND OF PERSON WHO NEVER GETS TOYS FROM THE QUARTER MACHINES, AND BUYS THE FIGURINES YOU WANT OFF EBAY INSTEAD!
You have no sense of adventure!
QUARTER MACHINES?
WHOA!
YOU DON'T KNOW ABOUT THOSE EITHER?!
You don't know anything!
O-OKAY...
Roshambocalyp
FINE, I'LL GIVE IT A TRY.
I'll do it...
WHY ARE THEY PICKING ON ME?

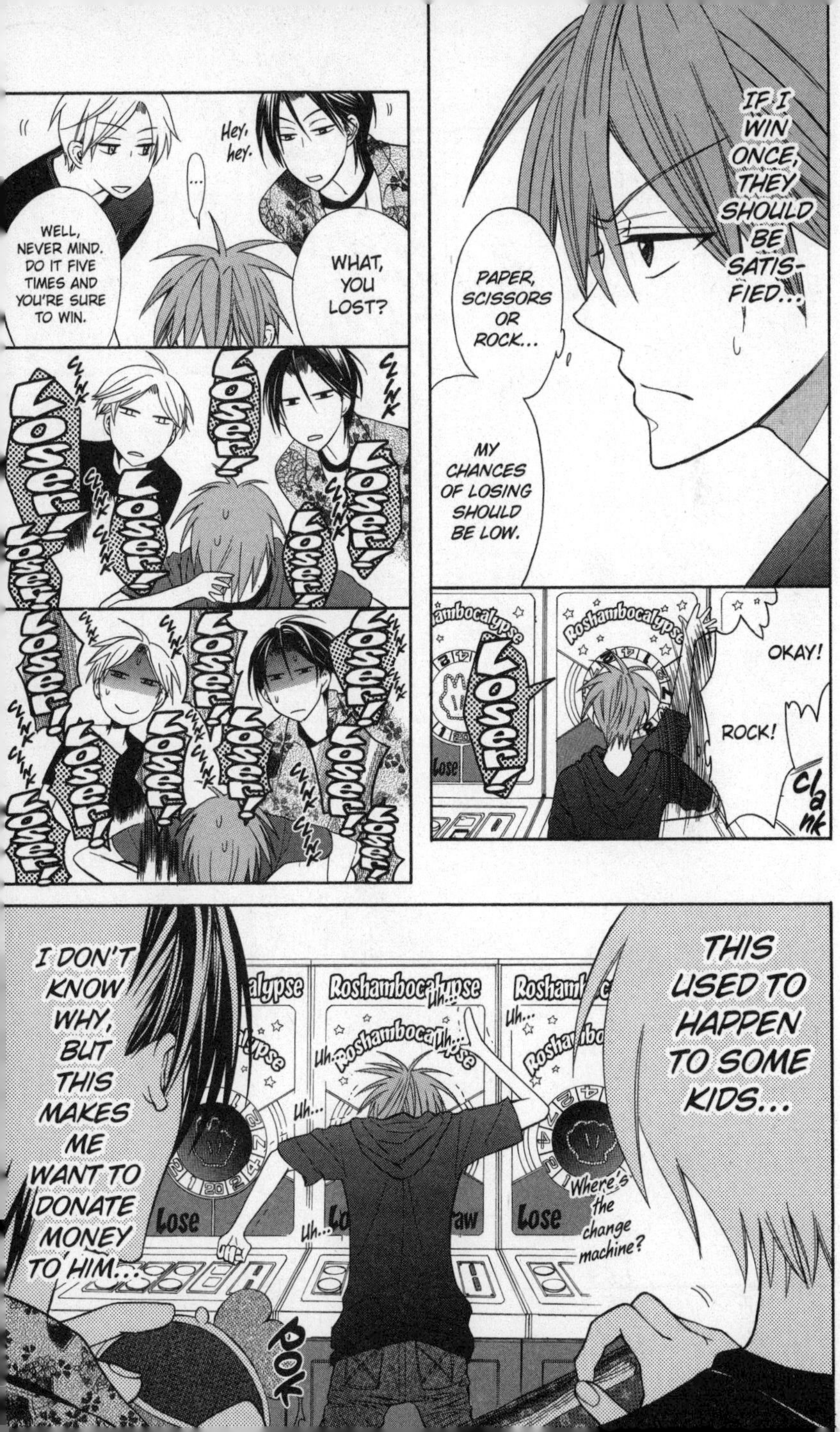
IF I WIN ONCE, THEY SHOULD BE SATIS-FIED...
PAPER, SCISSORS OR ROCK...
MY CHANCES OF LOSING SHOULD BE LOW.
OKAY!
ROCK!
Clank
Roshambocalypse
Loser!
Hey, hey.
WHAT, YOU LOST?
...
WELL, NEVER MIND. DO IT FIVE TIMES AND YOU'RE SURE TO WIN.
CLINK
Loser!
Loser!
Loser!
Loser!
THIS USED TO HAPPEN TO SOME KIDS...
Where's the change machine?
Roshambocalypse
Uh...
Uh...
Lose
I DON'T KNOW WHY, BUT THIS MAKES ME WANT TO DONATE MONEY TO HIM...
POK

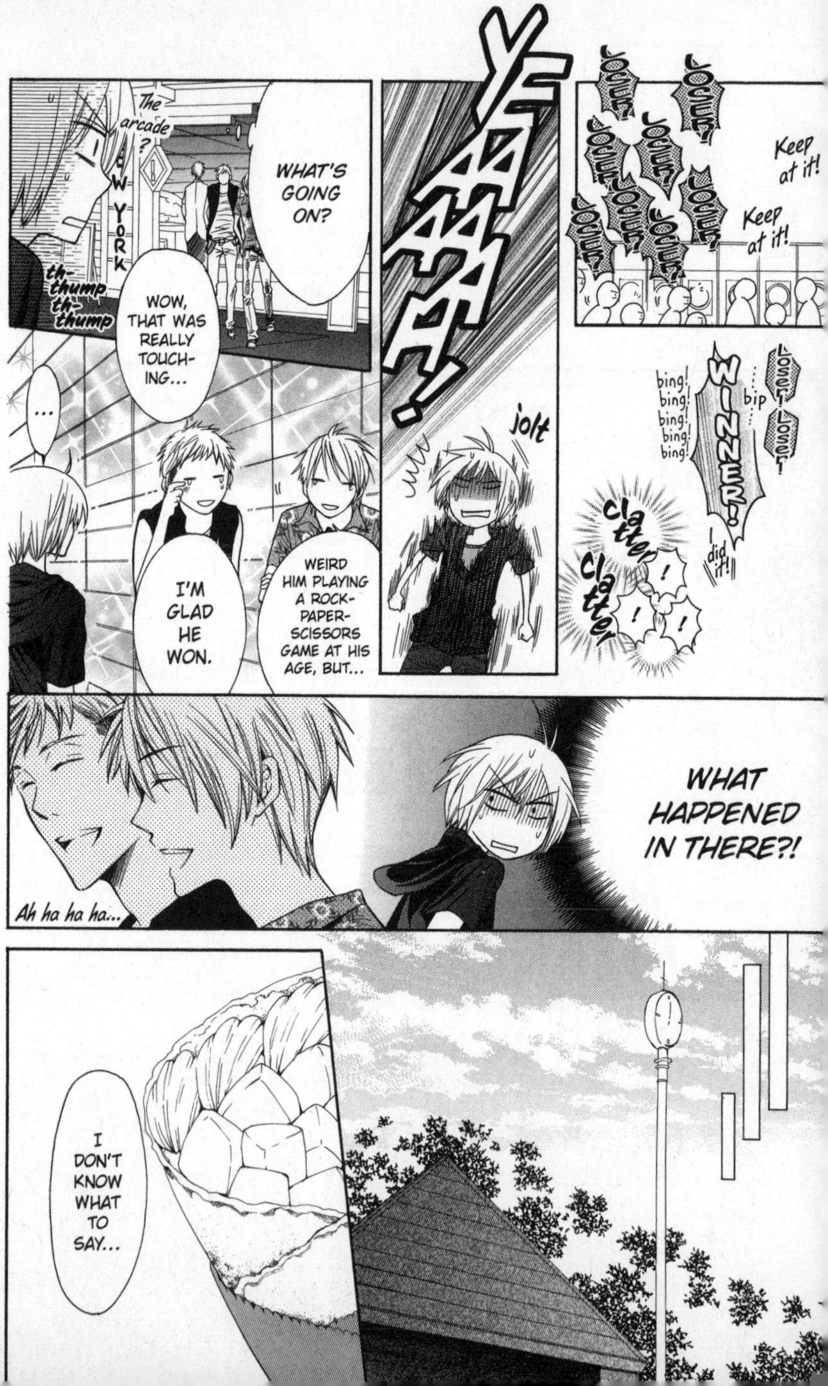
LOSER!
LOSER!
LOSER!
LOSER!
LOSER!
LOSER!
LOSER!
LOSER!
Keep at it!
Keep at it!
Loser! Loser!
bip
WINNER!
bing! bing! bing! bing! bing!
I did it!
Clatter
Clatter
!
!
!
YEAAAAAH!
jolt
WHAT'S GOING ON?
The arcade?
NEW YORK
th-thump th-thump
WOW, THAT WAS REALLY TOUCHING...
...
WEIRD HIM PLAYING A ROCK-PAPER-SCISSORS GAME AT HIS AGE, BUT...
I'M GLAD HE WON.
WHAT HAPPENED IN THERE?!
Ah ha ha ha...
I DON'T KNOW WHAT TO SAY...

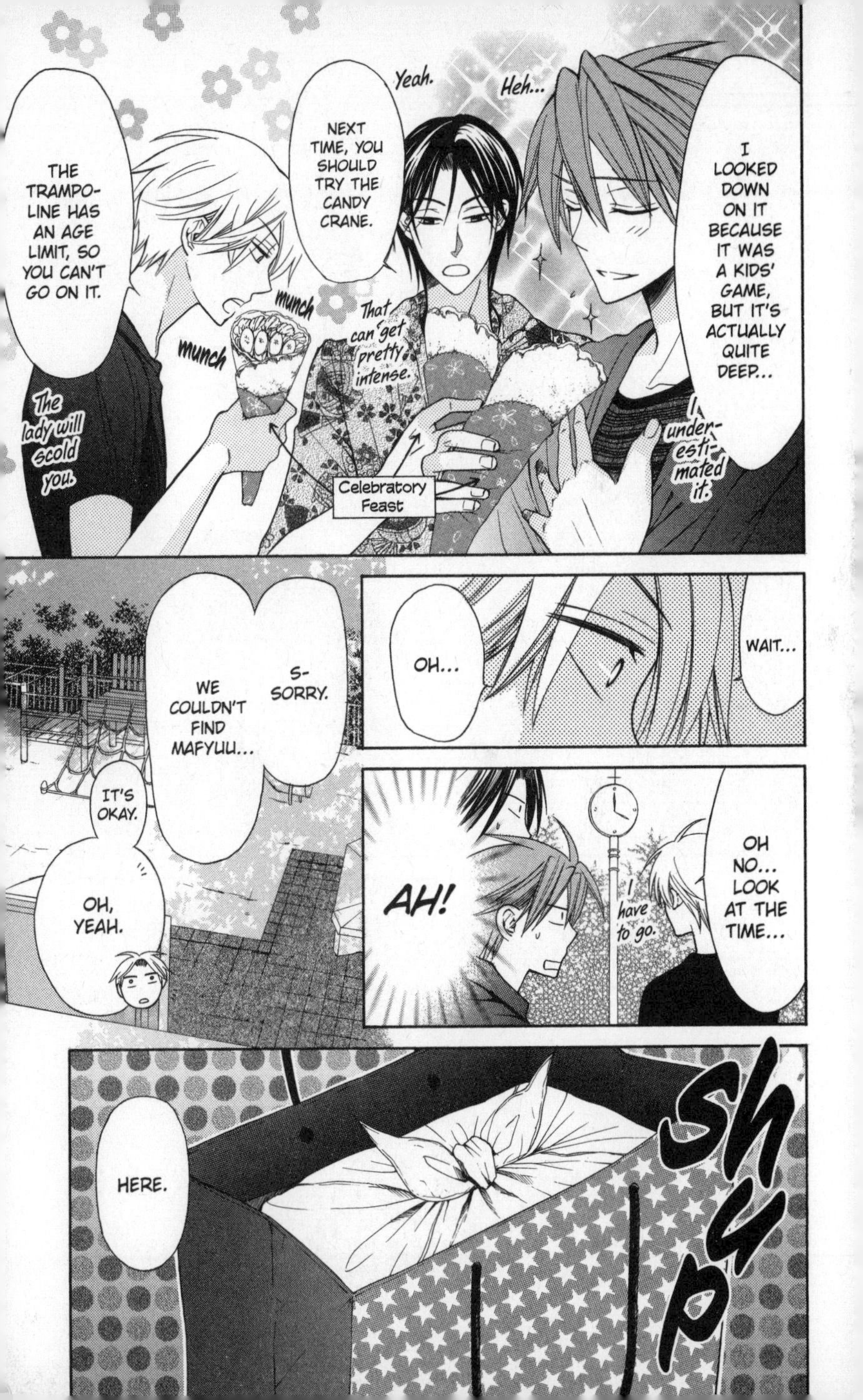
Heh...
I LOOKED DOWN ON IT BECAUSE IT WAS A KIDS' GAME, BUT IT'S ACTUALLY QUITE DEEP...
I underestimated it.
Yeah.
NEXT TIME, YOU SHOULD TRY THE CANDY CRANE.
That can get pretty intense.
Celebratory Feast
munch
munch
THE TRAMPOLINE HAS AN AGE LIMIT, SO YOU CAN'T GO ON IT.
The lady will scold you.
WAIT...
OH...
OH NO... LOOK AT THE TIME...
I have to go.
AH!
S-SORRY.
WE COULDN'T FIND MAFYUU...
IT'S OKAY.
OH, YEAH.
SHUP
HERE.

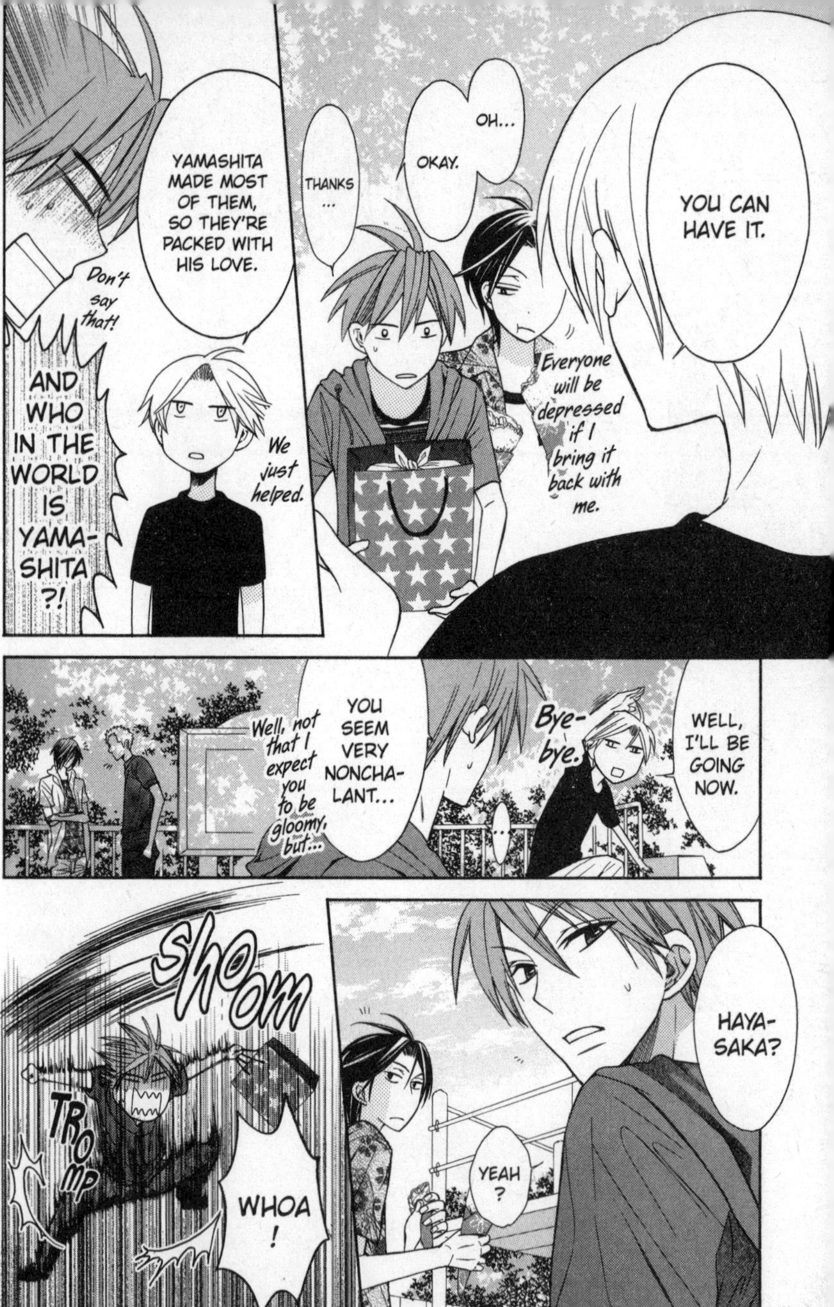
YOU CAN HAVE IT.
Everyone will be depressed if I bring it back with me.
OH... OKAY.
THANKS...
YAMASHITA MADE MOST OF THEM, SO THEY'RE PACKED WITH HIS LOVE.
We just helped.
Don't say that!
AND WHO IN THE WORLD IS YAMA-SHITA?!
WELL, I'LL BE GOING NOW.
Bye-bye.
...
YOU SEEM VERY NONCHA-LANT...
Well, not that I expect you to be gloomy, but...
HAYA-SAKA?
YEAH?
SHOOM
WHOA!
TROMP

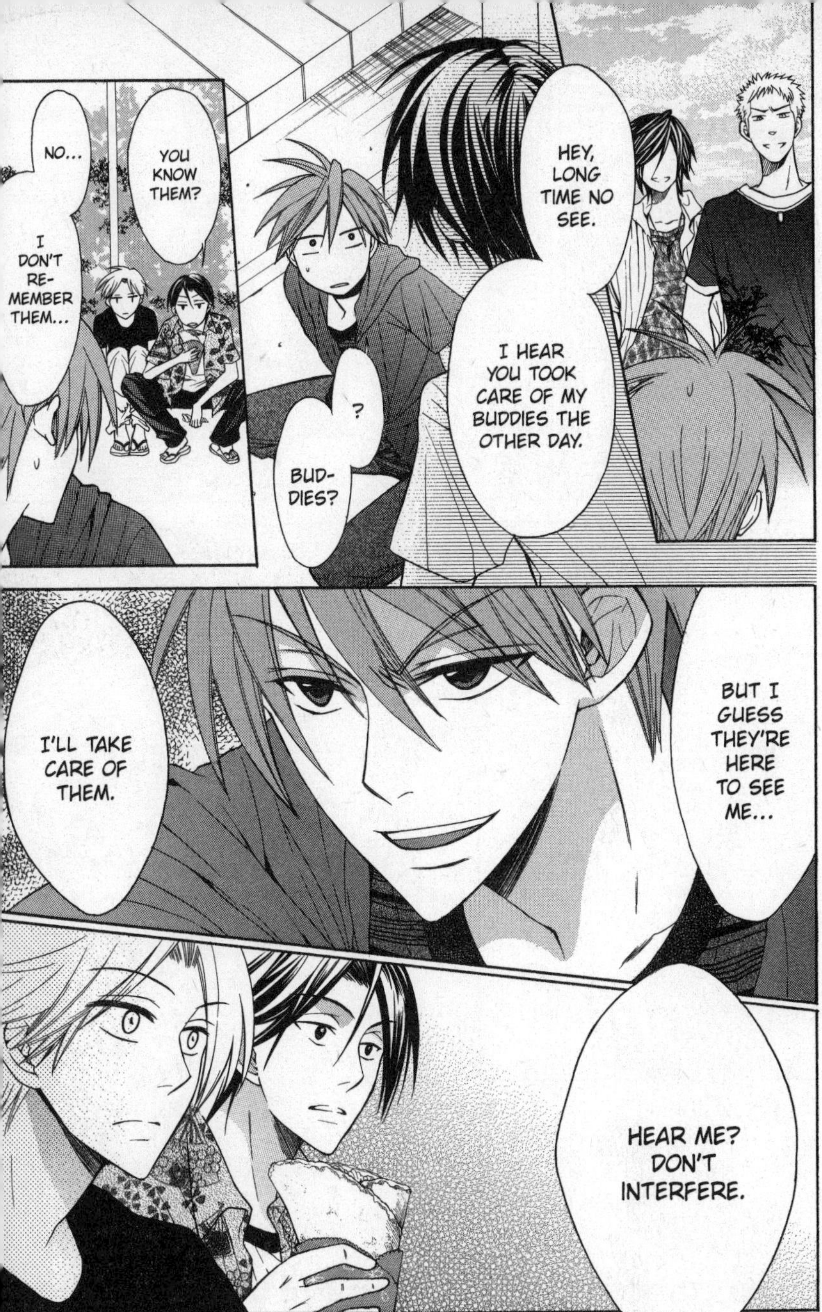
HEY, LONG TIME NO SEE.
I HEAR YOU TOOK CARE OF MY BUDDIES THE OTHER DAY.
?
BUD-DIES?
YOU KNOW THEM?
NO...
I DON'T RE-MEMBER THEM...
BUT I GUESS THEY'RE HERE TO SEE ME...
I'LL TAKE CARE OF THEM.
HEAR ME? DON'T INTERFERE.

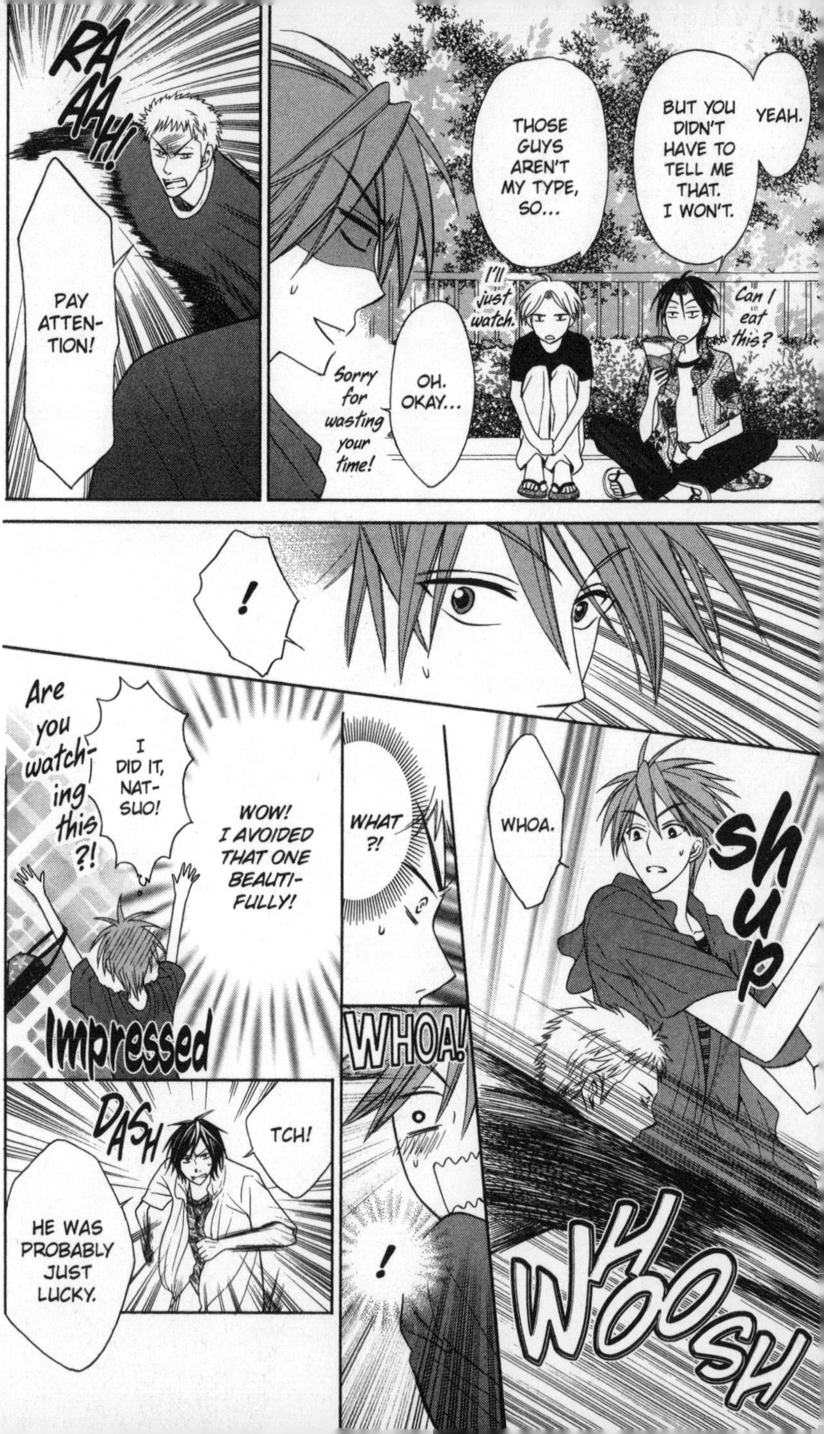
YEAH.
BUT YOU DIDN'T HAVE TO TELL ME THAT. I WON'T.
THOSE GUYS AREN'T MY TYPE, SO...
Can I eat this?
I'll just watch.
OH. OKAY...
Sorry for wasting your time!
RAAAH!
PAY ATTENTION!
!
WHOA.
shup
WHAT?!
Are you watching this?!
I DID IT, NATSUO!
WOW! I AVOIDED THAT ONE BEAUTIFULLY!
Impressed
WHOA!
!
WHOOSH
DASH
TCH!
HE WAS PROBABLY JUST LUCKY.

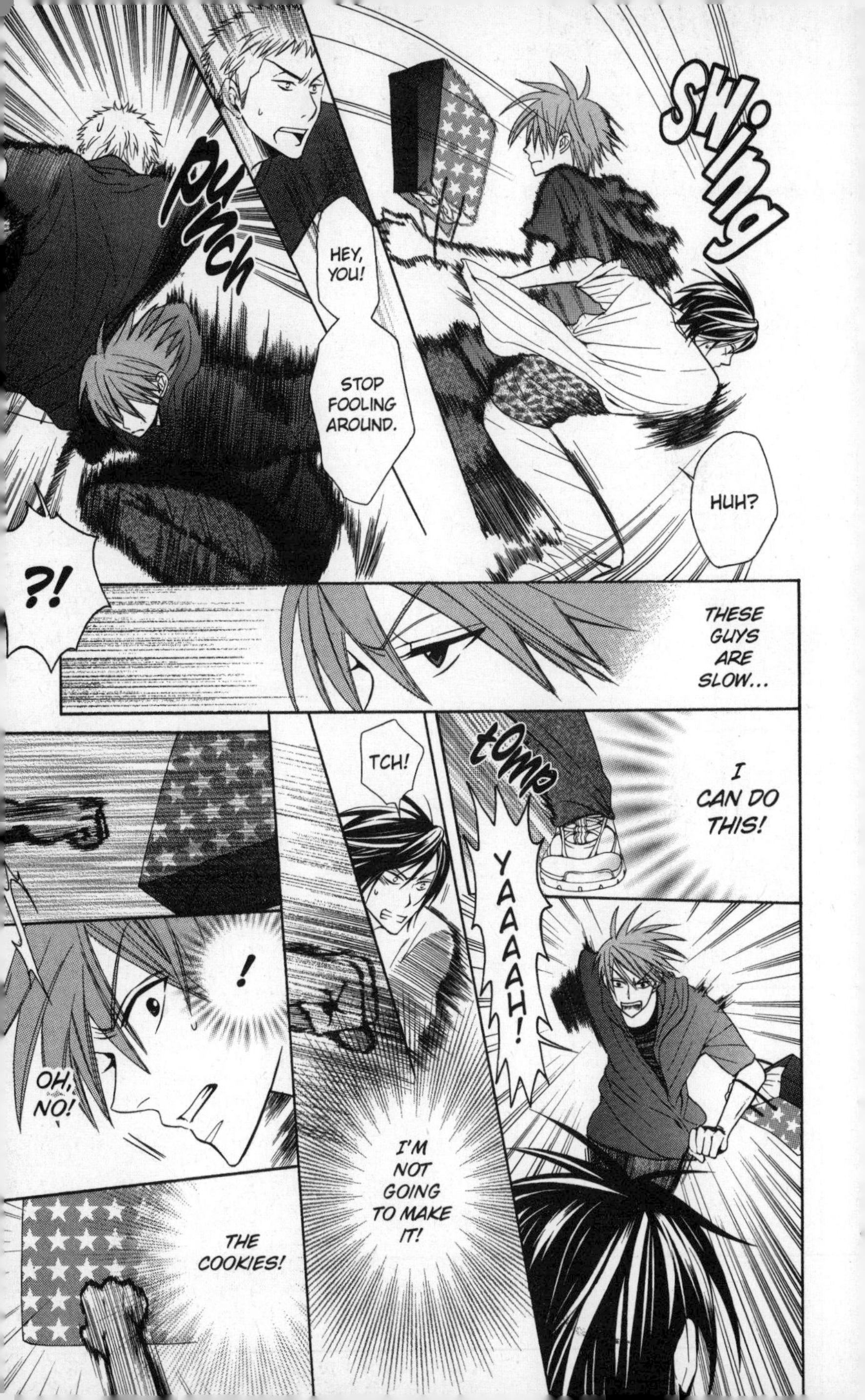
SWING
HUH?
HEY, YOU!
STOP FOOLING AROUND.
PUNCH
?!
THESE GUYS ARE SLOW...
I CAN DO THIS!
TOMP
TCH!
YAAAAAH!
!
OH, NO!
I'M NOT GOING TO MAKE IT!
THE COOKIES!

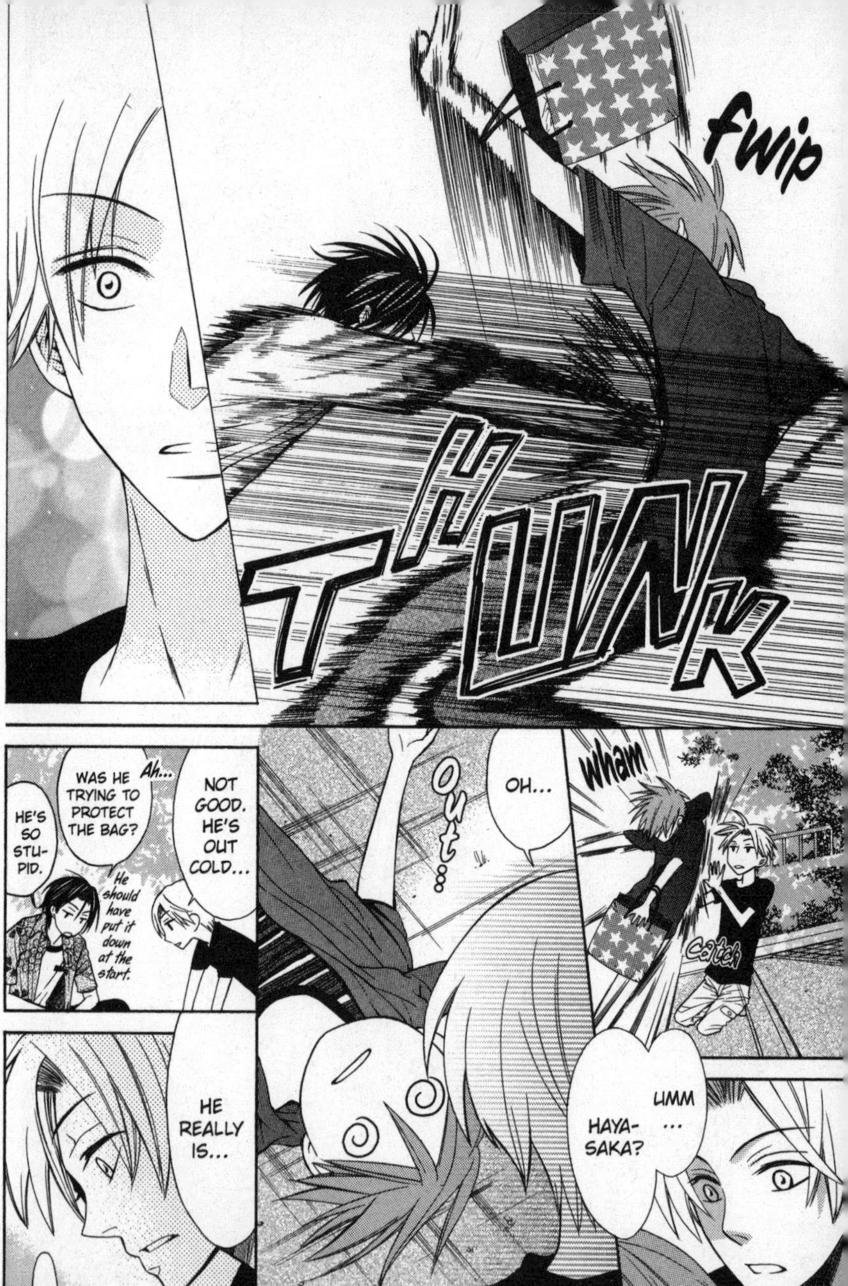

fwip
THUNK
wham
catch
OH...
out...
NOT GOOD. HE'S OUT COLD...
Ah...
WAS HE TRYING TO PROTECT THE BAG?
HE'S SO STUPID.
He should have put it down at the start.
UMM ...
HAYA-SAKA?
HE REALLY IS...
...

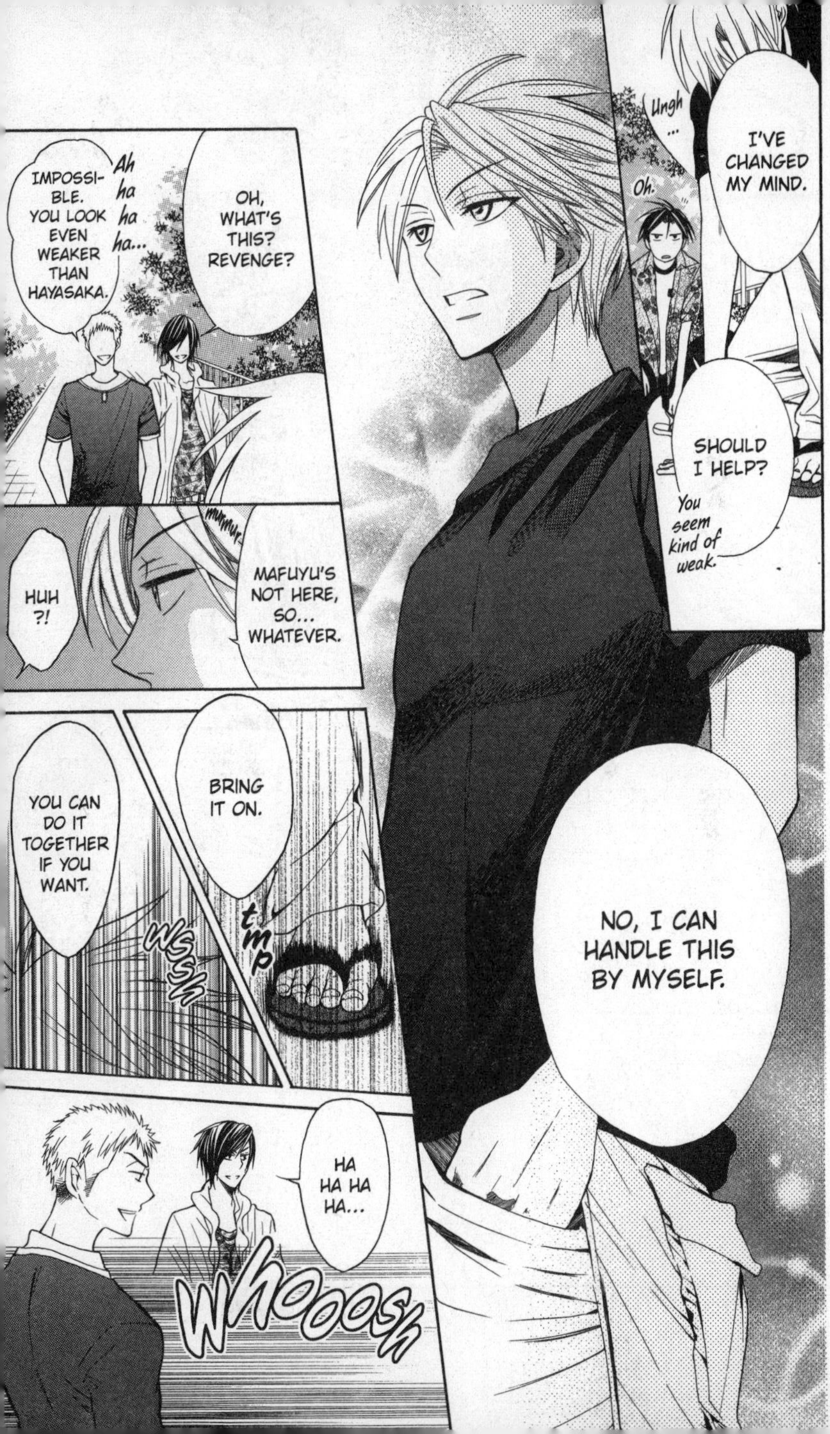
I'VE CHANGED MY MIND.
Ungh ...
Oh.
SHOULD I HELP?
You seem kind of weak.
NO, I CAN HANDLE THIS BY MYSELF.
OH, WHAT'S THIS? REVENGE?
Ah ha ha ha...
IMPOSSIBLE. YOU LOOK EVEN WEAKER THAN HAYASAKA.
murmur
MAFUYU'S NOT HERE, SO... WHATEVER.
HUH ?!
BRING IT ON.
tmp
WSSH
YOU CAN DO IT TOGETHER IF YOU WANT.
HA HA HA HA...
WHOOOSH

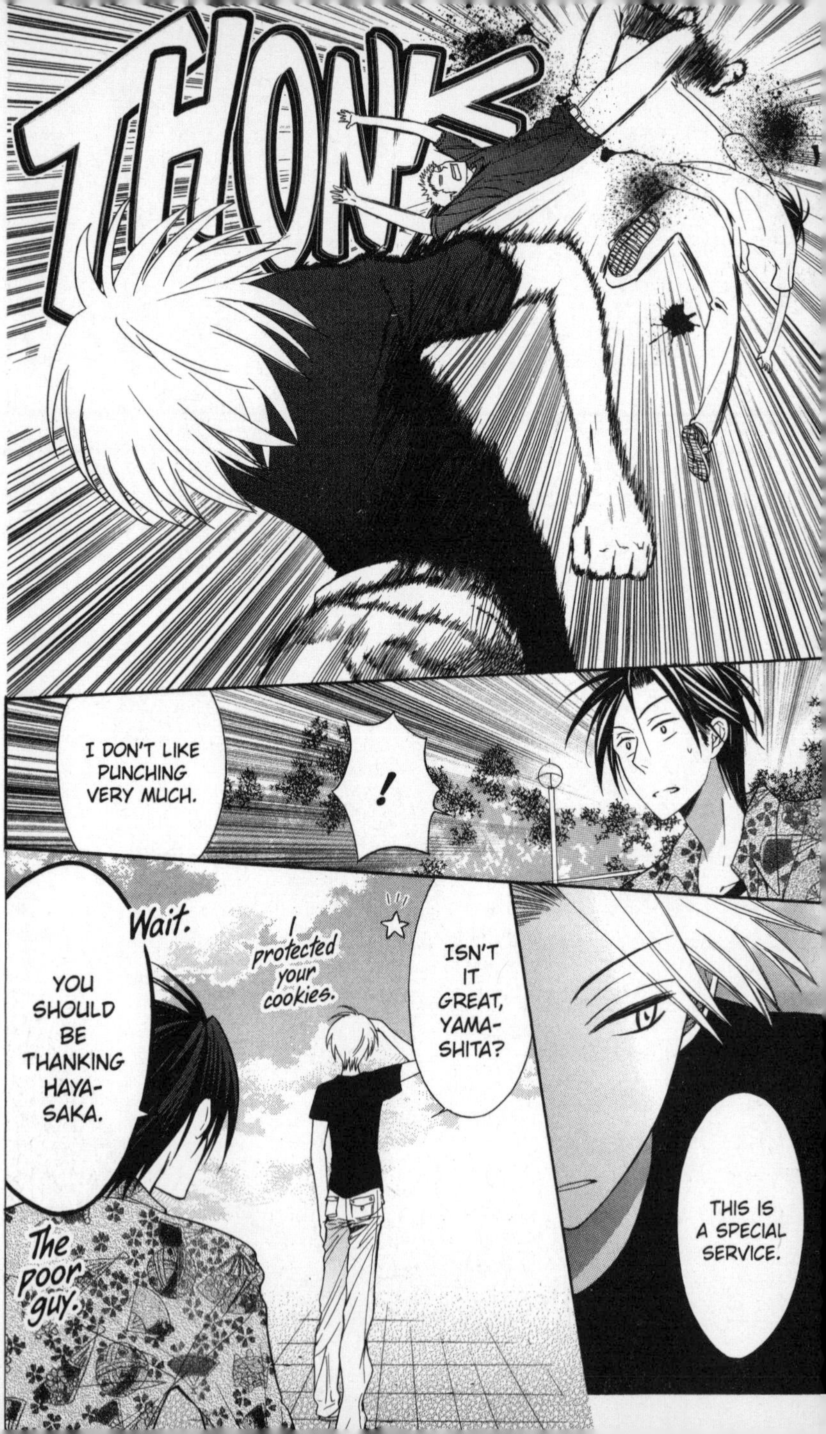
THONK
!
I DON'T LIKE PUNCHING VERY MUCH.
THIS IS A SPECIAL SERVICE.
ISN'T IT GREAT, YAMA-SHITA?
I protected your cookies.
Wait.
YOU SHOULD BE THANKING HAYA-SAKA.
The poor guy.

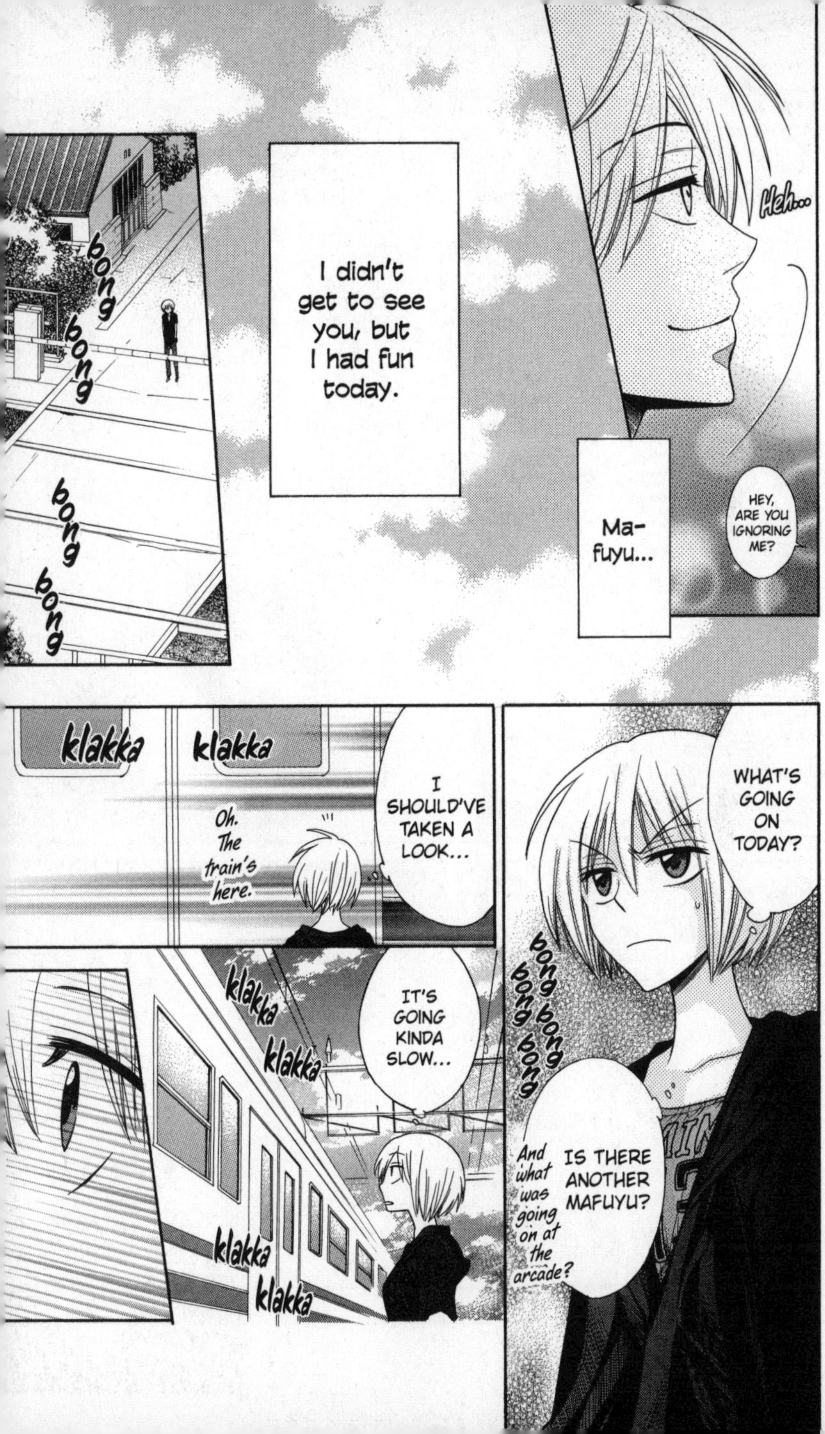
Heh...
HEY, ARE YOU IGNORING ME?
Ma-fuyu...
I didn't get to see you, but I had fun today.
bong bong
bong bong
WHAT'S GOING ON TODAY?
I SHOULD'VE TAKEN A LOOK...
Oh. The train's here.
klakka klakka
bong bong bong bong
IS THERE ANOTHER MAFUYU?
And what was going on at the arcade?
IT'S GOING KINDA SLOW...
klakka klakka
klakka klakka

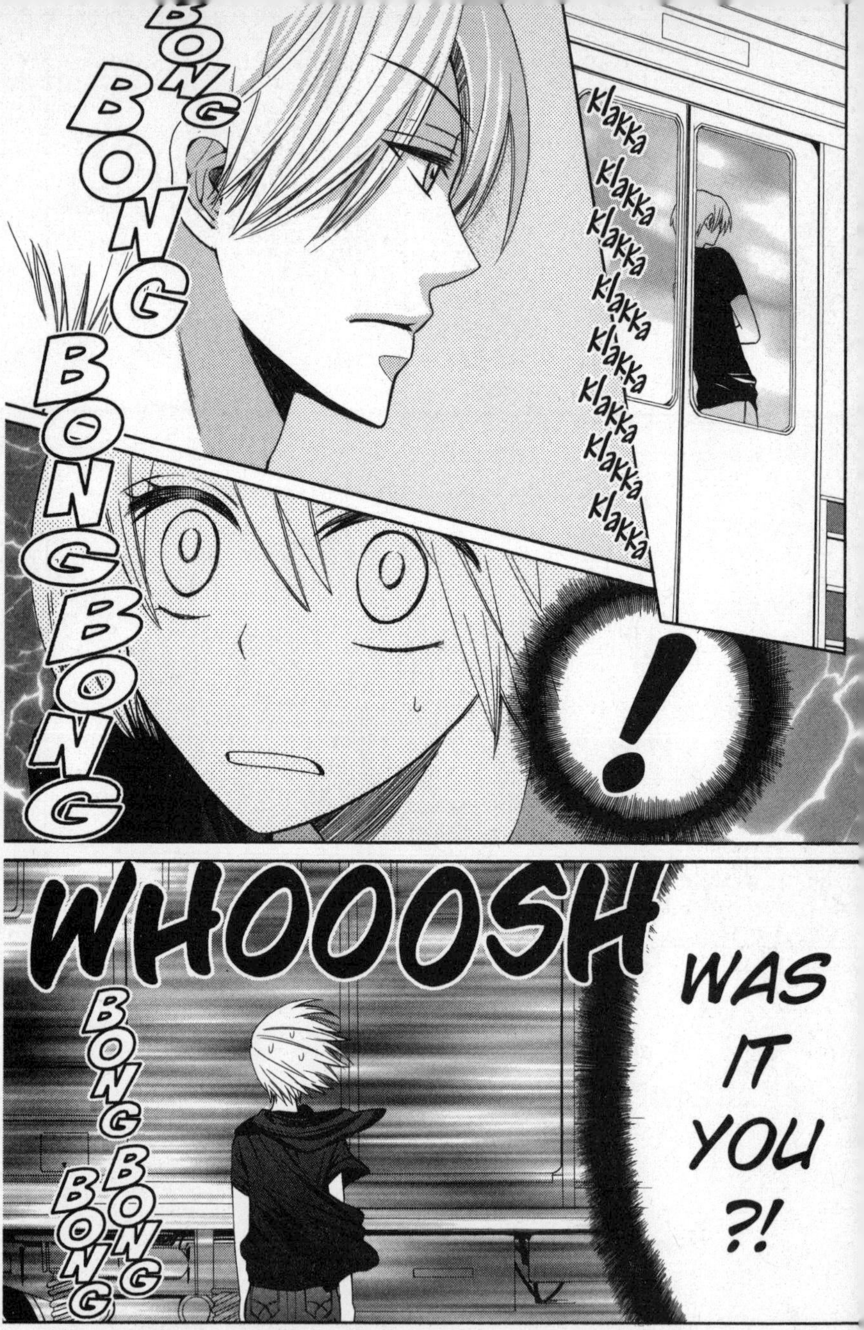

klakka klakka klakka klakka klakka klakka klakka klakka klakka
BONG BONG
BONG BONG
!
WHOOOSH
WAS IT YOU ?!
BONG BONG
BONG BONG

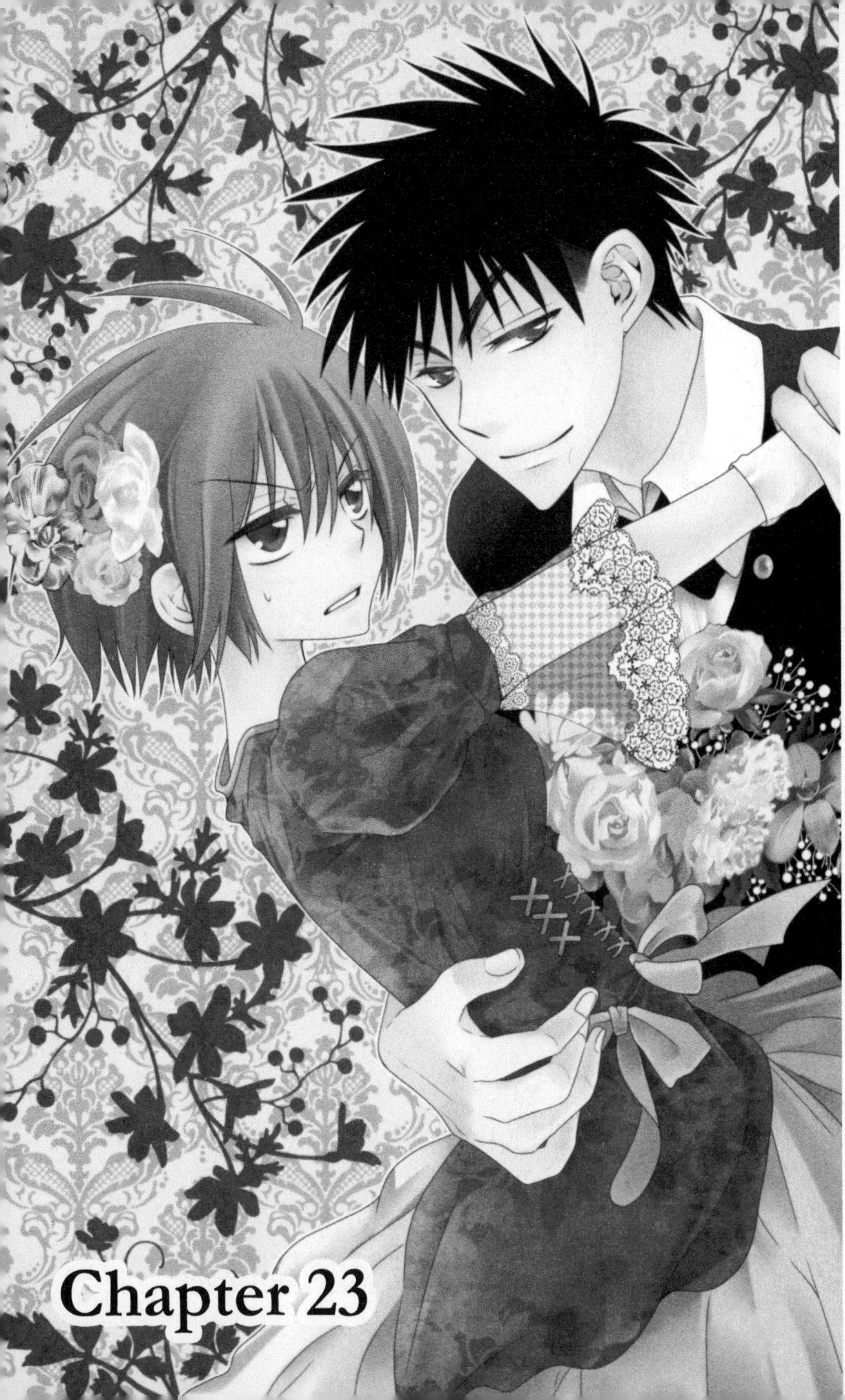
Chapter 23

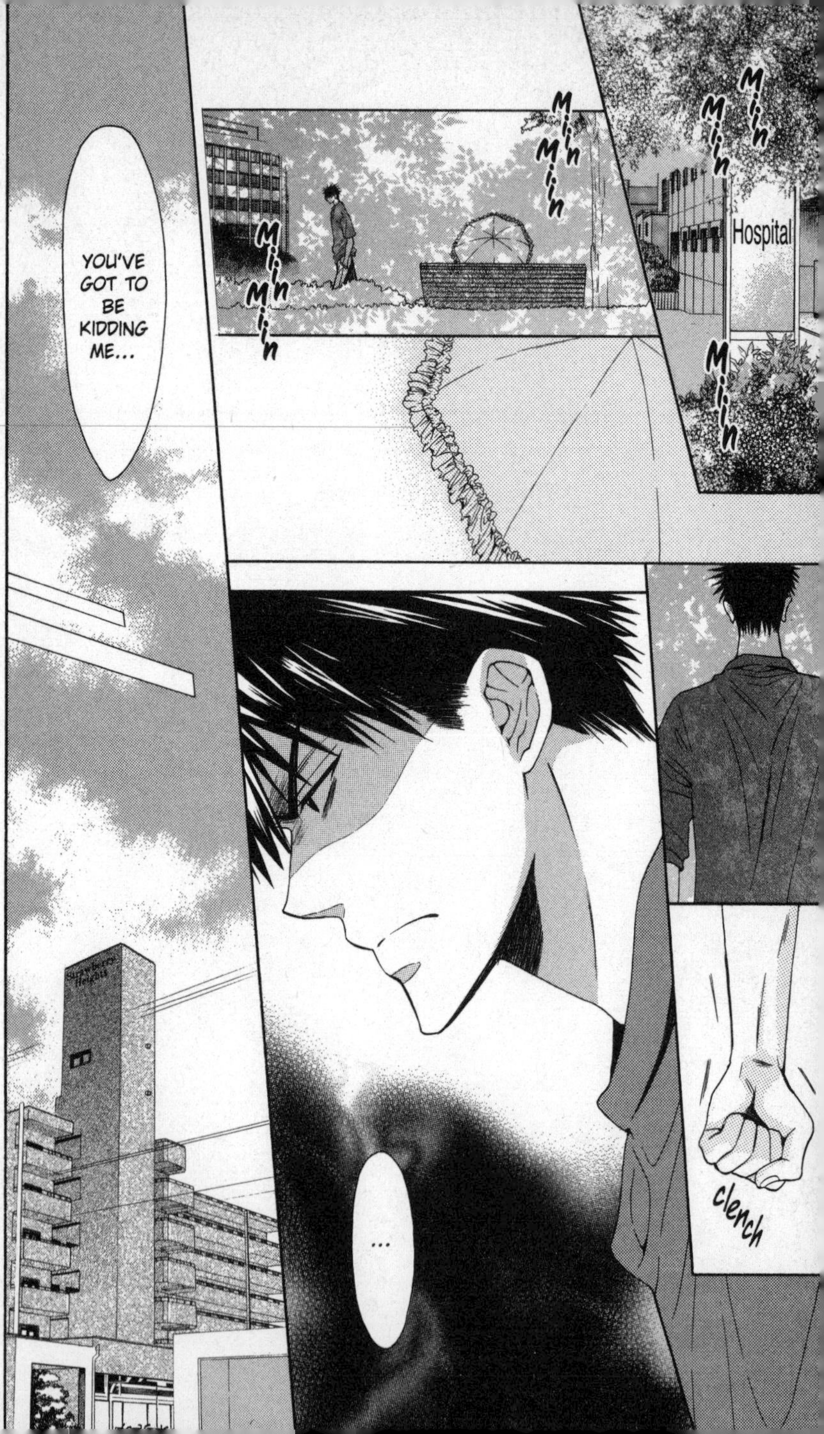

Miin
Miin
Hospital
Miin
Miin
Miin
Miin
Miin
clench
...
YOU'VE GOT TO BE KIDDING ME...

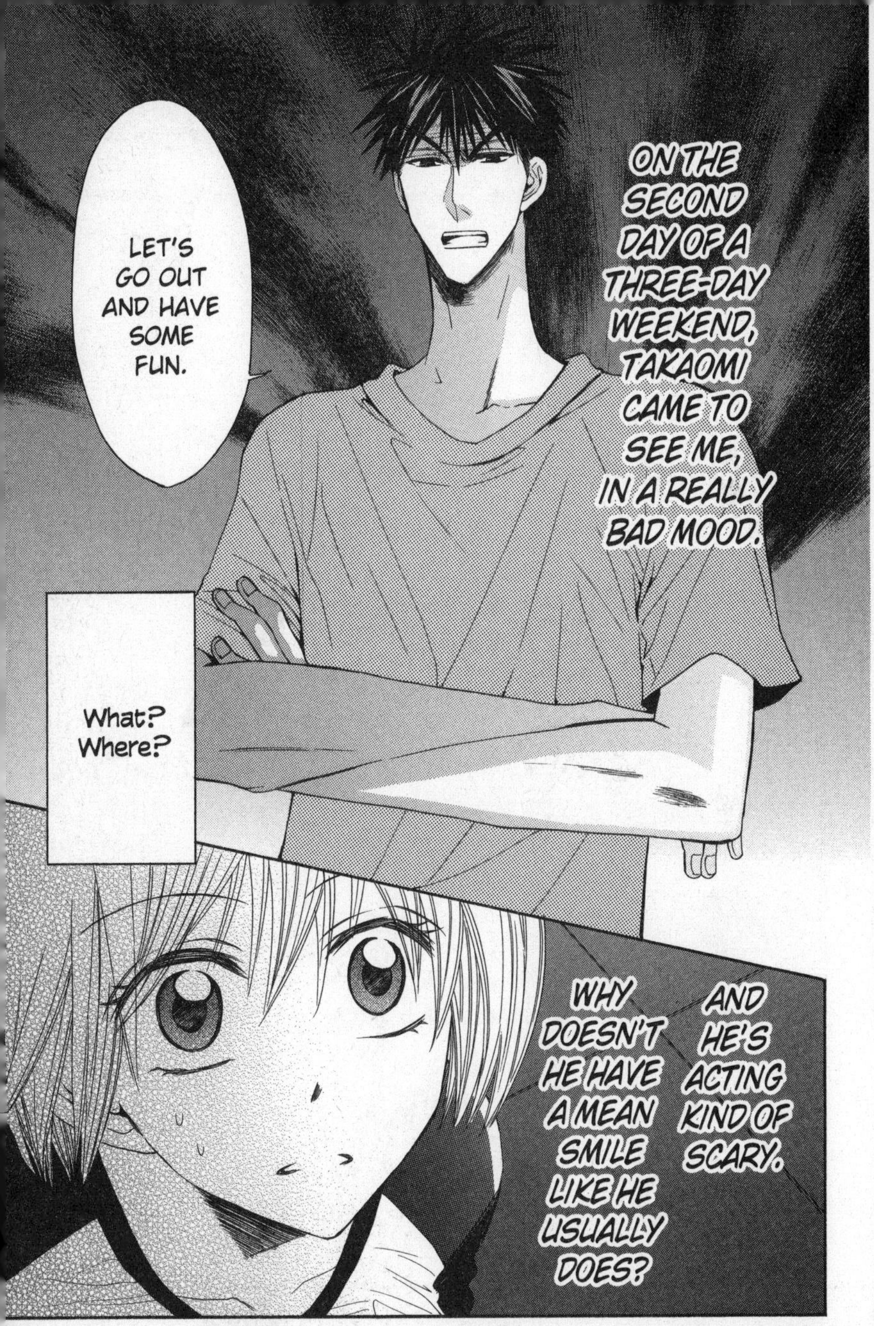

ON THE SECOND DAY OF A THREE-DAY WEEKEND, TAKAOMI CAME TO SEE ME, IN A REALLY BAD MOOD.
LET'S GO OUT AND HAVE SOME FUN.
What? Where?
AND HE'S ACTING KIND OF SCARY.
WHY DOESN'T HE HAVE A MEAN SMILE LIKE HE USUALLY DOES?

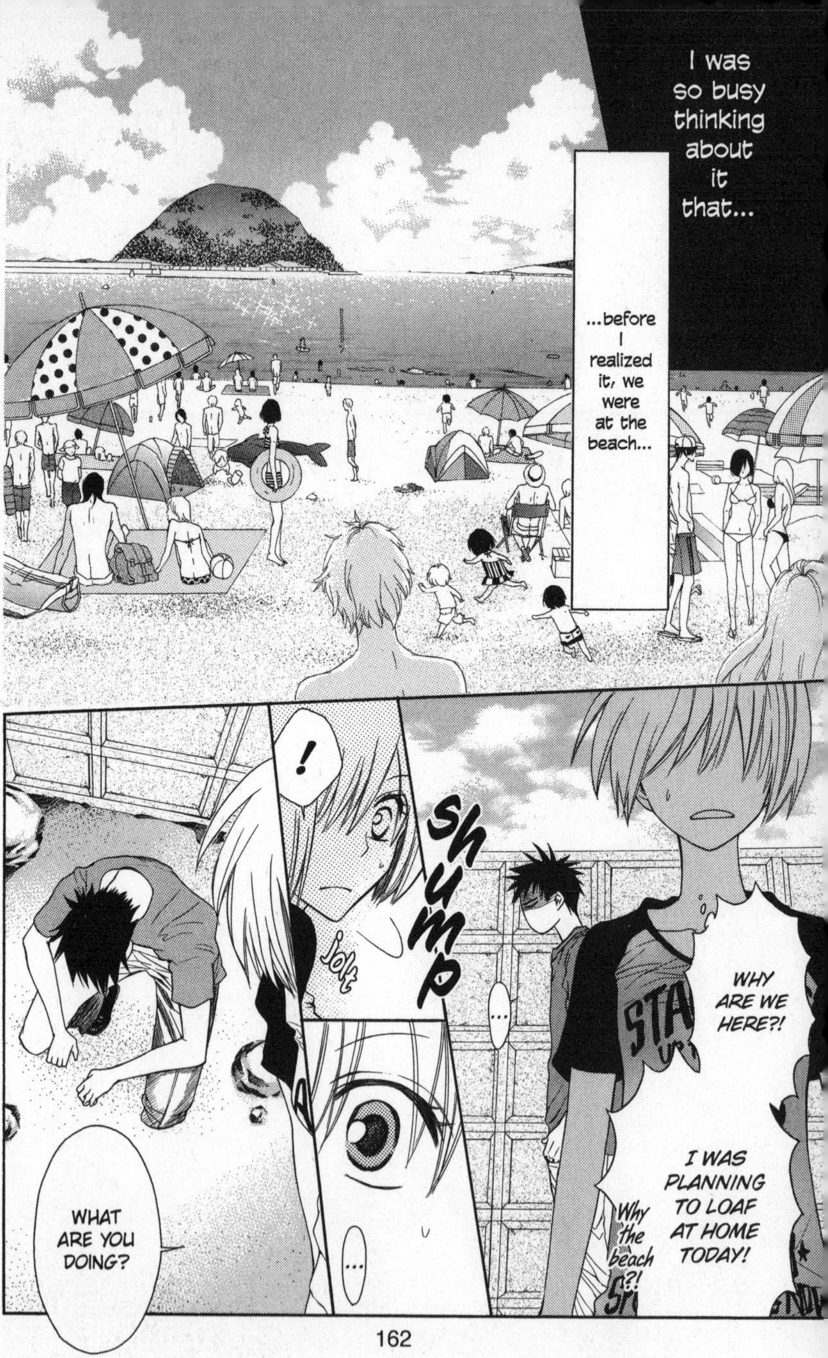
I was so busy thinking about it that...
...before I realized it, we were at the beach...
WHY ARE WE HERE?!
I WAS PLANNING TO LOAF AT HOME TODAY!
Why the beach?!
!
SHUMP
jolt
...
...
WHAT ARE YOU DOING?

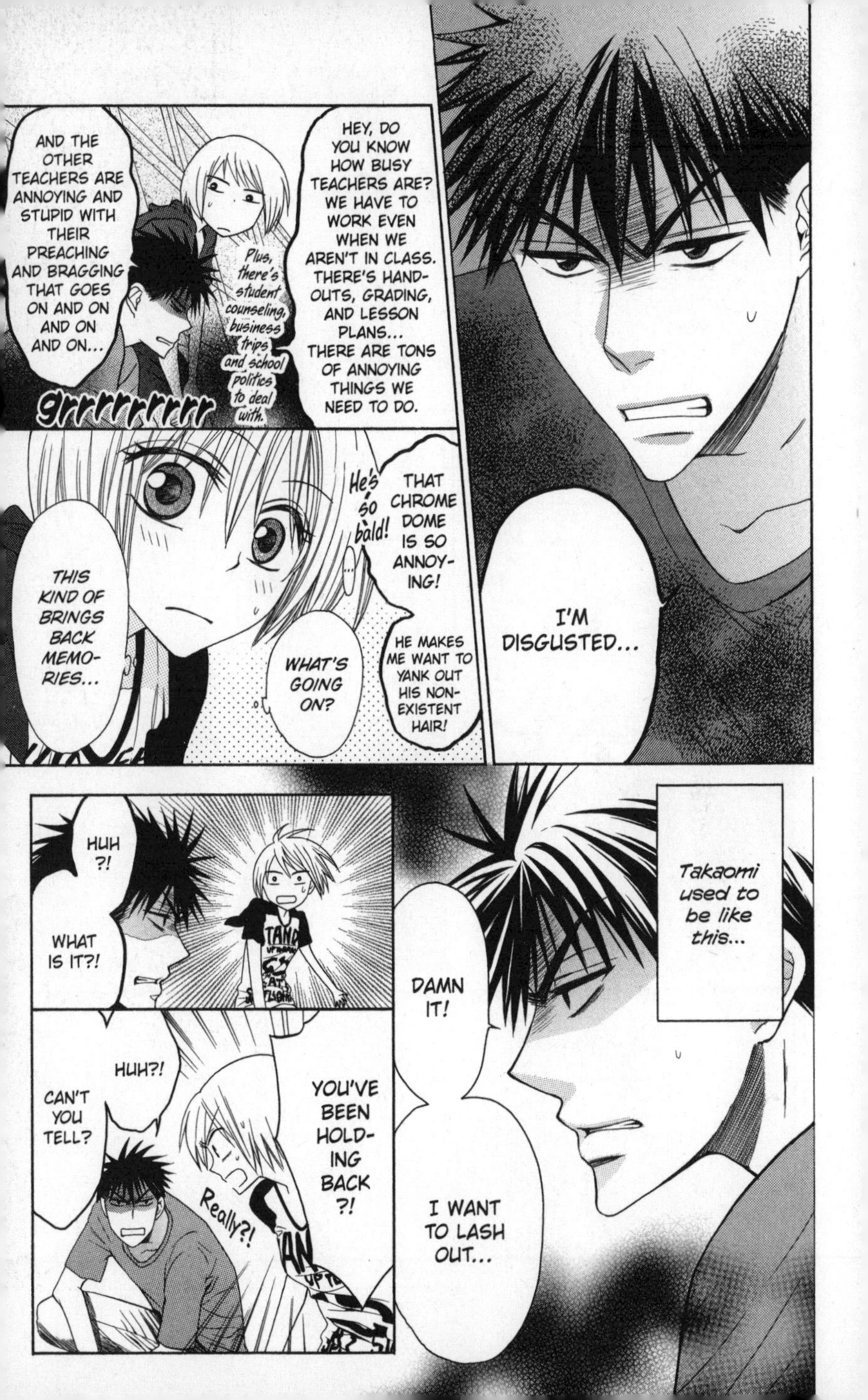
I'M DISGUSTED...
HEY, DO YOU KNOW HOW BUSY TEACHERS ARE? WE HAVE TO WORK EVEN WHEN WE AREN'T IN CLASS. THERE'S HAND-OUTS, GRADING, AND LESSON PLANS... THERE ARE TONS OF ANNOYING THINGS WE NEED TO DO.
Plus, there's student counseling, business trips and school politics to deal with.
AND THE OTHER TEACHERS ARE ANNOYING AND STUPID WITH THEIR PREACHING AND BRAGGING THAT GOES ON AND ON AND ON AND ON...
grrrrrrrrr
THAT CHROME DOME IS SO ANNOYING!
He's so bald!
HE MAKES ME WANT TO YANK OUT HIS NON-EXISTENT HAIR!
WHAT'S GOING ON?
...
THIS KIND OF BRINGS BACK MEMORIES...
Takaomi used to be like this...
DAMN IT!
I WANT TO LASH OUT...
HUH?!
WHAT IS IT?!
YOU'VE BEEN HOLDING-ING BACK?!
HUH?!
CAN'T YOU TELL?
Really?!

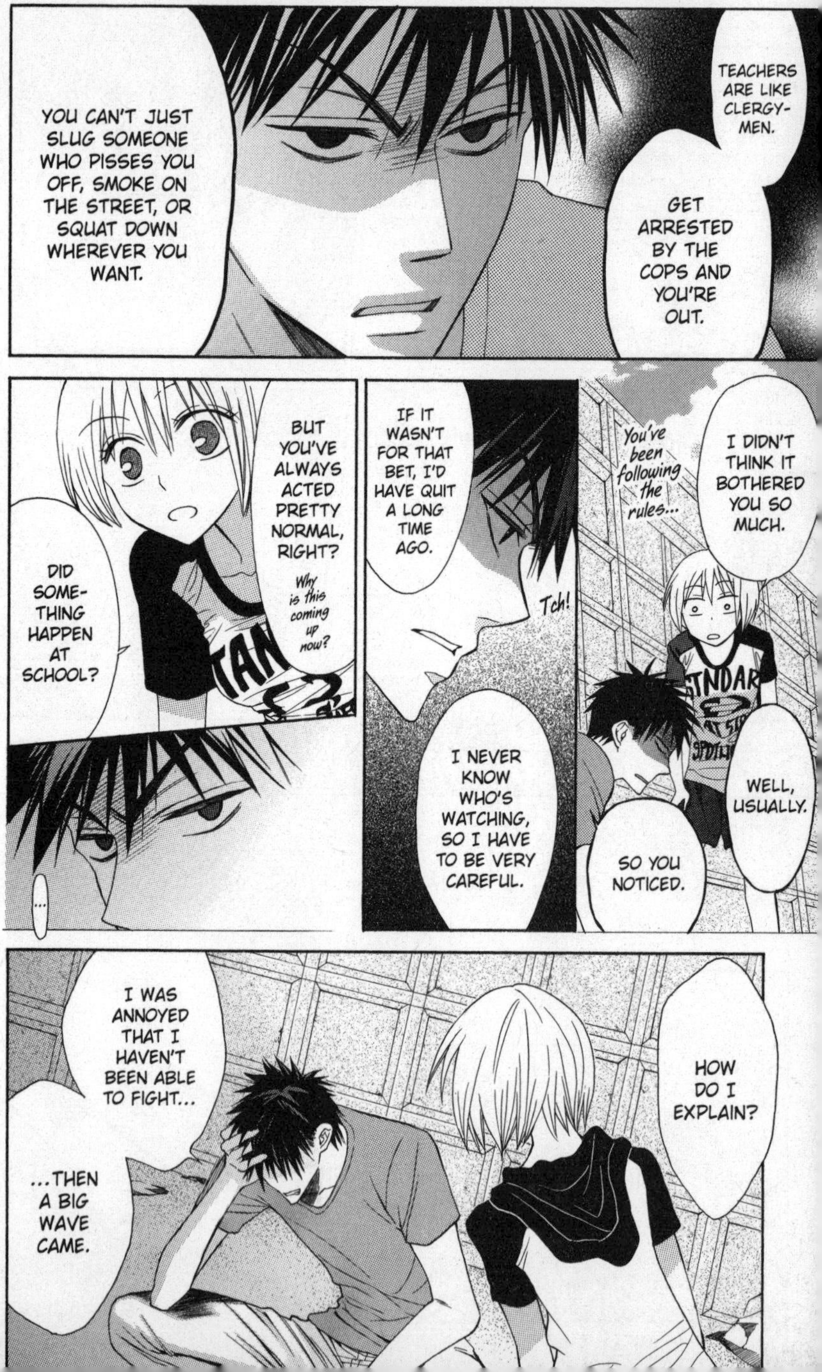
TEACHERS ARE LIKE CLERGYMEN.
GET ARRESTED BY THE COPS AND YOU'RE OUT.
YOU CAN'T JUST SLUG SOMEONE WHO PISSES YOU OFF, SMOKE ON THE STREET, OR SQUAT DOWN WHEREVER YOU WANT.
I DIDN'T THINK IT BOTHERED YOU SO MUCH.
You've been following the rules...
WELL, USUALLY.
SO YOU NOTICED.
IF IT WASN'T FOR THAT BET, I'D HAVE QUIT A LONG TIME AGO.
Tch!
I NEVER KNOW WHO'S WATCHING, SO I HAVE TO BE VERY CAREFUL.
BUT YOU'VE ALWAYS ACTED PRETTY NORMAL, RIGHT?
Why is this coming up now?
DID SOMETHING HAPPEN AT SCHOOL?
...
HOW DO I EXPLAIN?
I WAS ANNOYED THAT I HAVEN'T BEEN ABLE TO FIGHT...
...THEN A BIG WAVE CAME.

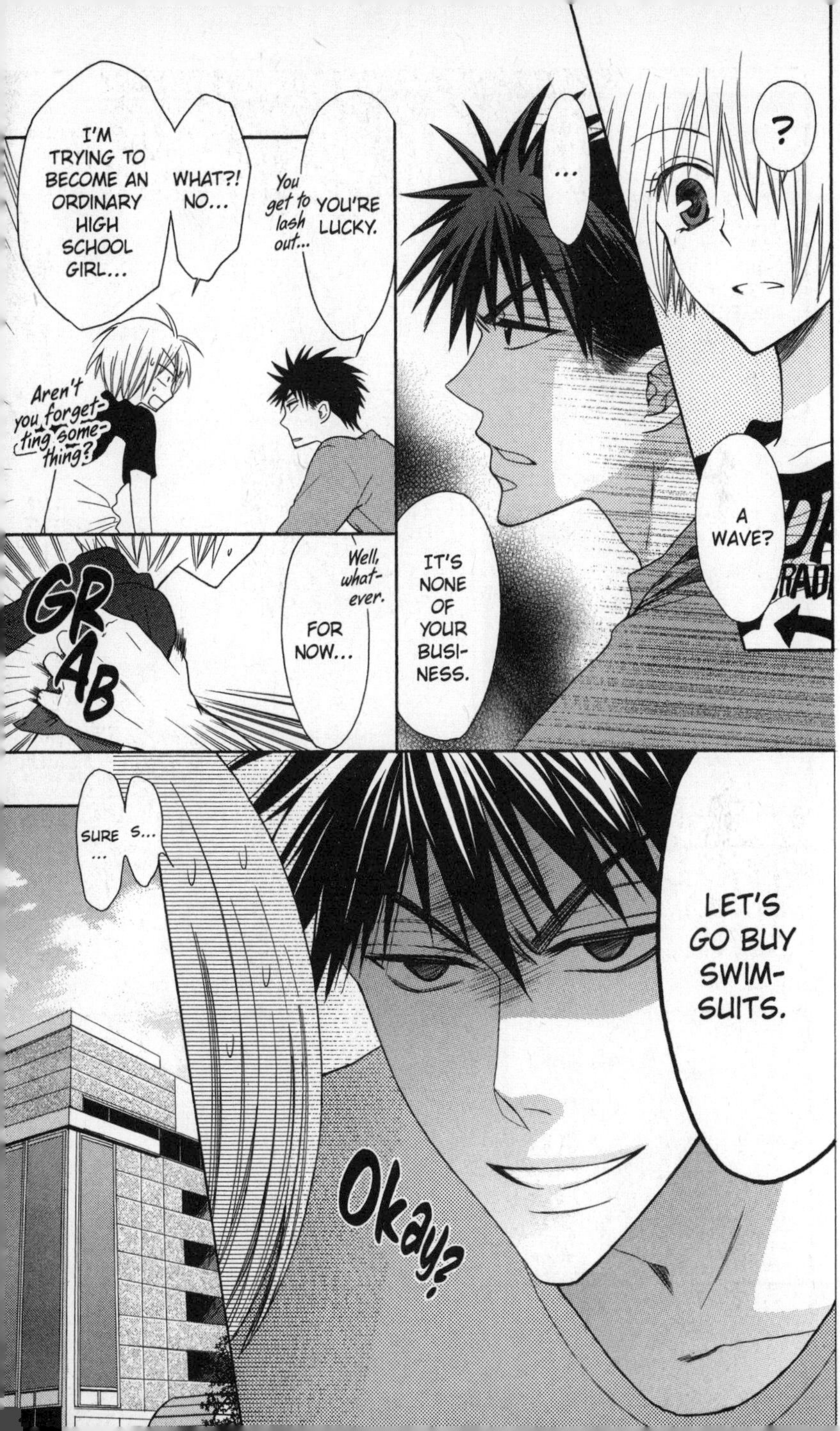
?
...
A WAVE?
IT'S NONE OF YOUR BUSINESS.
YOU'RE LUCKY.
You get to lash out...
WHAT?! NO...
I'M TRYING TO BECOME AN ORDINARY HIGH SCHOOL GIRL...
Aren't you forgetting something?
Well, whatever.
FOR NOW...
GRAB
LET'S GO BUY SWIMSUITS.
Okay?
SURE S... ...

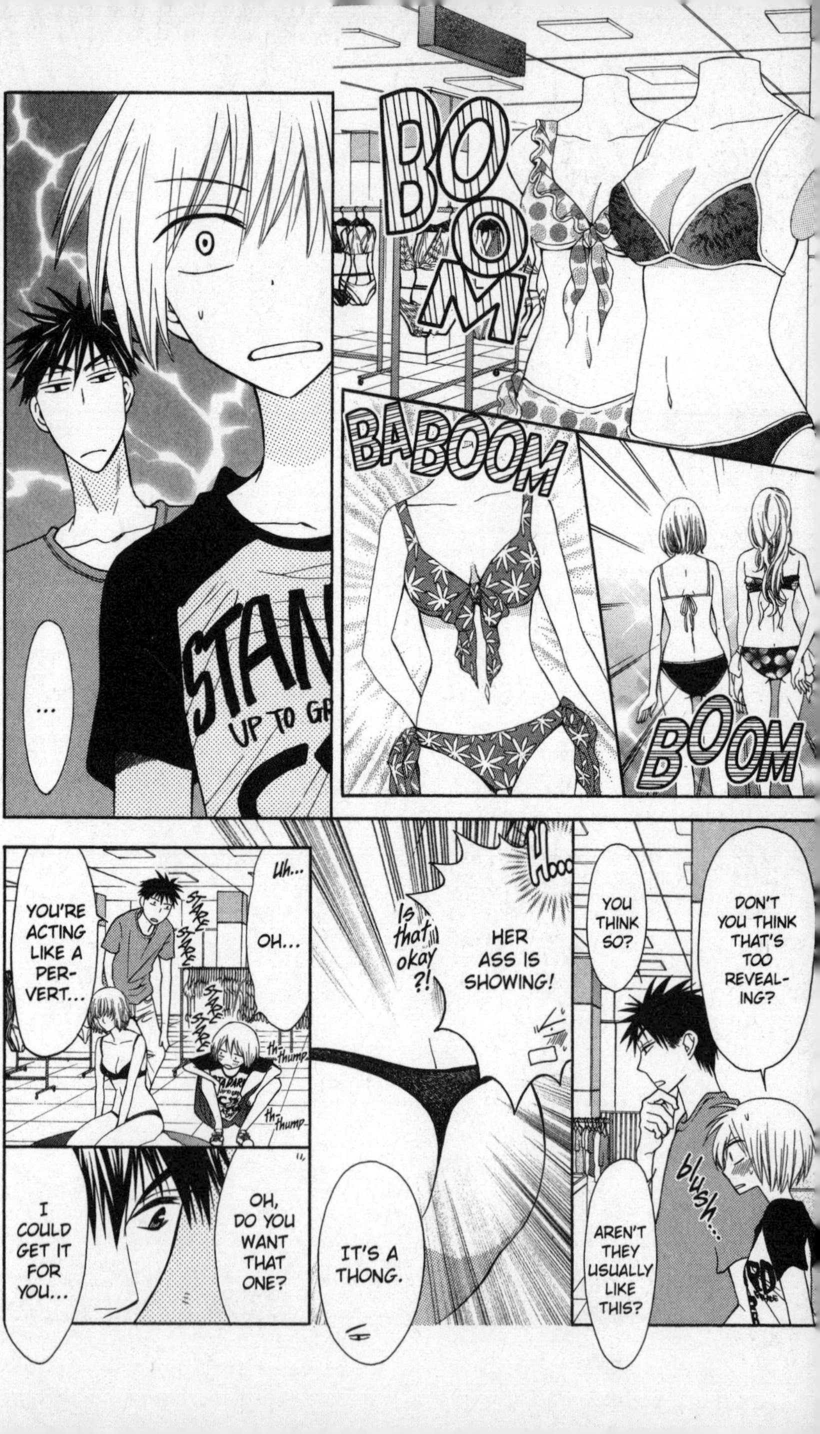
BOOM
BOOM
BABOOM
...
DON'T YOU THINK THAT'S TOO REVEAL-ING?
YOU THINK SO?
blush...
AREN'T THEY USUALLY LIKE THIS?
Hooo
HER ASS IS SHOWING!
Is that okay?!
IT'S A THONG.
Uh...
OH...
YOU'RE ACTING LIKE A PER-VERT...
STARE STARE STARE STARE
th-thump th-thump
OH, DO YOU WANT THAT ONE?
I COULD GET IT FOR YOU...

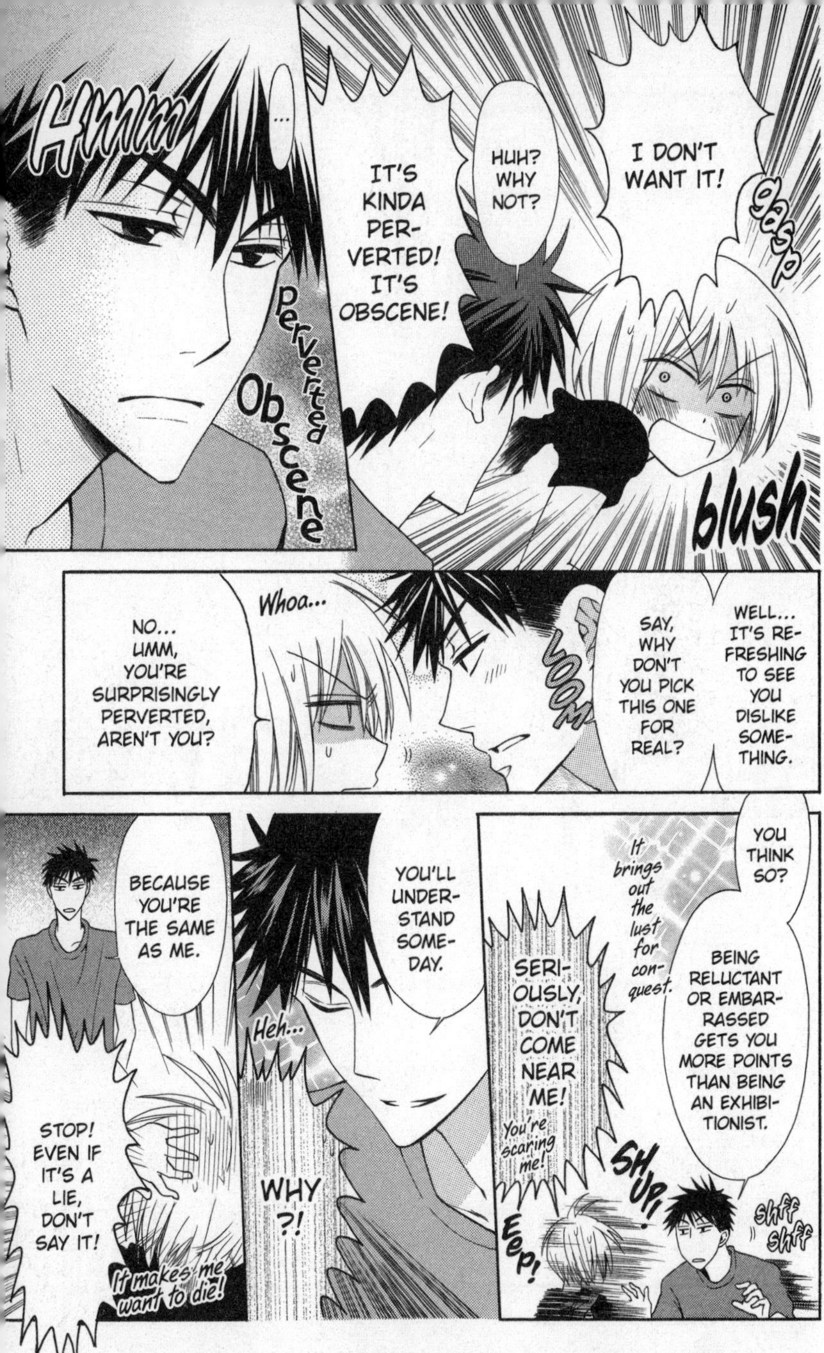
I DON'T WANT IT!
gasp
HUH? WHY NOT?
IT'S KINDA PERVERTED! IT'S OBSCENE!
blush
...
Hmm
Perverted
Obscene
WELL... IT'S REFRESHING TO SEE YOU DISLIKE SOMETHING.
SAY, WHY DON'T YOU PICK THIS ONE FOR REAL?
VOOM
Whoa...
NO... UMM, YOU'RE SURPRISINGLY PERVERTED, AREN'T YOU?
YOU THINK SO?
It brings out the lust for conquest.
BEING RELUCTANT OR EMBARRASSED GETS YOU MORE POINTS THAN BEING AN EXHIBITIONIST.
SERIOUSLY, DON'T COME NEAR ME!
You're scaring me!
SHUP!
shff shff
Eep!
YOU'LL UNDERSTAND SOMEDAY.
Heh...
BECAUSE YOU'RE THE SAME AS ME.
WHY?!
STOP! EVEN IF IT'S A LIE, DON'T SAY IT!
It makes me want to die!

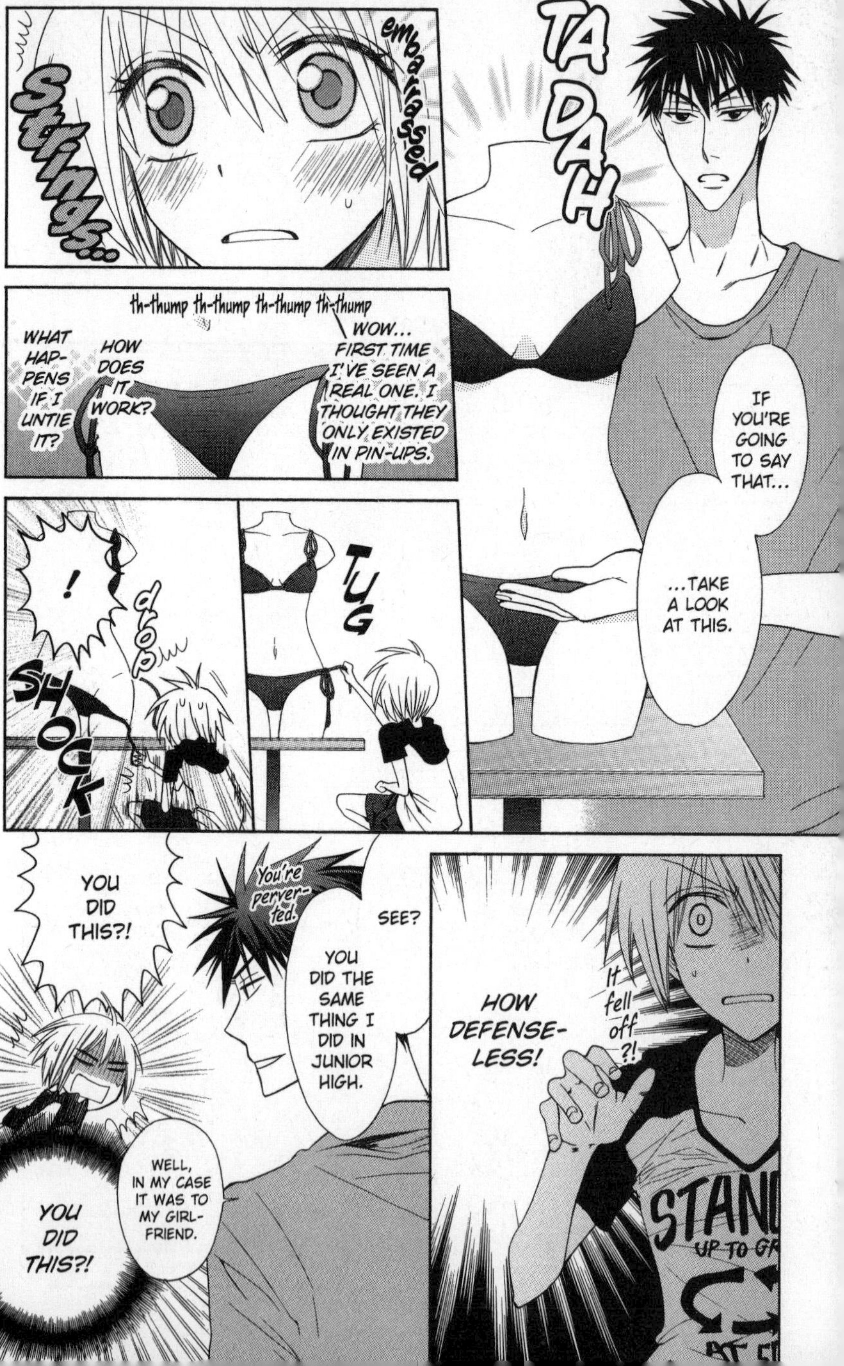

TA DAH
IF YOU'RE GOING TO SAY THAT...
...TAKE A LOOK AT THIS.
embarrassed
Strings...
th-thump th-thump th-thump th-thump
WOW... FIRST TIME I'VE SEEN A REAL ONE. I THOUGHT THEY ONLY EXISTED IN PIN-UPS.
HOW DOES IT WORK?
WHAT HAP-PENS IF I UNTIE IT?
TUG
!
drop
SHOCK
It fell off?!
HOW DEFENSE-LESS!
SEE?
YOU DID THE SAME THING I DID IN JUNIOR HIGH.
You're perver-ted.
YOU DID THIS?!
WELL, IN MY CASE IT WAS TO MY GIRL-FRIEND.
YOU DID THIS?!
STAND UP TO GR

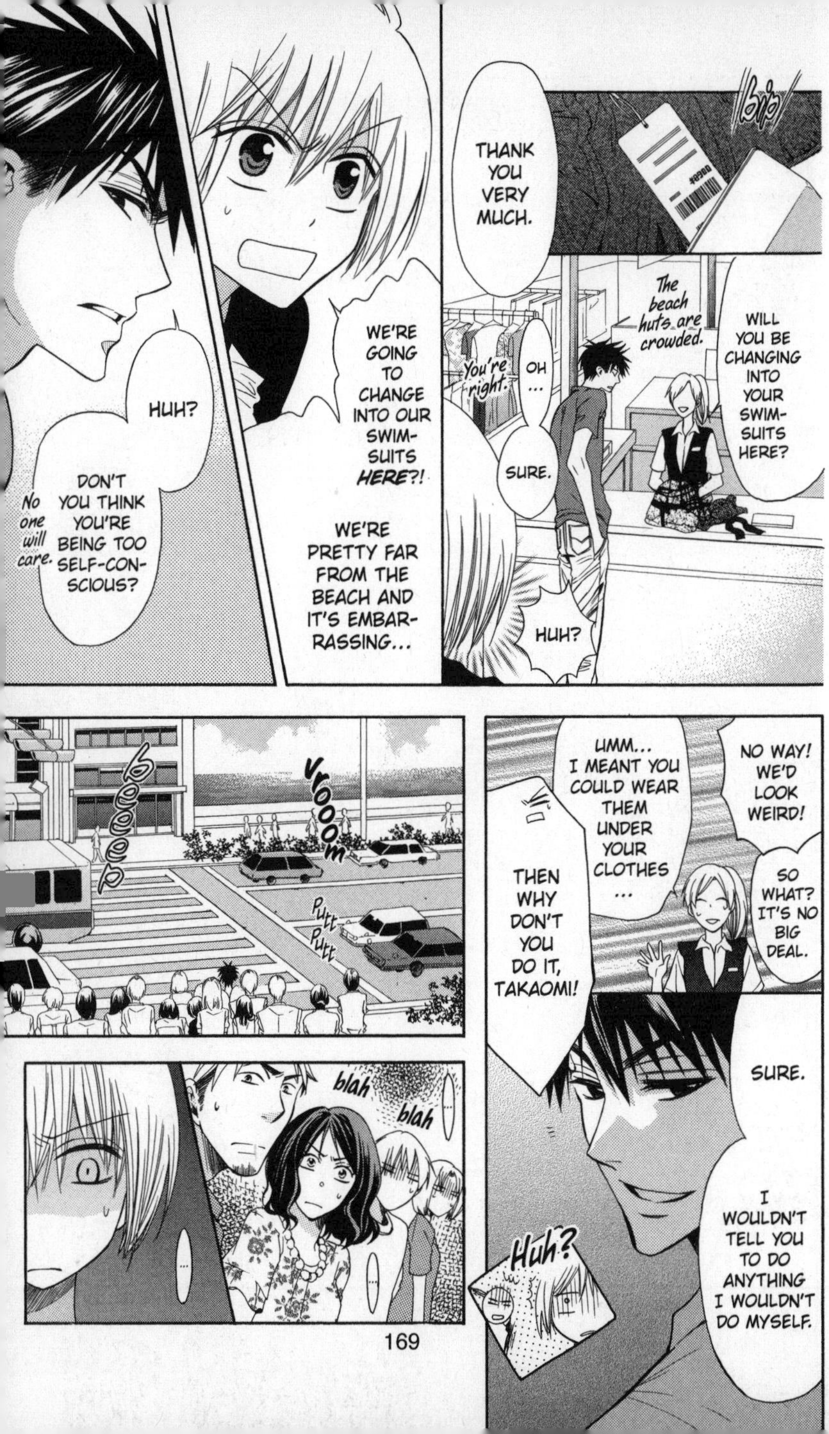
THANK YOU VERY MUCH.
The beach huts are crowded.
WILL YOU BE CHANGING INTO YOUR SWIM-SUITS HERE?
OH ...
SURE.
You're right.
HUH?
WE'RE GOING TO CHANGE INTO OUR SWIM-SUITS *HERE*?!
WE'RE PRETTY FAR FROM THE BEACH AND IT'S EMBAR-RASSING...
HUH?
DON'T YOU THINK YOU'RE BEING TOO SELF-CON-SCIOUS?
No one will care.
NO WAY! WE'D LOOK WEIRD!
SO WHAT? IT'S NO BIG DEAL.
UMM... I MEANT YOU COULD WEAR THEM UNDER YOUR CLOTHES ...
THEN WHY DON'T YOU DO IT, TAKAOMI!
SURE.
I WOULDN'T TELL YOU TO DO ANYTHING I WOULDN'T DO MYSELF.
Huh?
beeeep
vrooom
Putt Putt
blah blah
...
...
...

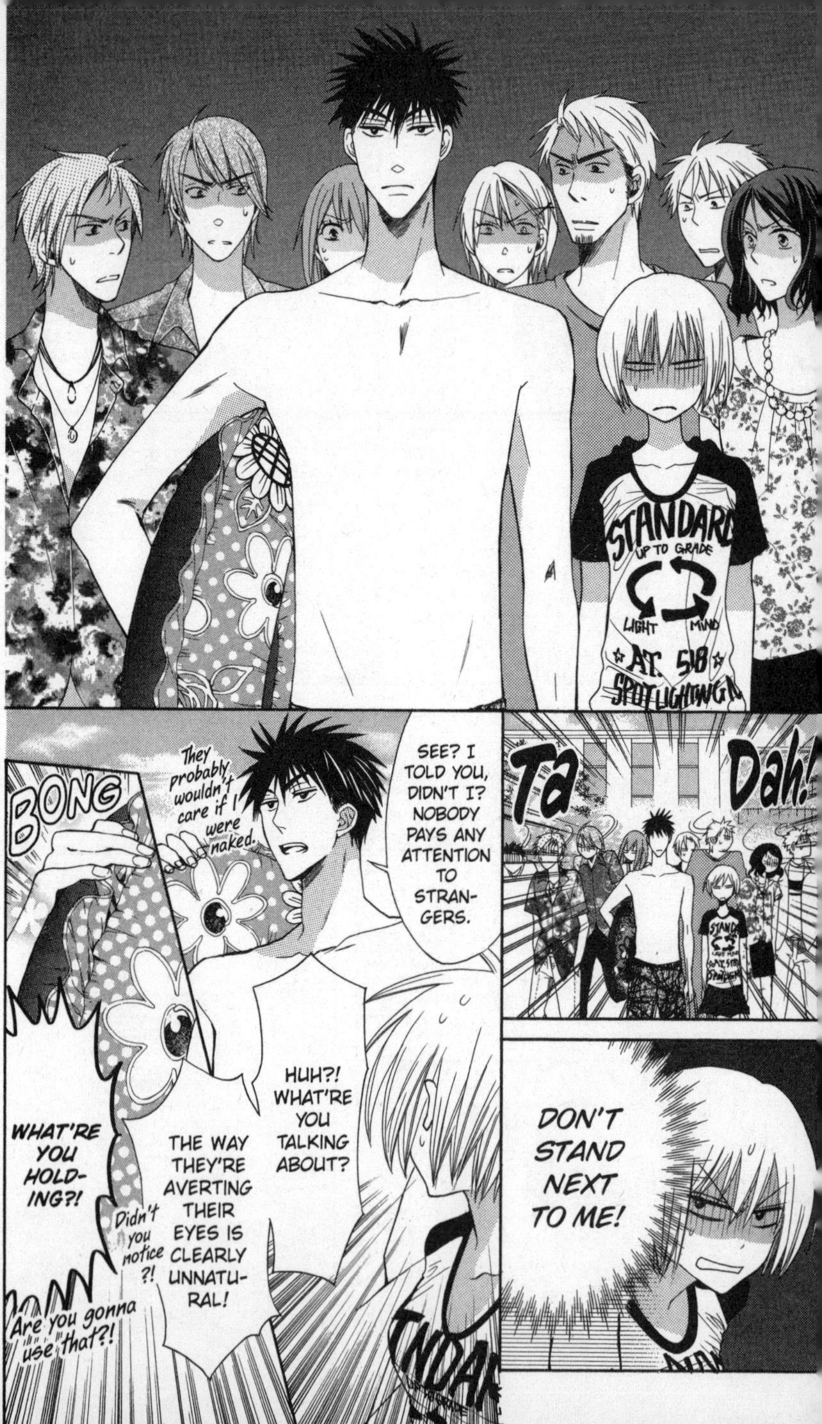
STANDARD
UP TO GRADE
LIGHT
MIND
Ta Dah!
DON'T STAND NEXT TO ME!
SEE? I TOLD YOU, DIDN'T I? NOBODY PAYS ANY ATTENTION TO STRANGERS.
They probably wouldn't care if I were naked.
BONG
HUH?! WHAT'RE YOU TALKING ABOUT?
THE WAY THEY'RE AVERTING THEIR EYES IS CLEARLY UNNATURAL!
Didn't you notice?!
WHAT'RE YOU HOLDING?!
Are you gonna use that?!

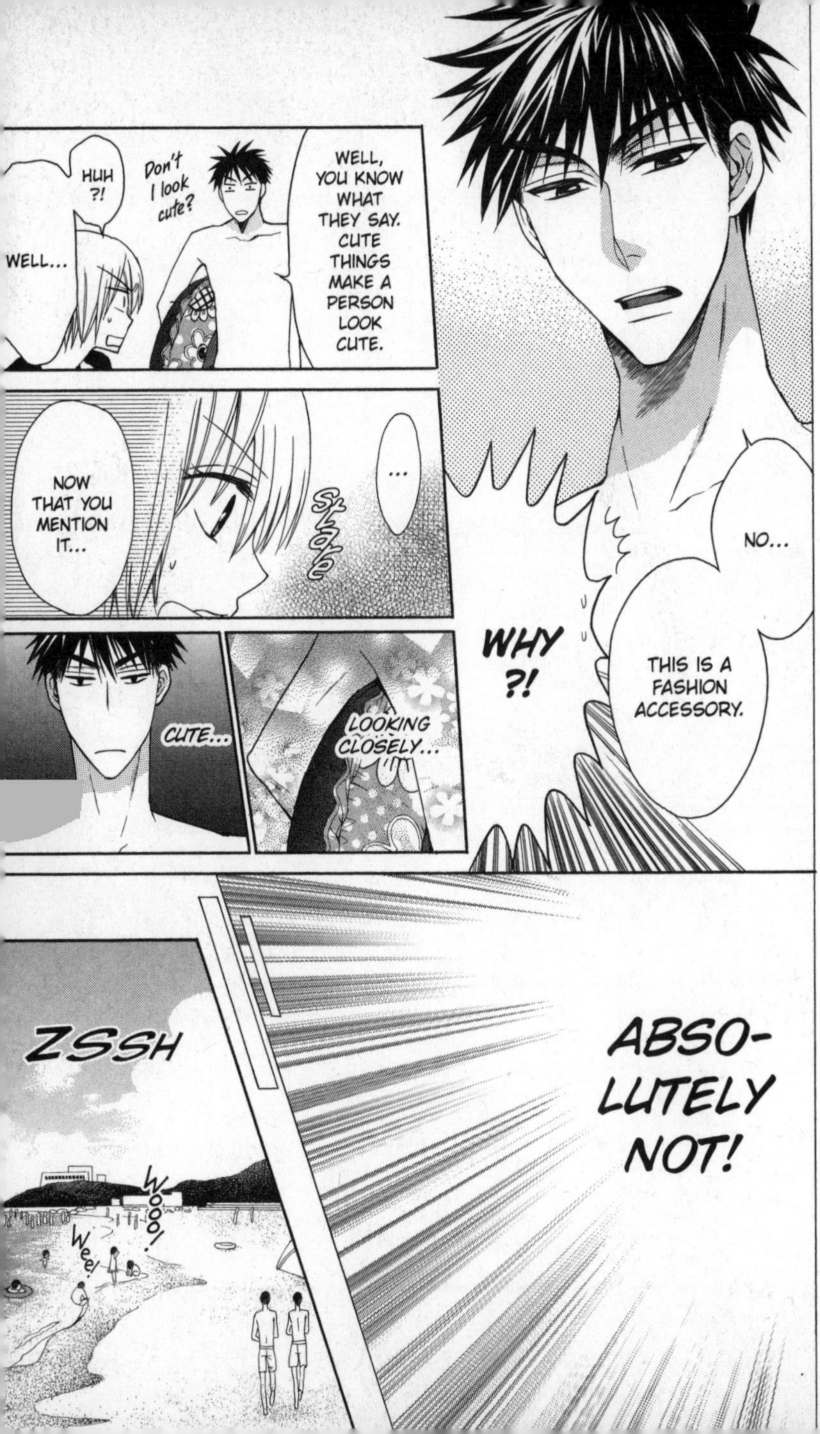
NO...
THIS IS A FASHION ACCESSORY.
WHY ?!
WELL, YOU KNOW WHAT THEY SAY. CUTE THINGS MAKE A PERSON LOOK CUTE.
Don't I look cute?
HUH ?!
WELL...
...
Stare
NOW THAT YOU MENTION IT...
LOOKING CLOSELY...
CUTE...
ABSO-LUTELY NOT!
ZSSH
Wooo!
Wee!

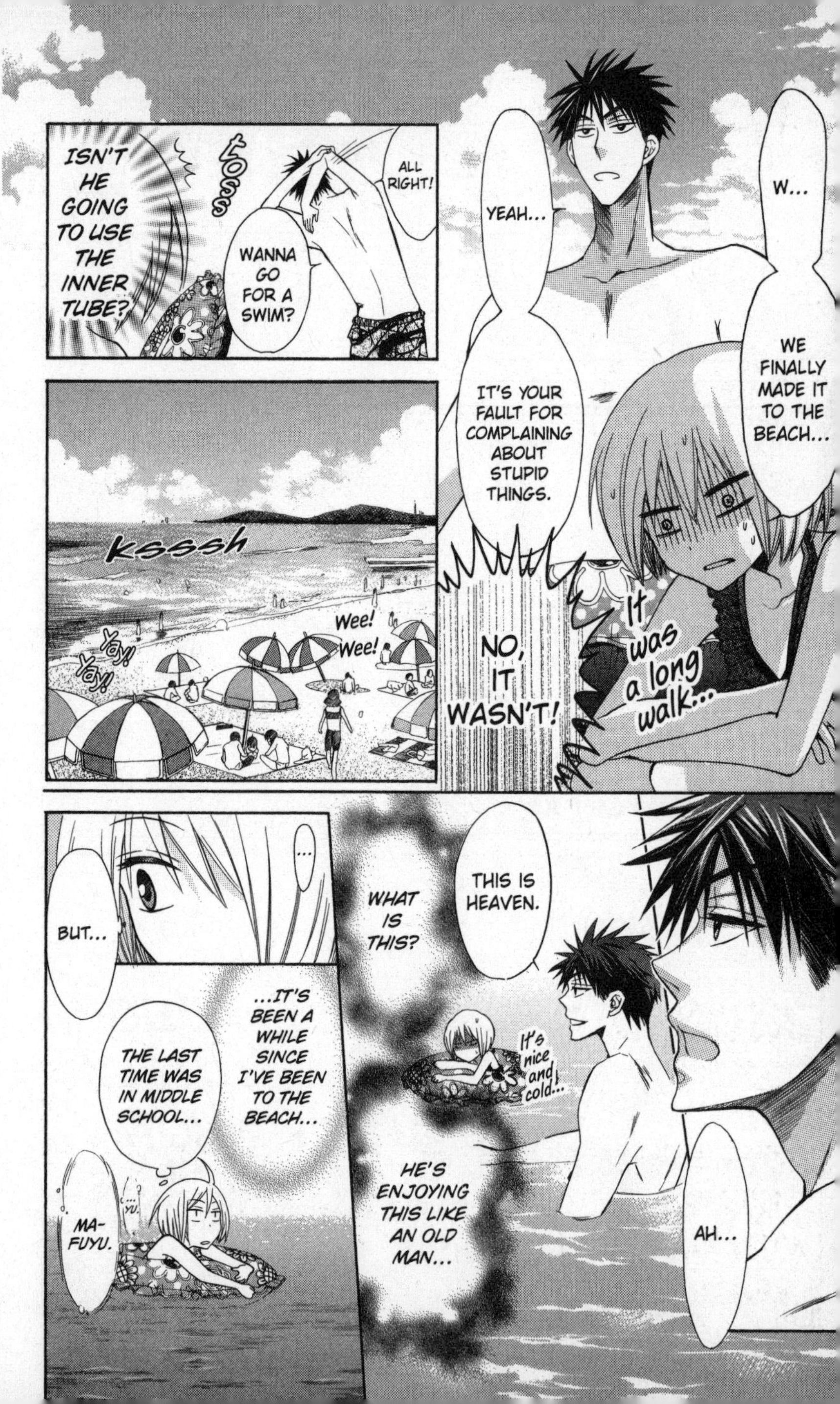
W...
WE FINALLY MADE IT TO THE BEACH...
YEAH...
IT'S YOUR FAULT FOR COMPLAINING ABOUT STUPID THINGS.
It was a long walk...
NO, IT WASN'T!
ALL RIGHT!
WANNA GO FOR A SWIM?
toss
ISN'T HE GOING TO USE THE INNER TUBE?
ksssh
Wee! Wee!
Yay! Yay!
THIS IS HEAVEN.
AH...
It's nice and cold...
WHAT IS THIS?
HE'S ENJOYING THIS LIKE AN OLD MAN...
...
BUT...
...IT'S BEEN A WHILE SINCE I'VE BEEN TO THE BEACH...
THE LAST TIME WAS IN MIDDLE SCHOOL...
MA-FUYU.

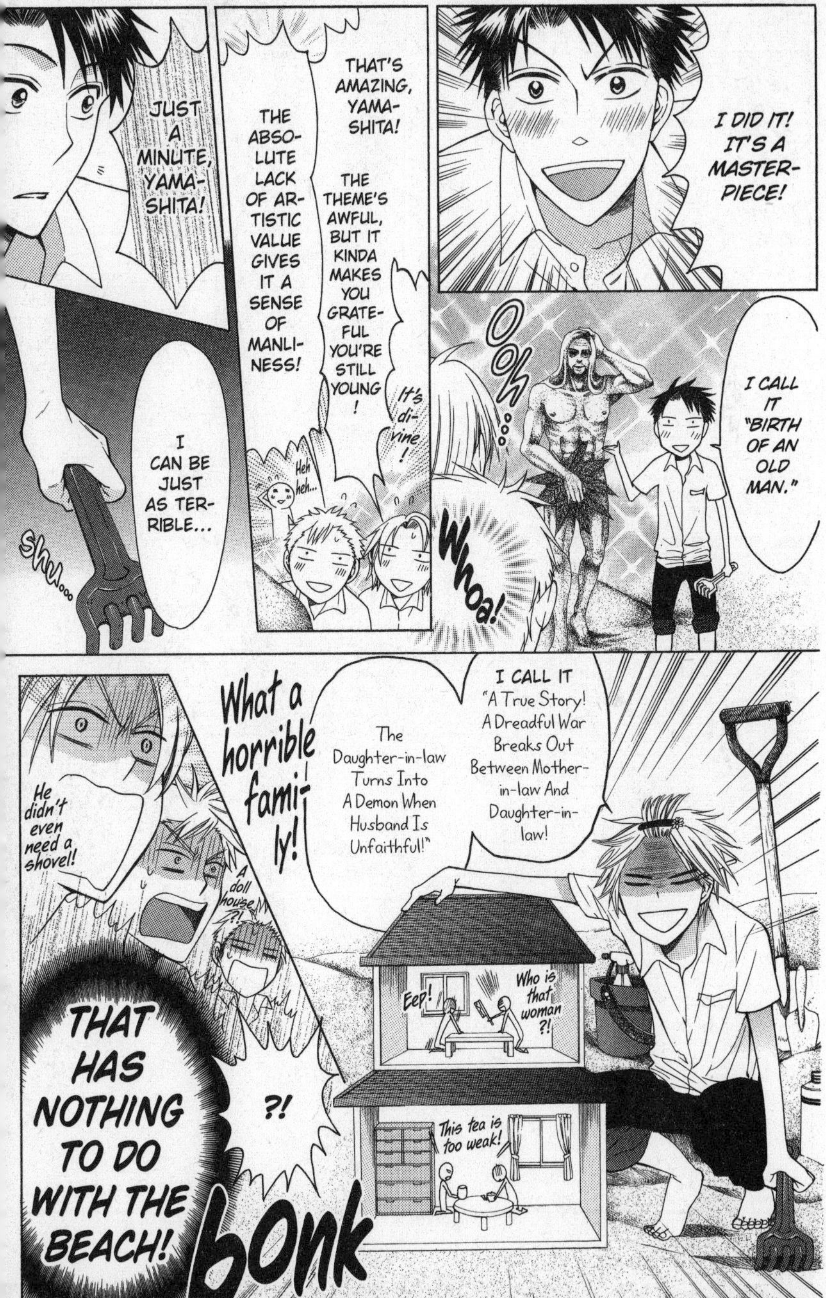
I DID IT! IT'S A MASTERPIECE!
I CALL IT "BIRTH OF AN OLD MAN."
Ooh...
Whoa!
THAT'S AMAZING, YAMASHITA!
THE THEME'S AWFUL, BUT IT KINDA MAKES YOU GRATEFUL YOU'RE STILL YOUNG!
THE ABSOLUTE LACK OF ARTISTIC VALUE GIVES IT A SENSE OF MANLINESS!
It's divine!
Heh heh...
JUST A MINUTE, YAMASHITA!
I CAN BE JUST AS TERRIBLE...
shu...
I CALL IT "A True Story! A Dreadful War Breaks Out Between Mother-in-law And Daughter-in-law!
The Daughter-in-law Turns Into A Demon When Husband Is Unfaithful!"
What a horrible family!
Who is that woman?!
Eep!
This tea is too weak!
He didn't even need a shovel!
A doll house?!
?!
THAT HAS NOTHING TO DO WITH THE BEACH!
bonk

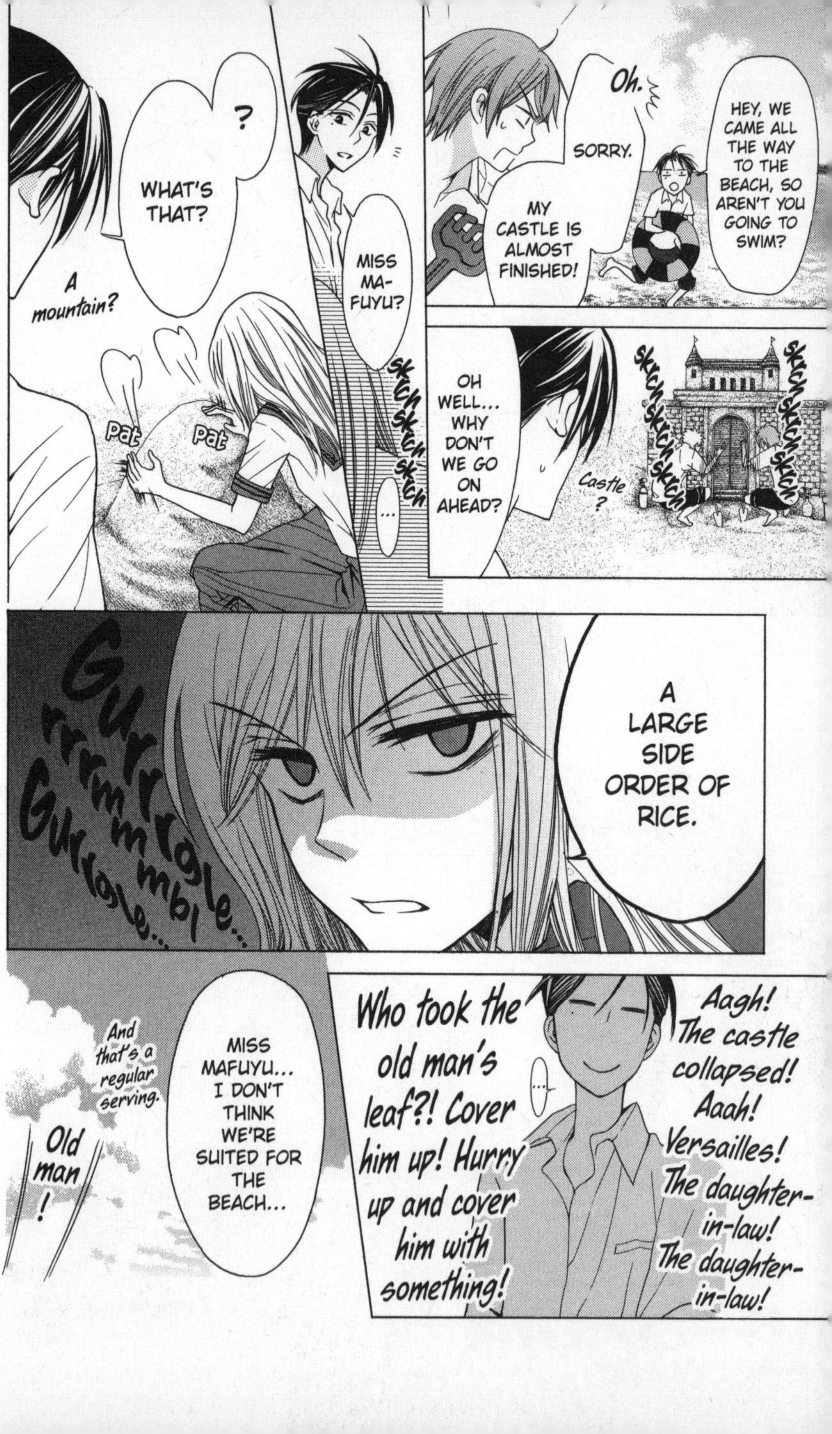
HEY, WE CAME ALL THE WAY TO THE BEACH, SO AREN'T YOU GOING TO SWIM?
Oh.
SORRY.
MY CASTLE IS ALMOST FINISHED!
skrch skrch skrch skrch
skrch skrch skrch skrch
OH WELL... WHY DON'T WE GO ON AHEAD?
Castle?
MISS MA-FUYU?
skrch skrch skrch skrch
...
?
WHAT'S THAT?
A mountain?
pat
pat
A LARGE SIDE ORDER OF RICE.
Gurrrgle... Grrrrmmbl Gurrrgle...
Aagh! The castle collapsed! Aaah! Versailles! The daughter-in-law! The daughter-in-law!
Who took the old man's leaf?! Cover him up! Hurry up and cover him with something!
...
MISS MAFUYU... I DON'T THINK WE'RE SUITED FOR THE BEACH...
And that's a regular serving.
Old man!

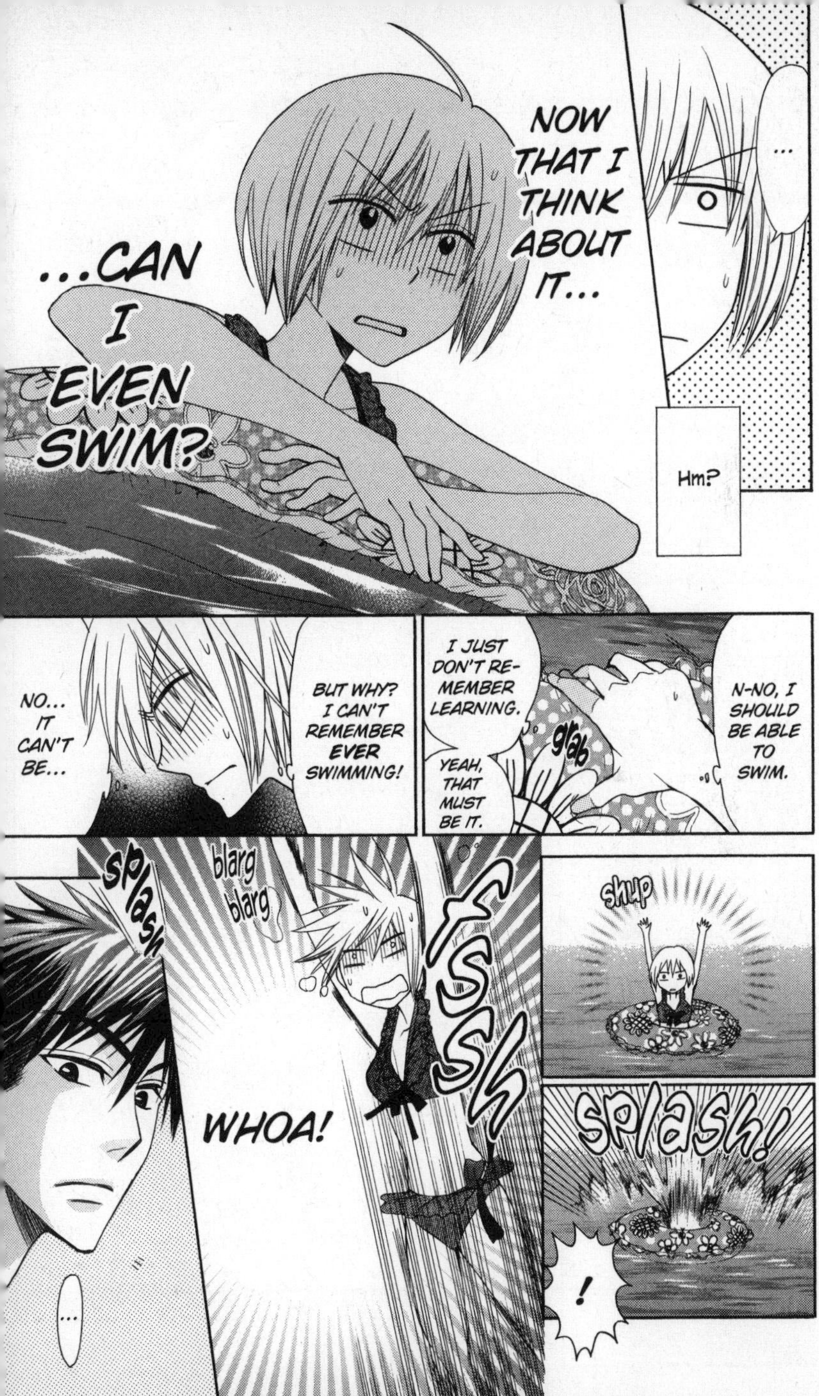
...
Hm?
NOW THAT I THINK ABOUT IT...
...CAN I EVEN SWIM?
N-NO, I SHOULD BE ABLE TO SWIM.
grab
I JUST DON'T RE-MEMBER LEARNING.
YEAH, THAT MUST BE IT.
BUT WHY? I CAN'T REMEMBER EVER SWIMMING!
NO... IT CAN'T BE...
shup
splash!
!
fssh
blarg blarg
splash
WHOA!
...

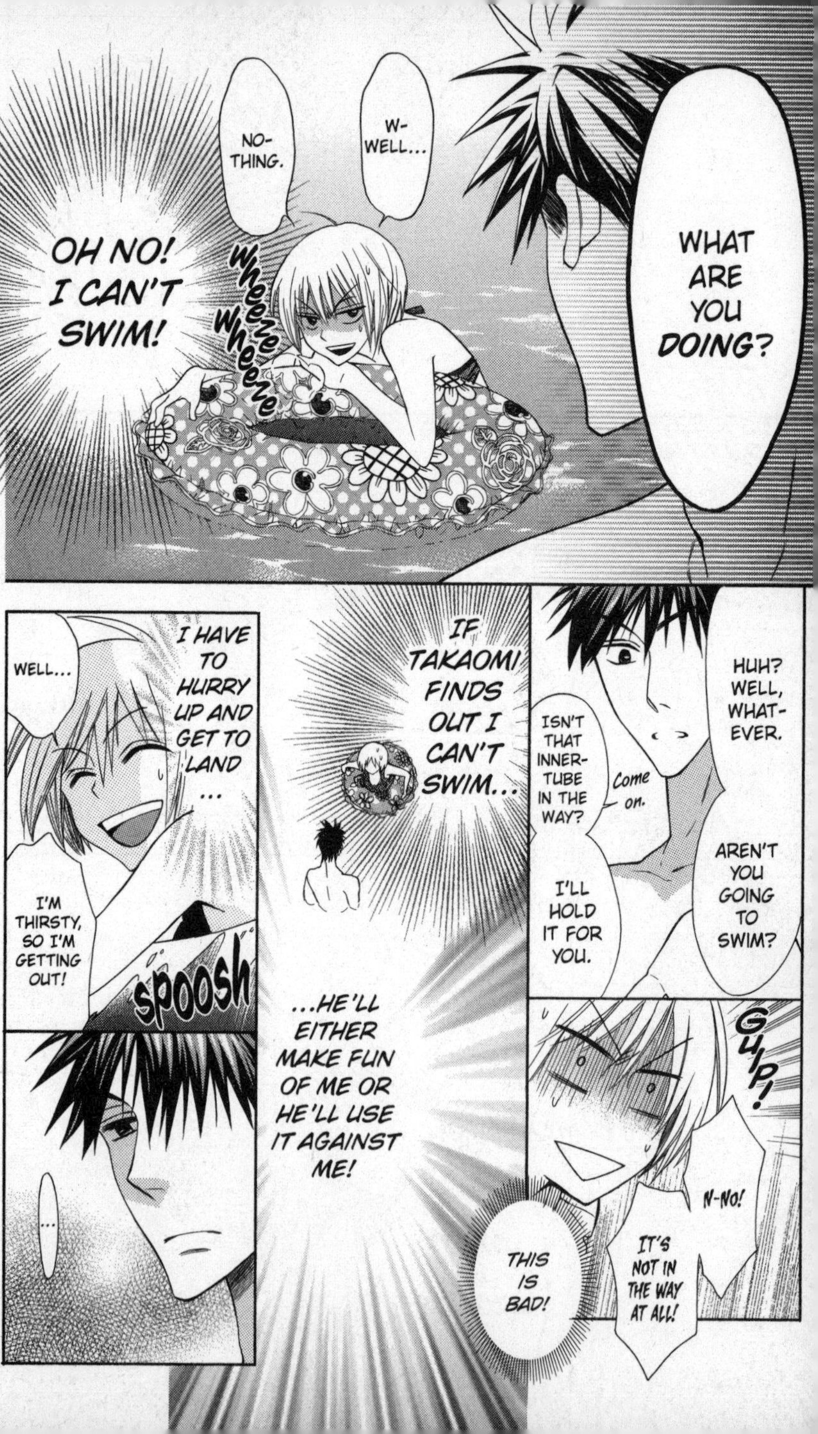
WHAT ARE YOU DOING?
W-WELL...
NO-THING.
OH NO! I CAN'T SWIM!
wheeze wheeze
HUH? WELL, WHAT-EVER.
AREN'T YOU GOING TO SWIM?
Come on.
ISN'T THAT INNER-TUBE IN THE WAY?
I'LL HOLD IT FOR YOU.
GULP!
N-NO!
IT'S NOT IN THE WAY AT ALL!
THIS IS BAD!
IF TAKAOMI FINDS OUT I CAN'T SWIM...
...HE'LL EITHER MAKE FUN OF ME OR HE'LL USE IT AGAINST ME!
WELL...
I HAVE TO HURRY UP AND GET TO LAND...
I'M THIRSTY, SO I'M GETTING OUT!
sposh
...

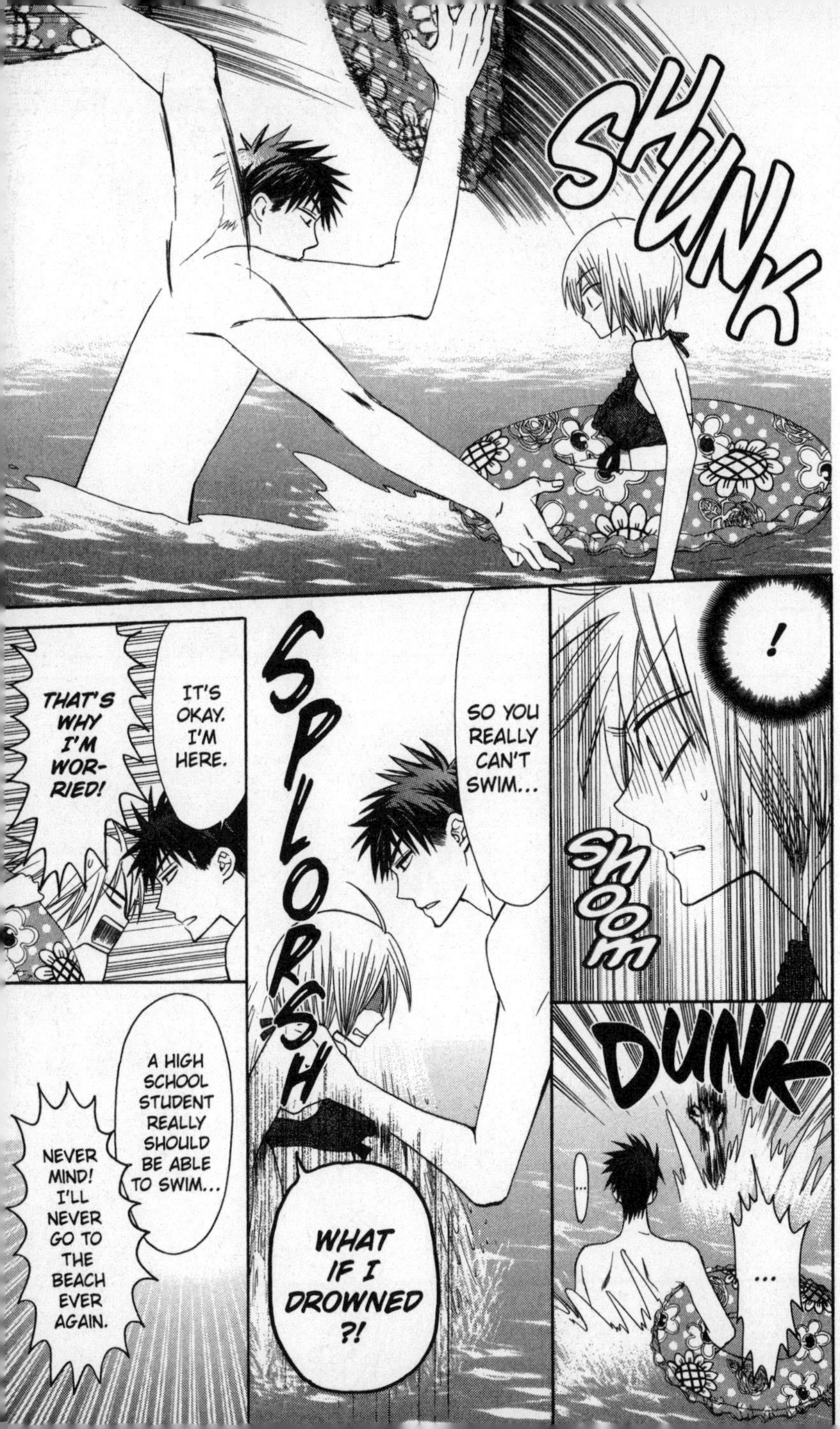
SHUNK
!
SHOOM
DUNK
...
...
SO YOU REALLY CAN'T SWIM...
SPLORSH
WHAT IF I DROWNED?!
IT'S OKAY. I'M HERE.
THAT'S WHY I'M WOR-RIED!
A HIGH SCHOOL STUDENT REALLY SHOULD BE ABLE TO SWIM...
NEVER MIND! I'LL NEVER GO TO THE BEACH EVER AGAIN.

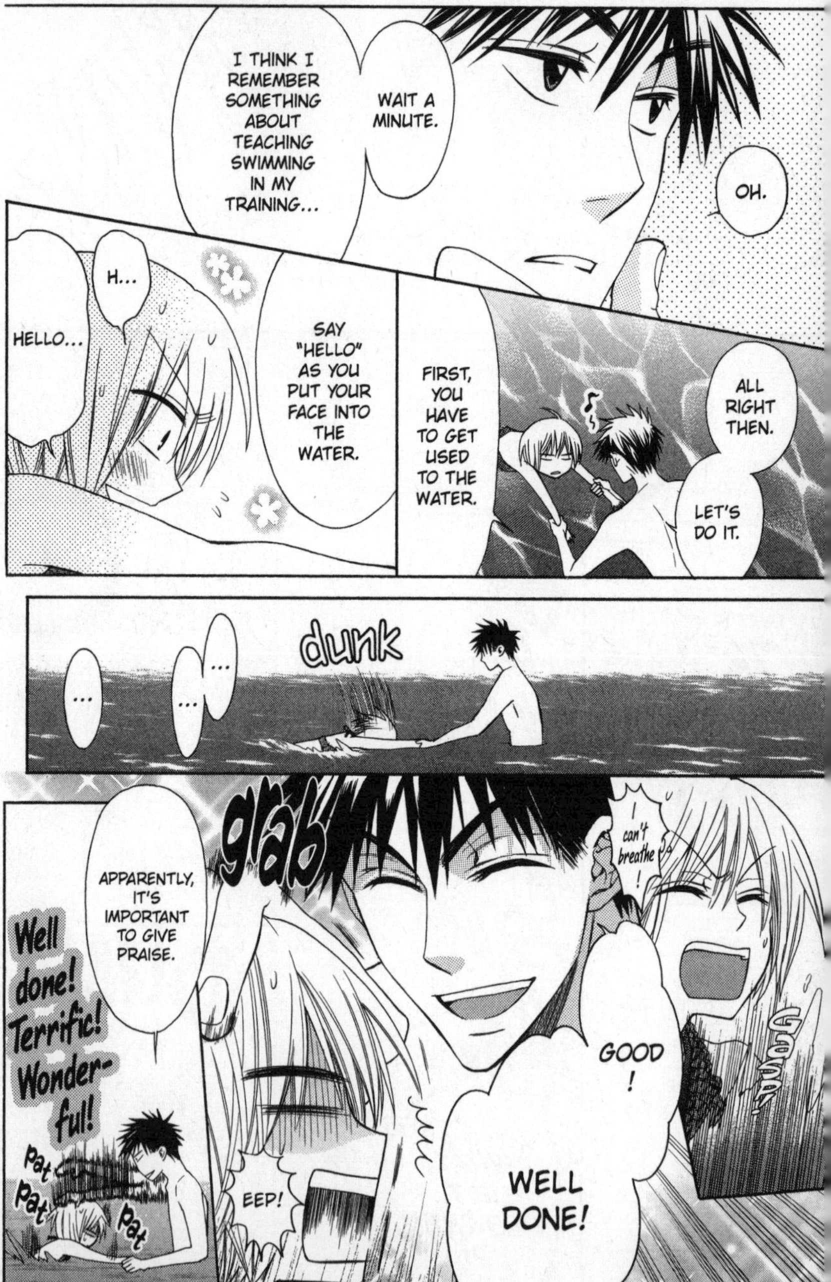
OH.
WAIT A MINUTE.
I THINK I REMEMBER SOMETHING ABOUT TEACHING SWIMMING IN MY TRAINING...
ALL RIGHT THEN.
LET'S DO IT.
FIRST, YOU HAVE TO GET USED TO THE WATER.
SAY "HELLO" AS YOU PUT YOUR FACE INTO THE WATER.
H...
HELLO...
dunk
...
...
...
grab
I can't breathe!
GOOD!
WELL DONE!
EEP!
APPARENTLY, IT'S IMPORTANT TO GIVE PRAISE.
Well done! Terrific! Wonderful!
Pat Pat Pat pat

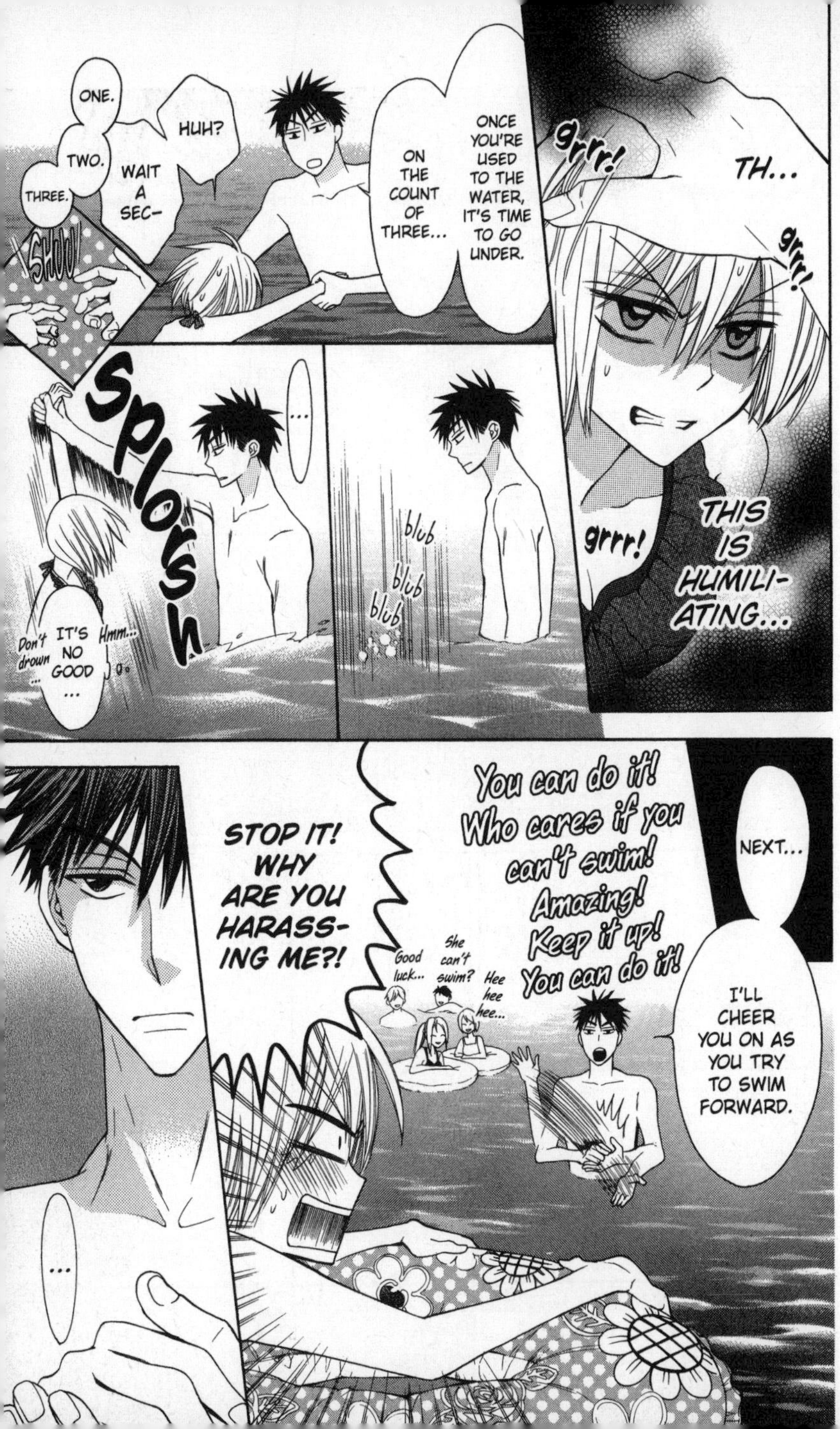
TH...
grrr!
grrr!
grrr!
THIS IS HUMILIATING...
ONCE YOU'RE USED TO THE WATER, IT'S TIME TO GO UNDER.
ON THE COUNT OF THREE...
HUH?
WAIT A SEC-
ONE.
TWO.
THREE.
SHOVE
blub
blub
blub
...
Splosh
Hmm...
IT'S NO GOOD...
Don't drown...
NEXT...
I'LL CHEER YOU ON AS YOU TRY TO SWIM FORWARD.
You can do it! Who cares if you can't swim! Amazing! Keep it up! You can do it!
She can't swim?
Good luck...
Hee hee hee...
STOP IT! WHY ARE YOU HARASSING ME?!
...

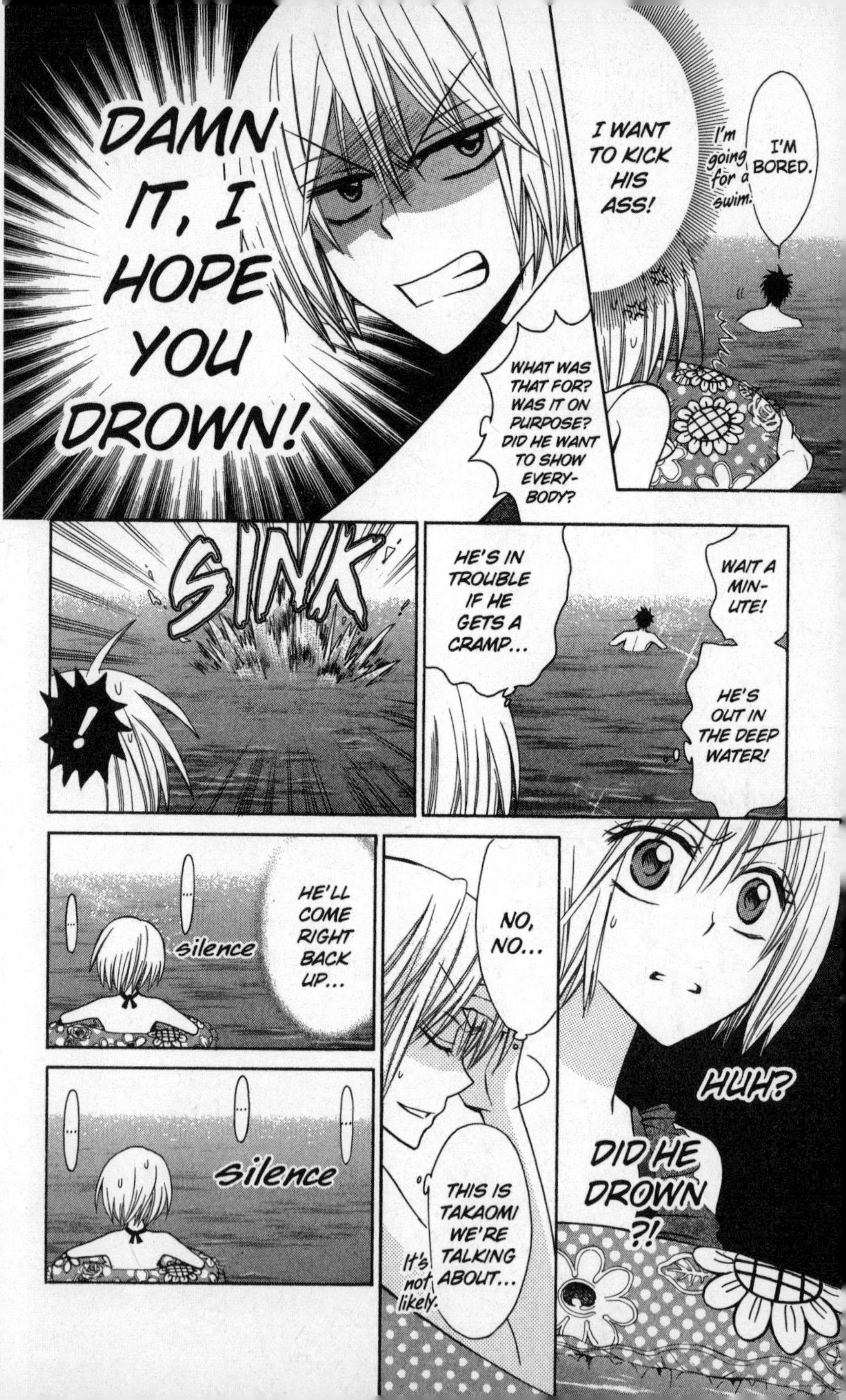
I'M BORED.
I'm going for a swim.
I WANT TO KICK HIS ASS!
WHAT WAS THAT FOR? WAS IT ON PURPOSE? DID HE WANT TO SHOW EVERY-BODY?
DAMN IT, I HOPE YOU DROWN!
WAIT A MIN-UTE!
HE'S OUT IN THE DEEP WATER!
HE'S IN TROUBLE IF HE GETS A CRAMP...
SINK
!
HUH?
DID HE DROWN?!
NO, NO...
THIS IS TAKAOMI WE'RE TALKING ABOUT...
It's not likely.
...
...
HE'LL COME RIGHT BACK UP...
silence
...
...
...
silence

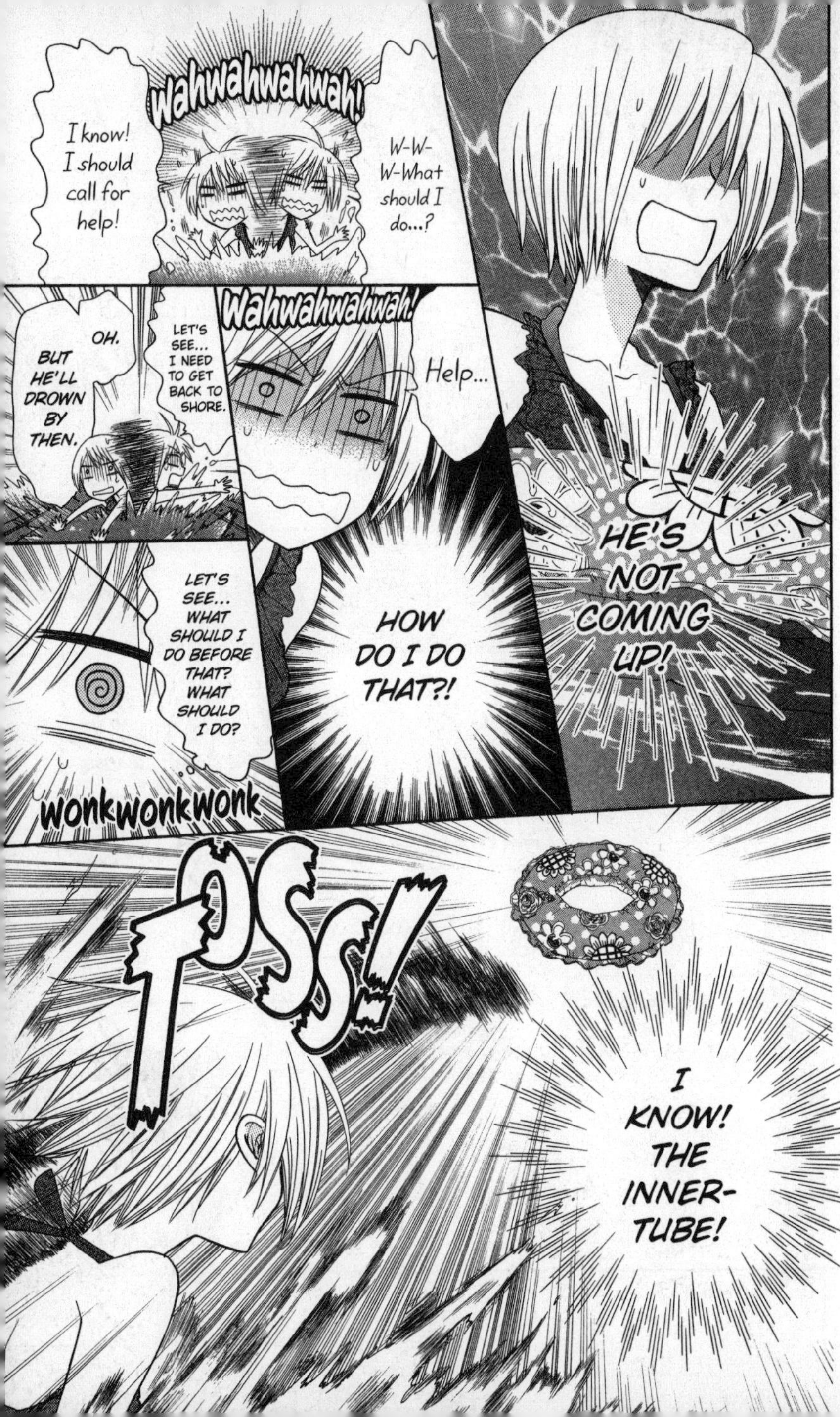
HE'S NOT COMING UP!
Wahwahwahwah!
W-W-W-What should I do...?
I know! I should call for help!
Wahwahwahwah!
Help...
LET'S SEE... I NEED TO GET BACK TO SHORE.
OH. BUT HE'LL DROWN BY THEN.
HOW DO I DO THAT?!
LET'S SEE... WHAT SHOULD I DO BEFORE THAT? WHAT SHOULD I DO?
wonkwonkwonk
I KNOW! THE INNER-TUBE!
TOSS!

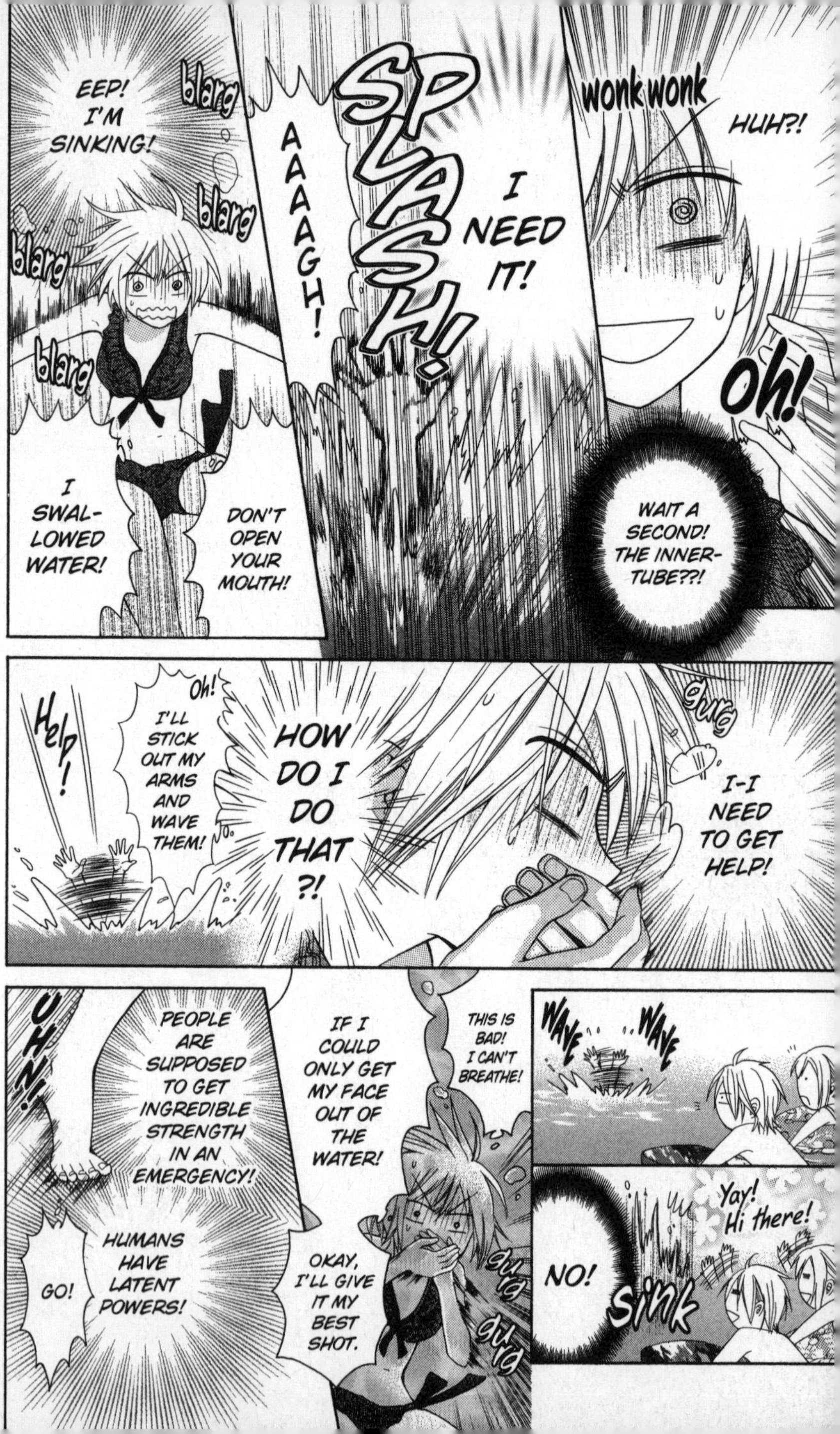
wonk wonk
HUH?!
Oh!
WAIT A SECOND! THE INNER-TUBE??!
SPLASH!
I NEED IT!
AAAAAGH!
EEP! I'M SINKING!
blarg
blarg
blarg
blarg
DON'T OPEN YOUR MOUTH!
I SWAL-LOWED WATER!
gurg
I-I NEED TO GET HELP!
HOW DO I DO THAT?!
Oh! I'LL STICK OUT MY ARMS AND WAVE THEM!
Help!
WAVE WAVE
Yay! Hi there!
sink
NO!
THIS IS BAD! I CAN'T BREATHE!
IF I COULD ONLY GET MY FACE OUT OF THE WATER!
gurg gurg
OKAY, I'LL GIVE IT MY BEST SHOT.
PEOPLE ARE SUPPOSED TO GET INGREDIBLE STRENGTH IN AN EMERGENCY!
HUMANS HAVE LATENT POWERS!
GO!
UHN!

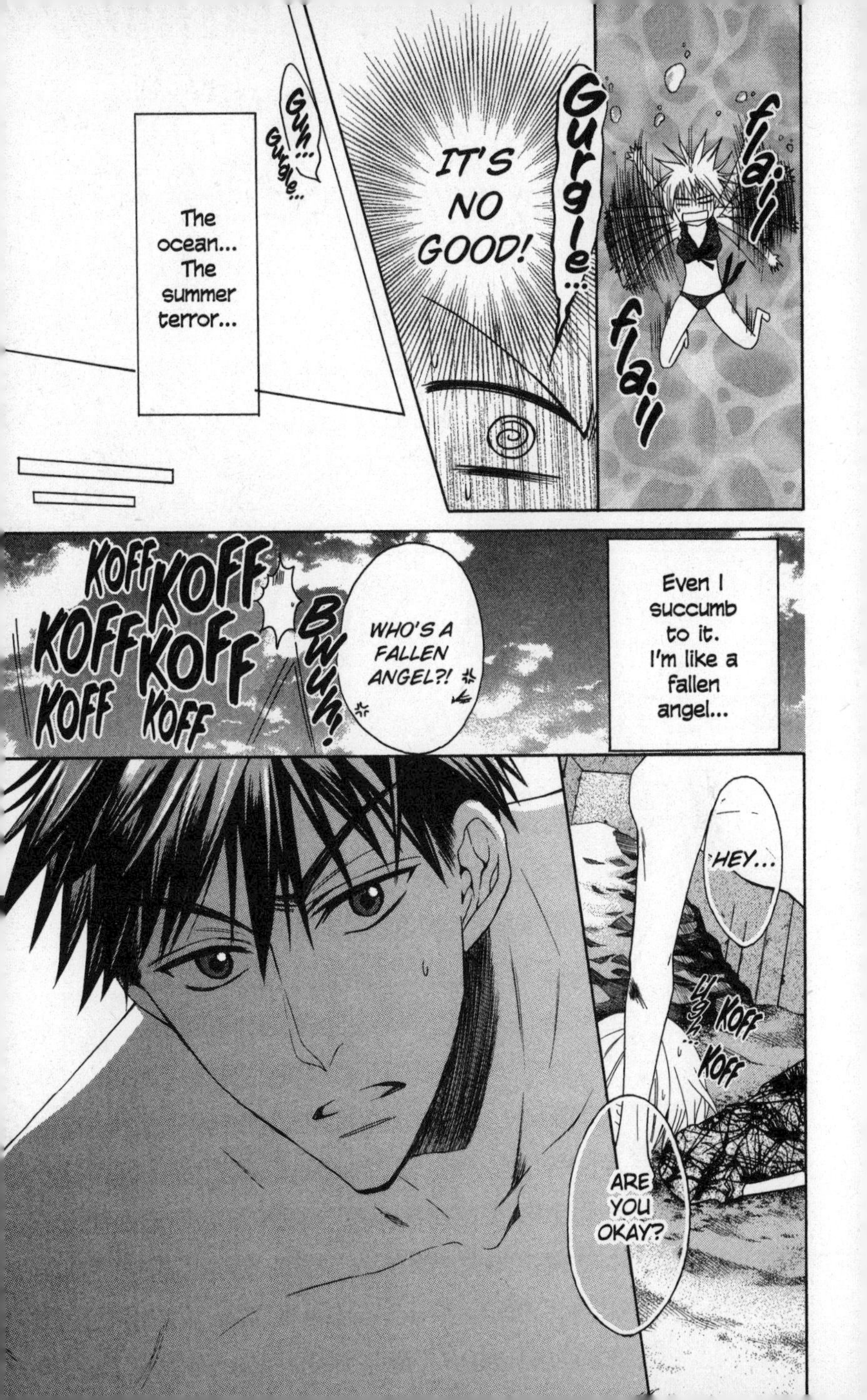
flail flail
Gurgle...
IT'S NO GOOD!
Gun...
Gurgle...
The ocean... The summer terror...
Even I succumb to it. I'm like a fallen angel...
WHO'S A FALLEN ANGEL?!
BWUH!
KOFF KOFF KOFF KOFF KOFF KOFF
HEY...
Ugh... KOFF KOFF
ARE YOU OKAY?

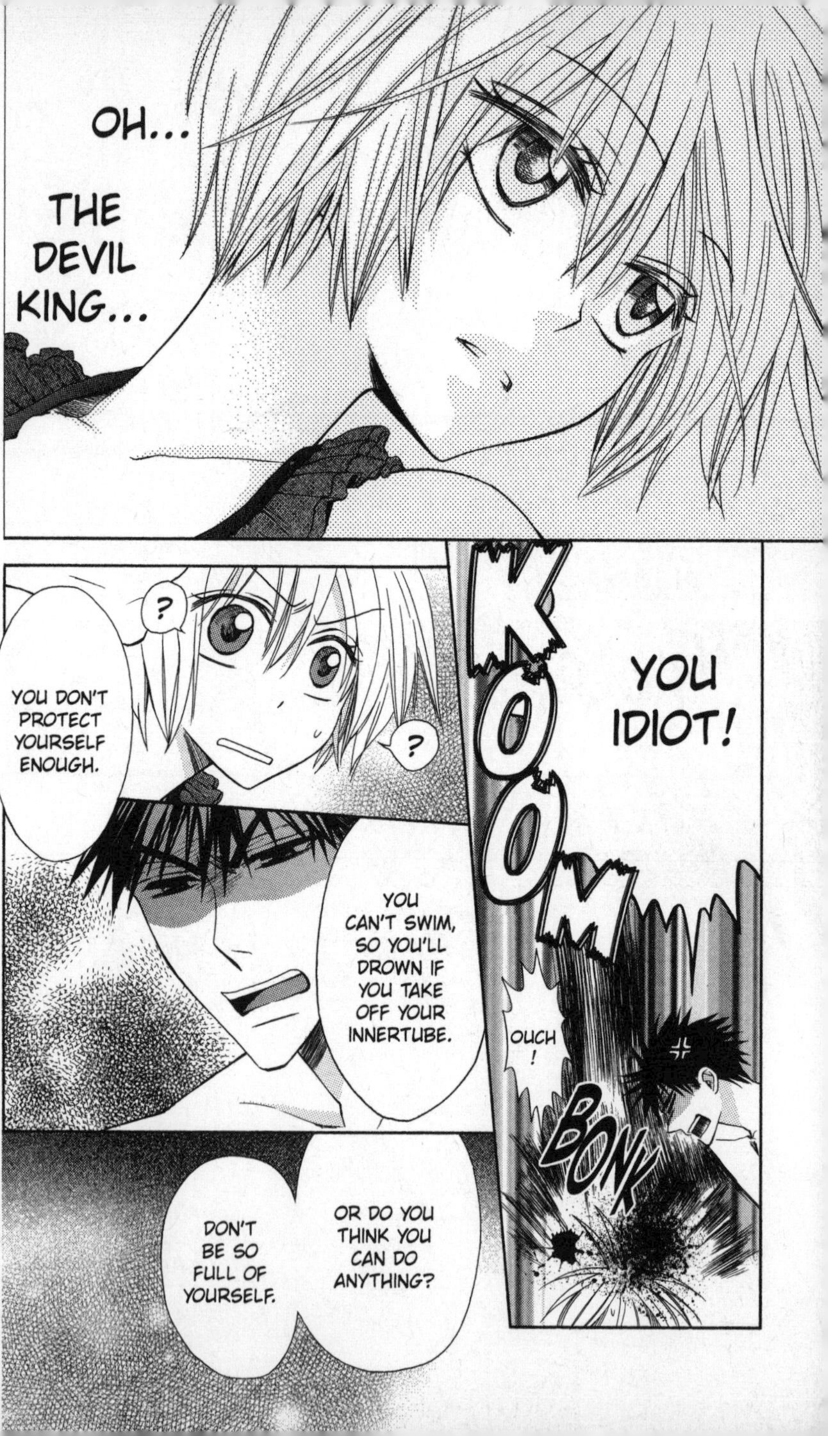
OH...
THE DEVIL KING...
KOOOM
YOU IDIOT!
OUCH!
BONK
?
?
YOU DON'T PROTECT YOURSELF ENOUGH.
YOU CAN'T SWIM, SO YOU'LL DROWN IF YOU TAKE OFF YOUR INNERTUBE.
OR DO YOU THINK YOU CAN DO ANYTHING?
DON'T BE SO FULL OF YOURSELF.

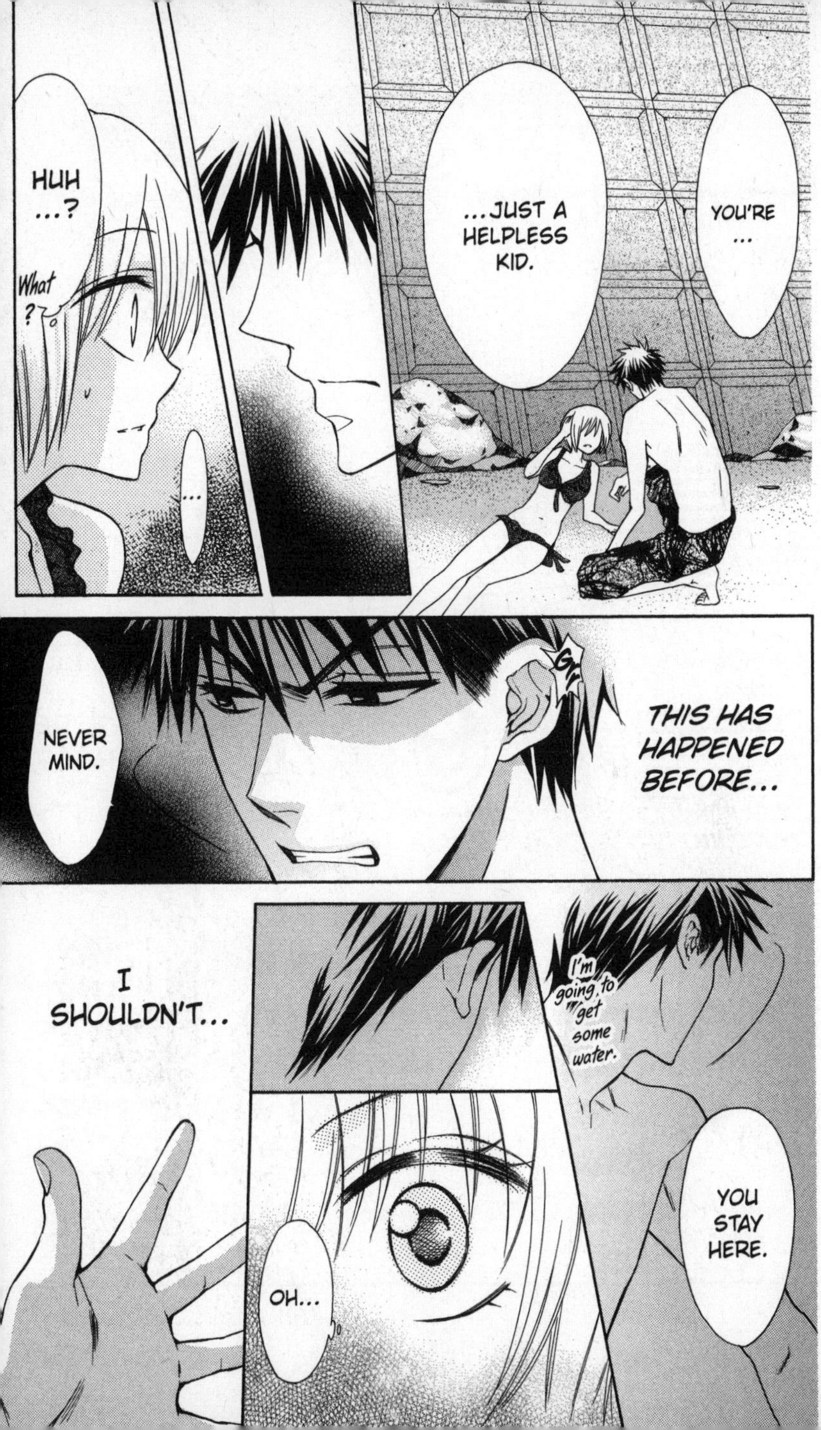
YOU'RE ...
...JUST A HELPLESS KID.
...
HUH ...?
What?
THIS HAS HAPPENED BEFORE...
Gr
NEVER MIND.
I'm going to get some water.
YOU STAY HERE.
OH...
I SHOULDN'T...

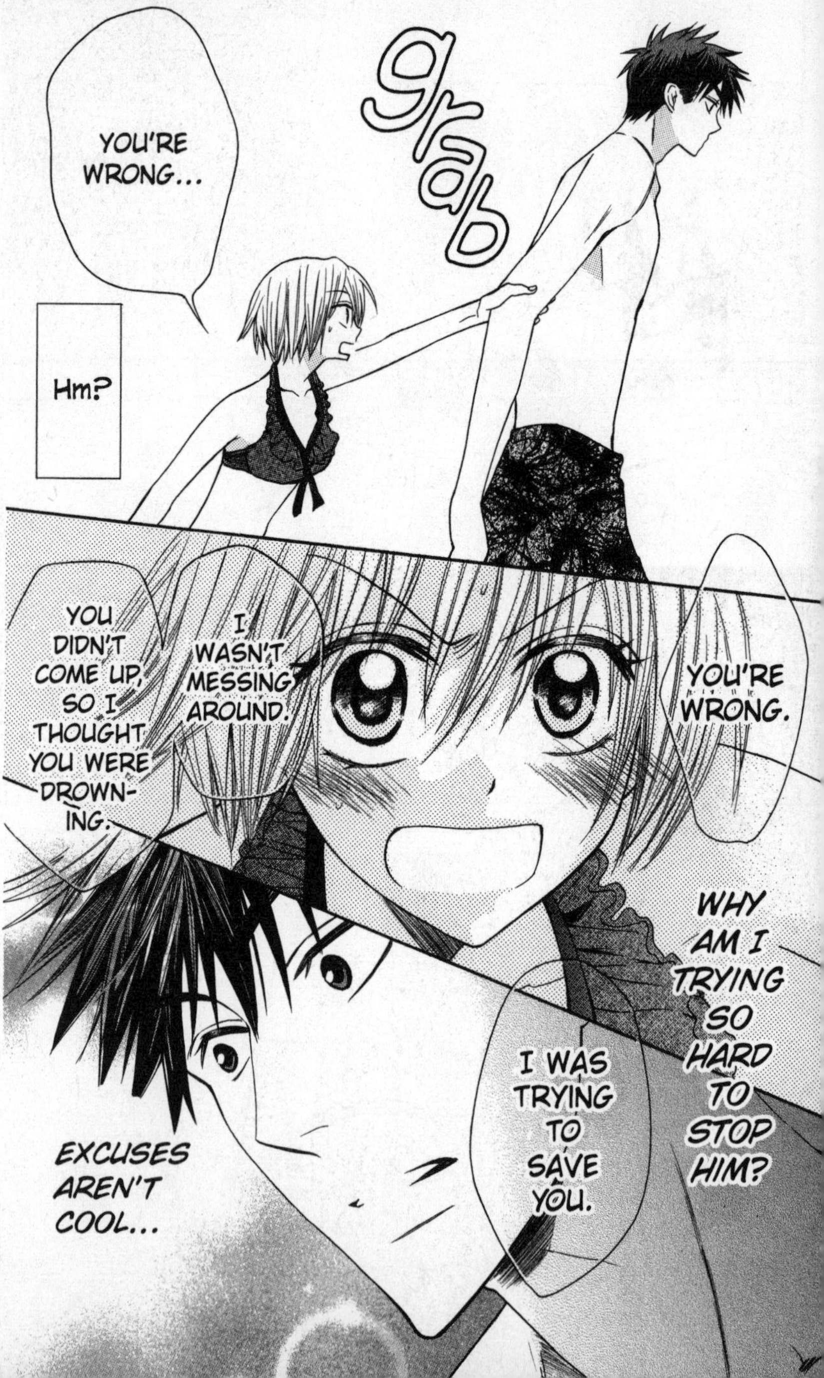
grab
YOU'RE WRONG...
Hm?
YOU'RE WRONG.
I WASN'T MESSING AROUND.
YOU DIDN'T COME UP, SO I THOUGHT YOU WERE DROWNING.
WHY AM I TRYING SO HARD TO STOP HIM?
I WAS TRYING TO SAVE YOU.
EXCUSES AREN'T COOL...

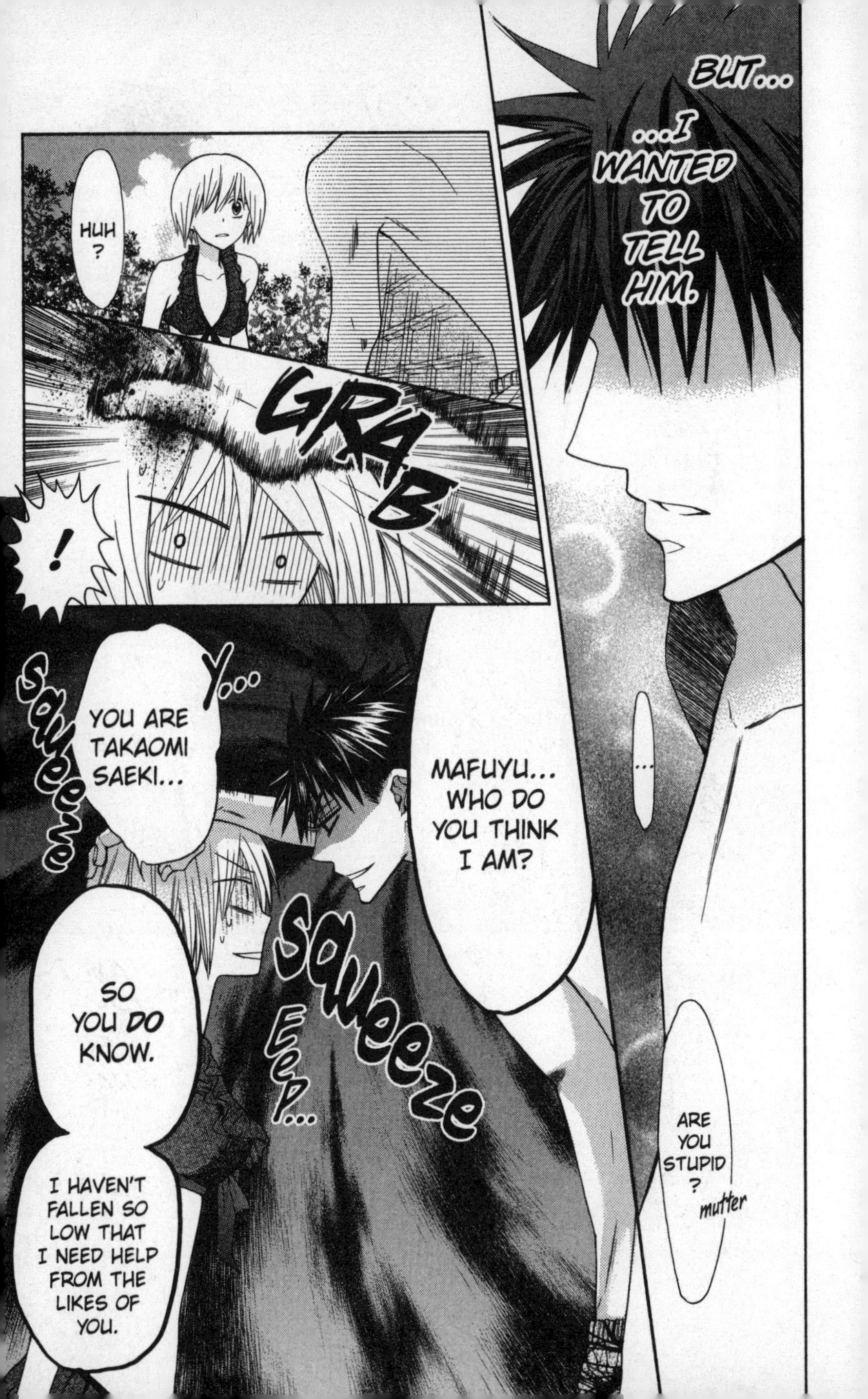

BUT...
...I WANTED TO TELL HIM.
HUH?
GRAB
!
MAFUYU... WHO DO YOU THINK I AM?
Y...
YOU ARE TAKAOMI SAEKI...
squeeze
squeeze
Eep...
SO YOU DO KNOW.
I HAVEN'T FALLEN SO LOW THAT I NEED HELP FROM THE LIKES OF YOU.
...
ARE YOU STUPID?
mutter

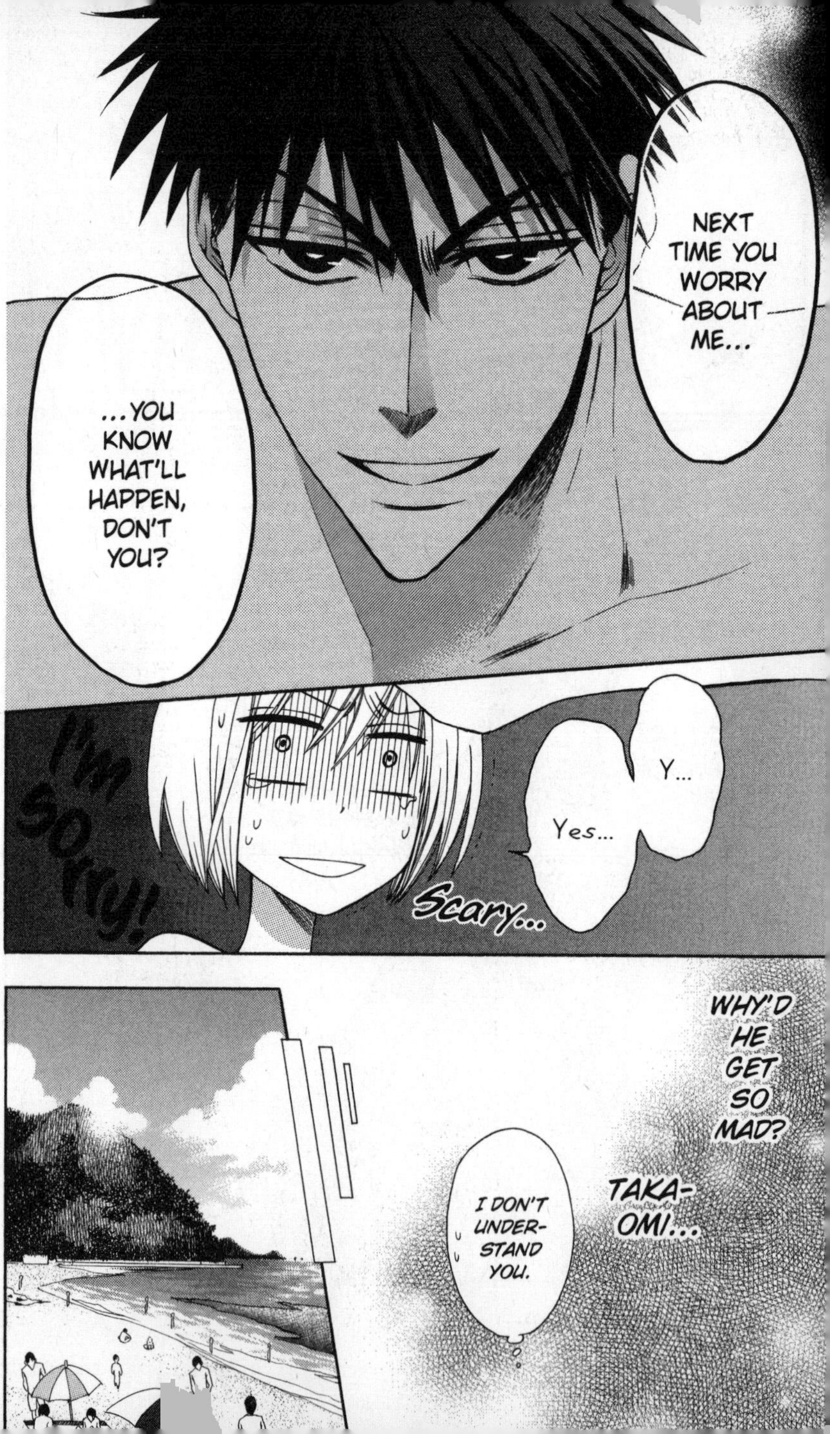
NEXT TIME YOU WORRY ABOUT ME...
...YOU KNOW WHAT'LL HAPPEN, DON'T YOU?
Y... Yes...
Scary...
I'm sorry!
WHY'D HE GET SO MAD?
TAKA-OMI...
I DON'T UNDER-STAND YOU.

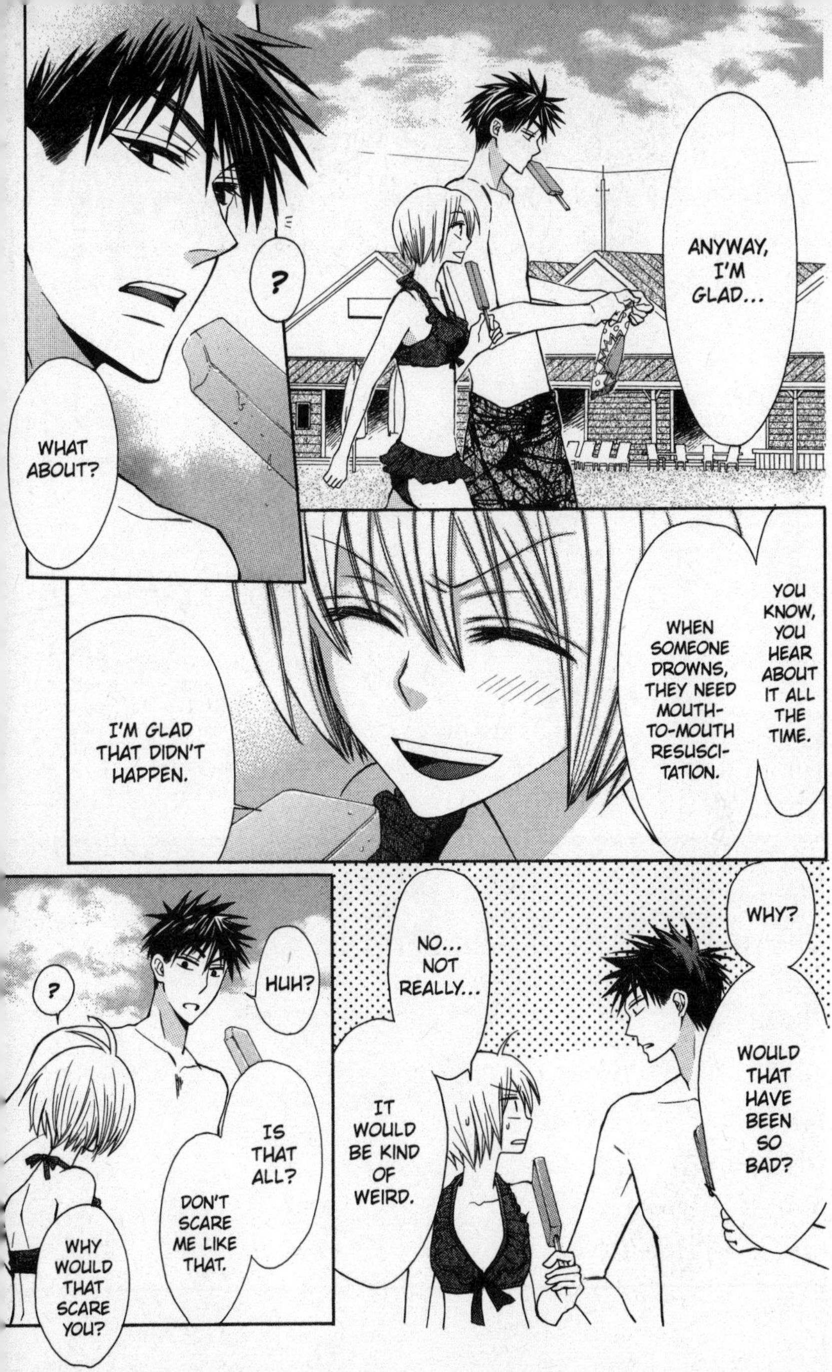
ANYWAY, I'M GLAD...
?
WHAT ABOUT?
YOU KNOW, YOU HEAR ABOUT IT ALL THE TIME.
WHEN SOMEONE DROWNS, THEY NEED MOUTH-TO-MOUTH RESUSCITATION.
I'M GLAD THAT DIDN'T HAPPEN.
WHY?
WOULD THAT HAVE BEEN SO BAD?
NO... NOT REALLY...
IT WOULD BE KIND OF WEIRD.
HUH?
?
IS THAT ALL?
DON'T SCARE ME LIKE THAT.
WHY WOULD THAT SCARE YOU?

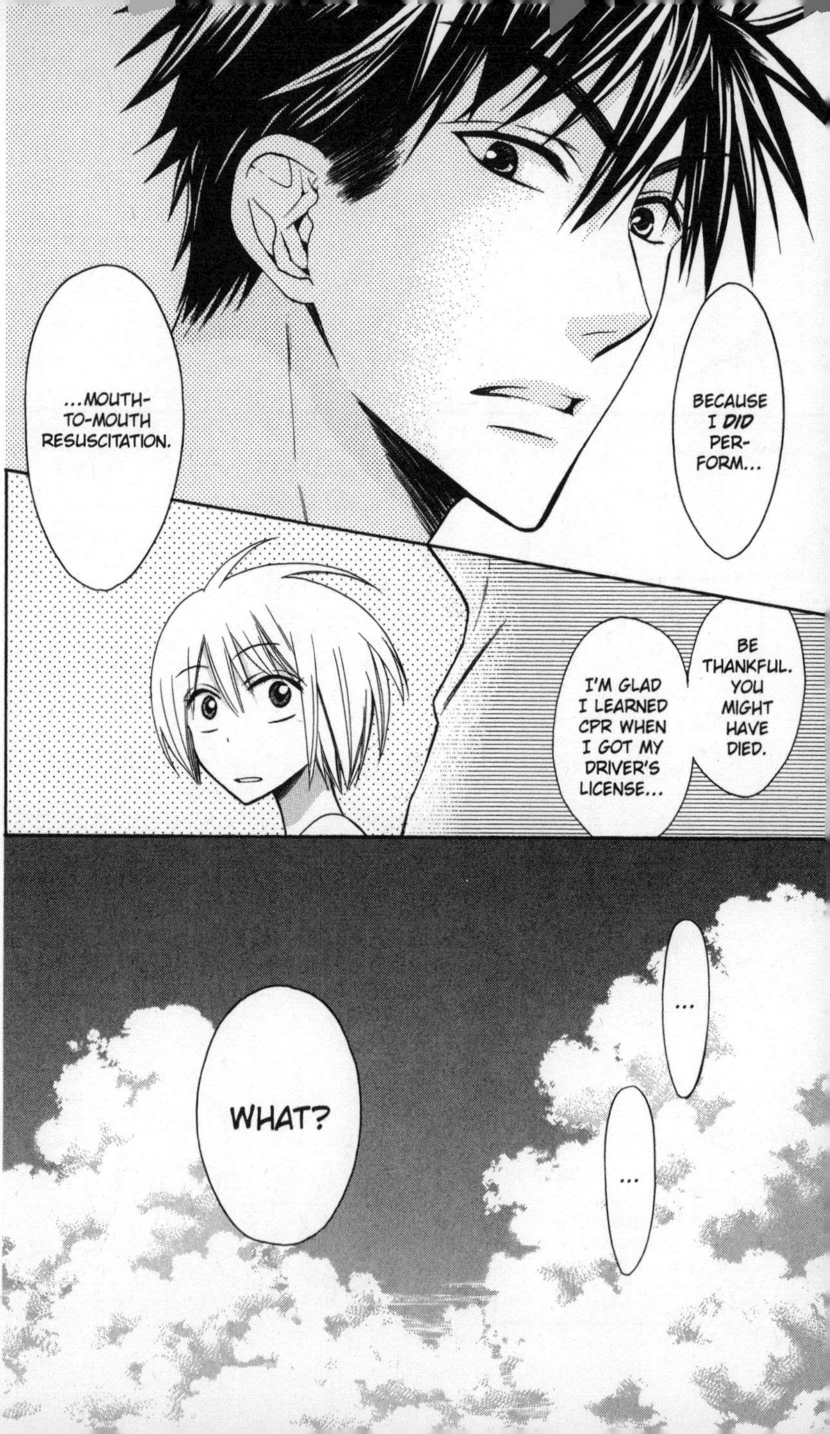
BECAUSE I *DID* PER-FORM...
...MOUTH-TO-MOUTH RESUSCITATION.
BE THANKFUL. YOU MIGHT HAVE DIED.
I'M GLAD I LEARNED CPR WHEN I GOT MY DRIVER'S LICENSE...
...
...
WHAT?

End Notes

Page 7, panel 3: Bancho
The leader of a unit, in this case the head
of a gang of delinquents.

Page 14, panel 7: Yakuza
The Japanese mob.

Page 79, panel 4: Hanafuda
Literally "flower cards," they are a set
of cards used to play various games.
Historically, hanafuda were also used
for gambling.

Page 79, panel 4: Kings
Also called the Ousama game, it is a party
game similar to truth or dare, where each
player is identified by a number, and the
"king" gives out embarrassing decrees.

Izumi Tsubaki began drawing manga in her first year of high school. She was soon selected to be in the top ten of *Hana to Yume's* HMC (*Hana to Yume* Mangaka Course), and subsequently won *Hana to Yume's* Big Challenge contest. Her debut title, *Chijimete Distance* (Shrink the Distance), ran in 2002 in *Hana to Yume* magazine, issue 17. Her other works include *The Magic Touch* (*Oyayubi kara Romance*) and *Oresama Teacher*, which she is currently working on.

ORESAMA TEACHER
Vol. 4
Shojo Beat Edition

STORY AND ART BY
Izumi Tsubaki

English Translation & Adaptation/JN Productions
Touch-up Art & Lettering/Susan Daigle-Leach
Design/Yukiko Whitley
Editor/Pancha Diaz

ORESAMA TEACHER by Izumi Tsubaki © Izumi Tsubaki 2009
All rights reserved. First published in Japan in 2009 by HAKUSENSHA, Inc., Tokyo.
English language translation rights arranged with HAKUSENSHA, Inc., Tokyo.

The stories, characters and incidents mentioned in this publication are
entirely fictional.

Printed in the U.S.A.

Published by VIZ Media, LLC
P.O. Box 77010
San Francisco, CA 94107

10 9 8 7 6 5 4 3 2
First printing, September 2011
Second printing, July 2014

www.viz.com   www.shojobeat.com

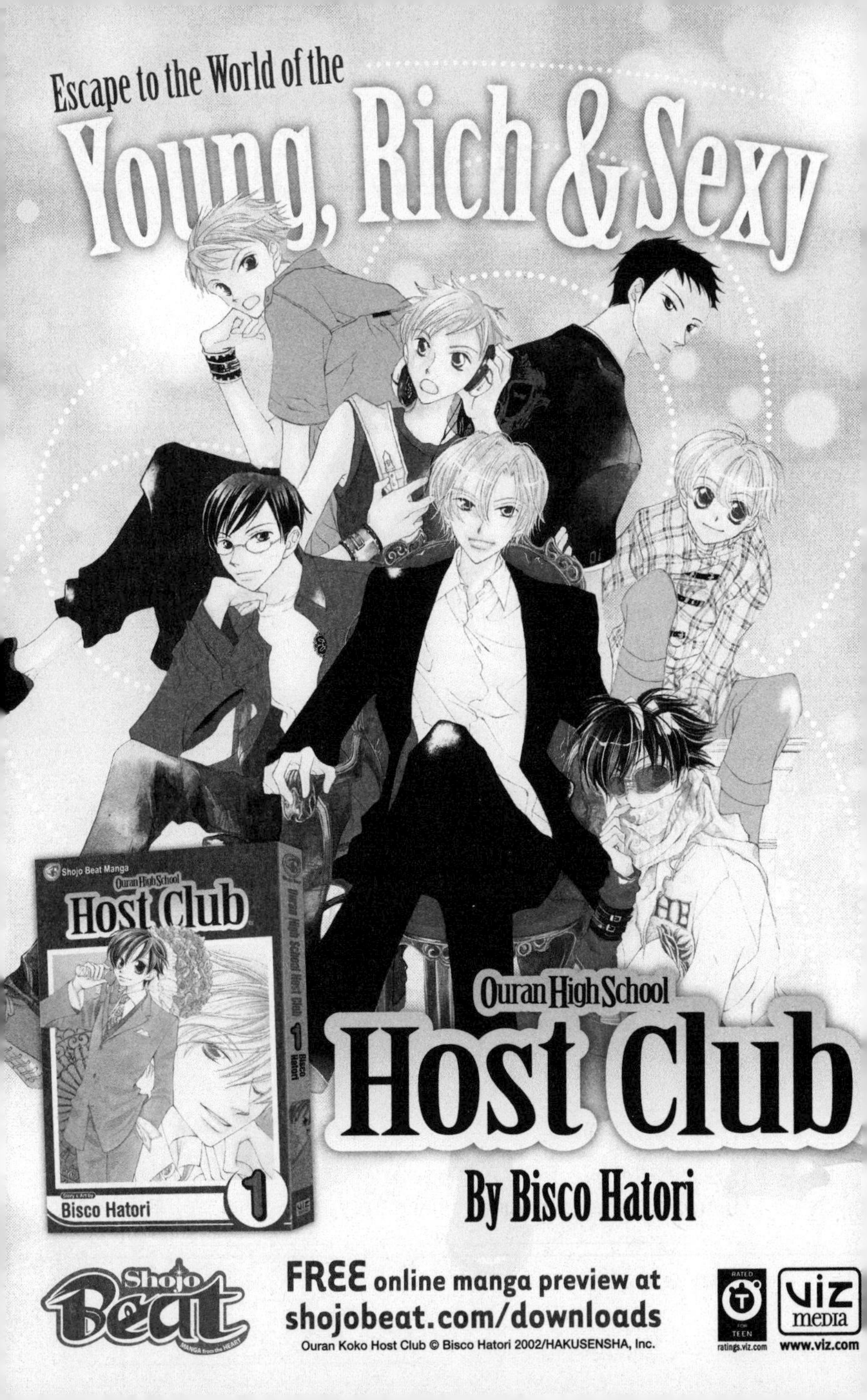
Escape to the World of the
Young, Rich & Sexy
Shojo Beat Manga
Ouran High School
Host Club
Bisco Hatori
1
Ouran High School
Host Club
By Bisco Hatori
Shojo Beat
FREE online manga preview at
shojobeat.com/downloads
Ouran Koko Host Club © Bisco Hatori 2002/HAKUSENSHA, Inc.
ratings.viz.com
VIZ media
www.viz.com

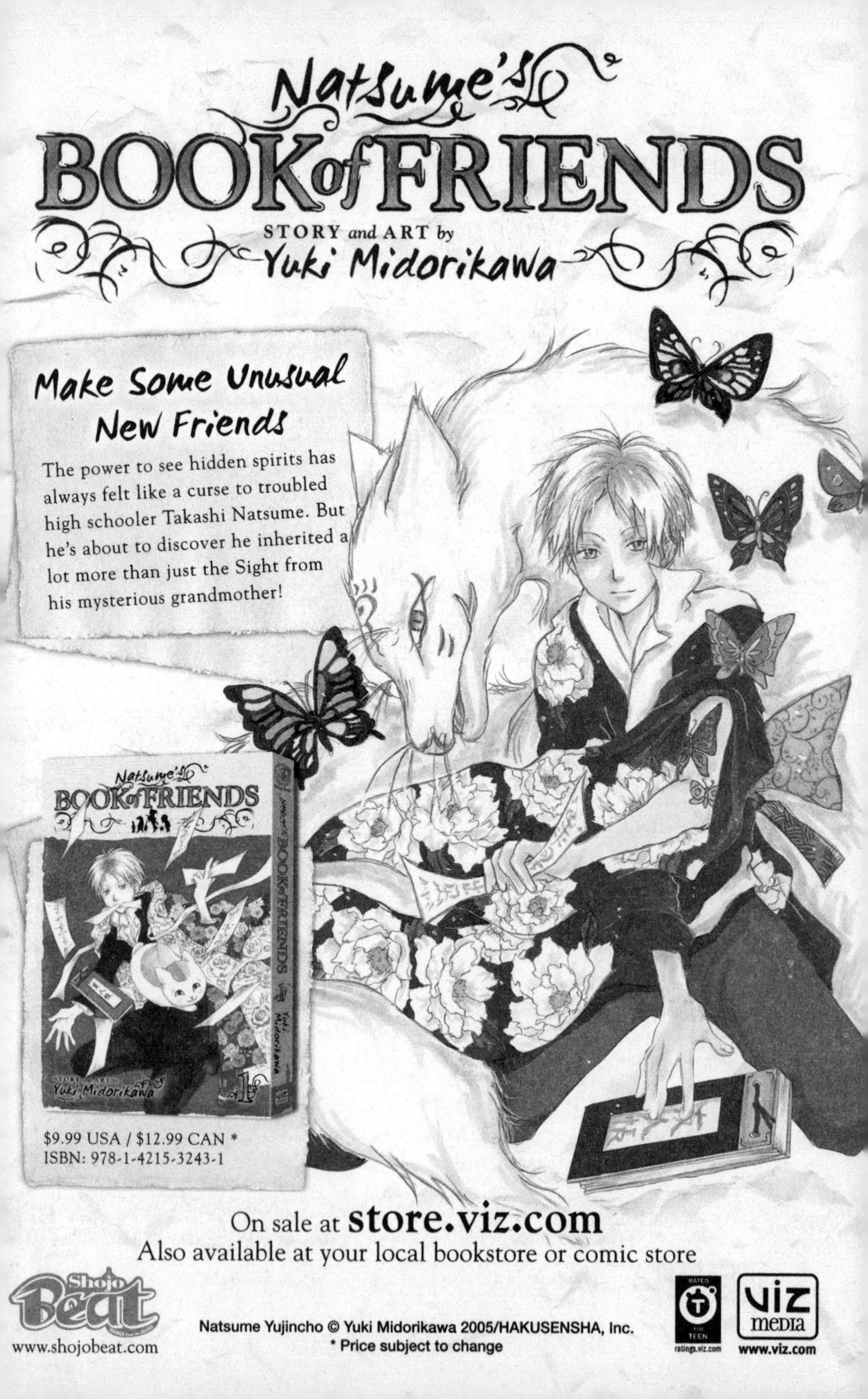

Natsume's
BOOK of FRIENDS
STORY and ART by
Yuki Midorikawa
Make Some Unusual New Friends
The power to see hidden spirits has always felt like a curse to troubled high schooler Takashi Natsume. But he's about to discover he inherited a lot more than just the Sight from his mysterious grandmother!
$9.99 USA / $12.99 CAN *
ISBN: 978-1-4215-3243-1
On sale at store.viz.com
Also available at your local bookstore or comic store
Shojo Beat
www.shojobeat.com
Natsume Yujincho © Yuki Midorikawa 2005/HAKUSENSHA, Inc.
* Price subject to change
RATED T FOR TEEN
ratings.viz.com
VIZ media
www.viz.com

Surprise!

You may be reading the wrong way!

It's true: In keeping with the original Japanese comic format, this book reads from right to left—so action, sound effects, and word balloons are completely reversed. This preserves the orientation of the original artwork—plus, it's fun! Check out the diagram shown here to get the hang of things, and then turn to the other side of the book to get started!

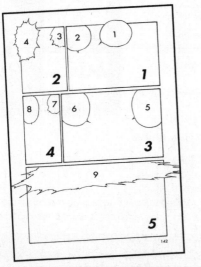